Essay Index

DATE DUE

DEC 1 8 2003			

THE WITHERED BRANCH

D. S. SAVAGE

THE
WITHERED BRANCH

Six Studies in the Modern Novel

ESSAY INDEX IN REPRINT

Core Collection Books, inc.
GREAT NECK, NEW YORK

FIRST PUBLISHED 1952
REPRINTED 1978

INTERNATIONAL STANDARD BOOK NUMBER 0-8486-3031-9

LIBRARY OF CONGRESS CATALOG NUMBER
78-58270

PRINTED IN THE UNITED STATES OF AMERICA

Contents

Acknowledgment

All but the last of the studies in this book, which were written over the period from 1944 to 1948, have appeared severally – in some cases in a shortened form – in the following publications: *Now, Focus, Humanitas, The New Spirit,* and *Writers of To-day.* Especially am I indebted to Mr. George Woodcock and to Dr. B. Rajan for their consistent editorial encouragement of work of a critical temper which, in the present constitution of the world of letters, could not expect wide agreement or acceptance.

D. S. S.

THE WITHERED BRANCH

Wisdom is common to all things. Those who speak with intelligence must hold fast to the common as a city holds fast to its law, and even more strongly. For all human laws are fed by one thing, the divine. It prevails as much as it will, and suffices for all things with something to spare. HERAKLEITOS

PREFACE

TRUTH AND THE ART OF THE NOVEL

'In the beginning was the Word . . .'

TOLSTOY, who has been well described as the most truth-loving writer in Russian literature, wrote in later life a pamphlet entitled *Bethink Yourselves!* in which he called on all his readers to halt in whatever they were doing, to detach themselves from whatever functional position they held in society, and seriously and radically to ask themselves *who* they were, *what* they were doing, and whether what they were doing was in conformity with their ultimate destiny as human beings. The call was to change a sleeping for a waking state. Now, it is not only the general life of society which is subject to a perpetual condition of habitual automatism; this condition affects even the production and the consumption of literature, so that in this field also the necessity arises from time to time for someone to rise up and issue a similar call to *Bethink Yourselves!* and in so doing to let loose the unpredictable dynamic of *the idea* in the midst of a mass of unquestioned assumptions, fixed opinions and established reputations. Why do we read novels and what are we really doing when we indulge in that habitual recreation? What *is* a novel, and – more largely – what is *art*? I begin with these awkward questions so that the reader to whom they are unwelcome can put this book back on the shelf before he gets involved in any unpleasantness. This is a book of criticism, not a collection of literary appreciations: behind it the idea is already at its incalculable work.

THE attempt to formulate a theory of the nature of a work of art resembles the attempt to formulate a theory of the nature of a man. Everyone knows what a man is, and likewise everyone knows what a work of art is – until he comes to think about it and to investigate what others have thought, when it transpires that there are endless theories, both of the nature of man and of

9

the nature, purpose and meaning of artistic activity. These are not idle questions. Misconceptions of the nature of man may have disastrous consequences in human life, and it is the same with art. The two questions are quite closely related, and as it helps an argument to rest in the first place upon an axiom, I begin with the assertion of the close and organic dependence of art upon life: that is, upon human experience. Art is personal, being rooted in the existence of a concrete and particular individual, the artist. An artist, more particularly a literary artist, and specifically a novelist, must create out of the particular situation in which he finds himself, and to which he has been brought by the interaction of his character (and all that goes to form it) with the circumstances of his time and place. His work will bear the stamp of all these factors. Every novel has a pattern which is imposed upon it by its author's essential being – and this applies no less when the work has the quality of universality. Of all art forms the novel is the most patently personal: it is always autobiographical in its origins. Autobiography itself is merely the simplest form of fiction; the autobiographical novel, so called, is in turn the simplest form of the novel proper; but the more complex forms are no less personal in their foundations. In the simple autobiographical narrative the author presents himself to himself as the central character, in whom the action meets and has its meaning. Complexity enters first of all with dramatization, which reflects an advance in objectivity consequent upon an apprehension of the inter-personal mutuality of living. Implicit in the dramatic form is the avowal of the interdependence of all human destinies, where the meaning of the action is centred not in one character but in each severally, according to his capacity.

To begin with, the general problem which confronts the novelist is that of transmuting the chaos of experience into the order of significant form. Experience in its raw state is incommunicable: that which is communicated is never experience but a mental construct which stands in a symbolic relation to it, mediating between writer and reader, and the craft of fiction consists in discovering and presenting such a construct. Writer and reader must meet on a ground which is objective in its presence to both, and it is the novelist's technical task to prepare it. Somehow he must translate his intrinsically incommunicable experience of reality into a reversed mirror-writing which will be reflected back again, right side up, in the mind of the reader, and first of all in his own mind as his own reader. The novel, that is to say, grounded in subjectivity, aspires towards objectivization – not in the sense of alienation from the subjective, but of its embodiment in apprehensible form. It is objectivization of this kind which alone can set the novelist free from a helpless and inartistic inentification with his experiencing self, making possible a form of self-transcension.

What is the operative factor in this interchange, which transforms the raw material of human experience into art? The American critic Mark Schorer follows a familiar course, which stands in need of examination, in calling it 'technique'. In an essay entitled 'Technique as Discovery', he writes forthrightly: 'The difference between content, or experience, and achieved content, or art, is technique.' This he elaborates as follows: 'When we speak of technique . . . we speak of nearly everything. For technique is the means by which the writer's experience, which is his subject-matter, compels him to attend to it: technique is the only means he has of discovering, exploring, developing his subject, of conveying its meaning, and, finally, of evaluating it. And surely it follows that certain techniques are sharper tools than others, and will discover more: that the writer capable of the most exacting technical scrutiny of his subject-matter will produce works with the most satisfying content, works with maximum meaning.' This writer goes on to define technique as 'any selection, structure, or distortion, any form or rhythm imposed upon the world of action; by means of which . . . our apprehension of the world of action is enriched or renewed'. In accordance with this definition, he speaks of Defoe's failure, in *Moll Flanders*, to distinguish his own values from those of the heroine, as a *technical* defect: 'Because he had no adequate resources of technique to separate himself from his material, thereby to discover and define the meanings of his material, his contribution is not to fiction but to the history of fiction, and to social history.' Discussing *Sons and Lovers*, he points to D. H. Lawrence's inability to separate himself as a writer from his experiential material – to sufficiently objectify his situation for the purposes of art; and this again he describes as a technical failure. 'All this, and the character of a whole career, would have been altered if Lawrence had allowed his technique to discover the fullest meaning of his subject.'

Clearly, in this dizzy elevation of 'technique', something has been left out of account. Misgiving is roused in the first place by the very inclusiveness of 'technique' as the word is here used; for something which means nearly everything may come frighteningly close to meaning almost nothing. The error, however, is so common that it indicates the importance of making a clear distinction between technique and a much more primary and fundamental activity, which I propose to call *vision*. In order to create the artistic entity which shall adequately objectify his subjectivity, the novelist must, of course, employ a technique, but his job will be not to make use of some impersonal instrument lying indifferently to hand, but to discover the method which is exactly suited to himself and to his subject, and this means in practice that he must *create* a technique for his always unique and particular purpose. As his vision penetrates the substance of his experience and subjects it to itself, it projects the *idea* of the form of the finished work, and the rest is a matter of experimental verification, of discovery and elimination in the chosen medium. No writer can possess himself of a technique for a creative purpose except through an act of imagination, and this applies even when a technique is apparently borrowed from another writer. Seen in this light, it would appear that Lawrence's difficulty lay on a far profounder level than that of technique; it was an interior, personal one – as common sense readily perceives. *Sons and Lovers* is an imperfect work of art not, at bottom, because of a defect of technique, but because of a failure of artistic imagination. Undoubtedly this deep defect is manifested in the structure and texture of the work, but to nominate it a technical fault is implicitly to deny depth to the novel and to misunderstand its nature.

So far we have two terms of the artistic synthesis, the subjective and the objective. It is in the simple opposition of these factors that two paths to artistic failure reveal themselves: the loss of balance which follows when subjectivity is regarded as all but self-sufficient and the corresponding deflection when the structure of objectivity is sought for its own sake. The first, which is the romantic error, leads to a formless expansiveness; the second, which is the classical, to an empty constructivism. But an integrated work of art contains within itself a resolution and equilibrium of the personal with the impersonal, the subjective with the objective, the particular with the universal. The subjective and the objective meet and fuse to illuminate and to concretize each other, forming a third entity, a diamond of compressed carbon. There has been a qualitative transformation. In order, therefore, to understand the nature of the artistic synthesis we must put our finger on the third term in which these disparate parts may be drawn together and resolved into unity. That term is Truth. I use the capital initial to emphasize that truth is an absolute.

ALL art arises from the creative need to raise content into its proper form. Form is that which orders content into significance; the 'significant' is that which has meaning, and meaning consists in a relation to truth. The artist – not the craftsman, the entertainer or the dilettante, but the authentic creator – is one who confronts his experience with a passionate and inflexible question as to its meaning, its inherent value, and who, working in his chosen medium, utilizes a particular technique to present the meaning he discovers, in symbolic form, to himself and to others. The discovery of meaning and its embodiment in the concrete artistic work is his justification and his triumph. To uncover the pattern in the formless flux, that which is meaningful in the midst of the sordid and the banal: to lay hold on this and to give it corporal, symbolic expression is the creative mission of the artist.

Truth, the absolute, forms in every integrated work of art the invisible centre around which everything in it coheres and in relation to which it becomes a communicator of value. Truthfulness is accordingly the first and absolutely indispensable prerequisite of all authentic art. There are degrees of truthfulness, and of authenticity: a novel may be constructed out of a secondary or a tertiary or even a negative relation to truth, but a great novel can be brought into being only as the outcome of a primary act of apprehension of truth. The apprehension of truth is *imaginative vision*. Imaginative vision is not a mere extension into nothingness, it is a vision of experience informed by meaning – in other words, it is a concrete perception of truth. For it is *truth* which performs the liberating act that lifts the novelist from immersion in his subjective states and enables him so to objectify his experience that it is communicable: to others, indeed, but first of all to himself. Art humanizes. Human life is that of personal movement and response, of communion, of communication, and thus of speech. Relationship is only possible through a mutual relationship to truth; speech is only possible through an avowal of and an aspiration towards truth. Art is speech.

The artist and the thinker are thus akin. 'Literature,' as John Peale Bishop acutely remarked, 'is the criticism of ideas by life.' While the novelist may well be devoid of the capacity for systematic abstract thought, there is no good novel which does not demonstrate in a highly concrete and complex state, a process of thought. The common factor between the thinker and the novelist is precisely their orientation to truth.

Truth being an absolute, a resolute personal orientation is an act of transcendence. The pursuit of meaning presupposes a vow, an act of dedication, and the acceptance of a vocation. It is here that life and art are most intimately drawn together. Before the novelist can embody meaning in his work, he must have discovered the pattern of meaning in experience. At its highest and most complete, his artistic task is secondary to and dependent upon a prior personal devotion to truth.

In the transcendent relation to absolute truth, the relative is imbued with meaning, the particular becomes fraught with universality, the temporal wears an aspect of the eternal. From this arises the permanence of great art and the perishability of the inferior work. Art draws its *autotelic* quality from its relation to the eternal. Great art is a vision of eternity, and the lesson it teaches is that life, in so far as it, too, embodies truth, is itself autotelic. Great art declares the inherent structure of the universe.

ORIENTATION to truth is essentially a religious act. It implies an act of faith in the truth and of constancy in devotion to it.

Accordingly, the interdependence of art and life is most clearly shown, in conditions of cultural unity and compactness, in religion, which is the very heart of culture. Religious dogma, cult and ritual are the communal concretion and consolidation of man's transcendent apprehension of truth. Religion in its primitive unity is both art-in-life and life-in-art. The elevation which it effects of men's experience into a unified archetypal pattern results socially in a drawing of the multiplicity of particular lives into symbolic or typical relation with the eternal, the universal and the absolute. In a condition of cultural unity truth is thus represented in however imperfect a form in the beliefs and practices which are held and performed in common and which hold society together in relation to a single centre in relation to which, in turn, each social function has a non-utilitarian meaning. In a condition of comparative disintegration, on the other hand, truth ceases to be represented in this unified and unifying way. This means that not only is the self-questioning modern man deprived of the inwardly and outwardly sustaining power of an established symbol of truth, but he lives in a world of manners similarly deprived of accepted significant patterns. Because the life of western man stands inescapably in a relationship to the Christian faith which has provided the foundation for his culture and his civilization, so his art is, willy-nilly, positively or negatively, in a similar relationship. The disintegration in which the modern novelist lives and moves is that of a *Christian* culture; what meaning it has is, inevitably, a religious meaning.

In such a state of radical disorder and confusion the conscious individual must turn ever more inwards to seek out the foundations of his life. It happens that there is no more satisfactory way of presenting his own situation to himself in all its diversity and complexity than that provided by the art of the novel, and it is suggestive that the part played by this literary form in human life has increased in importance commensurably with the decay of religion and the subsequent disintegration of cultural unity, while simultaneously the novel itself, in its higher forms, has increased proportionately in scope and depth, accompanying, in its progress towards artistic self-consciousness, the increasing self-questioning of modern man. In order to substantiate this statement one has only to compare the seventeenth-century prose romance, still close to poetry, with the realistic narratives of the eighteenth-century writers, and those in turn with the increasingly rich and subtle novels of the nineteenth century, which gave us not only Scott, Dickens and Balzac, but Stendhal, Dostoevsky, and Henry James. No longer a running commentary upon contemporary manners, the novel increasingly centres upon itself, accentuating its inherently autotelic quality. At the same time it compensates by greater richness, subtlety and elaboration for the essential impoverishment of the modern man's life consequent upon his alienation from the larger world.

In the latter part of the nineteenth century the novel would appear to have reached its apogee. Although since then the writing of fiction has expanded almost into a branch of industry, the effect of yet further cultural disintegration has been to isolate the artist from his milieu, with the consequence that 'creative' fiction has ceased directly to portray the social scene and has come increasingly to concern itself with the inner predicament of the individual. Since, as a man, the alienated novelist cannot in practice live in a state of pure flux, and since the very act of composition does in itself presume a search for intelligible form and thus for personal meaning, a situation arises in which the novel comes ultimately to be shaped by the novelist's human predicament, which, in a disintegrating culture, unavoidably takes the quite primitive and fundamental form of an absence of and a need for faith. It would be vain, and a misunderstanding of the novelist's role, to look to him for positive leadership in this matter. But by reason of the indirect relation to truth which obtains in the practice of his art, we may with assurance look to him for articulation of the condition in which he is enmeshed. It is here that the critical function finds its justification. As the novelist presents life to itself as art, so it falls to the critic to present art to itself as thought, drawing out its concealed meanings and tracing them to a common centre, and relating his findings to the general cultural situation.

LIKE the arts of thought and of fiction, that of criticism presupposes a disciplinary orientation to truth on the part of its practitioner, and like them its power is immeasurably reinforced when this orientation is not only artistic but first of all existential. The creative critic must have at command an uncommon admixture of faculties. Standing midway between the novelist and the philosopher, he must have something of the former's sensitiveness to the particularity and multifariousness of human experience, together with not a little of the latter's capacity for abstraction and generalization.

And here, once again, it is necessary to distinguish between an inadequate subjective or objective critical attitude and an approach which is an integral combination of both. To suppose that there can be a form of criticism which is entirely personal and subjective is as fallacious as to suppose that there can be brought into being a foolproof critical discipline which is impersonal, objective and automatic; and yet we do find critical theory to oscillate in great part between these two misconceived extremes. As with every other art, that of criticism is fundamentally personal, but the critic's purely subjective perceptions, responses and insights are endowed with objective quality, through the rigour of his relation to truth. It is out of such strict and inflexible orientation that critical theory establishes its principles and formulates its disciplines, which, once more, cannot be mechanically appropriated, but have to be possessed from within. Granted such a rigorous personal self-orientation on the part of the ideal critic, it follows that there can be no essential discontinuity between the mind he brings to his critical work and that which he takes to the rest of his human concerns. The same difference is effective here between the creative and the merely academic or popular critic as between that artist whose relation to truth is circumscribed by the specific discipline of his art, and that other whose orientation to truth is both artistic and existential – or, in other words, *religious*. It follows that the work of the creative critic will be powerfully affected by the *ideas* resulting from a relation to truth; it cannot be either impressionistically 'personal' or studiously unbiassed and colourless, like the popular forms of criticism which are encouraged and exalted by reason of the fear of ideas which animates the general mind.

In the six studies of modern novelists which compose this book an attempt has been made in every case at a sympathetic penetration to the heart of the work, and a consequent intuitive discovery of the underlying pattern which has shaped the sequence of the writer's novels. It will perhaps seem strange that I should use the word 'sympathetic' in connection with studies which will appear severe and even harsh, but that word nevertheless expresses my primary approach, and I use it to indicate that, doubtless with many failures, I stand not in an exterior but in an interior relation to the writers with whose work I deal. In the greater number of cases I had submitted myself more or less passively and at random to their influence over a long period of time before finding it necessary to my own development to separate myself from them in order to relate their work with increasing strictness to my own apprehension of truth. To the charge of a destructive negativeness, therefore, which may be brought against my treatment of them, I would reply that the severity towards a particular attitude or idea expressed must be considered in some degree as severity towards that part of myself which inclines or has inclined to the same direction. But in a time of general laxness, severity is its own justification. In the words of Blake, Establishment of Truth depends on Destruction of Falshood continually. I have little doubt that these novelists reveal in their work several distinguishable varieties of Falshood which, taken together, indicate an acute stage of spiritual malaise, as well as of cultural disintegration.

Just here another objection must be met. It will be charged that in concerning myself with the underlying formative forces which determine the novelist's work, I am overstepping the rightful terrain of criticism and raising issues which have little or nothing to do with literary values. The critic, runs this type of argument, should concern himself only with the purely literary qualities of the work before him, leaving the novelist to enjoy his personal vagaries as he pleases. The fact is, of course, that there are no such purely literary qualities which are not deeply connected with the inner movements of the novelist's personality. Flaws in the surface of a work are the outcome of a disrelation to truth, and disrelation to truth is a part of a more general disorientation of being. As, being an independent writer, I am not compelled to observe that rigid departmentalization of 'subjects' which is enforced by educational institutions, I see no reason why I should accept a widespread critical convention and draw an arbitrary line at the point where literature passes over into life. I can therefore state candidly that the typical modern novelists considered in this book reveal in their work several varieties of disorientation of being (or dehumanization) parallel with the deflection from truth which determines the structure of their work as a whole.

The varieties of slavery inherent in the human disposition which wait upon any such disorientation of being have been distinguished with great insight by Nicolas Berdyaev in his book *Slavery and Freedom*. Without in any way attempting to imitate Berdyaev's analysis, or to 'apply' his findings to the modern novel – a procedure which would in my view show critical insufficiency and bad faith – I am bound to say that my penetrations into the work of the writers dealt with in the ensuing pages confirm just such an insight into the conditions of inner subjection. Thus in the writings of Ernest Hemingway there is displayed a clear form of the slavery to war and to violence, in those of E. M. Forster there is marked slavery to the bourgeois spirit and to society, in Margiad Evans can be distinguished a pronounced form of slavery to passion and to nature, in Aldous Huxley the erotic lure is prominent, and in Joyce the aesthetic lure dominates everything, while in Virginia Woolf we see the elementary bewilderment of a mind incapable of formulating a clear view of her world of experience consequent upon inability to establish foundations in belief of whatever order. The lesson of the modern novel, as displayed in these figures, is that of the disintegration of the consciousness of modern man, resulting from his divided and depolarized being, sundered from its absolute centre. But while as a thinker I am interested in the organic manner in which, in these examples, one form of disorientation is connected with another, as a critic I note above all that each path here traced leads to a condition which may fitly be described as *the impossibility of speech*.

I BEGAN with a declaration of the dependence of art upon life. In order to understand this relationship in its larger sense it is necessary to make a formal distinction between two levels of life.

Life and art, in the context of culture, are engaged in a continuous cyclic interchange, to comprehend which we must
discriminate between the 'lower' level of the primary experiential flux and the 'higher', i.e. the distinctively human life of
values, of meaningful action and significant relationship.
Between the two stand those transforming agents of which art
is not the least important, which perform their function by
reason of their specialized relation to truth: in a state of cultural
unity it is religion which performs this office. The lower life is
transformed into the higher by means of the aspiration towards
and the embodiment of truth. Thus art is born out of life, and
the values it reveals again drawn into the current of social
living, to fertilize and once more give birth. Culture is the
result of this process, or rather, it is the process itself. It has two
faces, being at once a triumph – of form over the chaos of raw,
undifferentiated 'life' – and a failure – the failure to achieve
and to *incarnate* truth in existence, and thus to effect the real,
and not merely the symbolic, transfiguration of life. Yet without this transcendent endeavour towards the transfiguration of
life in the truth, culture itself would be emptied of meaning,
would shrivel and cease to exist.

Art is speech, and speech is ultimately impossible when there
is no absolute existential relation to truth. The relation to truth
which is implicit in the practice of art cannot be permanently
sustained when truth is withdrawn from existence. Not only will
life disorientated completely from truth succumb to chaos, but
art which originates from a life which is chaotic will eventually
also crumble from within. The instruments of technique will
perish, the structure of the artistic work will collapse, drama
will give place to a monologue which will end in the disintegration of language, of the sentence, even of the unitary word. The
word has meaning only in relation to the Word.

In its cultural aspect, indifference to truth has the effect of
upsetting the cyclic interchange of art and life, so that they
become confused, merge and lead to a common debasement.
The tendency towards this appears in artistic theory beforehand
in the forms of *vitalism* and *aestheticism* – the broken halves of an
entity formerly united by the aspiration towards truth. I consider them here first of all in their theoretical form. As a theory

of art in its relation to life, then, vitalism is a despair of art which demands its subordination to the service of some utilitarian aim on the level of society and nature; while aestheticism is a despair of life which exalts art into a sterile and vacuous self-sufficiency. The vitalistic heresy may be either directly naturalistic and 'pagan', as with D. H. Lawrence, or may take a sociological form, as in the varieties of Marxism. Poetry and the novel must lead to *more life* – either to a heightened sense of biological vitality, or to an intensified social activism. In any case its goal is no longer transcendent, but is displaced to the level of the primary experiential flux. The aesthetic theory is the converse of this, in its elevation of art at the expense of life. Life it sees as intrinsically meaningless and degraded; the revulsion it evokes can be alleviated only by retirement into a compensatory realm where all is refined, elegant and unsullied. Life is a deplorable reality, art a desirable dream. Both are linked with hedonism – truth being replaced by the pleasure-principle; and in each case there is a Utopian tendency in the final conclusion of art and life, the one being linked to notions of an idyllic state of nature, while the other inclines towards the aristocratic or plutocratic luxury of an artificial paradise. The vitalistic debasement of art to a functional purpose clearly leads to its extinction in a condition of sensational immediacy. The aesthetic denial of life progressively deprives art of content, forcing it ever further into insubstantiality.

To pass beyond the abstract theory to its emotional foundations, we find in E. M. Forster and in Margiad Evans a very plain substitution of ethical vitalism for spirituality, vitalism in this form being the quantitative valuation of life without regard to the qualitative distinctions which would be introduced by a relation to truth. On the other hand, the aesthetic attitude has profoundly conditioned the work of James Joyce and Virginia Woolf. It is of the greatest interest to see how in these cases an artistic sentimentalism is forced to give place at the last to a particularly gross vitalistic animality – a reduplication of the course of an earlier aesthete, W. B. Yeats. Thus art and life descend together to the level of undifferentiated 'lower' life, where the human image is dissipated in the phenomenal stream.

In these essays, then, I have endeavoured not merely to point out artistic failure but to some extent to uncover the existential roots of disintegration. It would be mistaken to condemn these novelists for their failures, not simply because their condition is also ours, but because of the real contribution which is made by the mere articulation of their situations, in their contributions to speech, which are contributions to our understanding of ourselves – even when it can be clearly shown that the course they have taken terminates in speechlessness. That man is inconceivable whose life stands in no relation to truth; every human thought, word and action stands in such a relation, but it may be at a multiple remove, to the furthest degree of automatism, or it may be wavering and negative and infirm, or contradictory of preceding and succeeding movements. These novelists, in the works which have grown from their searching of experience, have declared themselves and spoken their meaning, and it behoves their readers not to submit passively to the spell, but to examine that which is spoken and to relate it to their own understanding of life. So I have understood my critical task, and what follows, taken as a whole, is my critical contribution to our common understanding of our human predicament.

ERNEST HEMINGWAY

ERNEST HEMINGWAY is known as the author of a number
of miscellaneous novels and short stories, as well as two
books on blood sports. His best-known works, however,
are two 'novels of love and war', *A Farewell to Arms* and
For Whom the Bell Tolls, and his significant development, such
as it is (for only in a very special sense can he be said to develop
at all), may best be seen by a comparison of those two works. In
the second section of this essay such a comparison will be made,
but to begin with I propose to examine the essential or typical
qualities of the Hemingway presented to us in the general body
of his work.

Hemingway first received attention, when he was publishing
his earlier stories, as a *stylist*. And this is interesting, for the
content of his stories is in great part crude violent action, not
essentially dissimilar from the subject-matter of the stories found
in the cheap 'pulp' magazines of a primarily masculine appeal.
It may reasonably be assumed that Hemingway satisfies, on a
somewhat higher level of culture or of sophistication, the same
imaginative cravings fed among the semi-literate proletarian
masses of England and America by such productions as *War
Aces* and *Action Stories*. The difference is that where the writer of
'pulp' stories is writing deliberately to a known consumer-
demand, and where his products are, consequently, mechanical
and lacking in psychological content, Hemingway is consciously
an artist, writing to achieve an aesthetic effect, and is himself,
therefore, emotionally involved in his own work. It follows that
in his stories the emphasis is not, as in the 'pulp' magazines,
entirely on the crude, mechanical action, taking place in a
complete psychic vacuum. The psychological implications of
the violence of the 'pulp' mentality are made explicit. In reading Hemingway we are made aware that the violent action
itself, of so many of his stories, arises from the need for the

23

alleviation of a prior and underlying psychic vacuity – an emotional state which is sometimes in his work suggested with great skill.

Hemingway is, within very narrow limits, a stylist who has brought to something like perfection a curt, unemotional, factual style which is an attempt at the objective presentation of experience. A bare, dispassionate reporting of external actions is all that Hemingway as a rule attempts in presenting his characters and incidents. His typical central character, his 'I', may be described generally as a bare consciousness stripped to the human minimum, impassively recording the objective data of experience. He has no contact with ideas, no visible emotions, no hopes for the future, and no memory. He is, as far as it is possible to be so, a *de-personalized* being.

A brief glance at Hemingway's first book, a collection of tales entitled *In Our Time* (1925), will give us some notion of the essentials of his attitude and his equipment as a writer. These tales are really a series of brief, laconic sketches from the life of a man, together forming a fragmentary novel. The settings of the sketches alternate between the American countryside of Nick's boyhood, the scenes of war on the Italian Front, and post-war America and Europe. The action, however, is slight and subordinated to the predominant mood, conveyed with admirable honesty and artistic scrupulousness, which is one of utter and complete negation, almost of nihilism. 'Nick', wrote D. H. Lawrence, reviewing the book on its appearance in England, 'is a type one meets in the more wild and woolly regions of the United States. He is the remains of the lone trapper and cowboy. Nowadays, he is educated, and through with everything. It is a state of conscious, accepted indifference to everything except freedom from work and the moment's interest. Nothing matters. Everything happens. Avoid one thing only: getting connected up. If you get held by anything, break it. Don't get away with the idea of getting somewhere else. Just get away, for the sake of getting away. Beat it! . . . His young love-affair ends as one throws a cigarette-end away. "It isn't fun any more." "Everything's gone to hell inside me. . . ." He doesn't love anybody, and it nauseates him to have to pretend he does. He doesn't even *want* to love anybody; he doesn't want to go anywhere; he doesn't want to do anything. He wants just to lounge around and maintain a healthy state of nothingness inside himself, and an attitude of negation to everything outside' himself. And why shouldn't he, since that is exactly and sincerely what he feels?'

In Our Time, like much other of Hemingway's work, is fairly transparently autobiographical; it reads for the most part like a literal, though of course uncommonly discriminating, transcription of bare experience. A simple stylist like Hemingway, in search of a material upon which to exercise and develop his skill, would naturally turn first of all to the material nearest to hand – i.e. the material of simple personal experience. But a mind of Hemingway's negative and static quality will, it is evident, be unable to furnish sufficient material of a straightforward autobiographical kind for the simple craftsman to work on. Unlike a novelist of more complex and active mentality, gifted with psychological insight and the power to project, through the creation of character, a personal vision of experience – for whom, consequently, there would be no abrupt transition from 'autobiography' to 'fiction' – Hemingway is forced to turn for material to the plane, as I have said, of the 'pulp' magazine. His peculiarly negative view of human life quite naturally leads him to project his vision, when he leaves straight autobiography, into figures drawn from the lowest stratum of human existence, where life is lived as near as possible on an animal, mechanical level.

Here is a passage, from a work which is evidently of an autobiographical character rather than not, which has the advantage of representing Hemingway's characteristic factual style while at the same time presenting a fragment of typical subject-matter, which has its own implications on the human, moral plane. It is an incident in a military retreat from the novel *A Farewell to Arms*.

'I order you to cut brush,' I said. They turned and started down the road.

'Halt,' I said. They kept on down the muddy road, the hedge on either side. 'I order you to halt,' I called. They went a little faster. I opened up my holster, took the pistol, aimed at the one who had talked the most, and fired. I missed and they both started to run; I shot three times and dropped one. The other went through the hedge and was out of sight. I fired at him through the hedge as he ran across the field. The pistol clicked empty and I put in another clip. I saw it was too far to shoot at the second sergeant. He was far across the field, running, his head held low. I commenced to reload the empty clip. Bonello came up.

'Let me go finish him,' he said. I handed him the pistol and he walked down to where the sergeant of engineers lay face down across the road. Bonello leaned over, put the pistol against the man's head and pulled the trigger. The pistol did not fire.

'You have to cock it,' I said. He cocked and fired twice. He took hold of the sergeant's legs and pulled him to the side of the road so he lay beside the hedge. He came back and handed me the pistol.

'The son of a bitch,' he said.

The transition from writing on this level to the subsequent and alternative level of the human underworld involves no very considerable descent, it is clear. The following is from a sketch entitled 'The Killers'.

'What are you going to kill Ole Andreson for? What did he ever do to you?

'He never had a chance to do anything to us. He never even seen us.'

'And he's only going to see us once,' Al said from the kitchen.

'What are you going to kill him for, then?' George asked.

'We're killing him for a friend. Just to oblige a friend, bright boy.'

'Shut up,' said Al from the kitchen. 'You talk too goddam much.'

'Well, I got to keep bright boy amused. Don't I, bright boy.'

'You talk too damn much,' Al said. 'The nigger and my bright boy are amusing themselves. I got them tied up like a couple of girl friends in the convent.'*

The wider implications of the above examples of Hemingway's manner and matter are, of course, related to the almost complete extrusion of his vision of life upon the plane of the external – the plane of extreme objectivization where experience is alienated from its subject. To deprive life of its inwardness, and to see men, not as personalities, but as objects, as things, is to open the door, not for a morally condemnable cruelty or

* *Men Without Women* (1928).

brutality so much as for an even more devastating, because cold
and spiritless, contempt of human values and of human life,
which puts killing a man on the same level of actuality as cook-
ing an egg or blacking one's boots. For good measure, I give a
further, and incidentally later, example of Hemingway's objective eye for violence.

> The other fellow pulled the one who was hit back by the legs to
> behind the wagon, and I saw the nigger getting his face down on
> the paving to give them another burst. Then I saw old Pancho
> come around the corner of the wagon and step into the lee of the
> horse that was still up. He stepped clear of the horse, his face
> white as a dirty sheet, and got the chauffeur with the big Luger he
> had; holding it in both hands to keep it steady. He shot twice over
> the nigger's head, coming on, and once low.
> He hit a tyre on the car because I saw dust blowing in a spurt
> on the street as the air came out, and at ten feet the nigger shot
> him in the belly with the Tommy gun, with what must have been
> the last shot in it because I saw him throw it down, and old Pancho
> sat down hard and went over forwards. He was trying to come up,
> still holding on to the Luger, only he couldn't get his head up,
> when the nigger took the shot gun that was lying against the
> wheel of the car by the chauffeur and blew the side of his head off.
> Some nigger.*

Hemingway's de-personalized style, it appears, is the result
of no detached, arbitrary choice. It is a style actually perfectly
expressive of his outlook on life. In the flat, chaotic, elementary
world into which we are introduced by Hemingway's fiction,
everything is objectivized: inwardness, subjectivity, is eliminated, and man himself is made into an object, a thing. This
entire extrusion of personality into the outward sensational
world makes his characters the inwardly-passive victims of a
meaningless determinism. They inhabit a world which, because
it has been voided of inwardness, is entirely without significance.
The Hemingway character is a creature without religion,
morality, politics, culture or history – without any of those
aspects, that is to say, of the distinctively human existence.
    Such an outlook is a peculiar one in a writer because it

* *To Have and Have Not* (1937).

precludes the possibility of organic and interesting development. The Hemingway world is one of mechanical repetition, and in the series of Hemingway's nine or ten books there is no inward continuity to keep pace with the chronological sequence. It is therefore impossible to consider Hemingway as if there were some coherently developing pattern running through his progress as a writer. That there is a development of some kind, a *static* development, so to speak, I shall presently try to show. But the critic, I think, need feel no special obligation to consider Hemingway's works as a sequence. The pattern is essentially a fixed one, made by the running of the mind in a deterministic groove. Apart from the two 'war and love' novels which must be examined separately, there is only one book which throws any special light on Hemingway's mind, and that is the book on the Spanish bullfight entitled *Death in the Afternoon*, which serves the purpose of showing in a simple and explicit form Hemingway's fascinated preoccupation, which up to now I have refrained from commenting on, with the fact of death.

The profound spiritual inertia, the inner vacancy and impotence, which is a mark of all Hemingway's projected characters, issues in a deadening sense of boredom and negation which can only be relieved by violent, though still essentially meaningless, activity. The more violent the activity, the greater the relief from the sickening vertigo of boredom. But activity of this kind is in fact a drug, and like most other kinds of drug, for its effect to be maintained it must be taken in constantly increasing quantities. Ultimately, however, the state of boredom, certainly one of the most horrible of human experiences, reduces itself not merely to the absence of meaning, but to the total absence of a sense of life. Indeed, it is a feature of violent action that while it cannot produce a convincing sense of meaningfulness, it can at any rate produce an illusory sense of *life*. Violent action itself, however, is almost always destructive action. Its end is in death. And, ultimately, when the sense of life itself vanishes, there is only one way in which it may be recaptured, and that is by the violent, absolute contrast of life with death. Life regains its 'reality' in such cases – becomes, that is, aesthetically sensational and vivid in itself – only when it is brought up against the stark, black negation of the void.

Writing, in *Death in the Afternoon*, of his early interest in the bullfight, Hemingway says:

> I was trying to write then and I found the greatest difficulty, aside from knowing truly what you really felt, rather than what you were supposed to feel, and had been taught to feel, was to put down what really happened in action; what the actual things were which produced the emotion you experienced.

> . . . The only place where you could see life and death, i.e. violent death now that the wars were over, was in the bull ring and I wanted very much to go to Spain where I could study it. I was trying to learn to write, commencing with the simplest things, and one of the simplest things of all and the most fundamental is violent death. . . .

> So far, about morals, I know only that what is moral is what you feel good after and what is immoral is what you feel bad after and judged by these moral standards, which I do not defend, the bullfight is very moral to me because I feel very fine while it is going on and have a feeling of life and death and mortality and immortality, and after it is over I feel very sad but very fine.

Death in the Afternoon, which partakes of the nature of an esoteric introduction to a blood-cult, is written throughout in a tone of alternating naïve solemnity and cynical jocularity. But here, he seems to imply, in a senseless, mechanical and phoney world, is something which seems to be real and meaningful, and which may somehow be approached in a way which will impart a sense of significance and reality to living.

> . . . Someone with English blood has written: 'Life is real; life is earnest; and the grave is not its goal.' And where did they bury him? and what became of the reality and the earnestness? The people of Castilla have great common sense. They could not produce a poet who would write a line like that. They know death is the unescapable reality, the one thing any man may be sure of; the only security; that it transcends all modern comforts and that with it you do not need a bath-tub in every American home, nor, when you have it, do you need the radio. They think a great deal about death, and when they have a religion they have one which believes that life is much shorter than death. Having this feeling they take an intelligent interest in death. . . .

Such passages as this do at least reveal the nature, whatever one may think of its value, of the chief preservative of Hemingway's significance as a writer, that kind of desperate honesty which, once the bottom has been knocked out of things by painful and horrifying experience, cannot rest content with the pusillanimous compromises with which most people afterwards patch up their lives, and which one detects in the revulsion from the 'bath-tub in every American home', and in the manifest dread of any kind of 'faking' (in writing as in bullfighting) which is displayed throughout the book. A glance at one further facet of Hemingway's personal outlook, and we can pass on from this brief survey of his typical work. In *Green Hills of Africa* (1936), a tedious description of a hunting trip, there are two passages which are of interest for the light they throw on Hemingway as a writer. The first concerns *subject*.

I thought about Tolstoy and about what a great advantage an experience of war was to a writer. It was one of the major subjects and certainly one of the hardest to write truly of, and those writers who had not seen it were always very jealous and tried to make it seem unimportant, or abnormal, or a disease as a subject, while, really, it was just something quite irreplaceable that they had missed.

The second concerns, not subject, and not technique, exactly, but the writer's intention:

The reason every one now tries to avoid it, to deny that it is important, to make it seem vain to try to do it, is because it is so difficult. Too many factors must combine to make it possible. . . . The kind of writing that can be done. How far prose can be carried/ if anyone is serious enough and has luck. There is a fourth and fifth dimension that can be gotten. [And if a writer can get this] . . . Then nothing else matters. It is more important than anything he can do. The chances are, of course, that he will fail. But there is a chance that he succeeds. . . . It is much more difficult than poetry. It is a prose that has never been written. But it can be written, without tricks and without cheating. With nothing that will go bad afterwards. . . . First, there must be talent, much talent. Talent such as Kipling had. Then there must be discipline. The discipline of Flaubert. Then there must be the conception of what it can be and an absolute conscience as unchanging as the standard meter in Paris, to prevent faking. Then the writer must be intelligent and disinterested and above all he must survive.

Such, or something such, is the conception of himself which

Hemingway would like to project into the public mind. It is an interesting conception.

A novelist, of admitted literary merit, who lacks all the equipment generally expected of a practitioner of his art except a certain artistic scrupulousness and poetic sense, is something of a phenomenon. And while one would hardly suppose Hemingway could be considered as, intrinsically, a very important writer, yet, it is obvious, his purely symptomatic significance is considerable. For what does Hemingway represent but that, in a special form, which might be termed the *proletarianization* of literature: the adaptation of the technical artistic conscience to the sub-average human consciousness? Sociologically considered, Hemingway seems to me to epitomize a phase of culture in which all the inward values which have sustained that culture in the past are vanishing, and nothing much is left but the empty shell of civilization – the shell of technique. The characters of Hemingway reflect accurately the consciousness of the depersonalized modern man of the totalitarian era, from whom all inward sources have been withdrawn, who has become alienated from his experience and objectivized into his environment.

*

C. S. Lewis, in his *Preface to Paradise Lost,* drawing a distinction between the Primary Epic of Homer and the Secondary Epic of Virgil and Milton, points out that the former kind is deprived of the great subject possessed by the latter because 'the mere endless up and down, the constant aimless alternations of glory and misery, which make up the terrible phenomenon called a Heroic Age', admit of no historical pattern or design, which can only be given 'when some event can be held to effect a profound and more or less permanent change in the history of the world, as the founding of Rome did, or still more, the fall of man'.

No one event is really very much more important than another. No achievement can be permanent: today we kill and feast, tomorrow we are killed, and our women led away as slaves. Nothing 'stays put', nothing has a significance beyond the moment. Heroism and tragedy there are in plenty, therefore good stories in plenty; but no 'large design that brings the world out of the good to ill'. The total effect is not a pattern, but a kaleidoscope. . . .

Primary Epic is great, but not with the greatness of the later kind. In Homer, its greatness lies in the human and personal tragedy built up against this background of meaningless flux. It is all the more tragic because there hangs over the heroic world a certain futility. 'And here I sit in Troy,' says Achilles to Priam, 'afflicting you and your children.' Not 'protecting Greece', not even 'winning glory', not called by any vocation to afflict Priam, but just doing it because that is the way things come about. . . . Only the style – the unwearying, unmoved, angelic speech of Homer – makes it endurable. Without that the *Iliad* would be a poem beside which the grimmest modern realism is child's play.

It does not seem far-fetched to perceive some points of similarity between the Heroic Ages of the past and our own bloodstained epoch as it moves into an increasingly bleak future, and between the bards who recited the deeds of the ancient heroes and such a novelist as Hemingway – bearing in mind the retrogressive character of our own 'heroism', and, of course, putting the disparity between Homer and Hemingway into some proportion with that existing between, say, Hector or Agamemnon and Harry Morgan.

II

IN any serious considerations of the writings of Ernest Hemingway the fact must not be lost sight of that their author belongs to that generation of men whose formative adult years were spent on the battlefields of Europe during the first world war. It would scarcely be too much to say that Hemingway's special type of outlook is *a product of the battlefield*. Hemingway's comments upon war as a subject for the writer have already been noted. And it is a revealing fact that his two most coherent and most successful books, *A Farewell to Arms* (1929) and *For Whom the Bell Tolls* (1941), upon which his fame largely rests, are both 'novels of love and war'.

Each of these novels stands apart from the bulk of Hemingway's work by virtue of its embodiment of a sustained pathos; and this pathos, it is evident, is an aspect of its interior connection with Hemingway's own personal experience and vision of life. While much of Hemingway's writing is the product of a somewhat uneasy attitudinizing, *A Farewell to Arms* impresses one with its surprisingly genuine and unforced quality. It is naïve rather than cynical, bewildered rather than 'tough', and there is a minimum of deliberate sensational violence. Although published ten years after the end of the first world war, its clearly autobiographical character would seem to justify its being related to the early and comparatively unformed Hemingway, the Hemingway who was himself, in youthful immaturity, thrust by circumstances into the scarifying circumstances of war and left to digest his experience as best he could.

For a novelist with no coherent inner vision of human existence, the problem of form must present almost insuperable difficulties: difficulties which may be envisaged from a reading of Hemingway's two chaotic lesser novels, not considered here – *The Sun Also Rises* and *To Have and Have Not*. But in *A Farewell to Arms* this problem is solved by the exterior pattern of the events in which the curiously nameless hero is passively involved. The story is straightforward. An American enlisted in the medical section of the Italian Army, the hero meets, near the front, an English nurse called Catherine Barkley. They are indifferently attracted to one another, and there is a rather flat emotional encounter between them, very well described. (Catherine is mourning for her lover, killed in France, to whom she had put off her marriage.) Then the American is wounded and sent back to a hospital where he is nursed by Catherine, and they fall into an intimate sexual relationship. After his recovery, the American returns to the battle-front, but is involved in a disorderly retreat, is arrested and about to be shot by military police, but he frees himself, and 'through' with the war, makes his way to the town where Catherine is living and escapes with her down the lakes to neutral Switzerland. Here, away from the war and in outwardly idyllic circumstances, the whole accidental, haphazard series of events reaches its meaningless, accidental conclusion with Catherine's death at the maternity hospital in giving birth to a stillborn infant.

In this novel, the war, of which the central character is a more or less acquiescent and occasionally involved onlooker, is only the background and setting for the central story of the relationship between the soldier and the nurse. There is a real suggestion of pathos in the impersonal, unimpassioned account of their forlorn, uncomprehending, tacit endeavour to maintain

c

the illusion of the happiness and meaningfulness of their fortuitous relationship against their own deeper apprehension of lovelessness, frustration and fatality, although the emphasis is entirely on the objective occurrences, and the inward significance is never directly touched upon. The following passage will provide an example of Hemingway's honest realism in dealing with his 'love interest':

We walked down the corridor. The carpet was worn. There were many doors. The manager stopped and unlocked a door and opened it.

'Here you are. A lovely room.'

The small boy in buttons put the package on the table in the centre of the room. The manager opened the curtains.

'It is foggy outside,' he said. The room was furnished in red plush. There were many mirrors, two chairs and a large bed with a satin coverlet. A door led to the bathroom.

'I will send up the menu,' the manager said. He bowed and went out.

I went to the window and looked out, then pulled a cord that shut the thick plush curtains. Catherine was sitting on the bed, looking at the cut-glass chandelier. She had taken her hat off and her hair shone under the light. She saw herself in one of the mirrors and put her hands to her hair. She did not look happy. She let her cape fall on the bed.

'What's the matter, darling?'

'I never felt like a whore before,' she said. I went over to the window and pulled the curtain aside and looked out. I had not thought it would be like this.

'You're not a whore.'

'I know it, darling. But it isn't nice to feel like one.' Her voice was dry and flat.

'This was the best hotel we could get in,' I said. I looked out of the window. Across the square were the lights of the station. There were carriages going by on the street and I saw the trees in the park. The lights from the hotel shone on the wet pavement. Oh, hell, I thought, do we have to argue now?

'Come over here, please,' Catherine said. The flatness was all gone out of her voice. 'Come over, please. I'm a good girl again.' I looked over at the bed. She was smiling.

I went over and sat on the bed beside her and kissed her.

'You're my good girl.'

'I'm certainly yours,' she said.

There is, too, a queer, twisted pathetic quality in the lovers' final interview, when Catherine is on her deathbed.

> 'Do you want me to get a priest or anyone to come and see you?'
> 'Just you,' she said. Then a little later, 'I'm not afraid. I just hate it.'
> 'You must not talk so much,' the doctor said.
> 'All right,' Catherine said.
> 'Do you want me to do anything, Cat? Can I get you anything?'
> Catherine smiled, 'No.' Then a little later, 'You won't do our things with another girl, or say the same things, will you?'
> 'Never.'
> 'I want you to have girls, though.'
> 'I don't want them.'

These short passages are enough perhaps, to make plain something of the novel's relatively sympathetic quality. There is an absence of deliberate harsh violence; what violence there is comes, unsought, from the external circumstances of war, and is received passively. This is in keeping with the character of the young man, who is not a proletarian tough, but an average young bourgeois American. He is – not a sufferer, for although he endures suffering he refuses to accept it – but a victim, who has not yet become hard and cynical and addicted to violence as an end in itself. If, at the beginning of the story, he has a philosophy, it is a simple one of self-centred enjoyment, although towards the end, and after Catherine's death, this gives place to a naïve 'tragic' outlook, which is expressed in such reflections as these:

> Often a man wishes to be alone and a girl wishes to be alone too and if they love each other they are jealous of that in each other, but I can truly say we never felt that. We could feel alone when we were together, alone against the others. It has only happened to me like that once. I have been alone while I was with many girls and that is the way that you can be most lonely. But we were never lonely and never afraid when we were together. I know that the night is not the same as the day: that all things are different, that the things of the night cannot be explained in the day, because they do not then exist, and the night can be a dreadful time for lonely people once their loneliness has started. But with Catherine there was almost no difference in the night except that it was an even better time. If people bring so much

courage to this world the world has to kill them to break them, so of course it kills them. The world breaks every one and afterward many are strong in the broken places. But these that will not break it kills. It kills the very good and the very gentle and the very brave impartially. If you are none of these you can be sure it will kill you too but there will be no special hurry.

The harsh note of suppressed grief on which this story closes expresses the fatalistic stoicism which arises in the young American out of his inherent inner passivity as it is affected by his sense of futility and of loss. At such an intensity of suffering there are usually only two courses open to the human heart, a receptive softening or a cynical hardening. But we already know that a desperate, bitter hardness is a characteristic of Hemingway's work as a whole.

A survey of the ground covered by the greater part of Hemingway's writings shows it to be that indicated in the first part of this essay – the delineation of an eviscerated, chaotic world of futility and boredom lit up with flashes of violent action, where life is brought into a sensational vividness only by contrast with the nullity of death. The bulk of Hemingway's writing expresses consciously an outlook on life which is negative to the point of nihilism. Yet, abruptly, at the conclusion of the Hemingway opus we find a work – *For Whom the Bell Tolls* – of an undeniably sustained and positive character, which has been widely received as revealing a profound and positive insight into the human condition and the life of our time. What sort of enigma have we here?

That there is a reversal of attitude of a decisive kind is quite clear. For in this latter book we have a pattern, not of aimlessness, but of positive direction and sense of purpose, and a depiction, not of nihilistic despair, but of lyrical acceptance, where futility is replaced by meaningfulness, and instead of merely factual externality there is a significant, organic pattern to sustain the interior structure of the narrative. The pathos with which the story is imbued is a pathos quite different in quality from that of the Italian novel – it is a pathos which derives, not from a negative sense of victimization at the hands of life, but from a kind of subdued, lyrical ecstasy of acceptance. The story concerns a young American, Robert Jordan, who espouses the cause of the Republicans in Spain during the Civil War, enlists with the Government forces as a dynamiter, and is entrusted with a mission, involving almost certain death, behind the enemy lines. Under the guidance of the old peasant, Anselmo, he reaches the hiding-place, a cave in the mountains, of the group of guerrillas who are to assist him in blowing the bridge on the specified day. There he encounters a mixed group of primitive people, including Pablo, the surly and untrustworthy leader of the group, Pilar, his powerful, earthily-sagacious wife, and a girl, Maria, whom they have rescued, after she has been raped, from the fascists, and with whom he quickly establishes an intimate relationship. The atmosphere among the little group is tense, partly because of the antagonism which arises between Jordan and Pablo, and partly owing to the necessary hazards of existence in enemy territory. But what contributes most to the psychical intensity which permeates the life of this little group and draws them together in bonds of intimacy is their nearness to the fatality felt to be involved in the accomplishment of the mission which has brought them into combination with the newcomer. After surviving some hazardous circumstances, Jordan, with the others, blows the bridge, but is wounded while escaping and left to face certain death from the approaching enemy, which he does with a gun in his hand and in his sustained mood of subdued ecstasy.

Nothing more clearly brings out the completeness of the alteration of attitude in the later novel than the juxtaposition of the following passages from each book, the Italian and the Spanish, concerning the heroes' attitudes towards the emotional aura that surrounds every cause for which men are prepared to kill and to die.

This is from the earlier book:

> I did not say anything. I was always embarrassed by the words sacred, glorious and sacrifice and the expression in vain. We had heard them, sometimes standing in the rain almost out of earshot, so that only the shouted words came through, and had read them, on proclamations that were slapped up by billposters over other proclamations, now for a long time, and I had seen nothing sacred, and the things that were glorious had no glory and the sacrifices were like the stock-yards at Chicago if nothing was done

with the meat except to bury it. There were many words that you could not stand to hear and finally only the names of places had dignity. Certain numbers were the same way and certain dates and these with the names of the places were all you could say and have them mean anything. Abstract words such as glory, honour, courage or hallow were obscene beside the concrete names of villages, the numbers of roads, the names of rivers, the numbers of regiments and the dates.

Nothing could be more opposed to this than such sentiments as these expressed in the later novel:

> At either of those places you felt that you were taking part in a crusade. That was the only word for it although it was a word that had been so worn and abused that it no longer gave its true meaning. You felt, in spite of all bureaucracy and inefficiency and party strife, something that was like the feeling you expected to have and did not have when you made your first communion. It was a feeling of consecration to a duty toward all of the oppressed of the world which would be as difficult and embarrassing to speak about as religious experience and yet it was authentic as the feeling you had when you heard Bach, or stood in Chartres Cathedral or the Cathedral at Leon and saw the light coming through the great windows; or when you saw Mantegna and Greco and Breughel in the Prado. It gave you a part in something that you could believe in wholly and completely and in which you felt an absolute brotherhood with the others who were engaged in it. It was something that you had never known before but that you had experienced now and you gave such importance to it and the reasons for it that your own death seemed of complete unimportance; only a thing to be avoided because it would interfere with the performance of your duty. . . .

That a very peculiar transposition of emotional attitudes has been effected somewhere between the two novels is obvious. But by what agency has this startling reversal been brought about?

The answer is not far to seek. The characters in this novel prove on examination to be characters no less elementary than those in Hemingway's previous books, but to their elementary, stripped humanity has been added a rudimentary political sense. *Politics* appears to be the pivot which has enabled Hemingway to swing from a completely negative emotional polarity towards life to a positive one.

If this is the case, then it would appear that the claim of the

Spanish novel to real and positive significance – a claim which
has not been backward in coming from certain quarters –
depends very largely upon the quality of the political consciousness displayed in it. Now, a political awareness of such a valid
and enlightening character must, it is plain, be something very
complex and organic to its possessor's personality, must at least
affect, or be affected by, many other departments of its possessor's mind. Can this be said of Hemingway's political consciousness? It cannot.

I must pass over here the question of Hemingway's own
political affiliations, of which I know little except that in 1936,
with his compatriot, the socialist novelist, John Dos Passos,
Hemingway visited Loyalist Spain* and came back a strong
Communist sympathizer. In his writings, however, apart from
a propagandist play entitled *The Fifth Column*, the first work of
Hemingway's to show any social awareness is the novel *To
Have and Have Not*, published in 1937, which is a crude chronicle
of violent action (there are nine killings) upon which is superimposed, towards the end, a 'social' moral of the most elementary nature – a series of mechanical contrasts of the lives of
certain members of the parasitical bourgeoisie with the underprivileged workers. The hero, an individualist adventurer
named Harry Morgan, after a number of violent illegal
escapades, dies, shot in the stomach, uttering the following
profound observations:

'A man,' Harry Morgan said, looking at them both. 'One man
alone ain't got. No man alone now.' He stopped. 'No matter how
a man alone ain't got no bloody chance.'

He shut his eyes. It had taken him a long time to get it out and
it had taken him all of his life to learn it.†

* . . . Where, according to an article in the then radically leftist *Partisan
Review* (April 1938) ' . . . Dos Passos found bombs horrifying, bloodshed
gruesome, anarchists hounded by a Stalinist camarilla, the People's Front
conceding to Anglo-French imperialism and suppressing socialism; [and
where] Hemingway found bombs intriguing, bloodshed exciting, anarchists
treasonable, the People's Front noble, socialism nonsense . . .' etc. etc.

† It seems to have taken Hemingway quite a long time, too. In *Green Hills
of Africa*, published only a year previously, he was writing in this vein: 'If
you serve time for society, democracy, and the other things quite young,
and declining any further enlistment make yourself responsible only to yourself, you exchange the pleasant, comforting stench of comrades for something
you can never feel in any other way than by yourself' . . . etc.

In *For Whom the Bell Tolls*, the rudimentary quality of Robert Jordan's political consciousness is barely disguised, and we may safely take it that the quality of Jordan's insight accurately reflects Hemingway's own.

> You're not a real Marxist and you know it. You believe in Liberty, Equality and Fraternity. You believe in Life, Liberty and the pursuit of happiness. Don't ever kid yourself with too much dialectics. They are for some but not for you. You have put many things in abeyance to win a war. If this war is lost all of those things are lost. But afterward you can discard what you do not believe in. There is plenty you do not believe in and plenty that you do believe in.

So much, then, for the quality of Hemingway's political insight, which, from its appearance in his works, would seem to be very meagre indeed. It is enough, however, to justify a black-and-white taking of sides in an armed struggle. But politics is the pivotal point only for what is in effect a total transposition of emotional attitude. What the nature is of that reorientation which, it is plain to see, gives this novel its organic structure, and its sustained, epical positiveness, can now be made clear.

It is here that we touch upon the seeming paradox which makes it possible to speak of Hemingway's as a 'static' development. For what has occurred between the two novels is not a development, or unfoldment, at all, but a psychological shifting which has made possible a *retrogressive recapitulation* of an essentially identical theme. *For Whom the Bell Tolls* actually represents the same basic emotional situation as that stated in *A Farewell to Arms*, but turned, as it were, outside in. Whereas the accidental circumstances of war, sex and death, the poles of experience which provide the focal points for the emotional pattern, impose, in the earlier book, an external pattern on the narrative, reflecting the attitude of the central character as a passive victim, those identical circumstances are, in the later book, given an inward, positive significance and made intrinsic to the story, which attains thereby an interior coherence which is expressed stylistically in the rapt, exalted quality of the writing. It is exactly as though an emotional fixation, impressed on the mind by a certain original pattern of experience as the mind moved outward centrifugally to life, has determined, after a period of immobility, not a development, but an inward, centripetal, recapitulative movement, in which the accidentals become intrinsic; the negatives positive; the mechanical and outward the organic and inward. This whole process of reversal is aptly conveyed in the embarrassingly rhapsodic style of the Spanish novel, emotionally orientated as it is towards the central cult-acceptance of sexuality and death, which is in interesting contrast to the emotional and verbal asceticism of the Italian book.

Death provides the primary emotional focal point of the novel. From the moment he appears it is plain that Robert Jordan is going to his death. His own awareness of this fact serves not only to intensify his sense of the vivid immediacy of the little life which remains to him, but to throw depths of fortuitous significance into his physical union with the girl, Maria. Just as in the earlier novel, here too the emotional series is brought to an end by death. But for the death, accidental and as it were peripheral, of Catherine – death experienced as meaningless objective fact and deprivation – is here substituted a death which is deliberate and essential, embraced by the central character himself as the ultimate factor of subjective experience. And not only death is here embraced positively, and emotionally sanctioned, but also those other pivotal points of the Hemingway situation – sexuality (or 'love') and war.

The relationship of Catherine and the American 'Tenente' in the Italian novel is that of equals, and it retains some vestiges of human dignity which bring it within measurable distance of love, as distinct from animal sexuality. But that of Maria and Robert Jordan is one of uncontaminated animality, so uncontaminated indeed that Hemingway finds it possible to endow it with an absolute, 'mystical' significance. 'When I am with Maria,' ruminates Jordan, 'I love her so that I feel, literally, as though I would die, and I never believed in that nor thought that it could happen.' The emotional orgasm stimulated by his sense of proximity to death elevates every experience for Jordan into a realm of pseudo-mystical excitement. The mystico-sexual experiences of Robert Jordan reveal their nature, if that is in any doubt, by their existence in a psychic void, they

have no connection with and no effect upon his other activities –
although that perhaps is inaccurate, for there would appear to
be a direct connection with death and with killing. And here
the third significant transposition of attitude makes itself felt.
The hero of *A Farewell to Arms*, passively involved in war, as
passively accepts killing, and even himself dispassionately kills
when the necessity seems forced on him – which happens only
once in the book. And the context is not unfavourable to such
animadversions on war as the following:

'Tenente,' Passini said, 'we understand you let us talk. Listen.
There is nothing as bad as war. We in the auto-ambulance cannot
even realize at all how bad it is. When people realize how bad it
is they cannot do anything to stop it because they go crazy. There
are some people who never realize. There are people who are
afraid of their officers. It is with them that war is made.'
'I know it is bad, but we must finish it.'
'It doesn't finish. There is no finish to a war.'
'Yes, there is.'
Passini shook his head.
'War is not won by victory. What if we take San Gabriele?
What if we take the Carso and Monfalcone and Trieste? Where
are we then? Did you see all the far mountains today? Do you
think we could take all them too? Only if the Austrians stop
fighting. One side must stop fighting. Why don't we stop fighting?
If they come down into Italy they get tired and go away. They
have their own country. But no, instead there is a war.'
'You're an orator.'
'We think. We read. We are not peasants. We are mechanics.
But even the peasants know better than to believe in a war.
Everybody hates this war.'

In the later novel, however, war and killing are much more
enthusiastically undertaken.

'My rabbit,' Robert Jordan said and held her as close and as
gently as he could. But he was as full of hate as any man could be.
'Do not talk more about it. Do not tell me any more for I cannot
bear my hatred now.'
She was stiff and cold in his arms and she said, 'Nay, I will never
talk more of it. But they are bad people and I would like to kill
some of them with thee if I could. But I have told thee this only
for thy pride if I am to be thy wife. So thou wouldst understand.'

'I am glad you told me,' he said. 'For tomorrow, with luck, we will kill plenty.'

'But will we kill Falangists? It was they who did it.'

'They do not fight,' he said gloomily. 'They kill at the rear. It is not them we fight in battle.'

'But can we not kill them in some way? I would like to kill some very much.'

'I have killed them,' he said. 'And we will kill them again. At the train we have killed them.'

But there is no need for the multiplication of instances. So much must suffice. If the earlier and typical Hemingway, the underlying factors of whose work I have done my best to bring to light in the first part of this essay, represents an aspect of the widespread sickness of our civilization, the Hemingway of *For Whom the Bell Tolls* reveals that sickness in an advanced stage, sickness masquerading as health, and, accepted as such, precluded from the possibility of being resisted. Of social, or 'political' insight, in this book, there is none. Hemingway's sole claim to such insight rests upon his perception, of dubious worth in the context, of the inadequacy of individualism – 'No matter how a man alone ain't got no bloody chance' – and the superiority of what he had previously been pleased to term, in revulsion, 'the pleasant, comforting stench of comrades'. Hemingway's ostensibly 'profound' realization of the fact of human solidarity – which is all of moral insight that can be said to emerge from the Spanish novel – permitting, as it does, under scanty 'political' justification, the division of men and women into two armed camps equipped and ready for mutual slaughter – hardly possesses any intimate relationship to the epigraph from John Donne from which the novel takes its title.

As for the consequences of Hemingway's peculiar retrogression – a certain loss of sincerity and asceticism of style, the proneness to a peculiar sentimentalism, and the readiness to entertain the cheap substitutes for thought manufactured by political factions – we can safely leave these to the enjoyment of that enormous public which Hemingway has now found, and which, one presumes, shares, to a measurable extent, his outlook and values.

E. M. FORSTER

IN view of the present popular eminence of E. M. Forster, it is a striking reflection that the five novels upon which his public reputation is based were, with one exception, composed within a period of six years during the first decade of the present century. And even the exception, *A Passage to India*, although not published until 1924, was drafted some twelve years before that date.* E. M. Forster, it appears, is an Edwardian novelist, surviving into the contemporary world as a public personality on the basis of a past creativity which has been outlasted by its early products. In spite of this, Forster's is a name which 'counts': his books are reprinted in popular cheap editions, he lectures, broadcasts, contributes to symposia on such subjects as 'What I Believe', sits on committees, and in other ways represents 'culture' in the regions where it shades off into the realms of practical life. It is clear from all this that in some way Forster is a representative figure. When he makes public pronouncements, he voices the mind of a group and a class. As Rose Macaulay, a far from unsympathetic critic, has said of his later political writings, ' . . . in all of them he speaks with the voice of cultured, sensitive and democratic liberalism rather than with his own peculiar note, or rather, he is speaking with that part of his voice which sings in the choir with cultured, sensitive and democratic liberalism'. An examination of his mind should, therefore, lead us beyond the particular case to the general principles underlying it.

How Forster regards himself, or likes to be regarded by others, may be discovered from a reading of an essay on his work by Peter Burra which he has chosen to introduce the Everyman edition of *A Passage to India*. In this essay, asking why did Forster, who has 'felt so oppressively the attractions of abstract presentation', ever adopt the novel at all, Burra replies:

It is that he has ideas which need a more distinct articulation

* *Vide The Writings of E. M. Forster*, by Rose Macaulay.

than music or abstraction can make. He is an artist on the fringe of social reform. He is interested in causes. He has never cut himself off, as most artists sooner or later do, from the political and economic questions of the outer world. While he has never deliberately written, like Dickens, a novel with a purpose – an irrelevancy to the dangers of which this art form is particularly exposed – the fact nevertheless remains that *A Passage to India* is 'a book which no student of the Indian question can disregard' . . . Probably the writing of novels has not been the most important element in his life. We are constantly given the impression that there are better things in the world to do.

And this appreciation (it is hardly criticism), winding its laudatory course, concludes:

It is the Anonymous Prophecy that will remain with us, the transcendent beauty of the Mosque and Temple, and the athletic body of Stephen. It would be perhaps merely stupid to ask, in conclusion, for more. It is possible that the mind which saw so visionarily the significance of Stephen, and which could tell the Wilcoxes that 'nothing has been done wrong', has achieved their own wisdom; that the organism, being perfectly adjusted, is silent.

It is an odd explanation of a novelist's prolonged uncreativeness, this attribution of it to some perfect inner adjustment which has rendered speech superfluous! In the present exegesis a directly contrary view will be maintained: namely, that Forster's creative sterility from 1910 to 1924, and subsequently, is the result, not of inner adjustment, but of an inner exhaustion.

Forster is a significant writer. But significant writers are of two kinds. There are those, and they are the greater ones, whose creative work proceeds from an achieved centre of being, and whose continual creativeness is the expression of the constant extension of their grasp upon and penetration into reality. And there are those others, necessarily more numerous, whose work takes its shape from the exteriorization of an inner conflict – which derives, that is to say, from a condition which is antecedent to an achieved inner integration. These latter writers work out, in the course of their art, a more or less significant personal logic, and with its conclusion, if they have not succeeded in achieving a valid inner integration which will remove them to the plane of the creators, they relapse into nonsignificance. Forster is a writer of the latter type, and it will be

my purpose here to reveal the significant pattern which underlies his work and his silence.

The interest of that pattern lies in the fact that it takes us to
the heart of the liberal dilemma, the liberal confusion, and it is
the interest of Forster's novels that they reveal very clearly to
the perceptive eye the inner motions which preclude an attachment to the liberal outlook.

What are the characteristics of the liberal approach to life?
First of all, the liberal mind is a *medium* mind, a mind which fears
extremes and which therefore is predisposed towards compromise. It inhabits a middle region of life, that of people, and therefore its characteristic expression is a social and political one;
but it is incapable of moving beyond people, as they appear on
the social level, to an understanding of the principles and forces
which govern their lives, and this incapacity applies both to
spiritual and economic realities. The compromising tendency
of liberalism causes it to give mental hostages both to the realm
of ideals and to the world of affairs, but it is rooted in the latter
and in a crisis it is the latter which proves the stronger. Liberalism is a half-hearted creed, born out of stable and comfortable
material circumstances, in which it puts its main trust, making
a gesture of greater or less sincerity towards spiritual values –
but nothing more than a gesture, however sincere. Those
spiritual values, however, tend to become something rather less
than the ultimate and therefore terrifying ones. The absolute is
carefully excluded from the liberal way of life. The gesture
towards the spirit is arrested, and modified into a gesture towards culture; that, in turn, resolves itself into a salute to
civilization, and in times of stress the process of deterioration
will not always stop there.

The 'cultured, sensitive and democratic liberalism' which is
explicitly voiced by Forster's later journalistic writings is so
muddled and bewildered an affair that to examine it seriously
is to risk making oneself ridiculous. In his pamphlet, *What I
Believe* (1939), we find Forster reiterating his belief in 'personal
relationships', although personality itself has for him no ultimate
significance, and on his own admission 'Psychology has split
and shattered the idea of a "Person"'. Tolerance, good temper,
sympathy – 'these', says Forster, 'are what matter really'. But

it transpires that these liberal demi-semi-values exist only on the sufferance of 'force', which really upholds society. As to the social question, Forster would prefer, we gather, to any social change, a perpetuation of the old order of 'democratic' capitalism. But he praises 'democracy' while showing no awareness of its capitalistic and therefore incipiently totalitarian substructure: 'democracy' is considered solely from a superficial political point of view, the façade (Parliament, the Press) is naïvely accepted at its face-value. One is reminded of his treatment of 'the Indian question' in his fifth and last novel, where the ugly realities underlying the presence of the British in India are not even glanced at, and the issues raised are handled as though they could be solved on the surface level of personal intercourse and individual behaviour.

But the liberal confusion has another and graver aspect, in which it appears not as a failure merely but as a betrayal. 'I hate the idea of causes,' wrote Forster in 1939, 'and if I had to choose between betraying my country and betraying my friend, I hope I should have the guts to betray my country. . . . Probably,' however, he adds, 'one will not be asked to make such an agonizing choice.' Evidently Forster was not asked, for after the outbreak of war appeared *Nordic Twilight* (1940), an indictment, not very difficult to make in the circumstances, of Nazi culture and an exhortation addressed primarily, one supposes, to writers and those professing a concern with cultural values, to line up and join in the general totalitarian holocaust of total war – for the sake of 'culture'.

That 'cultured, sensitive and democratic liberalism' is not so innocent, so admirable, and so pleasant as it would represent itself to be becomes apparent only upon a much closer examination than is usually accorded it. Such an examination will be implied in what follows. Liberalism rests upon a fundamental spiritual failure, a spiritual equivocation, a spiritual betrayal. It is the outcome of an absence of faith in the spiritual realities which lie at the back of the variable values to which it presents its dubious salutations. Forster, in *What I Believe*, cleverly attempts to discredit faith by attributing that quality to the blind collective hysteria of the dupes of totalitarianism, thereby making it responsible for the evil and violence in the modern world. This, an age of unfaith, and consequently of greedy materialism and the worship of brute force, is characterized by Forster as 'an age of faith'. 'A child of unbelief,' as he elsewhere names himself, he begins his liberal Credo with the sentence, 'I do not believe in Belief', and wittily informs us that: 'My motto is: "Lord, I disbelieve – help thou my unbelief." '

The point of departure for the liberal betrayal cannot be put more clearly than in these words.

I

E. M. FORSTER'S first novel, *Where Angels Fear to Tread*, was published in 1905. In 1907 there appeared *The Longest Journey* and this was followed, in 1908, by *A Room With a View*. Each of these novels is concerned with the dual theme of personal salvation and the conflict of good and evil. Of the three it is *The Longest Journey* which is the most emotionally intense and personal, the others being more objectively conceived novels of social comedy, and here it may be convenient to consider the first and the third novels together – and perhaps this has even a chronological justification, for we are informed by Rose Macaulay that a draft of the first half of *A Room With a View* was made as early as 1903.

In each of these novels we have two opposed worlds or ways of life, and characters who oscillate between the two worlds. In *Where Angels Fear to Tread* the contrast and the conflict are between the world of 'Sawston', that is, of smug, respectable conventionality, and that of 'Italy', representing the free play of genuine natural feeling. Sawston is personified in Mrs. Herriton, insincere, calculating, cold, and moved by snobbery and her fear of public opinion; Italy by Gino, affectionate, impulsive and natural, a primitive whose very vulgarity has charm and warmth. In the drama that is played out between these opposites, it is Philip Herriton and Caroline Abbott who suffer the conflict between the two sets of values. Italy and the dramatic events which take place there have the effect of drawing out the nobility and passion of Miss Abbott's quiet nature, and it is through her that Philip, hitherto a man who has hovered distantly on the edge of existence, is drawn into life itself and given reality.

All through the day Miss Abbott had seemed to Philip like a
goddess, and more than ever did she seem so now. Many people
look younger and more intimate during great emotion. But some
there are who look older, and remote, and he could not think
that there was little difference in years, and none in composition,
between her and the man whose head was laid upon her breast.
Her eyes were open, full of infinite pity and full of majesty, as if
they discerned the boundaries of sorrow, and saw unimaginable
tracts beyond. Such eyes he had seen in great pictures but never
in a mortal. Her hands were folded round the sufferer, stroking
him lightly, for even a goddess can do no more than that. And it
seemed fitting, too, that she should bend her head and touch his
forehead with her lips.

Philip looked away, as he sometimes looked away from the
great pictures where visible forms suddenly became inadequate
for the things they have shown to us. He was happy; he was
assured that there was greatness in the world. There came to him
an earnest desire to be good through the example of this good
woman. He would try henceforth to be worthy of the things she
had revealed. Quietly, without hysterical prayers or banging of
drums, he underwent conversion. He was saved.

In *A Room With a View*, the antithesis is similar, but this time,
although the first part of the book is set against the background
of Italy, it is the radical Emersons, father and son, who represent life, truth, sincerity. The heroine, Lucy Honeychurch, is
torn between the values which they represent and those of the
pretentious, bookish Cecil Vyse and the insincere and intriguing
Charlotte Bartlett. Lucy has a moment of intense happiness in
Italy when she is kissed against a prospect of primroses by
George Emerson, but, a victim of the false proprieties as ex-
pounded and embodied by her cousin, Charlotte, she is implicated in a system of falsehoods. Persuading herself that she has
been outrageously insulted by a 'cad', she denies her natural
feelings, and shortly after becomes engaged to Cecil Vyse. The
Emersons, by a coincidence, come to live near Lucy's family in
Sussex, and after a game of tennis, when an incident occurs to
remind both George and Lucy of the previous episode in Italy,
George kisses her again, and afterwards pleads for her love.
Lucy deliberately repulses George, denying and suppressing
again her genuine feelings, and that same evening breaks off

D

her engagement to Cecil, after which, lifeless and empty –

. . . She gave up trying to understand herself, and joined the vast armies of the benighted, who follow neither the heart nor the brain, and march to their destiny by catch-words. The armies are full of pleasant and pious folk. But they have yielded to the only enemy that matters – the enemy within. They have sinned against passion and truth, and vain will be their strife after virtue. As the years pass, they are censured. Their pleasantry and their piety show cracks, their wit becomes cynicism, their unselfishness hypocrisy; they feel and produce discomfort wherever they go. They have sinned against Eros and against Pallas Athene, and not by any heavenly intervention, but by the ordinary course of nature, those allied deities will be avenged.

Lucy entered this army when she pretended to George that she did not love him, and pretended to Cecil that she loved no one. The night received her, as it had received Miss Bartlett thirty years before.

In each of these novels, there is a spiritual conflict. In Forster's words, describing Lucy's inner struggle,

The contest lay not between love and duty. Perhaps there never is such a contest. It lay between the real and the pretended. . . .

The 'real', however, seems to be associated with the natural; the 'pretended', with the falsities of convention which deny and frustrate the natural impulses and passions.

Italy makes no appearance in *The Longest Journey* (according to Rose Macaulay, ' . . . at once the most personal and the most universal of the five novels; and obviously the most auto-biographical . . .'), which is divided into three sections, 'Cambridge', 'Sawston', and 'Wiltshire'. Once again, these localities have their counterparts in the personalities of certain of the characters. Cambridge, which clearly represents the author's naïve conception of the good life, has its counterpart in the figure of Stewart Ansell; Sawston, again representing insincere conventionality, pretentious 'culture' and the worship of the false gods of prestige and success, has its human embodi-ment in the schoolmaster, Herbert Pembroke, and his sister, Agnes; while Wiltshire, which stands for the basic touchstone of nature, reality, the earth, is humanly projected into the figure of Stephen Wonham, the healthy, unreflective pagan.

Rickie, the little lame hero of the book, is drawn in turn into
the orbit of each of these worlds and undergoes an inward
struggle which, although it is more desperate and emotionally
intensified, is not unlike that of Lucy Honeychurch in *A Room
With a View.*

In many respects the theme of *The Longest Journey* recapitu-
lates that of *Where Angels Fear to Tread* and *A Room With a View*:
but its development is more complex, and the spiritual drama
more intense. It is, no doubt, this intensity which gives the
book its overcharged emotional atmosphere and its consequent
queer iridiscence as of something faintly morbid or perverse.

For the intensity does not seem justified by the terms of the
drama. Which means that the drama itself is emotionally
worked up to a point at which it becomes false to the terms of
reference within which the mind of the novelist is operating.

Throughout all of Forster's writings there is to be seen an
unfortunate tendency to lapse, at moments when the author
feels the necessity to indicate something beyond the level of
human relationships in their social setting (a level upon which
alone he is perfectly at ease), into 'poetical' vagueness of the
most embarrassing kind. An example of this is to be found
early in *The Longest Journey*, when Rickie glimpses Agnes and
her lover, Gerald Dawes, at a moment of erotic passion.

> Rickie limped away without the sandwiches, crimson and
> afraid. He thought, 'Do such things actually happen?' and he
> seemed to be looking down coloured valleys. Brighter they
> glowed, till gods of pure flame were born in them, and then he
> was looking at pinnacles of virgin snow. While Mr. Pembroke
> talked, the riot of fair images increased. They invaded his being
> and lit lamps at unsuspected shrines. Their orchestra commenced
> in that suburban house, where he had to stand aside for a maid
> to carry in the luncheon. Music flowed past him like a river. He
> stood at the springs of creation and heard the primeval monotony.
> Then an obscure instrument gave out a little phrase. The river
> continued unheeding. The phrase was repeated, and a listener
> might know it was a fragment of the Tune of Tunes. Nobler
> instruments accepted it, the clarionet protected, the brass en-
> couraged, and it rose to the surface to the whisper of violins. In
> full unison was Love born, flame of the flame, flushing the dark
> river beneath him and the virgin snow above. His wings were

infinite, his youth eternal; the sun was a jewel on his finger as he passed it in benediction over the world. Creation, no longer monotonous, acclaimed him, in widening melody, in brighter radiances. Was Love a column of fire? Was he a torrent of song? Was he greater than either – the touch of a man on a woman?

Forster's books abound in passages of this sort, which, however, represent merely an intensification of his normal 'sensitive' and 'charming' style. The prevalence of this sort of false, over-ripe writing indicates some basic uncertainty in Forster's grasp of life, and to apprehend the roots of that uncertainty it is necessary to investigate the disparity between the religious drama which he unfolds and the ultimate principles to which it is referred.

What are the characteristics of this religious drama? First of all, it proffers the possibilities of salvation or of damnation, as we may see in the cases of Philip Herriton and Lucy Honey-church in the other novels. Philip, granted a vision of 'infinite pity and . . . majesty' (which, incidentally, had an erotic source), 'underwent conversion. He was saved.' Lucy, conse-quent upon a denial and a lie, joins 'the vast armies of the benighted' and 'the night received her'. In *The Longest Journey* there are indications that the issue of salvation depends upon the acceptance or rejection of a 'symbolic moment'.

> It seems to me [says Rickie] that here and there in life we meet with a person or incident that is symbolical. It's nothing in itself, yet for the moment it stands for some eternal principle. We accept it, at whatever cost, and we have accepted life. But if we are frightened and reject it, the moment, so to speak, passes; the symbol is never offered again.

The symbol, for Rickie, was his illegitimate half-brother, Stephen. When his kinship with Stephen is revealed to him (although he is then under the mistaken impression that Stephen was the child of his father, whom he hated) he is inexpressibly shocked and disgusted, but his better impulse is to acknowledge him honestly and to inform him of the relation-ship. The impulse is quashed by Agnes, and Rickie succumbs inwardly to the false life represented by Sawston. When a later opportunity presents itself of acknowledging Stephen, and he again fails at the crisis, we are told that 'he remained conscientious and decent, but the spiritual part of him proceeded towards ruin'.

His inner ruination continues, but is interrupted by Stephen's appearance at Sawston, coincident with that of Ansell; who – when Stephen is callously turned away by Agnes – publicly denounces the inhumanity and hypocrisy of Rickie; and there follows Rickie's abandonment of the Sawston life and his reconciliation with Stephen, in which we must presumably see his movement towards 'salvation'.

Stephen, then, in this novel, is the touchstone of reality. He is the 'elemental character' who 'sees straight through perplexities and complications, who is utterly percipient of the reality behind appearance, both in matters of general truth and of incidents in the story', to quote from Burra's essay: and as this essay has Forster's own approval it may be illuminating to consider what further is said in it about Stephen.

In the person of Stephen [writes Burra] physical strength is exalted into the most exciting beauty and the whole novel reminds one constantly of the work which Lawrence produced a few years later. When he makes his first appearance, a third of the way through the book, the writing is lifted up like music to herald his approach. He is the product of an intensely passionate imagination working upon closely recorded detail of behaviour and conduct. He is life, at the centre and at the circumference – he is the world's essential simplicity, transformed by the author's vision. His significance is clear to the reader at once; no other character – except Mrs. Failing when the mood is on her – perceives it, until Ansell, the articulate philosopher, sums him up.

And this is how Ansell sums him up – possibly it is an illustration of how the writing is 'lifted up like music' when he appears:

A silence, akin to poetry, invaded Ansell. Was it only a pose to like this man, or was he really wonderful? He was not romantic, for Romance is a figure with outstretched hands, yearning for the unattainable. Certain figures of the Greeks, to whom we continually return, suggested him a little. One expected nothing of him – no purity of phrase nor swift-edged thought. Yet the conviction grew that he had been back somewhere – back to some table of the gods, spread in a field where there is no noise, and that he belonged for ever to the guests with whom he had eaten.

This, then, is the touchstone of reality and of salvation which Forster proposes and it is not difficult to penetrate its glaring inadequacies: it in no way justifies the emotional intensity of the drama which is indicated as taking place in Rickie's soul. Between the poles of conventionality and naturalness there is room for drama of a sort, but not a drama insufflated with the highly-pitched emotional excitement of *The Longest Journey*, or even indeed that of the other two novels. This is not to say that the drama which is proposed is intrinsically unreal; only that it is made unreal by being set in such limited and lateral perspectives: the drama is too intense for the slight terms of reference. A spiritual conflict is imported into a naturalistic framework, and the effect is one, inevitably, of sentimentality and falsification.

This confusion of the spiritual and the natural runs throughout the earlier novels. As in D. H. Lawrence (who, however, avoided Forster's irrelevant sweetness and charm), spiritual attributes are conferred upon biological phenomena. Thus in *Where Angels Fear to Tread*, Philip's 'conversion' follows upon the erotic emotions stirred in Caroline Abbott by the frankly sensual Gino. Similarly, in *The Longest Journey*, not only is Rickie's personal drama initiated by his witnessing of the erotic passage between Agnes and Gerald Dawes, but the 'acceptance' upon which his salvation depends centres around the result of his dead mother's illicit intercourse with her farmer lover – a Lady Chatterly situation. The importance which Forster confers upon sexual passion is shown both by the excessive excitement with which he approaches it, and the way in which he connects it with violent death – the finality of death being utilized to confer something of its own ultimate, absolute character upon the emotion stirred by sex.

To endow conventionality with all the attributes of the powers of darkness is, of course, grossly to overstate the matter. The world represented by the word 'Sawston' has genuine undercurrents of evil which we are made to feel, but which are simply not explicable in the terms of Nature versus Convention which are proposed. When we encounter such a sentence as this –

> Then he [i.e. Rickie] . . . prayed passionately, for he knew that the conventions would claim him soon . . .

we at once feel the somewhat ridiculous inadequacy of the antithesis which provides the frame of reference for the novel.

Not only in *The Longest Journey* is the question of salvation (raised in the action of the narrative and brought to an arbitrary conclusion there) left with a good many loose ends flying: the same is true of the other novels. What is to happen to Philip Herriton, now that his eyes have been opened to the wonder and beauty of life? What will happen to Lucy and George Emerson now that their difficulties are over and they are happily married? It is hard to see any more finality in their 'saved' state than that implied in the insufficient and question-begging symbol, towards the end of *The Longest Journey*, of 'Wiltshire' – the life of pastoral satisfactions.

The incompleteness and indeed the reversibility of Forster's moral symbolism is shown in his 'realistic' confusion of the attributes of the 'good' and 'bad' types. Having said, as Burra says in the essay already referred to, that Forster introduces an 'elemental' character into each of his books, whose wisdom 'puts into ironic contrast the errors and illusions of the rest', and having pointed out that 'In the case of the men the stress is laid on the athletic, of the women on the intuitive', one can point to characters who possess the external evidences of these qualities, and who yet turn out to be on the wrong side of the moral fence. George Emerson, Gino and Stephen may be said to be athletic', and therefore on the side of the 'real'. But equally athletic, though by no means on the side of the real, are Gerald Dawes and Agnes, while Stewart Ansell, undoubtedly a touchstone of values, is not athletic at all. Similarly in the case of the 'intuitive' women. Of them Mrs. Moore and Mrs. Wilcox and perhaps Mrs. Honeychurch are recognizably 'good' characters, while Mrs. Failing, a woman of the same basic type, and who possesses the additional symbolical advantage of living in Wiltshire, is as recognizably 'bad'. One might compare also Cecil Vyse with Philip Herriton and Stewart Ansell. This confusion is true to life, no doubt, but it is not true to the symbolical pattern of the novels, and it is necessary to ask what are the reasons for this ambivalence.

The most plausible explanation of Forster's 'realistic' confusion of good and bad types (a confusion which, it must be repeated, is out of place in a symbolical setting) lies in the very plain fact that the middle-class existence which Forster portrays, the life of the irresponsible, moneyed, parasitical bourgeoisie, is false, because it is based upon social falsehood, and nothing can ever be made really right within it. Consequently, no stable system of moral symbolism can be erected upon it.

This is not to say that his characters are by that fact deprived of the possibility of spiritual struggle; only that such a struggle which takes place within a spiritual arena circumscribed by its reference to the framework of their false social order, and whose outcome does not result in an overthrowing or a repudiation of the limits set around their lives by their privileged social and economic position, is thereby rendered devoid of real and radical significance. The life of Forster's characters, as members of the English upper middle-classes, is based on falsehood because it is based on unearned income, derived from nameless and unmentioned sources, and all their independence, freedom, culture, 'personal relationships' are only made possible by this fact. Their lives are lived in a watertight system abstracted from the larger life of society as a whole. They are out of touch with humanity, carefully, though for the most part unconsciously, preserving themselves, by means of their mental circumscriptions and social codes, from all encroachment of the painful and upsetting actualities which make their privileged existence possible. Unlike the rich of other times, their privileges carry with them no burden of responsibility, and thus possess no concrete social sanction. The penalty they pay for their social advantages is a heavy one – a fundamental unreality which vitiates the personal dramas which take place in the closed social circuit to which they are condemned. For an inner spiritual change which affects one's attitude to one or two other selected persons only, and does not extend itself to include every other human being irrespective of social distinction, is invalidated from the start. But at the point at which some attempt to deal with this question would seem necessary, Forster brings his stories to a close.

It is not difficult to perceive the connection existing between the false social circumstances which set limits to reality for the sake of their own perpetuation, and the inhibiting factors which

prevent Forster from reaching out to ultimates for the validation
of his religious drama. The novelist, despite his perception of
the reality of personal struggle towards salvation, is himself
unable to transcend the pattern imposed on reality by the self-
interest of the class to which he belongs, and instead, therefore,
of permitting the drama with which he is concerned to break
through the pattern and centre itself within the perspectives of
reality, he curtails the perspectives themselves and attempts to
persuade himself and his readers that the drama takes place
between the poles of Nature and Convention, with Nature
filling the place of God, or the Absolute.* The novelist's own
awareness that this will not justify a real spiritual dynamism in
his characters must eventually follow.

II

IT is possibly the realization of something of this which led
Forster to abandon the narrow personal drama and to embrace
the social issues which are clearly displayed in his fourth novel,
Howards End (1910). There is no doubt whatever as to the social
orientation of this novel and its characterization, nor as to its
bearing upon the logic of Forster's development. From the
point reached in *The Longest Journey* there were two possible
paths for one in Forster's situation: either to affirm the reality
of the spiritual, and thus to justify the drama of personal salvation, by placing the individual (and thus by inference his
social circumstances) in the ultimate perspectives of existence;
or to affirm the primary reality of the social and to reduce the
spiritual to an epiphenomenon dependent upon the social
pattern. The first alternative would have made possible a
continuation and development of the personal drama; and
thus, conceivably, the transformation of Forster into a genuine

* Of all the characters in the early novels who represent 'the real' as
against 'the pretended', not one derives his sanction from any other than a
natural principle. Stephen and Gino are a direct appeal to biological, not to
say physiological, values. In the case of Stephen it is made clear that he is a
crude atheist, while Ansell is evidently an ethical materialist. Old Mr.
Emerson, a religious figure, is an old-fashioned agnostic radical. The
clearest insight, however, into Forster's religiosity is to be derived from a
study of his early short stories where Nature is deified as Pan and conven-
tionalism is contrasted with the amoral universe of dryads, mermaids and
satyrs.

creator: the second could only have necessitated a transition from the personal to the social level, a movement from the centre to the periphery; which was, in fact, the result.

Howards End must be interpreted from this point of view. Here is an evidently allegorical contrast between the inner world of personal existence, represented by the cultured sisters Helen and Margaret Schlegel, and the outer world of the practical organization of living represented by the business-like, British-to-the-backbone, empire-building Wilcoxes. But before we move on to a consideration of the relationship between the two families, the focal point of the novel must be considered.

That focal point is money. Hardly are the Schlegels introduced before the subject of their investments is touched upon. Money, indeed, is the *leit-motif* which accompanies the Schlegels throughout the book. And it is poverty, in the character of Leonard Bast, which underscores their wealth and culture. The significance of this bringing to the surface of what, in order to permit the strictly personal drama, had hitherto been kept in concealment, hardly needs to be emphasized. *Howards End* is in one of its aspects a justification of economic privilege; but the recognition of the individual's dependence upon social circumstances destroys the possibility of the drama of personal salvation, and substitutes the drama of social relationships.

Leonard rises, spectre-like and accusing, from the depths of the world outside the social hot-house of the economically and culturally privileged, to confront the Schlegels with the harsh realities of their situation. But how subjectively and with what a suspicious bias he is presented will appear from the manner in which he is pushed on to the scene by his author:

> The boy Leonard Bast, stood at the extreme verge of gentility. He was not in the abyss, but he could see it, and at times people whom he knew had dropped in, and counted no more. He knew that he was poor, and would admit it: he would have died sooner than confess any inferiority to the rich. This may be splendid of him. But he was inferior to most rich people, there is not the least doubt of it. He was not as courteous as the average rich man, nor as intelligent, nor as healthy, nor as lovable. His mind and his body had been alike underfed, because he was poor.

Because he does not enjoy the financial advantages of the

Schlegels, Leonard Bast's aspirations towards culture are made to appear pathetic in their hopelessness. But the character of Leonard Bast is not the result of authentic, disinterested observation of life; he is unconsciously falsified, in a manner which will be considered below, to fit within the preconceived interpretation of reality which underpins the structure of the novel.

The argument of *Howards End*, at all times implicit and at times declared, is that culture and the good life depend upon economic security, which in the capitalistic world of the time means privilege. 'To trust people is a luxury in which only the wealthy can indulge; the poor cannot afford it' – such statements as this are intermittent in the early parts of the book. In Chapter VII the following conversation takes place between Margaret Schlegel and her aunt, Mrs. Munt, a conversation which sets the course for Margaret's progression throughout the story:

'I hope to risk things all my life.'

'Oh, Margaret, most dangerous.'

'But after all,' she continued with a smile, 'there's never any great risk as long as you have money.'

'Oh, shame! What a shocking speech!'

'Money pads the edge of things,' said Miss Schlegel. 'God help those who have none.'

'But this is something quite new!' said Mrs. Munt, who collected new ideas as a squirrel collects nuts, and was especially attracted by those that are portable.

'New for me; sensible people have acknowledged it for years. You and I and the Wilcoxes stand upon money as upon islands. It is so firm beneath our feet that we forget its very existence. It's only when we see someone near us tottering that we realize all that an independent income means. Last night, when we were talking up here round the fire, I began to think that the very soul of the world is economic, and that the lowest abyss is not the absence of love, but the absence of coin.'

'I call that rather cynical.'

'So do I. But Helen and I, we ought to remember, when we are tempted to criticize others, that we are standing on these islands, and that most of the others are down below the surface of the sea. The poor cannot always reach those whom they want to love, and they can hardly ever escape from those whom they love no longer. We rich can. Imagine the tragedy last June if Helen and Paul

Wilcox had been poor people, and couldn't invoke railways and motor-cars to part them.'

'That's more like Socialism,' said Mrs. Munt suspiciously.

'Call it what you like. I call it going through life with one's hand spread open on the table. I'm tired of these rich people who pretend to be poor, and think it shows a nice mind to ignore the piles of money that keep their feet above the waves. I stand each year upon six hundred pounds, and Helen upon the same, and Tibby will stand upon eight, and as fast as our pounds crumble away into the sea they are renewed – from the sea, yes, from the sea. And all our thoughts are the thoughts of six-hundred-pounders, and all our speeches; and because we don't want to steal umbrellas ourselves, we forget that below the sea people do want to steal them and do steal them sometimes, and that what's a joke up here is down there reality——'

. . .'Do tell me this, at all events. Are you for the rich or for the poor?'

'Too difficult. Ask me another. Am I for poverty or for riches? For riches. Hurrah for riches!'

'For riches,' echoed Mrs. Munt, having, as it were, at last secured her nut.

'Yes. For riches. Money for ever!'

'So am I, and so, I am afraid, are most of my acquaintances at Swanage, but I am surprised that you agree with us.'

That conversation occurs after the Schlegels' first encounter with Leonard Bast. After a second encounter, at which they find out something of his private life, the Schlegels attend a debating society at which the question is discussed of how a philanthropic millionaire ought to dispose of his money. 'Mr. Bast' is taken as the hypothetical poor man whose condition is to be improved by the millionaire's bounty, and Margaret, after listening to various propositions, intervenes with the suggestion that he should be given the money itself.

'Money's educational. It's far more educational than the things it buys. . . . When your Socialism comes it may be different, and we may think in terms of commodities instead of cash. Till it comes give people cash, for it is the warp of civilization, whatever the woof may be. The imagination ought to play upon money and realize it vividly, for it's the – the second most important thing in the world. It is so slurred over and hushed up, there is so little clear thinking – oh, political economy, of course, but so few of us think clearly about our own private incomes, and admit that independent thoughts are in nine cases out of ten the result of independent means. Money: give Mr. Bast money, and don't bother about his ideals. He'll pick those up for himself.'

On the other side of the Schlegels to Leonard Bast, however, and representing the organized, coercive practical life which guarantees to them that private income which makes their cultured existence possible, stands Henry Wilcox, efficient, practical, masterful, but spiritually and emotionally unintegrated. But the Wilcoxes' guarantees have a spiritual aspect – that of the 'outer life' which Forster takes as antithetical to the 'inner life' represented by the Schlegels. The Wilcoxes are introduced on this very note, which is struck almost immediately after Helen's return, at the beginning of the tale, from her visit to Howards End, Mrs. Wilcox's country house, where she has had a brief erotic passage with the Wilcoxes' youngest son, Paul.

'To think that because you and a young man meet for a moment, there must be all these telegrams and anger,' supplied Margaret.
Helen nodded.
'I've often thought about it, Helen. It's one of the most interesting things in the world. The truth is that there is a great outer life that you and I have never touched – a life in which telegrams and anger count. Personal relations, that we think supreme, are not supreme there. There love means marriage settlements, death, death duties. So far I'm clear. But here's my difficulty. This outer life, though obviously horrid, often seems the real one – there's grit in it. It does breed character. Do personal relations lead to sloppiness in the end?'
'Oh, Meg, that's what I felt, only not so clearly, when the Wilcoxes were so competent, and seemed to have their hands on all the ropes.'
'Don't you feel it now?'
'I remember Paul at breakfast,' said Helen quietly. 'I shall never forget him. He had nothing to fall back upon. I know that personal relations are the real life, for ever and ever.'
'Amen!'

The respective positions of Leonard Bast and Henry Wilcox have an obvious symbolic importance, in that the leanings of the Schlegel sisters are divided between the two. The impulsive and idealistic Helen reacts vehemently against Mr. Wilcox, and

her reaction drives her towards Leonard Bast, who has suffered
as a result of the business-man's human irresponsibility (and
whose character as a *victim* is further emphasized by the revelation that his bedraggled wife was once Mr. Wilcox's mistress).
Margaret, on the other hand, wiser and more level-headed, so
we are told, is drawn towards the Wilcox family and led to
associate herself with the values they represent.

> 'If Wilcoxes hadn't worked and died in England for thousands
> of years, you and I couldn't sit here without having our throats
> cut. There would be no trains, no ships to carry us literary people
> about in, no fields even. Just savagery. No – perhaps not even that.
> Without their spirit life might never have moved out of proto-
> plasm. More and more do I refuse to draw my income and sneer
> at those who guarantee it.'

The dramatic action of the book develops out of the schism
which takes place between the Schlegel sisters as each moves
further along her chosen path, Margaret towards the acceptance
of the 'outer life', expressed in her engagement to the widowed
Mr. Wilcox, and Helen towards her pursuit of a somewhat
vaguely conceived 'ideal'. The scales are, however, heavily
weighted against Helen, who is used as a mere foil to her sister's
maturer wisdom. That Helen's antagonism to her sister's
engagement to Mr. Wilcox is a modified one, and that inwardly
she is reconciled to it and even approves of it, appears from a
conversation between the sisters following an outburst of
Helen's to Mr. Wilcox on the subject of his responsibility for
the misfortunes of Leonard Bast.

> Margaret . . . gave her sister a thorough scolding. She cen-
> sured her, not for disapproving of the engagement, but for
> throwing over her disapproval a veil of mystery. . . . Helen was
> silent for a minute, and then burst into a queer speech, which
> cleared the air. 'Go on and marry him. I think you're splendid;
> and if anyone can pull it off, you will.' Margaret denied that there
> was anything to 'pull off', but she continued: 'Yes, there is, and
> I wasn't up to it with Paul. I can only do what's easy. I can only
> entice and be enticed. I can't, and won't, attempt difficult rela-
> tions. . . . But you, you're different. You're a heroine. . . .
> You mean to keep proportion, and that's heroic, it's Greek, and I
> don't see why it shouldn't succeed with you. Go on and fight with

him and help him. Don't ask *me* for help, or even for sympathy. Henceforward I'm going my own way. I mean to be thorough, because thoroughness is easy.'

The morality of the story and the conclusion we are supposed to draw from it are plain. 'Only connect . . .' exhorts the book's epigraph; and Margaret it is, we are asked to believe, who accomplishes the connection.

In this novel, however, once again Forster's work suffers artistically as the result of the confusion between the symbolical and the realistic treatment of his subject. A clearer and deeper mind, we can safely assume, taking the theme of the relationship of the inner life to the outer, would manipulate somewhat different symbols from 'Wilcoxes' and 'Schlegels' and would reach somewhat different conclusions from those of *Howards End*. For Forster has not in fact stated the real issue either helpfully or sincerely. What he has succeeded in doing, and in doing quite clearly enough, is to reveal, in the pre-determined and therefore falsified treatment of his subject, the central predicament and equivocation inherent in the compromising liberal mentality.

The crucial falsification is not that of the characters of the Wilcoxes, who are presented honestly and objectively enough, but of the Schlegels and Leonard Bast. And it is here, perhaps, that we touch upon the psychological compulsion which inclined Forster's mind towards his admixture of the symbolical and the realistic – namely, in its effect in securing the falsification of symbolical truth necessary for the adaptation of the realities represented by the words 'culture' and 'poverty' to the far from disinterested preconceptions of the bourgeois liberal point of view.

'It is private life that holds out the mirror to infinity; personal intercourse, and that alone, that ever hints at a personality beyond our daily vision.' Such, in characteristically Forsterian phraseology, is the Schlegel viewpoint. Suppose we grant, then, what is so almost squeamishly proffered – that, symbolically, the Schlegels represent the inner life of personality in contrast to the outer life of organization represented by the Wilcoxes. The question follows: Can there in fact ever be such a reconciliation between the two as is symbolized by Margaret's marriage to Mr. Wilcox? To speak more explicitly, can Culture only save itself from inward debility by an alliance with the State, can the life of the spirit maintain and strengthen itself only by a compromise with the Prince of this world?* Is such a reconciliation, or compromise, a spiritual achievement or a betrayal?

From the spiritual, personal and cultural point of view it is clearly a betrayal; it is the equivocal and deluded attempt to serve two masters which is spoken of in the New Testament. That Forster is uneasy about this is shown not only by his splitting of the Schlegel viewpoint into two, but also by his hesitant treatment of the relations between Margaret and Mr. Wilcox, for their relationship crashes on a critical issue, and is only saved, rather unconvincingly, by the entirely fortuitous circumstances which make Henry Wilcox, at the last moment, a 'broken man', and drive him humbly to his wife for protection.

What, indeed, is this 'connection', but the bridging of the two worlds which were, in the earlier novels, held apart as spiritual antitheses: the world of falsity and convention and the world of the genuine and natural: the 'pretended' and the 'real'? Twists of presentation aside, in what essential respect can the Wilcoxes be said to differ from the Pembrokes of *The Longest Journey*? Yet while, in the earlier novel, for the sake of the personal drama which is enacted between those antitheses, the Pembrokes are represented as something at all costs to be eschewed and shunned, in the later book, where the personal drama gives place to the social, the same type, with a few changes, is represented as admirable and to be courted.

What is the reason for this change of attitude and the decision to compromise? The answer, it is not difficult to perceive, lies in the weakness and invalidity of the inner life, of 'the real', as conceived by Forster, which, presented in naturalistic terms, has not sufficient inner vitality to maintain itself as a centre of spiritual energy in independence of the outer region of practical life. Forster's fundamental error consists of invoking the spiritual principle and then referring it for its ultimate sanction not to

* *Vide* Chapter XXVII: 'Talk as one would, *Mr. Wilcox was king of this world*, the superman, with his own morality, whose head remained in the clouds.' (My italics.)

God, to the supernatural – a resort which would have had the effect of thoroughly disequilibrizing Forster's mental pattern and bringing it to a new and revolutionary centrality – but to Nature. That Forster's ethical naturalism will not bear the spiritual burdens which are placed upon it we have already seen. This inability to support the personal values represented by the Schlegels by an appeal to any higher order of being than that embodied in the mundanely 'mysterious' figure of the first Mrs. Wilcox with her tiresome wisp of hay (with the dew still on it) deprives the antithesis between Schlegels and Wilcoxes of its absolute character and therefore of all real value as a statement of the relationship between the inner and outer realms of existence – or the realm of subjectivity and that of objectivization. For neither can the Schlegel sisters really be accepted as adequately symbolizing the life of the spirit, nor can Leonard Bast be regarded as a truthful representation of the urge towards culture unsupported by economic privilege. The Schlegels are simply what they are 'realistically' represented to be – two specimens of the leisured bourgeois parasite upon culture. And all that the book leaves us with is a statement of the real relations between 'cultured, sensitive and democratic' liberalism and the capitalistic structure of Edwardian society which permits and guarantees its harmless, ineffectual and even charming existence.

Here it is that Forster's confusion of symbolical and realistic treatment serves the purposes of so doctoring the issue that it conforms to the pre-requirements of an outlook obviously conditioned by its liberal bourgeois background. Forster's realistic presentation of the Schlegels enables him to get around the responsibility of declaring that his novel is an allegory of the inner life. Quite so. But if the Schlegels are only – the Schlegels, nothing more or less, then the book is deprived of inner significance. Forster's confused method enables him to retain the overtones of symbolical significance while presenting an apparently straightforward realistic narrative: it is no wonder that the book has been popular.

Perhaps we may exonerate Forster of the charge of sinister intent in deliberately falsifying his presentation of the Schlegels, at the price of denying them the symbolical significance which

E

they are presumed to possess. But it is much more difficult to avoid making the charge in the case of his presentation of Leonard Bast; and there is the further reflection to which this leads, namely, that Leonard is presented in such a way as to emphasize the Schlegels' claim to symbolical significance as the bearers of cultural values and the inner life. For the implication of Leonard's failure, owing to inferior social advantages, to attain the inner life, is that the inner life itself is made possible only by the possession of social advantages such as those the Schlegels enjoy, and from this it follows that, in the author's mind, the Schlegels do therefore possess symbolical significance.

Forster's evident determination that Leonard Bast should be made to fit the preconception that culture is secondary to economic security leads him to draw a portrait which is the least convincing fabrication in the book, and the one which most plainly calls into question the author's fundamental seriousness and responsibility as an artist. Now, it simply is not true that an inferior social position automatically deprives its victim of the possibility of attaining to the inner life, any more than it is true that the possession of social advantages guarantees spiritual development. It is not even true that the average rich man is, as Forster states, more courteous, intelligent and lovable than the average poor man.

The wretched Leonard is a lay figure, an effigy made to walk and talk in such a way as to bolster up the liberal philosophy which inspires the book. For culture is *not* dependent upon wealth; it is only to the parasites of the spirit that it appears as an object which can be externally appropriated. Nor can Forster's pressing of this point home find any response in the mind of the genuine champion of the dispossessed, for the depth of his concern with the sufferings of the underprivileged masses may be judged from the fact that it is Henry Wilcox with whom Margaret, 'keen to derive the modern capitalist from the warriors and hunters of the past', 'connects'.

Leonard is disposed of by death, and his elimination glossed over with an outburst of Forster's special lyricism:

. . . the time for telegrams and anger was over, and it seemed wisest that the hands of Leonard should be folded on his breast and be filled with flowers. Here was the father; leave it at that. Let Squalor be turned into Tragedy, whose eyes are the stars, and whose hands hold the sunset and the dawn.

III

THE foregoing delineation of the inner development of Forster's mind as revealed in his novels should have clarified the nature of the compromise or betrayal which lies at the root of 'cultured, sensitive and democratic liberalism', a compromise which cannot but vitiate its perpetrator's grasp of reality and deprive his mind of creative purpose. But if my interpretation of the interior dialectic of Forster's novels has any validity, then it follows that *A Passage to India* (1924) must have its relation to it. What, briefly, is that relationship?

With the resolution of the conflict between what is called, in *A Room With a View*, 'the real and the pretended', signified by the union of the Schlegels with the Wilcoxes, the novelist's own inner thought-conflict, expressing the inner conflict which lies at the bottom of all the novels, comes to an end, and there is no longer any imperative urge towards fictional creation. Forster has exhausted his theme, and the dramatic materials are lacking. More, his interest has moved outward, peripherally, from the personal drama to a concern with the generalized problems of society, and it is now possible to speak of him (*vide* Burra) as 'an artist on the fringe of social reform'. The only way in which the novelist can finally exploit his basic situation is by transporting his mechanical dramatic apparatus to some external situation which it happens approximately and fortuitously to fit. And so, in *A Passage to India*, we have the Anglo-Indian world of Turtons and Burtons on the one side and on the other that of Aziz and his compatriots, with Cyril Fielding, the liberal educationalist, in between, and Mrs. Moore, the counterpart of Mrs. Wilcox, anomalously bridging both worlds. But the apparatus hardly fits the drama, which, indeed, exiguous as it is, takes place, not in the battlefield of any individual soul, but on the plane of external action and political issues, where it is brought only to a precarious and inconclusive termination. The conflict is external to the author's mind.

A Passage to India is written at the extreme edge of Forster's creative impulse. It is hard to see how any but a mechanical and inwardly meaningless work of fiction could have succeeded it, and the fact that it has been followed by silence need cause us no great surprise. Certain features of the novel, however, have an interest in the light of the interpretation of Forster which I have proposed.

If the book can be said to have a hero, that hero must be Cyril Fielding, a character who evidently embodies his creator's own outlook upon life. In Fielding, we find a union of the qualities seen as separate in *Howards End*. Fielding is humane, cultured, enlightened, progressive, but he is also capable, reliable, and self-assured: he has a sense of the importance of 'personal relationships' but he also has 'grit' and his hands are definitely 'on the ropes'. Ideally, then, he should be an harmonious figure. Yet it seems that there is some dissatisfaction on his author's part with the finality of the values which he embodies.

. . . he felt dubious and discontented suddenly, and wondered whether he was really and truly successful as a human being. After forty years' experience he had learnt to manage his life and make the best of it on advanced European lines, had developed his personality, explored his limitations, controlled his passions – and he had done it all without becoming either pedantic or worldly. A creditable achievement; but as the moment passed, he felt he ought to have been working at something else the whole time – he didn't know at what, never would know, never could know, and that was why he felt sad.

Those feelings of self-dissatisfaction are again touched on at the end of the book, where Fielding is speaking to Aziz of his marriage to Mrs. Moore's daughter, Stella, who, he feels, unlike himself, is 'after something' – the 'something', whatever it is which is included in this vague gesture, being that, evidently, which is outside the scope of his limited, rationalistic scheme of life.

But the most significant factor in the novel is the emotional background provided by the Marabar Caves, around which the action centres. It is the visit of Aziz, Mrs. Moore and Miss Quested to the caves which precipitates the drama, and throughout the novel the echoing *'Boum-boum'* of the caves supplies an insistent undercurrent to the moods and thoughts of the characters.

The caves' horrible echo, is, however, a more elaborate repetition of something which has evidently lurked always at the edge of Forster's mind, for it has found expression in previous writings. It is indicated by the description of the infernal region in which a character in an early story finds himself after death, through his smug, unheroic life; and it is indicated also in the metaphor of the goblins 'walking quietly over the universe' to describe the Beethoven Symphony in *Howards End*. ('Panic and emptiness', the message of the goblins, being the words which Helen has previously applied to the inner life of the Wilcoxes.) The caves reiterate the same message of meaninglessness and nullity, but more insistently and overpoweringly. The echo murmurs: 'Pathos, piety, courage – they exist, but are identical, and so is filth. Everything exists, nothing has value.' And the terror of the Marabar lay in the fact that it 'robbed infinity and eternity of their vastness, the only quality that accommodates them to mankind'. Not only does the echo of the caves prolong itself throughout the story to which it provides such a menacing undertone, but it has the effect of undermining and disintegrating Mrs. Moore's hold on life, and ultimately, of destroying her. When we recollect that Mrs. Moore is to *A Passage to India* what Mrs. Wilcox is to *Howards End* – that she is the 'elemental character' who represents what appears to be the highest value to which Forster can appeal to sanction his interpretation of life, the metaphorical implications of her disintegration and its occasion are ominous, to say the very least. Nor is there anything in Forster's occasional and miscellaneous writings of the past twenty years to dispel the misgivings to which a consideration of the sequence of his novels, ending on this ominous note, gives rise.

VIRGINIA WOOLF

I

AMONG the women writers of our time there is none whose *prestige* stands higher than that of Virginia Woolf. It is because I believe this prestige to be unfounded that I am here proposing a drastic revaluation of her work. The legend of Virginia Woolf as an 'artist' pure and simple, projecting, in an experiential vacuum, sensitive and delicate word-patterns devoid of all but the most essentially aesthetic content, is one which can have taken root only in a society in which there exists the most lamentable indifference both to life and art. The following passage from a review of a typically adulatory book about Virginia Woolf's novels is representative of the prevalent inert and thoughtless acceptance of this legend:

> Of Mrs. Woolf's style this book does not directly treat, yet . . . here, if anywhere, the style *is* the writer . . . her best work is a sequence of illuminating moments woven into a complete design; and for that design her imagination used its own language – an impressionistic, highly charged, emotive prose that differs at times little, if at all, from poetry; its texture shot with grace, sensitivity, and subtle awareness. Over a human landscape of deliberately limited dimensions her delicate rhythms drift and play like soft clouds through which gleams the dappled sunlight of her pity and her humour, her sympathy for the sorrows and frustrations of her fellow men and women, and her ironic smile at their weaknesses and foibles. . . .

To the question, 'Yes – but what are Virginia Woolf's novels *about*? What view of life do they reflect? What particular insights do they display?' one receives no satisfactory answer.

That Virginia Woolf's novels are tenuous, amorphous and vague, that her prose expresses a state of sensitized generality, is true. Nevertheless, this condition has definite psychic roots, and in itself raises the question of value. What I shall attempt to do in this essay, therefore, is simply to lay bare the interior psychological pattern which runs through the series of her novels. It will then appear that beneath the imprecisions, vaguenesses and generalities of the particular w ɔrk there is an underlying, basic preoccupation which gives rise to those qualities: that the merely aesthetic approach to her work begs the question, and that beneath the aesthetic surface there runs a theme of a totally non-aesthetic character. In bringing this theme to light, in revealing the unconscious psychological process which determines the aesthetic form of the work, my aim is to explode the theory of aestheticism, and to show that no artistic work can exist in independence of its maker's human preoccupations and beliefs. All that is necessary to this end is to expose the interior logic of Virginia Woolf's development, which aestheticism is both unwilling and powerless to penetrate.

Virginia Woolf's work as a novelist falls roughly into three periods. There is the early period of conventional fictionalizing represented by her two first novels, *The Voyage Out* and *Night and Day*. There is the period of experiment marked by the discarding of those fictional properties which she was unable to utilize, and issuing in *Jacob's Room* – the first novel in what was to be recognized as her characteristic manner – and later, in an ascending scale, in *Mrs. Dalloway* and *To the Lighthouse*. And lastly, there is the descent into an increasingly despairing vacuousness and dissipation of perception through *The Waves*, *The Years*, and finally *Between the Acts*, marked by a disintegration of form expressing a surrender of all significance to the accidental process of time.

The Voyage Out (1915) and *Night and Day* (1919) are dull, third-rate novels in the conventional manner, interesting only because they reveal quite plainly the nature of the disabilities under which Virginia Woolf laboured. These two novels reveal that she lacked the first requirements of a good novelist: the ability to create living, credible characters whose life is projected into an interesting and significant narrative pattern. The structure of the first novel is incoherent. In substance, it is the story of Rachel Vinrace, an inexperienced girl of the professional classes, who is taken out to an island on the Amazon where there is a colony of holiday-making Europeans, and who makes a variety of haphazard human contacts, ponders on the meaning of life, is flustered by her discovery of sex, falls vaguely in love, goes on a picnic up the river, where she becomes ill and dies. The narrative is neither coherent nor sustained. Characters are introduced, become the focus of the action, and are then dropped. Indeed, it is not until she is nearly half-way through the book that the author makes up her mind that the story is to centre around Rachel, and not around one of the other half-dozen characters to whom, up to that point, no less attention has been paid.

Night and Day is a somewhat more orderly and externally competent piece of work. Here we have four chief characters, two young men and two young women, and the story is kept within the limits of their relationships, which are worked out to a conventional conclusion. It is, however, a story of no interest whatever, revealing no insight into the principles of human conduct – the dramatic movement is occasioned by the commonplace device of the 'love-interest' – and padded out (it is a work of five hundred pages) with irrelevant asides, descriptions and soliloquies. *Night and Day* might well qualify as the dullest novel in the English language. There can be few readers who have really traversed the book from beginning to end.

The uncertainty which characterizes Virginia Woolf's grasp of human character, experience, relationships, finds unintentionally ludicrous expression in her treatment of the relationship of her lovers, whom she presents as moved by the most comically unmotivated attractions and repulsions. The 'misty state of mind' in which Katharine Hilbery, the book's heroine, avers she had accepted William Rodney's offers of marriage, it is only too apparent is the common mental condition of Virginia Woolf's characters. Ralph Denham, the second male partner in this conventional foursome, for instance, explains to Katharine that –

> 'You can force me to talk as if this feeling for you were an hallucination, but all our feelings are that. The best of them are half illusions.'

This sense of vagueness and unreality is itself connected with an underlying sense of the planlessness of existence. A minor character, Evelyn Murgatroyd, in *The Voyage Out*, left alone after receiving a proposal of marriage, reflects, 'What did matter then? What was the meaning of it all?' and this question is never far from the lips of any character in these two novels. Towards the close of *Night and Day*, impelled to snatch at a meaningful conclusion for her otherwise random narrative, the author secures it with the simple overt statement that the lovers, Ralph and Katharine, merely by coming together, had some· how achieved valid intimations of the elusive 'significance' of human life.

> She had turned before she answered him. She had no wish to see anyone tonight; it seemed to her that the immense riddle was answered; the problem had been solved; she held in her hands for one brief moment the globe which we spend our lives in trying to shape, round, whole and entire from the confusion of chaos.
>
> 'It's all so easy – it's all so simple,' Katharine quoted, remembering some words of Sally Seal's, and wishing Ralph to understand that she followed the track of his thought. She felt him trying to piece together in a laborious and elementary fashion fragments of belief, unsoldered and separate, lacking the unity of phrases, fashioned by the old believers. Together they groped in this difficult region, where the unfinished, the unfulfilled, the unwritten, the unreturned, came together in their ghostly way and wore the semblance of the complete and the satisfactory. The future emerged more splendid than ever from this construction of the present.

Beneath *The Voyage Out* and *Night and Day*, it is obvious, are preoccupations of a quite basic and elementary kind with the primary conditions of human existence. And the first condition for existence at all is that implied in what we mean by the word 'belief'.

There is, in David Daiches' little book on Virginia Woolf, a discerning passage on this question of a writer's belief and its relation to method and style.

> . . . Virginia Woolf, unlike Jane Austen [says Daiches] was writing in a world in which there was no consensus of opinion concerning what 'reality' was, and, unlike some of her contemporaries, she was very much aware of that lack of agreement. The second and third decades of the twentieth century, which saw Virginia Woolf's flowering as a novelist, saw also the final dissolution of that common background of belief and attitude that made it possible for a writer to talk of Smith and Liverpool while

assuming certain unarticulated preconceptions concerning the nature and value of human life which made communication on what Virginia Woolf called the 'materialist' level at the same time statements about reality. Virginia Woolf had, as it were, to start from scratch, to provide each character with a world view in the light of which it was to be interpreted. The events recorded in her novels were not acted out against a solid background of belief, a stable emotional and intellectual pattern; they had, on the contrary, to be invested with their own philosophic and emotional background. Virginia Woolf had come face to face with the problem that challenged so many of her contemporary artists, the problem of producing significant art in an individualistic and sceptical age.

Art without belief – without, that is, community belief – is not easy to create. For here the artist has to throw his own sensibility around each work in such a way as to provide the reader or beholder with a philosophic background sufficient to serve as a key to the patterning of that particular work. As that key is no longer provided by the civilization in which both writer and reader live, it is up to the writer to provide one himself. Virginia Woolf has, therefore, to find a method of writing which enables her to tell a story while at the same time indicating the particular view of 'reality' which gives that story significance. This is the explanation of her constant concern with 'reality'.

. . . In an essay entitled 'How it strikes a Contemporary' she discusses this very point, the relation of art to community belief. Referring to the 'sense of security' that emerges from the work of Wordsworth, Scott and Jane Austen, she asks, 'From what, then, arises that sense of security which gradually, delightfully, and completely overcomes us?' And her reply is worth noting: 'It is the power of their belief, their conviction, that imposes itself upon us. . . . They have their judgment of conduct. They know the relations of human beings towards each other and towards the universe. Neither of them (i.e., Jane Austen and Scott) probably has a word to say about the matter outright, but everything depends upon it. . . . To believe that your impressions hold good for others is to be released from the cramp and confinement of personality.'

And this is precisely the point. The moderns, as Virginia Woolf saw them, lived in an age without common belief, and therefore could not be free from the cramp and confinement of personality. 'Our contemporaries afflict us because they have ceased to believe,' she complains in the same essay. Yet there was a way out of the difficulty. It might be possible to make a virtue of necessity, to find a way of writing which would call for dependence on the writer's personality, a way of writing out of a personal sense of truth so as to convey that sense to the reader as he reads. That is the course that Virginia Woolf took.

These remarks have their relevance: but it seems necessary to question the far too easy way in which they accept a writer's inert dependence upon beliefs which he receives at second-hand from 'society'. For where does 'society' in turn get those beliefs? Granted that the society to which Virginia Woolf belonged was without common beliefs, to explain the inner nature of her work by this is precisely equivalent to saying that she had no creative originality, that she passively and vacuously reflected, in personal terms, the spiritual decadence of that society. Daiches, however, evidently does not suppose that the question of belief is, in itself, of real and determining significance. He attributes to it nothing much more than an aesthetic *function*. The explanation of Virginia Woolf's 'constant concern with "reality" ', however, is something much more pressing than the need for finding 'a method of writing which enables her to tell a story while at the same time indicating the particular view of "reality" which gives that story significance'.

The question of belief in its most obvious form is occasionally touched on in *The Voyage Out*.

'I always think religion's like collecting beetles,' she said, summing up the discussion as she went up the stairs with Helen. 'One person has a passion for black beetles; another hasn't; it's no good arguing about it. What's *your* black beetle now?'

And again:

'They believe in God,' said Rachel as they regained each other. She meant that the people in the crowd believed in Him; for she remembered the crosses with bleeding plaster figures that stood where foot-paths joined, and the inexplicable mystery of a service in a Roman Catholic church. 'We shall never understand!' she sighed.

The Voyage Out was written, it is not hard to see, by someone with no particular beliefs about existence. The state of flux to which a general absence of belief necessarily leads is indicated in the following significant passage:

> Rachel felt much as Terence had felt that Evelyn was too close to her, and that there was something exciting in this closeness, although it was also disagreeable. She was spared the need of finding an answer to the question, for Evelyn proceeded, 'Do you *believe* in anything?'
>
> In order to put an end to the scrutiny of those bright blue eyes, and to relieve her own physical restlessness, Rachel pushed back her chair and exclaimed, 'In everything!' and began to finger different objects, the books on the table, the photographs, the fleshly leaved plant with the stiff bristles, which stood in a large earthenware pot in the window.
>
> 'I believe in the bed, in the photographs, in the pot, in the balcony, in the sun, in Mrs. Flushing,' she remarked, still speaking recklessly, with something at the back of her mind forcing her to say the things that one usually does not say. 'But I don't believe in God, I don't believe in Mr. Bax, I don't believe in the hospital nurse. I don't believe——' She took up a photograph and, looking at it, did not finish her sentence.

In *Night and Day* the problem of belief becomes somewhat more urgent. Of Mary Datchet in that novel her author writes –

> Having no religious belief, she was the more conscientious about her life. . . .

But, it later transpires –

> She could not see the world divided into separate compartments of good people and bad people, any more than she could believe so implicitly in the rightness of her own thought as to wish to bring the population of the British Isles into agreement with it. She looked at the lemon-coloured leaflet and thought almost enviously of the faith which could find comfort in the issue of such documents . . . feeling that faith, faith in an illusion, perhaps, but at any rate, faith in something, was of all gifts the most to be envied.

And we have seen that the lovers, towards the end of the same story, given an apparent, elusive intimation of life's 'significance', try to 'piece together . . . fragments of *belief*'.

Belief is inseparable from *meaning* and *reality*. And it is meaning and reality (or rather, her sense of life's meaninglessness and unreality) which trouble Virginia Woolf in her first two novels. As a novelist, Virginia Woolf began, not with any clear and steady vision of a pattern in human life, but with apparently no more compelling impulse than a mere desire to write, and a trust that the process of writing would assist towards the discovery of some inherent pattern in the random sequence of experience. The disorder and incoherence which, in her first novel, resulted from this aimless procedure, she endeavoured to overcome, in her second, by the imposition of a conventional pattern of character-relationships and, at the last, a hasty and unconvincing iteration of 'significance'.

II

THAT this solution failed to satisfy her appears from the immediately following period in her career, which is one of transition, marked by theorising and experiment directed towards the finding of a method of composition adapted to the limitations of her severely restricted perception of life. To this period belong the short tales and sketches which were collected in the little volume *Monday or Tuesday* (1921), and the well-known essay on 'Modern Fiction', in which she expressed her dissatisfaction with conventional writing and tentatively defined an attitude and a programme for the future of the novel.

This essay begins with a perfunctory reference to the classic English novelists and passes on at once to Wells, Bennett and Galsworthy, for whom she had conceived a marked distaste, representing as they did for her the most eminent and successful practitioners of the 'conventional' novel which had proved its inadequacy to the view of life that she increasingly considered it her task as a novelist to convey.

. . . Admitting the vagueness which afflicts all criticism of novels [she writes in this essay], let us hazard the opinion that for us at this moment the form of fiction most in vogue more often misses than secures the thing we seek. Whether we call it life or spirit, truth or reality, this, the essential thing, has moved off or on, and refuses to be contained any longer in such ill-fitting vestments as we provide. Nevertheless, we go on perseveringly, conscientiously, constructing our two and thirty chapters after a design which more and more ceases to resemble the vision in our minds. So much of the enormous labour of proving the solidity, the likeness to life, of the story is not merely labour thrown away but labour misplaced to the extent of obscuring and blotting out the light of the conception.

And then comes the well-known and portentous passage which points forward to her own later method of composition:

Look within and life, it seems, is very far from being 'like this'. Examine for a moment an ordinary mind on an ordinary day. The mind receives a myriad impressions – trivial, fantastic, evanescent, or engraved with the sharpness of steel. From all sides they come, an incessant shower of innumerable atoms; and as they fall, as they shape themselves into the life of Monday or Tuesday, the accent falls, differently from of old; the moment of importance came not here but there; so that, if a writer were a free man and not a slave, if he could write what he chose, not what he must, if he could base his work upon his own feeling, and not upon convention, there would be no plot, no comedy, no tragedy, no love interest or catastrophe in the accepted style, and perhaps not a single button sewn on as the Bond Street tailors would have it. Life is not a series of gig lamps symmetrically arranged; life is a luminous halo, a semi-transparent envelope surrounding us from the beginning of consciousness to the end. Is it not the task of the novelist to convey this varying, this unknown and uncircumscribed spirit, whatever aberration or complexity it may display, with as little mixture of the alien and external as possible? We are not pleading merely for courage and sincerity; we are suggesting that the proper stuff of fiction is a little other than custom would have us believe it.

. . . Let us record the atoms as they fall upon the mind in the order in which they fall, let us trace the pattern, however disconnected and incoherent in appearance, which each sight or incident scores upon the consciousness. Let us not take it for granted that life exists more fully in what is commonly thought big than in what is commonly thought small.

These paragraphs will repay the closest attention, for they mark the point of departure for the whole of their author's subsequent course as a novelist. Their personal application, as with all of Virginia Woolf's criticism ostensibly dealing with contemporaries, is evident. The description of the writer constrained 'not by his own free will but by some powerful and unscrupulous tyrant who has him in thrall' to write in such and such a way, is an apt one, not at all of Wells, Bennett or Galsworthy, but of Virginia Woolf herself, struggling with the composition of *Night and Day*, which she had just completed.

Virginia Woolf has been hailed as a prospector into new territory in the novel. In view of the claims made for her by admirers, it is interesting to recollect that she herself accepted the basic assumptions of the realistic writers of her period and departed from their methods only because forced to do so by her inability to extend her powers to their breadth of scope. Her method was one of retraction rather than extension – a narrowing of focus to take in only that which readily lent itself to appropriation by her extraordinarily limited vision. In a pamphlet, *Mr. Bennett and Mrs. Brown*, for example, written as late as 1924, we find her point of departure to be an unqualified agreement with a statement of Arnold Bennett's concerning the fundamental importance of the creation of 'character' to the novel; her reply to Bennett's criticism of the 'younger novelists', on the ground that they were incapable of the creation of character, taking the curious line that 'on or about December 1910', that is, at about the time these younger novelists (Virginia Woolf herself among them) began writing, 'human character changed', and consequently they were faced with entirely new problems of presentment, which their elders, Bennett, Galsworthy and Wells, owing to their overwhelming preoccupation with the material environment and political question were unable to help them to solve. For this reason, she concludes, doubtless with her own predicament still determining her words, 'we must reconcile ourselves to a season of failures and fragments'.

Jacob's Room (1922) is the first novel in which Virginia Woolf endeavours to put something of her new way of seeing and method of composition into practice. To 'record the atoms as they fall upon the mind in the order in which they fall' is not really a workable theory. And her actual method was a compromise between the practice of the conventional novelist and adherence to her own tentative formula. In *Jacob's Room* one notices less any innovation of a positive order than the simple and drastic employment of omission. There is no plot – the reader simply follows Jacob through this and that planless permutation in his history from childhood to his death in the war. The design of the novel follows from the mere juxtaposition of one passage of intrinsically trivial particularities with another, separated by a jump in time. While this simple omission is preferable to the accumulation of meaningless detail which had padded out the previous novel, there is no added intensity of vision, no motivating passion which might give the book an organic centre and thus create for the novel a significant form. The narrative comes to a blank space, Jacob's death (off-stage) and then abruptly stops. The novelist never comes to close quarters with her chief character, but portrays him in a wooden, detached, external manner which takes note of his way of sitting down, of reading a book, of lighting a pipe, and so forth, but which is powerless to evoke his inner life. Jacob is as void of content as any 'tough' character of Ernest Hemingway's, but instead of being precipitated into a region of violent external agitation, he moves with puppet-like impassivity through scenes of domesticated calm. It is a novel in two dimensions, and the general effect is of a silent shadow-play.

III

IT is not until *Mrs. Dalloway* (1923) that we reach a work in which it is possible to trace the drawing together in Virginia Woolf's mind of the impulsion towards belief on the one hand and on the other the inability to make any decisive movement of belief and thus to discriminate which led to the narrowing of vision to the elementary conditions of momentary experience. *Mrs. Dalloway* is curiously compounded of this dual movement of belief and unbelief.

In the early essay on 'Modern Fiction', Virginia Woolf charges the 'conventional' novelists whose manner she had attempted to follow, with writing of unimportant things, with spending their skill and industry on 'making the trivial and the transitory appear the true and the enduring'. 'For us at this moment,' she wrote, 'the form of fiction most in vogue more often misses than secures the thing we seek. Whether we call it life or spirit, truth or reality, this, the essential thing, has moved off.' What, then, is the enduring, the true, which it is the novelist's task to capture? She does not know; but she ventures to suppose that it may be found by a form of passive receptiveness to experience. 'Let us not take it for granted,' she wrote in that early essay, 'that life exists more fully in what is commonly thought big than in what is commonly thought small.' Unable to distinguish between this value and that she takes the barest unit of disparate experience and concentrates upon it, in the supposition or the hope that within that, if anywhere, must lie the secret of life's *indigenous* significance.

The inability to discriminate between levels of life, to make choices between 'good' and 'bad', 'right' and 'wrong', or 'desirable' and 'undesirable', besides thrusting the individual so affected back upon the naked and isolated moment of perception, places him furthermore in a position where, if any kind of positive 'significance' is to be attempted (and life can be endowed with significance only by an interior act of affirmation – of *belief*), then, inevitably, undifferentiated, elementary life has to be accepted unreservedly and in its totality. In *Mrs. Dalloway* we see not only the results of the period of experimental, impressionistic, *momentary* writing applied to the novel; we also see the attainment of a sustained, though of course ultimately spurious, 'significance' through the continuous act of complete and undiscriminating acceptance of every moment of undifferentiated existence, each separate atom of which is presumed to contain an equal fragment of *indigenous* meaning.

In *Mrs. Dalloway*, in fact, the specific absence of belief which is shown in the earlier novels is revealed in its reverse aspect. It takes on the appearance of belief – a positive acceptance and affirmation, not of any particular level of reality, but of *everything*, without discrimination: except, significantly enough, of that which would imply the possibility, or the need, of discrimination. 'One can only hope that they will have the same vision and the same power to believe, without which life would be so meaningless,' writes old Mrs. Hilbery, of Katharine and her fiancé in *Night and Day*: to believe, that is, not in any specific reality or value, but simply to believe, in everything, perhaps; in 'life'. And one can only take Clarissa Dalloway as exemplifying this 'belief' – a belief so total that it engulfs the whole of experience, and which on examination turns out to be a positive

F

inversion of unbelief. Besides representing the combination of
happiness and *belief*, Clarissa Dalloway is an incarnation of life
itself, the stream and efflorescence of natural, material, feminine
existence. A sentimental, worldly sort of average sensual
woman, she is presented lyrically and quite uncritically through
a rose-tinted haze, the trivialities of her pointless, sensational
life inflated to universal proportions.

But to go deeper, beneath what people said (and these judgments, how superficial, how fragmentary they are!) in her own
mind now, what did it mean to her, this thing she called life? Oh,
it was very queer. Here was So-and-so in South Kensington;
some one up in Bayswater; and somebody else, say, in Mayfair.
And she felt quite continuously a sense of their existence; and she
felt what a waste; and she felt what a pity; and she felt if only
they could be brought together: so she did it. And it was an
offering; to combine, to create; but to whom?

An offering for the sake of offering, perhaps. Anyhow, it was
her gift. Nothing else had she of the slightest importance; could
not think, write, even play the piano. She muddled Armenians
with Turks; loved success; hated discomfort; must be liked; talked
oceans of nonsense; and to this day, ask her what the Equator was,
and she did not know.

All the same, that one day should follow another; Wednesday,
Thursday, Friday, Saturday; that one should wake up in the
morning; see the sky; walk in the park; meet Hugh Whitbread;
then suddenly in came Peter; then these roses; it was enough.
After that, how unbelievable death was! – that it must end; and
no one in the whole world would know how she had loved it all;
how every instant . . .

The loquacious, breathlessly chattering style is a perfect
medium for the expression of the reflections of this empty-
headed, middle-aged bourgeoise matron, so ostentatiously and
rhapsodically thrilled by the mere continuous fact of existence
(though it is a leisured, idle, comfortable enough existence to be
sure). What is so curious about it is its quite genuine spontane-
ity, the essence from it of any hint of irony, of detachment,
which might reveal some disparity between the life-outlook
embodied in the character, and that of her creator. Here is
belief, then, on its most primitive level: a belief in 'life' – in

the successive moments of unco-ordinated sensational experience – as a 'good' in itself. Mrs. Dalloway is a child in her unreflective responsiveness to each moment of experience, but a child grown middle-aged, in whose deliberate retrogression to innocence there is a subdued strain of hysteria.

How far from the primal innocence of childhood Clarissa Dalloway has travelled is shown in such passages as the following, where the theology of middle-aged innocence is appropriately sketched in:

> Oddly enough, she was one of the most thorough-going sceptics he had ever met, and possibly (this was a theory he used to make up to account for her, so transparent in some ways, so inscrutable in others), possibly she said to herself, As we are a doomed race, chained to a sinking ship (her favourite reading as a girl was Huxley and Tyndall, and they were fond of these nautical metaphors), as the whole thing is a bad joke, let us, at any rate, do our part; mitigate the sufferings of our fellow-prisoners (Huxley again); decorate the dungeon with flowers and air-cushions; be as decent as we possibly can. Those ruffians, the Gods, shan't have it all their own way – her notion being that the Gods, who never lost a chance of hurting, thwarting and spoiling human lives, were seriously put out if, all the same, you behaved like a lady. That phase came directly after Sylvia's death – that horrible affair. To see your own sister killed by a falling tree (all Justin Parry's fault – all his carelessness) before your very eyes, a girl too on the verge of life, the most gifted of them Clarissa always said, was enough to turn one bitter. Later she wasn't so positive, perhaps; she thought there were no Gods; no one was to blame; and so she evolved this atheist's religion of doing good for the sake of goodness. . . .

Such, then, is the centre, if centre it can be called, around which Clarissa Dalloway's manner of responding to life coheres, or fails to cohere. And it has something in common with the aimless openness to life of the deranged consciousness of her *alter ego*, Septimus Warren Smith, the neurasthenic war-victim who darkly underscores her buoyancy with his submergence and her total acceptance of life with his total rejection – for he is to kill himself by jumping from a top-storey window on to the area railings.

The vague, fluid characters in this book – Clarissa herself, her whimsical, Puckish lover, Peter Walsh, and Septimus Warren Smith – are bathed in the tender warmth of their author's undiscriminating sympathy. It is interesting, that being so, to find that there are also portrayed two characters who are given at least potential definition by the decisiveness of their attitude to life, in which they stand in polar opposition to the indecisive fluidity of the other chief characters. And it is intriguing to watch the manner in which these two characters are pursued by their creator with a gratuitous vindictiveness which seems at first sight unaccountable.

To Clarissa Dalloway is opposed the maliciously-drawn minor figure of Miss Kilman, her daughter's teacher, who, she fears, is alienating the girl's affection from her. Between Mrs. Dalloway and Miss Kilman there is an unspoken but vibrant antagonism, which flashes out as Miss Kilman, leaving Mrs. Dalloway's house with the girl, encounters her employer on the landing.

> . . . Love and religion! thought Clarissa, going back into the drawing-room, tingling all over. How detestable, how detestable they are! For now that the body of Miss Kilman was not before her, it overwhelmed her – the idea. The cruellest things in the world, she thought, seeing them clumsy, hot, domineering, hypocritical eavesdropping, jealous, infinitely cruel and unscrupulous dressed in a mackintosh coat, on the landing; love and religion. Had she ever tried to convert anyone herself? Did she not wish everybody merely to be themselves? And she watched out of the window the old lady opposite climbing upstairs. Let her climb upstairs if she wanted to; let her stop; then let her, as Clarissa had often seen her, gain her bedroom, part her curtains, and disappear again into the background. Somehow one respected that – that old woman looking out of the window, quite unconscious that she was being watched. There was something solemn in it – but love and religion would destroy that, whatever it was, the privacy of the soul. The odious Kilman would destroy it. Yet it was a sight that made her want to cry.

Subsequently Miss Kilman is made to disgrace herself before Mrs. Dalloway's daughter, and is left, a pathetic figure, covered with humiliation.

Humiliation is the portion also of the other character who is so unsympathetic as to possess a definite, formulated attitude to life. Sir William Bradshaw, the nerve specialist who is called in to deal with the neurasthenic Septimus, is presented as a thick-skinned, domineering egotist, who applies to human beings a sovereign test of normality and sense of proportion.

Proportion, divine proportion, Sir William's goddess, was acquired by Sir William walking hospitals, catching salmon, begetting one son in Harley Street by Lady Bradshaw, who caught salmon herself and took photographs scarcely to be distinguished from the work of professionals. Worshipping proportion, Sir William not only prospered himself but made England prosper. . . .

But Proportion has a sister, less smiling, more formidable, a Goddess even now engaged – in the heat and sands of India, the mud and swamp of Africa, the purlieus of London, wherever in short the climate or the devil tempts men to fall from the true belief which is her own – is even now engaged in dashing down shrines, smashing idols, and setting up in their place her own stern countenance. Conversation is her name and she feasts on the wills of the weakly, loving to impress, to impose, adoring her own features stamped on the face of the populace. At Hyde Park Corner on a tub she stands preaching; shrouds herself in white and walks penitentially disguised as brotherly love through factories and parliaments; offers help, but desires power; smites out of her way roughly the dissentient, or dissatisfied; bestows her blessing on those who, looking upward, catch submissively from her eyes the light of their own.

In so mild a writer the vehement bitterness of this is surprising. It would seem that just as Clarissa Dalloway and Septimus Warren Smith are linked in an unconscious psychic sympathy, representing as they do the human mind's state of fluid and unprincipled openness to the undifferentiated phenomena of elementary existence, so the decisive attitudes of Miss Kilman and Sir William Bradshaw converge – and converge upon that threatening imperative towards *conversion*, the imposition of a definite view of life upon the fluid, the indefinite, which is felt as inexpressibly menacing to everything that Clarissa Dalloway herself values and represents. Pondering on Miss Kilman, and the challenge she is seen to present to her own undiscriminating acceptance, Mrs. Dalloway asks herself:

Why creeds and prayers and mackintoshes? when . . . that's
the miracle, that's the mystery: that old lady, she meant, whom
she could see going from chest of drawers to dressing-table. She
could still see her. And the supreme mystery which Kilman might
say she had solved, or Peter might say he had solved, but Clarissa
didn't believe either of them had the ghost of an idea of solving,
was simply this: here was one room; there another. Did religion
solve that, or love?

Sir William Bradshaw, like Miss Kilman, is disgraced. When
Septimus Warren Smith is in a condition of intense neurotic
excitement, he insists upon entering his room, with the result
that Septimus flings himself out of the window and is killed.
Towards the end of the story, at Mrs. Dalloway's party, the
climax of her day, she learns from Sir William Bradshaw, who
is one of the guests, of the young man's death.

What business had the Bradshaws to talk of death at her party?
A young man had killed himself and they talked of it at her party –
the Bradshaws talked of death. He had killed himself – but how?
Always her body went through it first, when she was told, suddenly, of an accident; her dress flamed, her body burnt. He had
thrown himself from a window. Up had flashed the ground;
through him, blundering, bruising, went the rusty spikes. There
he lay with a thud, thud, thud in his brain, and then a suffocation
of blackness. So she saw it. But why had he done it? And the
Bradshaws talked of it at her party!
    . . . But this young man who had killed himself – had he
plunged his treasure? 'If it were now to die, 'twere now to be most
happy,' she had said to herself once, coming down, in white. Or
there were the poets and thinkers. Suppose he had had that
passion, and had gone to Sir William Bradshaw, a great doctor,
yet to her obscurely evil, without sex or lust, extremely polite to
women, but capable of some indescribable outrage – forcing your
soul, that was it – if this young man had gone to him, and Sir
William had impressed him, like that, with his power, might he
not then have said (indeed she felt it now), Life is made intolerable;
they make life intolerable, men like that?
    Then (she had felt it only this morning) there was the terror;
the overwhelming incapacity, one's parents giving it into one's
hands, this life, to be lived to the end, to be walked with serenely;
there was in the depths of her heart an awful fear. Even now,
quite often if Richard had not been there reading the *Times*, so

that she could crouch like a bird and gradually revive, send roaring up that immeasurable delight, rubbing stick to stick, one thing with another, she must have perished. She had escaped. But that young man had killed himself.

Such then is the psychological structure of *Mrs. Dalloway.* Although, as a novel, it represents the peak of Virginia Woolf's achievement, just as it marks the highest, most buoyant point on the graph of her emotional progression, it shows no authentic advance over her earlier works: no movement of the mind, that is, into new territory. Apparently, affirmative in mood, its innocency is in fact, retrogressive and corrupt. And its apparent affirmation of life is merely the reverse aspect of its rejection of that which alone could give life meaning and value: i.e., a positive, spiritual affirmation which, facilitating the introduction of a principle of choice, of discrimination, would make life subject to differentiation and thus to the realization of meaning.

IV

AND yet, despite its at times cloying sentimentality, *Mrs. Dalloway* is perhaps Virginia Woolf's most satisfactory novel, for it has an organic structure which derives from the successful dramatic presentation of a view of life. It is in fact the only novel of Virginia Woolf's in which tension is achieved through the opposition of characters embodying contrary principles of conduct. The lack of such tension in the rest of her work results from the monistic conception of existence which sets all characters alike within the same undifferentiated flow of life, and makes inward and outward conflict alike inconceivable.

In the next novel, *To the Lighthouse* (1927), there are already signs of disintegration of form, concurrent with a loosening grasp upon experience which finds expression in a depletion of emotion. A buoyant, dashing surrender to the flux of life has given place to an anxious, anguished questioning of the flux. If *Mrs. Dalloway* is indicative of a state, however illusory, of achieved *being*, *To the Lighthouse* reveals an alienation from that being expressed as a concern for *meaning*.

The sentimentality of *Mrs. Dalloway* was communicated through the author's uncritical identification of her own viewpoint with that of her central character. But it is clear that such an identification could be effected only by a suppression of those mental qualities which in point of fact must have distinguished the 'intellectual' Virginia Woolf from such a feather-pated creature as Clarissa Dalloway is shown to be. *To the Lighthouse* is so much more subdued in tone than *Mrs. Dalloway*, and so lacking in the former novel's cloying and breathless sentimentality, precisely because there is no such simple identification of the writer with her central character. A significant alienation of identity appears in the presentation of Mrs. Ramsay, a modified and graver equivalent of Mrs. Dalloway, at one remove. Instead of being presented from *within*, she is approached externally, through the hazy and tremulous thoughts and emotions of her worshipper, Lily Briscoe.

Those critics, are, I think, mistaken who have supposed that the theme of this novel is contained in the story of the trip to the lighthouse. While that story indubitably provides a framework of incident for the support of the novel's content to which, however, it is not organically connected the substance of the book is contained in the verbal hoverings and quiverings around the relationship between Lily Briscoe and Mrs. Ramsay. Thus, the first part is devoted to Lily Briscoe's immediate thoughts and feelings about the living woman, who represents for her some mysteriously satisfying relationship with life that she herself, hovering on the edge of things, can hardly hope to achieve – for Mrs. Ramsay, *being* itself; for Lily Briscoe, *perception* of being: significance. The second part, 'Time Passes', records parenthetically the death of Mrs. Ramsay. And the final section of the novel concerns Lily's attempt to achieve a synthetic vision of existence, in which her memories of Mrs. Ramsay, and the wholeness, the integration of which she is emblematic, play a preponderating part. Finally, the climax of the book comes at the moment when it seems to her that Mrs. Ramsay actually returns to the house – she has a vision of her sitting placidly in her chair, knitting.

It is, assuredly, with Lily Briscoe's, if with anyone's, that the author identifies her point of view. To this detached, ineffectual spinster, with her 'artist's eye' – to her, the substantial, homely Mrs. Ramsay, with her house, her husband, and her eight children, represents a solid, tangible, satisfying rootedness in life which is so foreign to her experience as to be positively endued with mystery; and it is, consequently, with an aura of mysteriousness, of wonder, that she surrounds her in her reflections. Mrs. Ramsay is the exact counterpart of those matronly female characters who, in E. M. Forster's novels, represent those same 'mysterious' values of natural continuity, of unquestioning rootedness in the tangible, immemorial natural order.

In the first part of the book, near to the living woman, yet quite unable to penetrate into her character, Lily reflects upon her in such terms as these:

> Was it wisdom? Was it knowledge? Was it, once more, the deceptiveness of beauty, so that all one's perceptions, half-way to truth, were tangled in a golden mesh? Or did she lock up within her some secret which certainly Lily Briscoe believed people must have for the world to go on at all? Every one could not be as helter skelter, hand to mouth as she was. But if they knew, could they tell one what they knew? Sitting on the floor with her arms round Mrs. Ramsay's knees, close as she could get, smiling to think that Mrs. Ramsay would never know the reason of that pressure, she imagined how in the chambers of the mind and heart of the woman who was, physically, touching her, were stood, like the treasures in the tombs of kings, tablets bearing sacred inscriptions, which if one could spell them out would teach one everything, but they would never be offered openly, never made public. What art was there, known to love or cunning, by which one pressed through into those secret chambers? What device for becoming, like waters poured into one jar, inextricably the same, one with the object one adored? Could the body achieve it, or the mind, subtly mingling in the intricate passages of the brain? Or the heart? Could loving, as people called it, make her and Mrs. Ramsay one? For it was not knowledge but unity that she desired, not inscriptions on tablets, nothing that could be written in any language known to men, but intimacy itself, which is knowledge, she had thought, leaning her head on Mrs. Ramsay's knee.
>
> Nothing happened. Nothing! Nothing! as she leant her head against Mrs. Ramsay's knee. And yet, she knew knowledge and wisdom were stored in Mrs. Ramsay's heart. How then, she had asked herself, did one know one thing or another thing about people, sealed as they were? Only like a bee, drawn by some sweetness or sharpness in the air intangible to touch or taste, one

haunted the dome-shaped hive, ranged the wastes of the air over the countries of the world alone, and haunted the hives with their murmurs and their stirrings; the hives which were people. Mrs. Ramsay rose. Lily rose. Mrs. Ramsay went. For days there hung about her, as after a dream some subtle change is felt in the person one has dreamt of, more vividly than anything she said, the sound of murmuring and, as she sat in the wicker arm-chair in the drawing-room window she wore, to Lily's eyes, an august shape; the shape of a dome.

'It was not knowledge but unity that she desired.' But nowhere, in this first section of the book, does Lily succeed in 'pressing through into those secret chambers', in 'becoming . . . one with the object she adored'. The pattern is of frustration – a frustration reflected in the narrative in the postponement of the expedition to the lighthouse. In the ensuing vacant lapse of ten years, Mrs. Ramsay's death supervenes. And in the final section the novelist is faced with the formidable task of bringing the whole novel to a meaningful conclusion.

Deprived of the sense of secure certainty provided by the adored figure of Mrs. Ramsay, Lily Briscoe, on her return to the house with Mr. Ramsay, two of the children, and old Mr. Carmichael, the poet, is impelled to establish some kind of relationship with her – or, more accurately, with that which she represents – in spite of her death. For with Mrs. Ramsay and her unquestioning rootedness in the natural order has come to be associated the whole significance of life, so that with her obliteration from the scene, that significance has disappeared. So it is that this section of the book is devoted principally to Lily's bewildered and even passionate questionings for life's 'significance'. And the achievement of 'significance' is equivalent, it appears, to an actual *return* of Mrs. Ramsay.

Mrs. Ramsay, she thought, stepping back and screwing up her eyes . . . Mrs. Ramsay. When she thought of herself and Charles throwing ducks and drakes and of the whole scene on the beach, it seemed to depend somehow upon Mrs. Ramsay sitting under the rock, with a pad on her knees, writing letters. (She wrote innumerable letters, and sometimes the wind took them and she and Charles just saved a page from the sea.) But what a power was in the human soul! she thought. That woman sitting there, writing under the rock resolved everything into simplicity; made these angers, irritations fall off like old rags; she brought together this and that and then this, and so made out of that miserable silliness and spite (she and Charles squabbling, sparring, had been silly and spiteful) something – this scene on the beach for example, this moment of friendship and liking – which survived, after all these years, complete, so that she dipped into it to re-fashion her memory of him, and it stayed in the mind almost like a work of art.

'Like a work of art,' she repeated, looking from her canvas to the drawing-room steps and back again. She must rest for a moment. And, resting, looking from one to the other vaguely, the old question which traversed the sky of the soul perpetually, the vast and general question which was apt to particularize itself at such moments as these, when she released faculties that had been on the strain, stood over her, paused over her, darkened over her. What is the meaning of life? That was all – a simple question; one that tended to close in on one with years. The great revelation had never come. Instead there were little daily miracles, illuminations, matches struck unexpectedly in the dark; here was one. This, that, and the other; herself and Charles Tansley and the breaking wave; Mrs. Ramsay bringing them together; Mrs. Ramsay saying 'Life stands still here'; Mrs. Ramsay making of the moment something permanent (as in another sphere Lily herself tried to make of the moment something permanent) – this was of the nature of a revelation. In the midst of chaos there was shape; this eternal passing and flowing (she looked at the clouds going and the leaves shaking) was struck into stability. Life stands still here, Mrs. Ramsay said. 'Mrs. Ramsay! Mrs. Ramsay!' she repeated. She owed this revelation to her.

What is the meaning of life? The emphasis here is very different from that in *Mrs. Dalloway*. Life, no longer a 'lark' and a 'plunge', as in the opening sentence of that novel, but a dark enigma, hides its purpose from its puzzled and groping creatures. But 'the great revelation had never come . . . perhaps never did come'. There were only little fragments, little flashes, of 'significance', united by the presence of Mrs. Ramsay, typifying the inscrutable natural order. But perhaps, after all, this *was* a revelation. Perhaps, that is to say, there was no larger meaning, but only a succession of little elusive fragments of 'significance', and one must make the most of these. Thus, it appears, we are back at the state of affairs which preceded the fervent and enthusiastic acceptance of momentary sensation which gave *Mrs. Dalloway* its special character.

It is hardly surprising that this meagre 'revelation' should be felt by Lily Briscoe to be still unsatisfactory. It contents her for a very short while. And then, a little further on, this exasperated clutching at life's elusive 'significance' is taken up afresh in her impassioned inward questioning of Mr. Carmichael.

Against her will she had come to the surface, and found herself half out of the picture, looking, a little dazedly, as if at unreal things, at Mr. Carmichael. He lay on his chair with his hands clasped above his paunch not reading, or sleeping, but basking like a creature gorged with existence. His book had fallen on to the grass.

She wanted to go straight up to him and say, 'Mr. Carmichael!' Then he would look up benevolently as always, from his smoky vague green eyes. But one only woke people if one knew what one wanted to say to them. And she wanted to say not one thing but everything. Little words that broke up the thought and dismembered it said nothing. 'About life, about death; about Mrs. Ramsay' – no, she thought, one could say nothing to nobody. The urgency of the moment always missed its mark. Words fluttered sideways and struck the object inches too low. . . .

'What does it mean? How do you explain it all?' she wanted to say, turning to Mr. Carmichael again. For the whole world seemed to have dissolved in this early morning hour into a pool of thought, a deep basin of reality, and one could almost fancy that had Mr. Carmichael spoken, a little tear would have rent the surface of the pool. And then? Something would emerge. A hand would be shoved up, a blade would be flashed. It was nonsense of course. . . .

. . . She addressed old Mr. Carmichael again. What was it then? What did it mean? Could things thrust their hands up and grip one; could the blade cut, the fist grasp? Was there no safety? No learning by heart of the ways of the world? No guide, no shelter, but all was miracle, and leaping from the pinnacle of a tower into the air? Could it be, even for elderly people, that this was life? – startling, unexpected, unknown? For one moment she felt that if they both got up, here, now on the lawn, and demanded an explanation, why was it so short, why was it so inexplicable, said it with violence, as two fully equipped beings from whom nothing should be hid might speak, then, beauty would roll itself up; the space would fill; those empty flourishes would form into shape; if they shouted loud enough Mrs. Ramsay would return. 'Mrs. Ramsay!' she said aloud, 'Mrs. Ramsay!' The tears ran down her face.

The conclusion, the moment of vision, to which these questionings lead, is, although it provides the climax of the novel, strangely indeterminate and unconvincing.

Suddenly the window at which she was looking was whitened by some light stuff behind it. At last then somebody had come into the drawing-room; somebody was sitting in the chair. For Heaven's sake, she prayed, let them sit still there and not come floundering out to talk to her. Mercifully, whoever it was stayed still inside; had settled by some stroke of luck so as to throw an odd-shaped triangular shadow over the step. It altered the composition of the picture a little. It was interesting. It might be useful. Her mood was coming back to her. One must keep on looking without for a second relaxing the intensity of emotion, the determination not to be put off, not to be bamboozled. One must hold the scene – so – in a vice and let nothing come in and spoil it. One wanted, she thought, sipping her brush deliberately, to be on a level with ordinary experience, to feel simply that's a chair, that's a table, and yet at the same time, It's a miracle, it's an ecstasy. The problem might be solved after all. Ah, but what had happened? Some wave of white went over the window pane. The air must have stirred some flounce in the room. Her heart leapt at her and seized and tortured her.

'Mrs. Ramsay! Mrs. Ramsay!' she cried, feeling the old horror come back – to want and want and not to have. Could she inflict that still? And then, quietly, as if she refrained, that too became part of ordinary experience, was on a level with the chair, with the table. Mrs. Ramsay – it was part of her perfect goodness – sat there quite simply, in the chair, flicked her needles to and fro, knitted her reddish-brown stocking, cast her shadow on the step. There she sat.

Lucy, the artist, is able to finish her picture. And, in conclusion:

Yes, she thought, laying down her brush in extreme fatigue, I have had my vision.

'Symbolically,' writes Mr. Daiches in his estimation of it, 'the past returns and shapes the present. Mrs. Ramsay comes back into Lily Briscoe's picture, as she had been part of the original design ten years before, and out of this meeting of two very different personalities across the years the final insight results. Across the water at the same moment Mr. Ramsay, by his praise of James's handling of the boat, is exorcising the ghost of James's early resentment, also ten years old, and all the threads of the story are finally coming together. It is a masterly piece of construction.' But, really, does this fleeting appearance of a phantom Mrs. Ramsay do anything of the kind? And what, after all, does it imply – in what way does it answer Lily Briscoe's protracted questioning of 'the meaning of life'? What, finally, is the reader really meant to make of this whimsical apparition itself? These questions are simply not answered – are not, in fact, even asked by Lily Briscoe.

Had this 'vision', which is the climax of the book, any validity, it would mean that Virginia Woolf herself had at last achieved a creative inner integration, that her protracted quest for the meaning of experience had resulted in the attainment of a balanced and potent view of life which would provide a germinal point of departure for further and positive creation. The fact that it was in reality but a calculated, mechanical device for introducing a point into an otherwise pointless novel, is borne out not only by its own unsatisfactory effect but by its failure to provide a starting-point for a wider and more vital extension of meaning into Virginia Woolf's vision of existence.

V

THE principle which, in the foregoing pages, I have been trying to establish, is that at the centre of this novelist's work there lies, not some abstract 'aesthetic' principle, but a plain and simple preoccupation with the most primary and central necessity of human life – the necessity of belief.

To accept life, to respond to experience, without any prior belief in the primacy of this or that order of reality is to become the victim of utter inward disorder. And this is accentuated when the state of society is such as to provide no readily acceptable conventions of the good and the bad, the desirable and the undesirable. In such a case, only an original act of faith, a decisive and positively dynamic spiritual affirmation can provide a focal centre for the introduction of meaning into experience, which in turn will introduce a principle of order into life. Such an order presumes discrimination: an acceptance of *this* presumes a corresponding rejection of *that*: and thus there is erected a scale of values upon which may be built a more or less orderly and significant experiential pattern. The discovery of meaning and the introduction of order depend upon an initial act, and upon subsequent, continual interior activity. They are introduced by the dynamism of the subject. Now the distinguishing feature of Virginia Woolf's apprehension of life lies precisely in its passivity; and further-more, she subscribed unwittingly, as we have seen, to a view of life which placed a primary emphasis upon the object. One recalls the passive function ascribed to the mind ('The mind *receives* a myriad impressions') and the atomistic conception of experience ('From all sides they come, an incessant *shower of atoms*') revealed in the essay 'Modern Fiction'. This sort of initial inward inertia at once obviates the very possibility of meaning, which cannot conceivably subsist inherently in the world of objects. Virginia Woolf's search for 'significance' on the primitive level of primary sensational perceptions, therefore, was chimerical from the beginning. And indeed, it is a typical feature of the characters in her novels to be altogether lacking in the capacity for discriminating within experience. They are passively caught up in the stream of events, of 'life', of their own random perceptions. The furthest Virginia Woolf could move in the direction of a positive act of belief was towards the undiscriminating and finally pointless embracing of everything, which is featured in *Mrs. Dalloway* – a comprehensive gesture which itself obviated the very possibility of order achieved through discrimination, since it was precisely discrimination which was repudiated. This very gesture, when its perpetuation became impossible – and only two years after the affirmations of *Mrs. Dalloway* there came the questionings of *To the Light-house* – resulted in an inevitable surrender to eventual explicit meaninglessness.

A simple *monism*, let us call it, was fundamental to Virginia Woolf's outlook upon life. From this derives her incapacity to portray character. For the omission of a principle of differentia-tion in human life – a principle which is obviously dualistic in that its operation results in a continual extension of an *either/or* choice – makes quite impossible the definition of character, which is itself built up upon the tension of choice between this and that value, this and that course of conduct, and grows through inward affirmations, struggles, and decisions. This lax and vitiating monism is expressed in the absence from her characters of any interior struggle or development. At best they grope for an elusive 'significance' within the texture of atomized, elementary perception; at worst are helplessly caught away in the disintegral temporal stream. Being so void of interior definition, and having no points of opposition, such characters could hardly be expected to maintain dramatic relationships with each other. And this elementary monism, which renders it impossible to make distinctions of values, to introduce discriminations within the total process of life, to grasp the nature of personality, must have the effect, eventually, of merging everything in one vast, undifferentiated flux. It is exactly this which is to be seen in the last three novels, *The Waves*, *The Years*, and *Between the Acts*.

Experience in *The Waves* (1930) is generalized by being located in a void, out of which the six characters, or voices, take turns in delivering isolated, introspective monologues in a stylized diction, bearing upon their common lives. The narrative, thus taken up by each in turn, proceeds from their childhood through the several stages of their lives to beyond middle age, when the novel terminates with a melancholy, inconclusive summing-up. Each section of the novel is preceded by a piece of poetical prose expressing, in terms of the progress of the day from morning to night, the process of human life from childhood to age. Over the earlier parts of the book there preside the beams of a rising sun, while over the latter part fall the shadows of a world in which the sun is declining, while throughout there sounds the menacing beat of the Waves, signifying the primal flux out of which life emerges and into which it must dissolve.

So generalized and so shadowy is the novel that not much can profitably be said about it. It is a medley of impressionistic scenes, a complex of sometimes sensitive but unrelated observations, strung together only by a sense of the transience of life. The sense of realness, of tangible, common-sense, yet somehow mysterious and worshipful rootedness in life which had previously been projected into the figures of Mrs. Dalloway and Mrs. Ramsay, here surrounds the remoter, more abstract figure of Percival, who, himself silent, is presented only through the comments of the speaking characters.

Percival's death in India at the age of twenty-six (taking place, like Mrs. Ramsay's, off-stage) provides a climactic point in the book, and the deprivation in the lives of the six characters which his death brings is combined with the symbolism of the rising and declining day. With his death, the others are slowly permeated by the vaguely-suggested sense of the treacherousness of life, and towards the end the virtual surrender to meaninglessness is expressed by Bernard in his summing-up.

The Years (1937) is a more tedious, protracted and commonplace repetition of *The Waves*. In structure it shows a relapse to the conventional which is curious – it is *Night and Day* without the plot-structure, stretched out and dissolved in the featureless, disintegrating stream of sixty years. A diffuse group of characters, even shadowier in outline than those in any of the previous novels, are seen at various intervals in their passage through life, drifting emptily down the stream of time. But in spite of this surrender, there is no passionate concern with the nature and meaning of time. Nor is there even any nostalgic endeavour to capture and convey the subtler vibrations of 'period' atmosphere; and the selection of incidents seems quite desultory. The predominant mood is of a vacant lassitude. Formlessness reaches its apogee.

She had always wanted to know about Christiantity – how it began; what it meant, originally. God is love, The kingdom of Heaven is within us, sayings like that she thought, turning over the pages, what did they mean? The actual words were very beautiful. But who said them – when? Then the spout of the tea-kettle puffed steam at her and she moved it away. The wind was rattling the windows in the back room; it was bending the little bushes; they still had no leaves on them. It was what a man said under a fig tree, on a hill, she thought. And then another man wrote it down. But suppose that what that man says is just as false as what this man – she touched the press cuttings with her spoon – says about Digby? And here am I, she thought, looking at the china in the Dutch cabinet, in this drawing-room, getting a

G

little spark from what someone said all those years ago – here it comes (the china was changing from blue to livid) skipping over all those mountains, all those seas. She found her place and began to read.

But a sound in the hall interrupted her. Was someone coming in? She listened. No, it was the wind. The wind was terrific. It pressed on the house; gripped it tight, then let it fall apart. Upstairs a door slammed; a window must be open in the bedroom above. A blind was tapping. It was difficult to fix her mind on Renan. She liked it, though. French she could easily read of course; and Italian; and a little German. But what vast gaps there were, what blank spaces, she thought leaning back in her chair, in her knowledge! How little she knew about anything. Take this cup for instance; she held it out in front of her. What was it made of? Atoms? And what were atoms, and how did they stick together? The smooth hard surface of the china with its red flowers seemed to her for a second a marvellous mystery. But there was another sound in the hall. It was the wind, but it was also a voice, talking. It must be Martin. But who could he be talking to, she wondered? She listened, but she could not hear what he was saying because of the wind. And why, she asked herself, did he say we can't tell a lie to save our souls? He was thinking about himself; one always knew when people were thinking about themselves by their tone of voice. Perhaps he was justifying himself for having left the Army. That had been courageous, she thought; but isn't it odd, she mused, listening to the voices, that he should be such a dandy, too? He was wearing a new blue suit with white stripes on it. And he had shaved off his moustache. He ought never to have been a soldier, she thought; he was much too pugnacious. . . . They were still talking. She could not hear what he was saying, but from the sound of his voice it came over her that he must have a great many love affairs. Yes – it became perfectly obvious to her, listening to his voice through the door, that he had a great many love affairs. But who with? and why do men think love affairs so important? she asked as the door opened.

And so the vague thoughts drop from Christianity to teacups, from teacups to love-affairs, in a process of mental dissipation. Only towards the end (as in *The Waves*) does the imminence of her conclusion persuade the novelist to cast about for a few grains of 'significance'. And so, in the concluding section, those characters who are still surviving are suddenly endowed with a proclivity to ponder about Life. Eleanor Pargiter, to whose reflections we have just listened, first introduced in 1880 as a young girl, now an old woman, is made to reflect as follows:

My life, she said to herself. That was odd, it was the second time that evening that somebody had talked about her life. And I haven't got one, she thought. Oughtn't a life to be something you could handle and produce? – a life of seventy-odd years. But I've only the present moment, she thought. Here she was alive, now, listening to the fox-trot. Then she looked round. There was Morris; Rose; Edward with his head thrown back talking to a man she did not know. I'm the only person here, she thought, who remembers how he sat on the edge of my bed that night, crying – the night Kitty's engagement was announced. Yes, things came back to her. A long strip of life lay behind her. Edward crying, Mrs. Levy talking; snow falling; a sunflower with a crack in it; the yellow omnibus trotting along the Bayswater Road. And I thought to myself, I'm the youngest person in this omnibus; now I'm the oldest. . . . Millions of things came back to her. Atoms danced apart and massed themselves. But how did they compose what people called a life? She clenched her hands and felt the hard little coins she was holding. Perhaps there's 'I' at the middle of it, she thought; a knot; a centre; and again she saw herself sitting at her table drawing on the blotting-paper, digging little holes from which spokes radiated. Out and out they went; thing followed thing, scene obliterated scene. And then they say, she thought, 'We've been talking about you!'
. . . Does everything then come over again a little differently? she thought. If so, is there a pattern; a theme, recurring like music; half remembered, half foreseen? . . . a gigantic pattern, momentarily perceptible? The thought gave her extreme pleasure: that there was a pattern. But who makes it? Her mind slipped. She could not finish her thought.
. . . It's useless, she thought, opening her hands. It must drop. It must fall. And then? she thought. For her too there would be the endless night; the endless dark. She looked ahead of her as though she saw opening in front of her a very long dark tunnel.

Depressing as all this is, it remains vague and undefined. The nearest approach to a definite attitude within this pervasive general temper in which all the characters are monistically submerged is provided by a younger woman at the same party:

Peggy, marooned when the dance started, over by the bookcase, stood as close to it as she could. In order to cover her loneliness she took down a book. It was bound in green leather; and had, she noted as she turned it in her hands, little gilt stars tooled upon it. Which is all to the good, she thought, turning it over, because then it'll seem as if I were admiring the binding, . . . But I can't stand here admiring the binding, she thought. She opened it. He'll say what I'm thinking, she thought as she did so. Books opened at random always did

'*La médiocrité de l'univers m'étonne et me révolte,*' she read. That was it. Precisely. She read on . . . '*la petitesse de toutes choses m'emplit de dégoût. . . .*' She lifted her eyes. They were treading on her toes. ' . . . *la pauvreté des êtres humains m'anéantit.*' She shut the book and put it back on the shelf. 'Precisely,' she said.

After the aimless vacancy of the substance of the tale and such concluding reflections as these, the book's final sentence comes with a glib indication of a superimposed 'significance' almost shocking in its irrelevance.

Then she turned round into the room. 'And now?' she said, looking at Morris, who was drinking the last drops of a glass of wine. 'And now?' she asked, holding out her hands to him.

The sun had risen, and the sky above the houses wore an air of extraordinary beauty, simplicity and peace.

VI

THE annihilation of personality in the stream of non-personal being which is the logical consequence of Virginia Woolf's basic monism is expressed several times in *Night and Day*:

The great torrent of vans and carts was sweeping down Kingsway; pedestrians were streaming in two currents along the pavements. She stood fascinated at the corner. The deep roar filled her ears; the changing tumult had the inexpressible fascination of varied life pouring ceaselessly with a purpose which, as she looked, seemed to her, somehow, the normal purpose for which life was framed; its complete indifference to the individuals, whom it swallowed up and rolled onwards, filled her with at least a temporary exaltation.

This undisguised, but intermittent, note of individual personal immolation is kept at bay through *Jacob's Room*, *Mrs. Dalloway*, and *To the Lighthouse*, only to emerge once more on the downward emotional curve of *The Waves*.

'But listen,' said Louis, 'to the world moving through abysses of infinite space. It roars; the lighted strip of history is past and our Kings and Queens; we are gone; our civiliz..tion; the Nile; and all life. Our separate drops are dissolved; we are extinct, lost in the abysses of time, in the darkness.

In *The Years*, the process of time is confessed as sovereign. Human beings are simply and unresistingly swept away in the irreversible flux. It is the negation of spirit, the acceptance of dissolution, and it is perfectly in keeping with the incredible fragmentariness and incoherence of that novel.

The surrender to the process of time which had taken possession of Virginia Woolf's work from *To the Lighthouse* onwards, which is itself symptomatic of the relinquishment of meaning in personal life, is, in *Between the Acts* (1941) made absolute: but this enthroning of meaninglessness is effected in what is evidently a last desperate gesture towards the delineation of meaning. The book's 'extraordinary vacancy and pointlessness, the apparent absence of concern for any appearance of grasp or point', as F. R. Leavis describes it, is in fact the outcome of a pathetic gesture towards a final, desperate sort of significance. Here the time-pattern is extended to embrace, not one or two individual life-times, but the whole collective period of the human story. A naïve, self-cancelling 'significance' is indicated by a simple placing of the trivial moments of the inherently pointless characters in this tale against the immensities of racial history. The entire work is merely an elaboration of this intrinsically futile gesture, of which its inner story, that of the village pageant-play, is the type.

On the book's opening page, we have this immediate reference back to history:

> Her family, she told the old man in the arm-chair, had lived near Liskeard for many centuries. There were the graves in the churchyard to prove it.

And on the second page:

> From an aeroplane, he said, you could still see, plainly marked, the scars made by the Britons; by the Romans; by the Elizabethan manor house; and by the plough, when they ploughed the hill to grow wheat in the Napoleonic wars.

This historical and prehistorical background is reiterated at every opportunity:

> Only something over a hundred and twenty years the Olivers had been there. Still, on going up the principal staircase . . . there was a portrait. A length of yellow brocade was visible half-way up; and, as one reached the top, a small powdered face, a great head-dress slung with pearls, came into view; an ancestress of sorts. Six or seven bedrooms opened out of the corridor. The butler had been a soldier; had married a lady's maid; and, under a glass case, there was a watch that had stopped a bullet on the field of Waterloo.

The very boy who delivers fish has to be presented with a backward glance at his ancestry:

> Mitchell's boy – had to deliver right over the hill at Bickley; also round by Waythorn, Roddam, and Pyeminster, whose names, like his own, were in Domesday Book.

When someone knocks over a coffee-cup, the individual who catches it turns it over and sees, from the markings, that it was made at Nottingham at about 1760. Even the stones in the ground point a moral:

> This dry summer the path was strewn with stones, He kicked – a flinty yellow stone, a sharp stone, edged as if cut by a savage for an arrow. A barbaric stone; a prehistoric.

Old Mrs. Swithin, who on the day of the pageant is living in the village with her brother, Mr. Oliver, and his daughter, Mrs. Giles Oliver (Isa), at his country house, is awakened in the morning by the song of birds, and –

> . . . Forced to listen, she had stretched for her favourite ready – an Outline of History – and had spent the hours between three and five thinking of rhododendron forests in Piccadilly; when the entire continent, not then, she understood, divided by a channel, was all one; populated, she understood, by elephant-bodied, seal-knecked, heaving, surging, slowly writhing and, she supposed, barking monsters; the iguanodon, the mammoth, and the masto-don; from whom presumably, she thought, jerking the windows open, we descend.

The Pageant, a description of which forms the greater part of this peculiar novel, is designed by the producer, Miss La

Trobe, to show the villagers their organic continuity with history – their absorption, as it were, in the unbroken stream of time. That is the theory, which the novelist emphasizes as a fact at every opportunity.

> The audience was assembling. . . . Among them were the representatives of our most respected families – the Dyces of Denton; the Wickhams of Owlswick; and so on. Some had been there for centuries, never selling an acre. . . . Roughly speaking, had Figgis been there in person and called a roll call, half the ladies and gentlemen present would have said: '*Adsum*; I'm here, in place of my grandfather or greatgrandfather,' as the case might be.

The titled woman who patronizes the pageant is described as 'the old lady, the indigenous, the prehistoric':

> Then the great lady in the bath chair, the lady whose marriage with the local peer had obliterated in his trashy title a name that had been a name when there were brambles and briars where the Church now stood – so indigenous was she that even her body, crippled by arthritis, resembled an uncouth, nocturnal animal, now nearly extinct – clapped and laughed aloud – the sudden laughter of a startled jay.

It is all like that. The barn, in which refreshments are served during the interval, is 'the Barn, the Noble Barn, the barn that had been built over seven hundred years ago and reminded some people of a Greek temple, others of the middle ages, most people of an age before their own, scarcely anybody of the present moment'. And the climax of the moronic pageant is the section called 'Ourselves', when Miss La Trobe arranges for a host of actors with mirrors to flash them in the faces of the assembled audience.

The novel has one or two curious implications. To ascribe some peculiar sort of indwelling 'significance', not to the individual life, but to the collective history of mankind, the life of the race, is by emphasizing more continuity, to place human values at once within primarily biological categories. So it is that, oddly enough for this supposedly delicate and refined woman novelist, the biological pseudo-values of race, nature and sex are emphasized continually throughout her tale. During an intermission in the pageant, when Miss La Trobe is

anxiously waiting for something to fill the hiatus in the performance, the emotional continuity is appropriately provided
by the mindless bellowing of a herd of cows:

> Then suddenly, as the illusion petered out, the cows took up the
> burden. One had lost her calf. In the very nick of time she lifted
> her great moon-eyed head and bellowed. All the great moon-eyed
> heads laid themselves back. From cow after cow came the same
> yearning bellow. The whole world was filled with dumb yearning.
> It was the primeval voice sounding loud in the ear of the present
> moment. Then the whole herd caught the infection. Lashing their
> tails, blobbed like pokers, they tossed their heads high, plunged
> and bellowed, as if Eros had planted his dart in their flanks and
> goaded them to fury. The cows annihilated the gap; bridged the
> distance; filled the emptiness and continued the emotion.

These 'values' are applied to the human characters.

Mrs. Giles Oliver (Isa), for example, is introduced with a
reference to her sexual yearnings for a certain gentleman farmer
she has met; a little later she reads in the current *Times* about
the brutal rape of a girl by some troopers, and this incident
recurs to her mind at intervals throughout the day. When her
husband, Giles Oliver, from whom she is estranged, comes to
the house from his work at London:

> 'He is my husband,' Isabella thought, as they nodded across the
> bunch of many coloured flowers. 'The father of my children.'
> It worked, that old cliché; she felt pride; and affection; then pride
> again in herself, whom he had chosen. It was a shock to find, after
> the morning's look in the glass, and the arrow of desire shot
> through her by the gentleman farmer, how much she felt when
> he came in, not a dapper city gent, but a cricketer, of love; and
> of hate.

This phrase is repeated at intervals up to the end of the book –

> . . . 'the father of my children,' she muttered. The flesh poured
> over her, the hot nerve wired, now lit up, now dark as the grave
> physical body.
>   . . . Yet he was extraordinarily handsome. 'The father of my
> children, whom I love and hate.' Love and hate – how they tore
> her asunder! . . .

– when, after the lengthy description of the pageant which is to fill the onlookers with a sense of their racial-historical continuity, Giles and Isa at last come together and,

> Left alone together for the first time that day, they were silent. Alone, enmity was bared; also love. Before they slept, they must fight, after they had fought, they would embrace. From that embrace another life might be born. But first they must fight, as the dog fights the vixen, in the heart of darkness, in the fields of night. . . .

Thus impersonality is transformed into animality. Meanwhile, old Mrs. Swithin has returned to her meditations.

> It was time to read now, her Outline of History. But she had lost her place. She turned the pages looking at pictures – mammoths, mastodons, prehistoric birds. . . . 'England,' she was reading, 'was then a swamp. Thick forests covered the land. On top of their matted branches birds sang.' . . . 'Prehistoric man,' she read, 'Half-human, half-ape, roused himself from his semi-crouching position and raised great stones.'

Finally, night descends.

> The house had lost its shelter. It was night before roads were made, or houses. It was the night that dwellers in caves had watched from some high place among rocks. . . .

So ends the last book of this 'pure artist'.

MARGIAD EVANS

A STUDY of the cultural products of the last hundred years reveals an amazing heterogeneity of modes of human life and thought. This is to be expected in a period during which, following widespread apostasy from Christianity, no common faith has existed to sustain and unify cultural endeavour, nor is this heterogeneity the result of a creative flowering, but of a process of dissolution. Human life is disintegrating into fragments, and the individual, instead of achieving, or at least pursuing, wholeness, tends to adopt a fragmentary view of life, which results in a distortion of personality and its submission to lower elements.

A remarkable and little apprehended stream of this kind, running through the culture of the present day, issues from a peculiar and distinctive cult of nature, a reversion to a pre-Christian immersion of the soul in the natural universe. John Cowper Powys and his brother Llewelyn are eminent contemporary representatives of this cult in the world of letters. Brief passages from a recent book of the former indicate some of the basic features of the cult. This writer, not without philosophical pretensions as the author of *In Defence of Sensuality* and *A Philosophy of Solitude*, advocates 'a philosophy of life which regards the whole purpose of this Dimension of the Multiverse as the fullest possible enjoyment of life in general by each individual in particular'. Of this 'fullest enjoyment' Powys says:

> The most intense as well as the most lasting enjoyment possible to man is not to be attained through love or lust or power or possession or action, but through a very special sort of sensation, the sensation of embracing the whole Inanimate Mystery of which our present Dimension is composed.

Rhapsodizing over the irresponsibility of old age, which, he claims, sets men and women free to devote themselves to this 'fullest enjoyment of living', he exclaims:

> But oh! the escape from the appalling debt we owe to our fellow-men that is offered by the inanimate or sub-animate!

The more we learn to eat it, drink it, ravish it, be ravished by it, fuse with it, merge with it, sink into it, lose ourselves in it, the more fully we shall possess our souls in peace, the better will our solitude be protected and our subtlest egoism fulfilled.

In these passages we have, allowing for idiosyncrasies of expression, a fairly typical presentation of some of the chief features of the cult of nature. A cult of solitude, of sensuality, of enjoyment, of biological vitality, and of merging, it is antipersonal and antisocial, anticultural and materialistic. It is sufficient here merely to indicate these matters and to comment on the didactic presentation of the principles of the cult in J. C. Powys' work. This presentation, presupposing a settled basis of formulated experience, distinguishes him from those who are themselves spiritually involved in a process of turning towards nature as a release from the burdens and strains of the distinctively human life which is frustrated by the conditions of the modern world.

Such a turning towards and dissolution of personality in the fluid universe of nature is to be seen in progress in the writings of D. H. Lawrence. Yet, because Lawrence was a complicated person, the progression in Lawrence's case was intricate. A much simpler, but no less revealing, example of the process of the repudiation of personal life and spiritual values for the sake of immersion in the life of nature is to be found in the work of a distinguished contemporary, Margiad Evans.

A writer of considerable force and honesty, her earlier books, *Country Dance*, *The Wooden Doctor*, *Turf or Stone*, and *Creed* – all novels of more than common merit – are bitter, passionate cries of protest against the frustrations of personal life. The mood of her work is curiously reminiscent of that of *Wuthering Heights*. These novels followed close upon one another, having been published within a period of five years. There was then a significant seven years' silence between the publication of her fourth novel, *Creed* (1936), and her last book, *Autobiography* (1943), which clearly bears the markings of an individual version of the cult of nature.

Not an autobiography in the usual sense of the word, this book is a series of nature articles and notes written under such headings as 'A Little Journal of Being Alone', 'The Winter Journal', 'The Autobiography of an Afternoon', containing nothing about the author except as she exists in relationship with nature. It is clear that this is not intended to be an appetizer for the special public that seems to delight in little volumes about the English countryside; the title 'Autobiography' has for the author a quite definite significance, implying nothing less than that life in relationship with nature is the true, the essential life. 'This autobiography,' she writes, 'is the record of my gravest (that is happiest) inner existence. . . .' She says early in the book:

> Oh, how long it is since I have looked at the greatness of Nature miserably, through my own dreariness! *Now* it is my great refuge, my independent godliness which I worship without self-pity. It's a beautiful change from the tortured symbolism in which creation is molten and twisted into the form of *self*, to the simple and ever open sight of love! The fields are my grass life, the sun, the wind, the weather. If this power over my solitary hours persist, I am blessed.

Such is the spirit of her book. In keeping with this, elsewhere in it she confesses, 'Life to me is solitude'; and again, 'Don't talk to me of morals. To draw a moral is to draw a bolt.'

> Writing saddens me. Vision is turned into effort. Only in the *inner physical* eye is the radiance reflected. Life to me is solitude. My senses are all solitary. Through solitude I breathe. Memory is solitude and seeing. My senses are all solitary. They desert me when I am not alone, or rather leave me paralysed at the point of desertion. I thought this as I turned into the wind. Leaning on a gate I looked up at the sky in joy of my loneliness. The earth was reared up against the tossing clouds. And as I achieved the stripped summit of the hill and my eye swept the vigorous lines, the spaced and wintry trees that made the identity of the place, I put from me the intermediate self and spoke to the spirit, I, asking it, to what is it apt? The answer came by sight and feeling – to the earth itself and not to the people of it. My passionate and only belief is in another order of being from my own: my joy is in the hills and the different notes of the wind, and the (to me) unbaptized stars.

II

THE novels of Margiad Evans glow with a dark, sombre, passionate light. This is in evidence in her first and shortest work, *Country Dance* (1932), a tale, purporting to be founded upon an old manuscript diary kept by the central character of the story, of a bitter rivalry between two jealous, surly men of the Welsh Border over a girl, half Welsh, half English, as sullenly passionate as they. Unlit by any gleam of love, it ends, inevitably, in the murder of the girl by the rejected lover. Beneath the tale itself runs an emotional awareness of the dark grief of existence; the book's motto reads:

> . . . Place thy hand, unless thou believest me,
> Under my breast and beware of hurting me;
> Thou shalt hear if thou listen
> The sound of the little heart breaking.

Although written with a terse, incisive power, *Country Dance* did not achieve any great degree of success with the reading public.

The Wooden Doctor (1933), the second novel, won immediate recognition for the author's talent as a writer and straightway went into several impressions. This clearly personal novel is the history, told in the first person, of the childhood, adolescence, and youth of Arabella Warden, given a sporadic emotional continuity by the description of her unrequited passion for a middle-aged Irish doctor who is the one person in her desolate childhood to show her human tenderness.

The note of desolation is sounded in the opening pages, and the tale proceeds with a bitter, restless feverish ardour.

> In our home there was no peace. My father did more than drink occasionally; he was an habitual drunkard. No word was ever more accurately or deservedly applied; no family was ever rendered more miserable by its justice.
> . . . We grew up accepting him at first with terror and disgust, finally with bitter resignation. We have heard our mother called by names that would have shamed a harlot, not below the breath, but as one might sing praises. We have stood shivering behind bolted doors with our hands over our ears that we might not hear him scream of the horrors that he saw, and shut our eyes to those that were no delirious fancy.
> . . . Sometimes for our own sake, and his own, we have wished him dead, drowned, buried, or for ourselves that freedom. . . .
> . . . One and all, year in, year out, we nursed the prospect of escape. We quarrelled among ourselves, fretted, isolated by our

eccentricities, we sharpened our claws in one another's flesh. Our home among the quiet fields became a cage of savagery.

That note is sustained throughout the novel. Brought up in such surroundings, Arabella is morose, wild, and rebellious. In her teens she goes as a pupil-teacher to a school in France, but she is no happier there than at home.

> For years afterwards I hated the French. If I had been happy at the Cours Saint-Louis it might have dispelled my impression that the world was a grievous place.

Returning to England, she is attacked by a mysterious and painful malady:

> In the night the pain came back. It was like a fox in a bag scratching and rending to get out. My spirits trailed in the dust. The claws penetrated my sleep, dragged me awake and I sat up in my bed. I knew that I was ill. . . .
> One night we went to the cinema. . . . We were laughing. Suddenly out of the darkness the fox sprang with flaming feet and famished jaws, rending, biting, tearing. I wished that I could faint and be delivered from this agony, but my strength increased with the torture. A man in front of me had rather long hair. I wanted to seize it in both hands and pull his head backward: I felt I could have pulled it off.

Meanwhile she has drawn no nearer towards the doctor:

> One day after the doctor had gone my mother observed: 'He is beginning to look old.'
> Sadness filled me at these words. To me he was unchanged, but she was right, and I felt that living and loving were slipping by. . . .

There follows an incisive description of the experience of illness and the life of hospitals, written with savage stoicism. Then:

> One night I looked from my window. What a stormy sky I saw, and the moon shining livid behind black clouds; the hills rose up to them and mingled indistinguishably.
> There could be no comfort in humans. And my mind could find no god. I seized a pencil and wrote angrily.
> 'There's no doctor.'
> 'There's only me.'

'Am I to spend the rest of my life in the vapours? The gods forbid.'

In the morning I looked at what I had written with wonder. It was sunny.

All woes grow dim in the sun.

The Wooden Doctor learns of Arabella's passion for him and gently rejects her.

. . . the cut was dealt to me that divided my life into two parts. The period I approach was one of intense misery to me: I cannot write about it now without trembling; yet I am urged to do it. . . .

She goes to stay with a married cousin.

My cousin had a beautiful face. Those delicate features, those laughing, shining eyes, that cunning mouth, all that fascination so frequently before me, so contentedly blooming beside the husband she adored, tortured me. Savagely I envied her, not for what she had, but for what she might have had. To myself I cried: 'J'ai perdu, perdu, perdu; elle auriait gagnée!'

Full bitterness was mine, but my habit of deception hid it all. Outwardly I led a commonplace and happy existence: inwardly I seethed with jealousy and shame, and an aching loss.

I could not attract the man I loved: henceforth I should walk in utter humiliation. Twenty lovers would not atone for it. I look at those words now that I have written them down, admitting their truth. Arabella, from the heights of folly and the depths of despair I trounce you, denounce you, curse you, flout you for a fool.

I wish I could inspire one half the devotion I have given!

Her inner state is one of isolation:

I began to feel now more than ever before that confession was foolish and to be found out contemptible. That belief cut me off from all but superficial contact with other people.

Heavily, heavily the days trundled by. I was glad when the hours passed quickly and the evenings came. I strained my eyes ahead, tugged at the leash . . . for what?

I did not want to die – there were many things that interested me – but I did wish that I had never been born.

So the tale runs on. The portrait of Arabella is not a pretty one: tortured, rebellious, and proud, she is filled with 'fierce

resentment' of the happiness of others. She begins to write a
book, and to finish it goes to a farmhouse in Wales, where she
meets a young man called Oliver, who makes love to her and
begs her marry him. She promises to do so, but on returning
home finds that her devotion to the doctor makes marriage
impossible.

Abruptly the story closes:

> All this took place some time ago.
> My book was published.
> Oliver sends me red tulips on my birthday.
> And the Irishman married a young girl a few months after my
> return.
> And that's the end.

Clearly, this is a very simple novel, covering a restricted area
of sensibility. Its merit is its passionate intensity and the savage
honesty which presents a firmly limned outline of felt experience. Its limitations are as apparent as its virtues: what would
seem to be lacking in the attitude to life which it reveals is any
potentiality of development. The author's patent identification
of herself with her heroine, who lives solely in her egoistic
passional life, and who, utterly without humility and the
capacity for self-forgetfulness, is unable in any way to transcend
her particular circumstances, suggests an inadequate equipment for continuous fictional creation. The story in *The Wooden
Doctor* is, in fact, slight, secondary entirely to the implicit
attitude which it reveals toward experience. The nature of that
attitude is sufficiently indicated by the extracts given above.
The 'humiliation' of which it is a record is a measure of
Arabella's pride which remains unaffected to the end. It even
has a demoniac quality. The interest of the book centres
entirely upon the presentation of events and scenes which group
themselves around the inner passionate protest of Arabella. The
protest is against existence itself, for not shaping itself to her
egoistic desires. The result is a stark simplicity which, however,
seems to hold within it no potential unfoldment, inasmuch as the
book possesses no positive philosophical, moral, religious, or
social content. There is no novelist's interest in human beings
for their own sake: everything centres around the morose

Arabella and her exclusive preoccupation with her own sorrows. *Turf or Stone* (1934) is a less successful work, although it has considerable emotional interest. The hero of the book, Easter Probert, a half-gipsy groom and outcast from society, although outwardly a wild, sullen, malicious creature, is really – though unconsciously – searching for a woman's tenderness and love. The story opens with a description of Easter's marriage to a rather superior, genteel girl whom he has seduced, Mary Bicknor, a companion-servant to a wealthy old lady. He treats her brutally from the time of the wedding, quarrelling with her outside the very church and leaving her to walk home while he jumps into a passing bus. Easter is groom for Matt Kilminster, an idle, bored, dissolute 'gentleman', married to a frivolous, luxury-loving, self-pitying wife with three children. Having conceived an attachment for Easter's wife, Matt arranges for the groom to be away from the house for three days in the week in order to indulge his passion for Mary. Denied the tenderness for which he is always hungering, Easter sinks further into a bitter, violent nihilism until at last Mary, incensed at his treatment of her, lays information of his cruelty with the police and applies for a separation. Matt's young daughter, Phoebe, goes to Easter's squalid lodging to plead with him to keep her father's name out of the matter to avoid disgrace: although he does not agree to do so, he keeps his mouth shut at the court hearing and makes no defence against Mary's charges. Shortly afterwards he is killed in a brawl.

Turf or Stone is again a novel of passion rather than of character. The characters move in a heavy, oppressive atmosphere of empty meaninglessness, lifted only by occasional outbursts of debauchery or rage. Their world is utterly without light or love. Existence drags painfully. Unable to look for grace from above, they are at the mercy of the dark forces which rise from the lowest depths of their natures. 'Morose', 'dreary', 'baleful', 'sullen', 'gloomy', 'threatening', 'brooding', 'sombre', and 'bitter' are adjectives which litter each page. Matt Kilminster typifies this picture of existence: he –

led an increasingly blank existence. He was sometimes tortured by the vacancy of everything. Lately he had taken to drinking....

H

[He was driven] deeper, deeper, into a vague mental state where nothing held any significance.

'My blind island,' he called it to himself. . . .

He fell into a sombre calm, and his thoughts were all sad:

'How is it people are happy in this world, or even at their ease?'

By contrast with Matt and the others, it becomes clear as the tale proceeds that Easter in some way represents for the author the assertion of a value. As a hero, Easter recalls certain of the characters of D. H. Lawrence. Though presented in all his native viciousness and squalor, the only hint of idealization occurring in the retrospective glance at his childhood, it is nevertheless implied that circumstances have made him what he is and that in contrast to the other characters he has virtue. Besides being insolent, violent, and malicious, he has courage, animal gracefulness, and vitality.

If the story is told from the viewpoint of any one of the characters, it is that of Matt's eldest daughter, Phoebe. As the tale unwinds, there are subtle hints of the emotional significance which the groom holds for the growing girl. An example is the description of Phoebe's interview with Easter:

He put one foot on the bench, laid his elbow on his knee, and cupped his chin, while he stared at her eyes which she could not meet without a spasm of shame and something besides, something sharp and acute which stirred her so deeply that she began to shake. He desired Phoebe ardently, had done so for a long time, almost unaware; even as he sneered at the purity of her face it fascinated him. He experienced once more the voluptuous and painful craving for unsought caresses. The furious rancour which he had fostered for the last two years was beginning to give way before a sense of isolation which at times sapped his manhood and caused wild outbreaks of unconscious weeping at night. He was discovering that no creature of seven skins can be an outcast without suffering at least intermittent grief and yearning.

Phoebe was silent.

'There's no sense in your staying,' he resumed obstinately, 'why, God blast it all, you innocent toy, you don't know what you're asking of a man! It's my nature to be revengeful; you're asking me to change my nature . . . you might as well say "hop out of your skin, Easter, you'd be handsomer in a new one".'

'I do believe you have a cleaner skin underneath.' For the first time he was moved a little beyond his predatory senses. She heard him sigh.

'Perhaps,' he went on, 'But you wouldn't touch it! You don't even offer me anything. You'd make a new man if you could, but you won't take the new man near you and keep him against harm. You're Miss Kilminster and I'm a groom, and that's enough.'

He broke off, watching her. Her heart was beating so hard that he could see the throbs shaking her breast. Had he been aware to what extent she was fighting her own rising instincts he might have gone forward and taken his revenge on Matt without leaving the shed.

When Phoebe hears of his death, the story ends with the words: 'she began to cry dreadfully and heavily, in a deathly senseless manner, as if every sob would kill her'.

Turf or Stone, in so far as it is not written as direct auto-biography centring around the narrator, but as a drama concerning a group of characters, told in the third person, reveals in the author an increase in that objectivity necessary for novelistic creation, which makes possible the dramatic explication of a morality, the projection of a pattern of thought. Although the novel lacks structure, the character of Easter reveals a movement towards the dramatic presentation of an inner attitude, which alone gives significance to a novelist's work.

That inner attitude is seen clearly in the writer's subsequent novel, *Creed* (1936).

III

THIS bold title discloses that the novel, like all significant modern literature, is scriptural in character. Despite its lack of an overt morality, so is *The Wooden Doctor*, which discloses, although not in philosophical terms, a definite attitude toward experience. In *Turf or Stone*, the attitude implicit in the earlier book is made more explicit; in *Creed* it is given full and definite expression. This is without doubt the best of Margiad Evans's novels. Considered aesthetically, it is one of the very few significant modern works of fiction. As the title implies, an attempt is made to formulate and express a religious attitude to life.

The chief character is Francis Dollbright, ironmonger's

clerk, a religious bigot, stern and upright, worshipper of a harsh, tyrannical Ancient of Days, the eternal Judge and condemner of human sin. The story opens with an account of a sermon preached by an old Welsh parson, Ifor Morriss, who is overcome by sincerity in his pulpit and preaches his own private gospel of the irrelevance of sin and the impossibility of damnation.

> 'Ah, I tell you man cannot perish! I know it, for God loves him; not as a saint but as a blackened sinner he is loved. . . .
> My friends, although we should be murderers and blasphemers, although we are eaten through with meanness, cowardice, deceit, cruelty and the unnamed sins of our lusts, we should never be afraid to lift our foreheads to His face: although we are conscious of a determined will to continue in our vile courses, let us worship and say:
> ' "Lord, I know you are in me, and I thank You for Your presence. In the midst of our wickedness and our resolution to continue, let us kneel and avow: I know that You have not abandoned me." '

Shocked by this blasphemy, Dollbright interviews and anathematizes the parson after his sermon. Morriss laughs at Dollbright, who returns home in a state of inner turmoil, which moves him to assert his moral values by severing connections with his employer, John Bridges, an ill-living, passionate, unbelieving man who lives with a woman to whom he is not married. Dollbright announces this decision to his wife, who bitterly resents the placing of the demands of his conscience before her well-being, despite which he notifies his employer of his intention to quit. Meanwhile his wife discovers that she is ill with cancer and must undergo an operation, while Dollbright finds that his action earns him the contempt rather than the respect of other people. Eventually he wavers, and the discovery of his wife's illness forces him to go hat in hand to Bridges to beg for the return of his job.

Interwoven with the story of Dollbright is that of the stricken, beseeching passion of the young Bellamy Williams for haunted, compassionate Menna Trouncer. They feel 'fated' to love each other, but Menna tries to run from her fate and to deny Bellamy.

'Oh, Menna, Menna, Menna, I'd scarcely be in such despair if I saw you dead or loving another man! Dead you'd be out of chance, and loving would give you substance and a heart which I'd twist towards me. But I can't strain at nothing, and nothing is all I've got to beg you by. What do you hold to? What can't you spare when you've spared everything? What's your most inner and last hope? I'll pray and implore you by that to take me and love me . . . love me. I want the looks that you hide from me, the time that you spoil, all the joys that you kill and keep back. I want my sleep from you, my life, my rest. I'm deserted and sleepless without you. I want your hands on my head – it's all pain and longing! Take me, Menna darling, dear love——!' Tightly as he held her, forcing her face close to his own with his hard right hand over her ear and his gasps crossing her lips, she scarcely felt the pressure on her living body. But each word melted her. She looked at him, lifted her hand and put it against his neck; then her eyes yielded and his own name seemed uttered in them rather than in sound. Neither would move; they were walled up in passion, in a rigid pause, a stricken knowledge of what was inevitable between them. All softness and elasticity departed, even the tremulousness of breathing. Their eyes were like caldouses. At last he spoke, but with indescribable difficulty, as though something bolted and barred within him were making noises behind a door.

'Now . . . is it . . . love?'

She could not answer, could do nothing but gaze while her hand began to stir on his neck and she learned the line of his lips forever.

'If we two part,' he toiled on in the same weak, yet urgent tone, 'we shall always hanker after each other. You'll never forget me; I have burned into you.'

'Yes——'

In a desperate spasm they simultaneously clutched each other and stood blind and reeling with their faces stricken together. Then the strength ran out of them. Bellamy fell against the wall, covering his eyes, and Menna sank down on the floor at his knees.

In his bewilderment and inner struggle, Dollbright encounters Menna's hideous mother. This woman, powerfully drawn by the author, provides a spiritual centre for the book. Under the surface of their lives, all these characters, Dollbright, Ifor Morriss, Menna Trouncer, and Bellamy Williams, meet and are psychically united; their basic stuff is the same and finds its crude expression in the figure of Mrs. Trouncer.

Once more [Dollbright] noticed her short dirty neck disappearing in the wrinkles of a silk handkerchief. Suddenly he felt an abominable seduction dwelling in her swarthy flesh. She shook . . . He looked at her with grim disgust.

'It isn't church and chapel and gory black hats that makes life,' she said.

'Nor whiskey and the gutter,' he retorted.

'Talking of the gutter you name yourself. Sodding churchwarden!' she screamed, glaring and advancing as he shut the inner door that Florence might not hear. When he turned round he found her face almost touching his ear; the large pores stood out like a rash, the nose was nearly black. Without the slightest warning but the audible clash of her teeth, she shot her fist out and struck him on the right arm above the elbow with her left.

He saw the blow whirling in the air like a chipped stone falling. She did not repeat it, she was too breathless.

'You . . .!' he shouted, 'touch me again and I'll call a constable.'

'If I'd the strength, I'd tear up the stones in the street to heave at you. I'd squash your bloody nob in the Mill, myself the wheel, and bless every fall of bad that comes your way . . . I'd stamp you down in Hell, where I've been and seen not one devil but ten thousand holding up their arms at the whole —— lot of us and sending up rockets that burst your eyes. Blast you to ruins! My tongue's gone down me gullet——'

Standing in the doorway she glared at him as if she would nail him to the wall.

'Church bug – climb up the cross!'

The underlying psychic unity of these passion-driven characters expresses itself in Dollbright's fascinated recognition of that which he has in common, despite appearances, with the terrifying, bestial drunkard, Mrs. Trouncer.

He could not find words to form his thoughts, nor images to hold them. They were too vague, immense, and inevitable. He had a sense of elemental diablerie quite apart from any human will. Men and things were part of it, as agents but no more. It was a dark illumination of the intellect, a search, a quest into the wizard powers. It was a faith prouder than any, savagely intolerant of happiness and goodness. It made Ifor Morriss smug, Bridges empty as the skull he preached.

It made Mrs. Trouncer great.

Instincts go deeper than reasons, sin than sanctity. Dollbright was, he bitterly and fearfully acknowledged, a swaddled ignoramus before this woman's violent force. She made him ashamed of his religion, weary of it and distrustful; she interfused God and temptation. She was scored and branded. He hated her still, but he could think of her without the limitation of disgust. He ceased to curse himself for the abominable perversion of his desire. Self-blame was lost in an almost supernatural fear. He felt she was a giant figure in his destiny . . . she fated him.

What was she, less obviously than a blasphemous hag? She swilled spirits until her face was swinish and gloating, but what inexplicable look of initiation was that in her eye? Of what soul was her face the defiant scar? What end had she visioned and dared?

He knew that whatever these things were, they lay not in her, but beyond her; and that they had travelled to him through her. . . . He was changed in the dark. All the time he was conscious of a new omnipotent idea of evil as a profound unearthly cause, a demonic over-soul, charged with life, and tangible only as breath.

As if to underline this discovery, to put beyond doubt her plain meaning, Margiad Evans makes a personal interpolation to the reader. 'I own that I am here. . . .'

I have never read any books on theology; but I have heard what I thought was God's voice in strange mouths. I have heard his name sound wonderful and holy in a furious row outside the pub, and I have heard sanctified congregations worshipping literature.

As for God – imaginations have bestowed the power and the glory upon him, but in fact he has only his name. He is like a madman, whose property very truly is his, only he is not allowed to make use of it. And like a madman is God in that to manifest his strength he has to break through the restraining bonds of those very ones who declare his calamitous insight, and fear his fires.

No. It requires not Christ to symbolize the poverty of God. It is so evident! With half the world pouring divinity on his altars, with all the building and decking of his houses, the painting of his revelations, he is still only a word among worse words.

His kingdom on earth is in oaths and men's deaths and despairs. He is in every man's mouth, though he die with each one. Wherever there's shame and cruelty and wickedness, tongues drag him in as the one thing that can stand up to them – he is preached in all the sins and proclaimed in curses.

Dollbright fights in agony of mind against his conversion to this new and terrible 'faith'. In the throes of his struggle he is driven to the edge of suicide, further tormented by the importunings of his elderly lodger, Benjamin Wandby, who has chosen to make Dollbright judge over his inflamed conscience: he cannot forget that he was imprisoned years ago for attempted murder. Meanwhile Bellamy and Menna at last come together: Menna has turned on her mother, the obstacle to their union, now deliberately hastening her inevitable death through drinking. When for the first time Menna spends the night with Bellamy she returns home in the early morning to find Dollbright and Benjamin Wandby in the house and her mother dead, having fallen in a drunken stupor through an open trap door into the cellar. Wandby is astounded that Dollbright, the condemner of others' sin, has no word of reproach for Menna. Dollbright has come to the end of his struggle. The book concludes with this tremendous finale:

> He saw himself stooping over the monstrous figure lolling brokenly on the black mouldy steps, its garment slowly, slowly tearing from the nail. He smelled the horrible odour of drink and dirt and decay mixed with slimy wood and the rawness of stored potatoes. The hideous incident paused in his mind's eye, invoking horror, sickness . . . and deep unaccustomed pity. What staggering enforced journey had plunged her into that dark earthly hole with the fallen lantern shining on the brink? What whole abandonment by every human soul had she discovered in the night? She spoke of love?
>
> Unlike Benjamin, he was less affected by the tragedy of Menna's development than by her mother's ghastly end. She had crashed across his unchosen track like a lightning-stricken tree whose shadow was consumed by fire and death. This was her act in his destiny. This was the power over him which he had felt with a supernatural shrinking from the inevitable demonism of her eye, the demoniacal authority of her wild, half hinted speech, which was subterraneously linked to the breaking forth of his own fierce ungoverned spirit.
>
> That spirit had moved him all his life. Pounded down, subdued and overloaded, leashed and lashed by his inexorable unnatural

faith, he had struggled to make of that restless genitor a sacrifice to eternity. And it had burst upwards under his feet. And he had quoted it before he knew that he had heard its gagged voice speak. . . . For a long time he had not thought at all. Every day he had come and gone to his work, he had sat with his wife, he had suffered the terrible nothing in his breast and his brain. Last night, with blood on his hand and holding the matted head upon his arm, he had felt a great opening in his mind as though air were rushing into a vacuum. He could not think then: he was almost strangled, speechless in thought and undelivered.

Now words were working in him, excitement seized him. He felt his existence enclosed in a tremendous destiny. The knots in his breast relaxed in a rushing thaw. He shouted wildly, he walked about the empty shop like a man clean mad, possessed by freedom.

'I can lament or defy. And I'm defiant. From your millions you have lost me, and all your aeons will never bring me back. Order could not compel me; pain shall not subdue me, and tears are not repentance. The more powerful you, the weaker I; but the more you gather the less you never lose! Oh, God, I have taken separate existence from you, and you cannot pour my one soul back into your self!'

It grew dusky with a white, blind twilight, like the film of cataract. Benjamin Wandby came and knocked at the window. Dishevelled, passionate, Dollbright stood in the door.

'I thought I'd find you here,' said the other; 'I've come to tell you she's dead.'

'Dead, dead?' he echoed like a foreign word. He was free of death.

IV

THE meaning of *Creed* – that is, the significance of the inner orientation reached by Dollbright – is plain. But this meaning is by no means clearly apparent to the casual reader with no very clearly defined spiritual standards by which to measure the terms of the doctrine offered in this book.

It is easy for such a reader to run through the book and to read into it the conversion of Dollbright from proud religious bigotry to a humbler and more Christlike acceptance of suffering and sinful humanity. Yet the quotations given above should be sufficient to dispel this impression and to make clear he nature of Margiad Evans's creed. There is little point in maintaining a polite assumption that this novel has no necessary relation to its author's personal attitude. To repeat, between all the characters there is a profound psychic connection: Menna's and Bellamy's erotic passion, Dollbright's religious fervour, Ifor Morriss's creed, and Mrs. Trouncer's demoniac instinctive vitality – all these are aspects of one fundamental attitude, summed up in the author's declared acknowledgment of a deity who is 'preached in all the sins and proclaimed in curses'.

The religious argument of the book is that God is really to be identified with the telluric passionate depths of existence. That which Dollbright eventually comes to accept is a notion of the deity in which no separation is made between the divine and demoniac, holy and unholy. He finds himself no longer able to condemn, not because he has conquered intolerance with understanding and love, but because he has now no standpoint from which to make distinctions, between sin and sanctity, good and evil, salvation and perdition. All are fused in one passionate and insatiable act of undiscriminating acceptance, in which rings, however, a strange note of rebellion. This desperate creed is based upon and necessitates an exaltation of passion. But such an exaltation is inseparable from a fearful underlying boredom and vacuity. In this connection, the relationship between the feverish violence which distinguishes the characters in *Creed* and the dreary futility which is the pervasive emotional atmosphere of the preceding novel, *Turf or Stone*, should be considered. This exaltation of passion has nothing whatever to do with love: there is no question of love between Menna and Bellamy. It is a dark passion, in essence destructive and murderous – witness Bellamy's thoughts at the boxing match he attends, Menna having refused his solicitations:

> These weren't men. They were 'sports' who didn't know what it was to feel savage rage in your limbs and strangulation in your heart. Bellamy felt himself go rolling over and over, clenching that wet streaky body, hugging the breath out of it, cracking its ribs against the reef of his own bones. To break a man against yourself – that must be joy, to fly, to fell a tree, to beat a woman whom you passionately desired, to go to war . . . perhaps to go to war . . . that was a future. . . .

This exaltation of passion is connected with a lofty and intractable pride.

It is a characteristic of passion to be both destructive and self-consuming. It incinerates the energy on which it feeds. It leads not to renewal of passion, but to exhaustion, vacancy. It is bred in vacancy, flourishes in it, and burns out to leave the vacancy more achingly unbearable than before. Exalted into a 'faith', it is a creed of desperation. Personality and the personal values cannot flourish in its sultry atmosphere. It cannot lead to creativeness. Its direction is not lifeward but towards death and perdition. Margiad Evans's prolonged silence of seven years following the publication of *Creed* was thus not without significance. The creed of passion, bad in itself, is doubly bad for the novelist, if only for the obvious reason that it does not permit of the differentiation of character, its tendency being to merge individual personalities into a common emotional stream. *Creed* itself shows no subtle awareness of personality: each character is but a powerful projection of a certain aspect of the author's egoistic life-attitude. This raw stuff of passionate existence is monotonously the same wherever it is found. On these premises Margiad Evans would seem, as a novelist, to have little scope or variation, none for development, without a rupture in continuity. That her book is archetypal may be glimpsed from her treatment of Bellamy and Menna. They are powerless in the grip of their passion; the passion as a quality in itself rather than they as individual beings is the theme of her narrative. But passion as such has a monotonous uniformity. As a sincere and non-professionalized novelist, Margiad Evans would find little satisfaction, one presumes, in mere repetition. In this sense *Creed* represents the conclusion of an inner process, not a beginning; it contains no creative potentialities.

The conclusion to Margiad Evans's development, however, is to be found in her last book, not a novel, but an autobiography; not even an autobiography, but a sheaf of nature-notes. In fact, her *Autobiography* (1943) marks a final repudiation of personal values and calmly despairing desire for the merging of the soul into the life of the natural universe. Passion had faded out, leaving only the desire for rest, peace, and self-obliteration, which the author finds in an identification of herself with the phenomena of nature. The opening passages of the first section, 'A Little Journal of Being Alone', indicate the tone of the book.

Midwinter and all dulled but the wind and the stars. The dead of the dark winter; stretching behind me the dim patch of silent days alone. The wind is a tooth in the breast . . . the dark suns give no light.

There was no sky – only the breathy air and a heaviness behind the trees like the dull butt of an iron bar. I watch the moribund chickens standing about on one leg with their claws crimped like a bunch of twigs. A draught that seemed to splinter the bones, ran an icy tune along the hedge and leapt with the wind, dragging after it the straws combed by the brambles out of this morning's load. In, in, shut everything in. Oh, the happiness of being alone – it's like having only one door to yourself and that bolted and firm walls around. The taste of it is in my food, the sound of my footsteps. I enjoy it even when terrified of my own alarming presence in the welcoming void.

Down in the orchard getting wood, I said, 'That's the smoke of my fire.' In a moment I shall light my last candle and go to bed. I'm going to sleep on my elbow and my shadow lurches over the page. There's a noise far away in the dark which seems to know where I am. Why do all such things recall Death?

It needs no particularly sensitive ear to capture the melancholy undercurrent of this writing. To merge with nature is to merge with that which is transient, perishable; indeed this book smells of mortality.

. . . One is in everything. One lives through the universe and beyond. Though I think what I see I don't see with my eyes alone. Never shall I see Nature passing without falling in with its order, myself mixing and coming to consciousness in all life.

All existences merge, even physically. Things more than resemble one another, they are more than kin, they are one manifestation. Likenesses are symbols. How should we not grow like one another when the same element brims up in us all, when we ourselves are conscious sometimes that our separate existence is an intermittent form assumed, we cannot tell why?

The life which is opposite to me, be what it is when I reach out to it, responds to me. There is no picture, no form of life, and in no form but as an unseen element, it floods the earth and sky. As nothing individual it returns. As nothing individual I go out.

Lapsing and losing myself I seem to breathe through distant trees; to look around the world from stones in the fields, and down on it from the budding mountain. It has seemed to me that ever since I was a child creation desired me as I desired creation. All of us sought one another.

The sympathy I longed for was not human sympathy, nor any human idea of it. It wasn't tenderness I wanted, nor mutual recognition, mutual pleasure; it was nothing I could describe in human language. I call it reciprocity, but that is apt to be too much. The further I can get from being a human being, the clearer can I feel in me the idea of an elemental conception. I need to feel it and have always needed it. I need and desire an extension, a plurality of being. . . . I don't wrap myself in solitude, I go naked in it. I discard my particularity, I discard myself. I don't want other humans to be solitary with me because their humanity on top of mine is too much for impersonality to discard. . . .

To make a full examination of this particular modern cult would require a volume; a brief comment is all that can be managed here. A life lived only in a relationship to nature, and not also in relationship to nature's complement, history, to say nothing of personal relationships, is less than half an existence. Devotees of the cult have, in the first place, little sense of personality and, in the second, little sense of history, of society; or, if they have a sense of these realities, it is negative and reactionary. An odd inner vacuity runs through most of the literary works of the cult, which at the same time evinces an absence of development. One who limits himself to that which he is in relationship with nature constricts his humanity; he becomes less than, not more than, human. Margiad Evans speaks of 'love', but the test of love is not a relationship with the inanimate, but with another person; for her, however, 'Life . . . is solitude'. The praise of solitude is found, too, in Richard Jefferies, whose Story of My Heart is a classic work of the nature cult, and in J. C. Powys. Books written from such an aspect can have no development, no form, because no beginning and no end; the writer inhabits a world in which time has been absorbed, or evicted, by space. Autobiography, despite the brilliant incisiveness of some of its descriptions, is finally tedious, because it is both repetitive and shapeless.

What is the value of simple descriptive jottings about the

trees and the weather, however incisively performed? What is the point of nature-writing?

> If you want to write with absolute truth and with the ease of a natural function, write from your eyes and ears, and your touch, in the very now where you find yourself alive wherever it may be. Carry your paper and book with you and conceal yourself in the fields. Watch and be in what you see or in what you feel in your brain. . . .

But to what end? If the essential meaning and value of life is to be found in this immediate communion with the natural universe, why reproduce one's observations, sensations, impressions, in the abstract mental medium of language? This is an inescapable problem for every despiser of society, of humanity, of culture, of the spirit. Margiad Evans continues her reflections:

> Even so there is a fading, a merging, a loss of something which no pondering and no effort can bring back. We are bound to return sometime and to begin 'copying out'. Once that starts . . . well to be within walls, even close under an open window where you can see rooks flying and calling under the clouds, is to be in comparative darkness. However light the room in which you work, it has few living shadows and little space compared to the field in which you saw so clearly. You may picture it with all the vividness in your power, but where is the grass you actually saw, the real grass with separate blades, with moss in it and roots and the light roughing it? It is not in you. Recollect the trees as you may, something is gone out of the vision. You cannot call up the colour of the bark, the seaminess, the firm flakes. A joy which rested on the ground and filled the sky, is not to be described. The brain wearies toiling with language, and the captive sight follows the bird's flight over the elm tops with a deep unconscious longing to return to the 'now' which seemed so unbreakable when you rested in the field only a short while ago.

Quite so. And silence would seem to be the inevitable conclusion of the inner dialectic to which the author has submitted herself.

There is a point at which too emphatic a 'love of life', physically speaking, meets and merges with a longing for death. There is in the cult of nature an underlying dreariness, however it be disguised with a mask of 'joyousness' and 'optimism'. Margiad Evans reiterates her happiness, but the effect of her writing is of a deep hollow sadness. The transient sensual happiness on which some of the more superficial, dogmatic, and loquacious devotees of the cult place emphasis has a ghoulish character; it is a happiness snatched from the grave: nor can they altogether conceal from themselves their awareness of this fact. There is in nature not only a life-giving and a generative, but also a death-dealing principle, and an acceptance of nature as God implies the acceptance of both its aspects. In *The Story of My Heart* Jefferies's paeans to nature modulate insensibly into strains such as these:

> Could I have my own way after death I would be burned on a pyre of pine-wood, open to the air, and placed on the summit of the hills. Then let my ashes be scattered abroad – not collected in an urn – freely sown wide and broadcast. That is the natural interment of man – of man whose Thought at least has been among the immortals; interment in the elements. Burial is not enough, it does not give sufficient solution into the elements speedily; a furnace is confined. The high open air of the topmost hill, there let the tawny flame lick up the fragment called the body; there cast the ashes into the space it longed for while living.

The deathward trend of *Autobiography* is equally explicit. 'I used to feel,' writes Margiad Evans, 'that in some profound way my body was becoming my soul.' From that, the acquiescence, so foreign to the Christian consciousness, in annihilation, is not far distant: and so we find such paragraphs as this:

> It was pure delight to lie there with my dear home winds coming over the tops of the elms and my own country lapping around its incomparable hills . . . to lie and rest and wonder whether real death can be so perfect.

And this:

> Walking between the oak trees and the stile, I thought of death, as I do every day and every hour. Not death with its kneeling and services, and decay; but of short corruption to cleanness, and the white bone in its starry beauty on the turf. . . . I am not lonely. I should only be lonely if I happened alone, if I existed alone, if I had to make myself breathe. If I had created myself and must decide for myself when to die, then I should be lonely, and should

not ask myself why I didn't envy the strolling people their laughter, the children out of school their childhood. I don't envy them because on earth I find myself in everything, because in view of death we are all the same age.

Upon that note the Autobiography closes.

ALDOUS HUXLEY

THE reputation of Aldous Huxley -- that initial reputation, through which his claim upon popular esteem still persists, was made, it should be recollected, in the era of post-Great War 'disillusionment', whose predominant mood was faithfully reflected in the bright and bitter humour, the sardonic portrayal of human futility, which marked the early novels and tales. In his earlier days Huxley was read with enthusiasm by many of his contemporaries, not only in England, who felt that, in his sophisticated hedonism, his freedom from outworn loyalties, even his licence, he spoke for a generation. He was detached, ironical, and he knew how to be amusing with that wryness which revealed an awareness of the corruption at the bottom of the glass of pleasure.

Huxley's work as a whole has taken the form of a thinly disguised autobiographical sequence; its shape has been determined by its author's changing attitude to life, which has always found its corresponding intellectual expression (reviewers were wont, as a matter of course, to prostrate themselves before his overwhelming 'intellect'); and the problem for the critic lies in the difficulty of keeping a just balance between the attitude to life underlying and conditioning the specific artistic productions; these productions (the novels) themselves; and the resultant ideas which the novelist has abstracted, as it were, from the creative process, and which he now arrays formidably and somewhat menacingly before his public.

For, as it happens, that early entertainer ('that different person', Huxley writes in a recent new preface to one of his old novels, 'who was oneself in youth . . .') is a figure from whom the later and at first glance strangely altered Huxley would wish rather pointedly to dissociate himself. Today there confronts us, not the sardonic portraitist of futility, but the prophet and the philosopher of Enlightenment, of Liberation, through

a species of contemplative mysticism, or mystical contemplation. And this prophet, or teacher, quite overshadows, if he
has not finally liquidated, the artist.

What, in fact, is the nature of the teaching which emerges?
It is rather a simple doctrine. Man's final end, according to
Huxley's most recent work, a compendium entitled *The Perennial Philosophy* (1946), is nothing less than 'unitive love-know-
ledge of the Divine Ground', a knowledge which one must
attain by 'making oneself loving, pure in heart and poor in
spirit', through a 'discipline more arduous and unremitting than
any imposed by ecclesiastical authority' – a discipline which
involves, indeed, a total dying to self.

Salvation, deliverance, enlightenment are apostrophized; but
always the emphasis, in this version of mysticism, is upon self-
obliteration; and self-obliteration, it appears, in an impassive,
non-personal, not-God (as with strange candour the 'Divine
Ground' is here described). Time and all its works, being evil,
must be annihilated: the goal is *Nirvana*, complete cessation of
the pain which comes through individuation, separation from
the abysmal One.

> Man must live in time in order to be able to advance into
> eternity, no longer on the animal, but on the spiritual level; he
> must be conscious of himself as a separate ego in order to be able
> consciously to transcend separate selfhood; he must do battle with
> the lower self in order that he may become identified with that
> higher Self within him, which is akin to the divine Not-Self; and
> finally he must make use of his cleverness in order to pass beyond
> cleverness to the intellectual vision of Truth, the immediate,
> unitive knowledge of the divine Ground.

The mystics – Catholics, Quaker, Hindu, Buddhist, Taoist,
Sufi, and the rest – have pointed out the way; Huxley annotates
it: we refuse it at our peril.

Whether in fact the new doctrine can be so completely dis-
sociated from its literary antecedents is something which we
owe it to truth and to ourselves to investigate rather than to
take on trust. A hundred years ago Søren Kierkegaard in a
masterly essay categorically described the fundamental disorientation which afflicts all human existence not lived under

the rubric, Faith, as the 'sickness unto death'; the sickness unto death being – despair. To designate Aldous Huxley as the novelist of despair – if despair is the emotional potentiation of futility, the central theme of his work – will seem unquestionably fitting to the earlier 'Pyrrhonic aesthete', and if it should arouse some surprise, here and there, when applied with even greater emphasis to the later Huxley, in his 'Perennial' avatar, that surprise will, I trust, be modified in the light of what is said below.

That there is, in reality, more than a marked affinity between Huxley's earlier and his later work and ideas we shall discover if, disregarding whatever overt attitudes the abstract theorist would have us accept, we scrutinize the underlying structure of the novelist's and the thinker's world. The fictional universe which he creates and populates possesses certain well-defined features which might all be said to be explicable in the light of a fundamental *discontinuity*. If we say of Huxley's characters that they are static and isolated, that a certain impersonal detachment shows itself in their creator's attitude towards them, and that at the same time their existence presumes a context of pointlessness, we shall have sketched a readily recognizable picture of Huxley's constant frame of reference. For, by a curious irony, while Huxley himself would claim a radical discontinuity between the divergent attitudes to life – 'Pyrrhonic hedonism' and contemplative mysticism – which in turn grow out of and condition his earlier and his later work, in fact the two originate in a common dislocation of being: the one exaggeration of attitude finds its balancing counterpart in the other; and the irony is pointed in the fact that discontinuity itself can even be said to be the only continuous factor in decisive operation throughout Huxley's artistic career. Huxley's development follows not a spiral but an hour-glass pattern. The psychological structure underlying *Crome Yellow*, *Antic Hay*, and *Those Barren Leaves* becomes modified as the novelist's dissatisfaction with his non-committal relationship to life draws him towards a closer engagement, only to reassert itself with finality as he crosses over into a yet further detachment which is the obverse of the earlier attitude, and which reinforces its pronounced bias towards the impersonal, the non-human.

I

THE mental structure upon which Huxley was to raise his successive fictional edifices is discoverable with little difficulty in his first novel, *Crome Yellow* (1921). A dualism of mind and matter, of spirit and body, of the ideal and the actual is fundamental to it, and is the source at once of Huxley's pessimism, of the purely static and episodic quality of his work, and of his humour. Futility and frustration, humorously presented, the disparity between intention and accomplishment, are the themes of this slight, episodic narrative which tells of a short holiday spent by a young poet, Denis, at the country house of Crome, during the course of which he encounters a succession of interestingly odd characters, is pursued by a young female while himself unsuccessfully pursuing another, and eventually allows himself to be bundled off for home just as he seems to be within reach of amorous success. The appropriate note is struck in the opening paragraph:

> Oh, this journey! It was two hours cut clean out of his life; two hours in which he might have done so much, so much – written the perfect poem, for example, or read the one illuminating book. Instead of which – his gorge rose at the smell of the dusty cushions against which he was leaning. . . .

And it is maintained with fair consistency throughout.

The character of Denis is indeterminate. He is young and very uncertain of his own feelings and beliefs, and is moreover somewhat isolated from human contacts. Denis's response to living is involuntarily moralistic; theoretically he is a hedonist:

> 'I've always taken things as they come,' said Anne. 'It seems so obvious. One enjoys the pleasant things, avoids the nasty ones. There's nothing more to be said.'
>
> 'Nothing – for you. But, then, you were born a pagan; I am trying laboriously to make myself one. I can take nothing for granted, I can enjoy nothing as it comes along. Beauty, pleasure, art, women – I have to invent an excuse, a justification for everything that's delightful. Otherwise I can't enjoy it with an easy conscience.
>
> '. . . Pleasure is one of the mystical roads to union with the infinite – the ecstasies of drinking, dancing, love-making. As for women, I am perpetually assuring myself that they're the broad

highway to divinity. And to think that I'm only just beginning to
see through the silliness of the whole thing!'

Of Huxley's two themes, the first, the disparity of the ideal
and the actual, is expressed characteristically in the account
from Mr. Wimbush's History of Crome, of the Elizabethan
baronet's sanitary arrangements; 'the necessities of nature are
so base and brutish that in obeying them we are apt to forget
that we are the noblest creatures of the universe', so that
accordingly the privy must be a book-lined room at the top of
the house, commanding 'an extensive and noble prospect'. It
finds expression also in the interpolated anecdote of the three
lovely sisters who in public maintained a pretence of wan,
etherial spirituality, while surreptitiously gorging themselves
at elaborate private repasts in their chamber; while of the
second, a deliberate hedonism coupled with an underlying
sense of personal futility, Mr. Scogan in this novel is the mouthpiece:

'Worried about the cosmos, eh?' Mr. Scogan patted him on the
arm. 'I know the feeling,' he said, 'It's a most distressing symptom.
What's the good of continuing to function if one's doomed to be
snuffed out at last along with everything else? Yes, yes. I know
exactly how you feel. It's most distressing if one allows oneself to
be distressed. But then why allow oneself to be distressed? After all,
we all know that there's no ultimate point. But what difference
does that make?'

We shall see that throughout his successive works Huxley has
never departed from these foundations.

Antic Hay (1923) is at once more serious and more farcical, a
mordant blaze of characters and incidents against a starker
background of futility. Yet there is a pronounced thread of
morality running through the tale's desperate gaiety. When we
are introduced first to Theodore Gumbril we find him 'specula-
ting, in his rapid and rambling way, about the existence and the
nature of God', and then, a little later, disturbed by a pricking
conscience over his 'first serious and deliberate lie' – in childhood.

The element of broad farce enters with Gumbril's invention
and marketing of trousers with pneumatic seats. On the
strength of his hopes from this venture he leaves his job as

schoolmaster and embarks upon a random course of dissipation during which he encounters such exponents of depravity as Myra Viveash, whose voice 'seemed always on the point of expiring, as though each word were the last, uttered faintly and breakingly from a death-bed . . .'; Coleman, whose career of debauchery is carried out on principle and is accompanied by blasphemy; and Mr. Mercaptan, whose speciality is seduction according to the precepts of Crebillon *fils*, upon a white satin sofa in his tastefully decorated apartment. The thread of quasi-moral narrative – that which concerns Gumbril's relations of simple, genuine affection with the girl Emily, whom he is led to abandon at a whim of Mrs. Viveash's – is slight in proportion to the whole novel, which concerns the erratic futilities of Gumbril and the others as they are whirled around in the dry wind of boredom, vanity and despair.

Beneath the amusing surface there is a clear enunciation of the theme of futility:

> 'It's appalling, it's horrible,' said Gumbril at last, after a long, long silence, during which he had, indeed, been relishing to the full the horror of it all. Life, don't you know. . . .

And when, after his betrayal of Emily, he goes, with Mrs. Viveash, the dreary, anguished, pleasure-hunting round of night-clubs in an episode which palely reflects the Walpurgis-nacht scenes of *Ulysses*, the night perpetuates itself with yet further revelations of human depravity and the farcical point-lessness of things, until finally:

> 'Tomorrow,' said Gumbril at last, meditatively.
> 'Tomorrow,' Mrs. Viveash interrupted him, 'will be as awful as today.' She breathed it like a truth from beyond the grave prematurely revealed, expiringly from her death-bed within.

Those Barren Leaves (1925), the novel following, is the first to be written from a serious questioning of life. Each of the major characters who are gathered at the wealthy Mrs. Aldwinkle's Italian villa – Calamy the disenchanted man of the world, whose temper provides a point of location for the mood of the book, Cardan, and Chelifer – shares with the other two a common disillusionment with the human state. But whereas Cardan has pursued to the end a course of genial parasitical pleasure-seeking, Chelifer is a self-torturing romantic who takes a perverse delight in seeking out and identifying himself with life's most dingy aspects, while Calamy himself has simply wearied of the amorous round of the idle, affluent set, and is on the verge of a vaguely-envisioned quest for the 'way'.

'. . . It seems to me,' says Calamy, when Mr. Cardan, true to character, is praising 'love' as the most enjoyable of indoor sports, '. . . that I'm beginning to have had enough of sports, whether indoor or out-of-door. I'd like to find some more serious occupation.' And he continues, in response to Mr. Cardan's profession of amorality, in this vein:

'You're fortunate. . . . It's not all of us whose personalities have such a natural odour of sanctity that they can disinfect our septic actions and render them morally harmless. When I do something stupid or dirty I can't help feeling that it is stupid or dirty. My soul lacks virtues to make it wise or clean.

'And I can't dissociate myself from what I do. I wish I could. One does such a devilish number of stupid things. Things one doesn't want to do. If only one could be a hedonist and only do what was pleasant! But to be a hedonist one must be wholly rational; there's no such thing as a genuine hedonist, there never has been. Instead of doing what one wants to do or what would give one pleasure, one drifts through existence doing exactly the opposite, most of the time – doing what one has no desire to do, following insane promptings that lead one, fully conscious, into every sort of discomfort, misery, boredom and remorse.

'. . . I don't like running after women, I don't like wasting my time in futile social intercourse, or in the pursuit of what is technically known as pleasure. And yet for some reason and quite against my will I find myself passing the greater part of my time immersed in precisely these occupations. It's an obscure kind of insanity.

'. . . And what's the most depressing of all . . . is the feeling that one will go on like this for ever, in the teeth of every effort to stop. I sometimes wish I weren't externally free. For then at any rate I should have something to curse at, for getting in my way, other than my own self. Yes, positively, I sometimes wish I were a navvy.'

While Mr. Cardan, for his part, in spite of his espousal of the theory and practice of hedonism, is forced continually to realize

that he is in a blind alley, finding, towards the end of his career
of pleasure, only bodily decrepitude and death. Alone, his
reflections tend to take on a morbid tinge:

> It would be tiresome to end one's days with recurrent fever and
> an enlarged spleen. It would be tiresome for that matter, to end
> one's days anyhow, in one's bed or out, naturally or unnaturally,
> by the act of God or of the King's enemies. Mr. Cardan's thoughts
> took on, all at once, a dismal complexion. Old age, sickness,
> decrepitude; the bath-chair, the doctor, the bright efficient nurse;
> and the long agony, the struggle for breath, the thickening dark-
> ness, the end, and then – how did that merry little song go?

> More work for the undertaker,
> 'Nother little job for the coffin-maker.
> At the local cemetery they are
> Very busy with a brand new grave.
> He'll keep warm next winter.

> Mr. Cardan hummed the tune to himself cheerfully enough.
> But his tough, knobbly face became so hard, so strangely still, an
> expression of such bitterness, such a profound melancholy, ap-
> peared in his winking and his supercilious eye, that it would have
> frightened a man to look at him.

The tone then is markedly more serious. And for the first
time we find the disparity fundamental to Huxley's outlook
emphasized as a cleavage between 'the flesh' and 'the spirit'.
Thus, while Chelifer derives a mordant satisfaction from the
ironic contrast which he delights to point between man's
aspirations and the ·brute facts of his animal existence, the
elderly Mr. Cardan's ruminations take a melancholy turn, and
the disparity is seen like this:

> Only the tragedy of the spirit can liberate and uplift. But the
> greatest tragedy of the spirit is that sooner or later it succumbs to
> the flesh. Sooner or later every soul is stifled by the sick body;
> sooner or later there are no more thoughts, but only pain and
> vomitings and stupor. The tragedies of the spirit are mere strut-
> tings and posturings on the margin of life, and the spirit itself is
> only an accidental exuberance, the products of spare vital energy,
> like the feathers on the head of a hoopoo or the innumerable
> populations of useless and foredoomed spermatozoa. The spirit
> has no significance; there is only the body. When it is young, the

body is beautiful and strong. It grows old, its joints creak, it becomes dry and smelly; it breaks down, the life goes out of it and it rots away. However lovely the feathers on a bird's head, they perish with it; and the spirit, which is a lovelier ornament than any, perishes too. The farce is hideous, thought Mr. Cardan, and in the worst of bad taste:

But at this point we must pause to collect the threads which have so far been taken up, in order to trace them to their common centre in that basic disjunction of personality which is the psychological source of all the disjunctions in the Huxley world-picture. Let us begin with the two principal obsessions which have so clearly emerged this far – 'hedonism' and 'futility'.

Huxley's central character, whichever of his books we take up, is distinguished primarily by the fact that he places so little value upon his existence as a man that he is implicitly prepared to forgo his claim upon personal destiny and meaning, albeit with an uneasy conscience, for the immediate gain of a random succession of disrelated sensations. Inwardly inert, led this way and that by mere appetite, he becomes immersed consequently in a world which is deprived of value. Unaware that meaning and purpose do not reside as objective facts in the world of things but are interior realities which await for their realization upon interior dynamic movement, oblivious to the truth that personality is not a substance with which we are endowed by nature, but an inward integration which may be achieved only by the decisive choice of oneself, he arbitrarily attributes his own purposelessness to the universe as a whole. 'Hedonism' and 'futility' thus complement each other.

In *Crome Yellow* the chief character, Denis, is young, his hedonism an aspect of the common bewilderment of youth. Gumbril, in the second novel, is an older man, and hedonism gathers a cynical tinge, while futility is emphasized. Calamy, in the present novel, represents a further stage still – he is the disillusioned hedonist; and now the disparity of the Huxley world is presented from a new aspect. As a disillusioned hedonist Calamy has wearied of a life without *meaning*, he is beginning to look for another path, and hence the concept 'spirit' for the first time makes its appearance; but 'spirit' itself, superimposed upon the existing psychological pattern, takes the impress of the fundamental duality of mind, and appears as directly anti-thetical to 'matter', or 'the flesh', as something in some way beyond the limits of the sensual plane upon which human life is actually lived. Thus we find that Calamy unquestioningly assumes that the 'way' of which he is in quest must lie some-where beyond the region of ordinary human experience, and that it is to be found in opposition to the path of sensual indulgence from which that experience is inseparable.

He speaks in this manner to Chelifer and Mr. Cardan just prior to his departure for the mountain retreat:

' . . . there is a whole universe within me, unknown and wait-ing to be explored; a whole universe that can only be approached by way of introspection and patient uninterrupted thought. Merely to satisfy curiosity it would surely be worth exploring. But there are motives more impelling than curiosity to persuade me. What one may find there is so important that it's almost a matter of life and death to undertake the search.'

'H'm,' said Mr. Cardan. 'And what will happen at the end of three months' chaste meditation when some lovely young tempta-tion comes toddling down this road, "balancing her haunches", as Zola would say, and rolling the large black eye? What will happen to your explorations of the inward universe then, may I ask?'

'Well,' said Calamy, 'I hope they'll proceed uninterrupted.'

'You hope? Piously?'

'And I shall certainly do my best to see that they do,' Calamy added.

'It won't be easy,' Mr. Cardan assured him.

'I know.'

'Perhaps you'll find that you can explore simultaneously both the temptation and the interior universe.'

Calamy shook his head. 'Alas, I'm afraid that's not practi-cable. It would be delightful if it were. But for some reason it isn't. Even in moderation it won't do. I know that, more or less, by experience. And the authorities are all agreed about it.'

This brings us at last to the structure of Huxley's novels, all of which – it is one of their principal defects – are remarkable for their lack of total dramatic movement and impetus. And this is precisely explicable as a consequence of the absence of dynamic movement in the mind of the novelist himself, a defect which is naturally communicated to his creatures, whose intercourse with each other, prepared and sustained by the accidents of social life, is virtually confined, as we have ofter. heard it remarked, to sexuality and cerebration. No character in the course of this novel undergoes in the course of it any modifications of outlook or temperament, each remains immobile within the limits marked out for it from the first. Of Calamy, we know nothing of the particular events and motives which move him towards the tentative renunciation which begins to take effect at the novel's close. Mr. Cardan is a lay figure as rigid as any in a morality play, and Chelifer is a study only in deliberate self-stultification. And such figures as the doctrinaire socialist, Mr. Falx, and the preposterous Mrs. Aldwinkle herself, are merely caricatures sardonically sketched by the satirist of social types. Only with the immature – in this case with Irene and the young Lord Hovingden, in their naïvely innocent courtship, does the novelist show any movement of human sympathy. Between such inwardly static characters, it is clear, there can be no dramatic interplay and thus no movement of the novel as an entity. So that instead of the movement of life we are presented with episodes, blocks of incident and conversation broken up peremptorily by external change.

But this is something which deserves further exploration, for it is evidently bound up with the whole question of movement and purpose. Movement in a work of fiction is required, of course, to be significant – to bear some purposeful relation to an end. In that vivid portrayal of purposeless activity, *Antic Hay*, the dance of futility is necessarily non-dramatic and presupposes the stasis of character – which in turn is static just because, according to the context, the possibility of purposeful movement is non-existent; life itself is purposeless. In the succeeding novel there is some endeavour to move beyond this static condition dictated by life's total futility. Yet all that the novel succeeds in doing in this respect is to lay bare at great length the absolute cleavage between 'matter' and 'spirit' which underlies the idea of pointlessness. Nowhere in it is there any questioning of the reality and the appropriateness of this dualism.

The novel ends inconclusively. Calamy retires to his mountain retreat, but it is uncertain whither his lonely quest will lead him; whether, indeed, it will lead anywhere. All we are told is that, looking at the distant skyline, he feels 'somehow reassured'.

II

THAT there is a progression of a sort within the first three novels is clear. And while *Point Counter Point* (1928) seems to show a divergence from what was later to appear as Huxley's main line of development, it nevertheless derives from the same basic pattern – though the emphasis is changed – while it continues the movement towards human responsibility already hinted at in the portrait of Calamy.

That *Point Counter Point* represents a movement away from the detached manipulation of puppet-characters towards a sympathetic approach to human life is a fact not entirely contradicted by the novel's ill-success in this aim, which is most signally exhibited by the emergence in its pages, for the first time, of a patently deliberate autobiographical character, the novelist Philip Quarles, whose personal views and problems, identical with Huxley's own, are placed directly before us.

The central problem in Philip Quarles's life is his personal isolation; 'All his life long he had walked in a solitude, in a private void, into which nobody, not his mother, not his friends, not his lovers had ever been permitted to enter.' Although, we are given to understand, he is a man of exceptional intellectual endowments, his convictions are fluid, his response to life indeterminate:

> If there was any single way of life he could lastingly believe in, it was that mixture of pyrrhonism and stoicism, which had struck him, an enquiring schoolboy among the philosophers, as the height of human wisdom and into whose mould of sceptical indifference he had poured his unimpassioned adolescence. Against the pyrrhonian suspense of judgment and the stoical imperturbability he had often rebelled. But had the rebellion ever been really serious? Pascal had made him a Catholic – but only so long as the volume of *Pensées* was open before him. There were moments when, in the company of Carlyle or Whitman or bouncing Browning, he had believed in strenuousness for strenuousness' sake. **And then there was Mark Rampion. After a few hours in Mark**

Rampion's company he really believed in noble savagery; he felt convinced that the proudly conscious intellect ought to humble itself a little and admit the claims of the heart, aye and the bowels, the loins, the bones and skin and muscles, to a fair share of life.

This last sentence provides the clue to the book's central 'idea' – a variation on the spirit-flesh duality, but with the scales weighted this time towards 'the flesh' – not now in the name of an irresponsible hedonism but of a biological vitalism obviously borrowed, in large measure, from D. H. Lawrence, who is caricatured admiringly in the novel in the painter, Mark Rampion, who preaches, in part, as follows:

> 'This damned soul,' he went on, 'this damned abstract soul – it's like a kind of cancer, eating up the real, human, natural reality, spreading and spreading at its expense. Why can't he be content with reality, your stupid old Beethoven? Why should he find it necessary to replace the real, warm, natural thing by this abstract cancer of a soul? The cancer may have a beautiful shape; but, damn it all, the body's more beautiful. I don't want your spiritual cancer.'

The spirit-matter dualism has not been resolved, but instead of an orientation towards the spirit *à la* Calamy, we have, not indeed a despairing acceptance of the futility of sensual-human life, but an attempt at its justification in terms of nature, vitality, health. Thus, to take but one typical example:

> John Bidlake [a sexagenarian philanderer] made no apologies for the kind of love he had to offer. So far as it went, it entirely justified itself. A healthy sensualist, he made his love straightforwardly, naturally, with the good animal gusto of a child of nature.
> . . . It was a love without pretensions, but warm, natural, and, being natural, good so far as it went – a decent, good-humoured, happy sensuality.

This novel, however, shows Huxley at his most inept. Badly constructed, incoherent, puerile in conception and presentation, and written in shoddy journalese, it reveals the fatal juvenility which, beneath the sophisticated surface, vitiates his understanding of life. The attempt to extend an inherently limited scope results in the crowding of the pages with flat caricatures of

living personages, their characters and activities interpreted in
terms no more searching than their relationship, 'wholesome'
or 'perverted', to sex and physical life. With the conclusion of
the novelette called *Brave New World* (1932) – a satirical projection into the future of the way of life implicit in a deliberate
hedonism, which need not concern us here – the shadow of
D. H. Lawrence lifts from Huxley's pages, and with his next
work we are back to the main line of his development – to the
haunting preoccupation with the futility of life and the possibility of finding a way of escape from its pointlessness and
tedium.

III

FOUR years after *Brave New World* and eight after *Point Counter
Point* there appeared Huxley's crucial novel, *Eyeless in Gaza*
(1936); crucial, because it represents a direct attempt to deal
with the problems raised by his earlier works, and because it
stands at the mid-point of his career as a novelist. Here the
characters, previously formalized to excess, gain in definition
and humanity, and genuine drama begins to emerge, centring
around the autobiographical figure of the writer, Anthony
Beavis, and his movement from a self-indulgent, cynical detachment towards personal regeneration and the acceptance of
human responsibility.

The autobiographical novelist-character in *Point Counter
Point*, we have seen, was signally isolated from the world, from
other persons. The following extract from his notebook links
him indubitably with Anthony Beavis, who has come to
precisely the same realization, and who, moreover, takes at
last the hazardous step of implementing it in action:

> Till quite recently, I must confess [Philip Quarles writes] I took
> learning and philosophy and science – all the activities that are
> magniloquently lumped under the title of 'The Search for Truth'
> – very seriously. I regarded the Search for Truth as the highest
> of human tasks and the Searchers as the noblest of men. But in
> the last year or so I have begun to see that this famous Search
> for Truth is just an amusement, a distraction like any other, a
> rather refined and elaborate substitute for genuine living; and
> that Truth-Searchers become just as silly, infantile and corrupt

in their way as the boozers, the pure aesthetes, the business men, the Good-Timers, in theirs. . . . Shall I ever have the strength of mind to break myself of these indolent habits of intellectualism and devote my energies to the more serious and difficult task of living integrally?

The personal theme of *Eyeless in Gaza* is Anthony's realization of the fatal error which has distorted and vitiated his life as a human being; but there is also an impersonal theme – that of the process of time. Once more the opening paragraph sets the key:

> The snapshots had become almost as dim as memories. This young woman who had stood in a garden at the turn of the century was like a ghost at cock-crow. His mother, Anthony Beavis recognized. A year or two, perhaps only a month or two, before she died. . . .

And the structure of the novel, the erratic alternation of pages from the remote past, the near past and the present of Anthony's history, while it reveals the temporal preoccupation, at the same time perfectly expresses the essential discontinuity of Anthony's existence as a result of his crucial, though always unacknowledged, refusal to go forward to claim his personal destiny as a human being, to 'become himself'.

Anthony has chosen not to be humanly responsible, chosen not only 'the part of the detached philosopher' but of the detached sensualist, desiring neither to love nor to be loved. The crisis in his life occurs on his forty-second birthday when with his mistress of the moment, Helen – who happens to be the daughter of a former mistress, Mary Amberley – he is lying on the roof of his retreat in southern France, 'in a golden stupor of sunlight and fulfilled desire'. Despite his volition, his wish to sever himself from his past and to live only in the immediate enjoyment of the present, perspectives of memory, invoked by this and that apparently trivial sense-association, persistently open up before him:

> Even the seemingly solid fragments of present reality are riddled with pitfalls. What could be more uncompromisingly *there*, in the present, than a woman's body in the sunshine? And yet it had betrayed him. The firm ground of its sensual immediacy and of

his own physical tenderness had opened beneath his feet and precipitated him into another time and place. Nothing was safe. Even this skin had the scent of smoke under the sea. This living skin, this present skin; but it was nearly twenty years since Brian's death. . . . What if that picture gallery had been recorded and stored away in the cellars of his mind for the sole and express purpose of being brought up into consciousness at this present moment? Brought up, today, when he was forty-two and secure, forty-two and fixed, unchangeably himself, brought up along with those critical years of his adolescence, along with the woman who had been his teacher, his first mistress, and was now a hardly human creature festering to death, alone, in a dirty burrow? And what if that absurd childish game with the flints had had a point, a profound purpose, which was simply to be recollected here on this blazing roof, now as his lips made contact with Helen's sun-warmed flesh? In order that he might be forced, in the midst of this act of detached and irresponsible sensuality, to think of Brian and of the things that Brian had lived for; yes, and had died for – died for, another image suddenly reminded him, at the foot of just such a cliff as that beneath which they had played as children in the chalk pit. Yes, even Brian's suicide, he now realized with horror, even the poor huddled body on the rocks, was mysteriously implicit in this hot skin.

Anthony's spiritual crisis, its antecedents and outcome, has been subterraneously prepared out of his unwilling but inescapable realization of the treacherous quality of time, with its accompaniments, age and death; and this is reproduced in the narrative, which takes us consecutively through various stages of Anthony's history, always returning to the point of departure – the sunlit roof. It is precipitated by the shock of an unexpected and startling incident. Out of an aeroplane flying immediately above there falls a yelping dog, to drop like a missile on to the roof, spattering the reclining lovers with its blood. Recovering from the shock, Anthony feebly passes it off as a joke, but 'for all answer, Helen covered her face with her hands and began to sob'.

For a moment Anthony stood quite still, looking at her crouched there, in the hopeless abjection of her blood-stained nakedness, listening to the painful sound of her weeping. 'Like seccotine': his own words re-echoed disgracefully in his ears. Pity stirred within him, and then an almost violent movement of love for this hurt and suffering woman, this *person*, yes, this person whom he had ignored, deliberately, as though she had no existence except in the context of pleasure. Now, as she knelt there sobbing, all the tenderness he had ever felt for her body, all the affection implicit in their sensualities and never expressed, seemed suddenly to discharge themselves, in a kind of lightning flash of accumulated feeling, upon this person, this embodied spirit, weeping in solitude behind concealing hands.

He knelt down beside her on the mattress, and, with a gesture that was meant to express all that he now felt, put an arm round her shoulder.

But at his touch she winced away as if from a defilement. With a violent, shuddering movement she shook her head.

This is the crisis which jerks Anthony into an abrupt awareness of his mistaken path. The rest of the novel conducts us through the corridors of Anthony's past history, his long, mistaken path being traced to its primal root in his early liaison with Mary Amberley, by whom he is idly prompted to betray his friend's trust and ultimately to cause Brian's suicide, by wantonly seducing the girl to whom he is betrothed, while concurrently, we are shown his later progress towards responsible participation in human affairs and the eventual acceptance of an ascetic, neo-Buddhist 'spirituality'.

The story, written with manifest sincerity, is a serious attempt to state a genuine human predicament and to find a way around it. Yet the statement, and the solution, when all is allowed, leave one with a disturbed feeling that all is not well, that somewhere there is a hiatus, a dislocation and a spiritual failure.

Anthony's conversion takes place at the point where he is made abruptly to realize that he has denied the inwardness of another person; that he has denied love for the sake of a detached sensuality. But as the narrative proceeds, we become aware that his personal discovery of love is turning from its proper object and becoming generalized, at first into hypothetical beneficence for humanity and at last into a cold moralism which derives its sanctions from a peculiarly impersonal metaphysic.

K

Returning to the antecedents of his conversion, we find that the tentative emotion of love (for Helen) becomes confused and finally submerged in the emotion of disgust (for Helen's mother, his once charming mistress, now a drunkard, a dope-addict, a squalid wreck). Simultaneously, this disgust fuses with the horror of time, of the accumulation of moments which leads inexorably to decay and death. The horror of time, as it accumulates in human life as age, is in turn associated with disgust for the physical body which experiences and expresses this accumulation. So that we are back at the position stated so clearly, eleven years before, in *Those Barren Leaves*. When, in his thirties, Anthony re-encounters Mary Amberley after an estrangement of more than ten years' duration, his predominant emotion is not pity but horror:

> 'Doing what one doesn't want,' she repeated, as though to herself. 'Always doing what one doesn't want.' She released his hand, and, clasping her own behind her head, leaned back against the pillows in the attitude, the known and familiar attitude, that in the Hôtel des Saints-Pères had been so delicious in its graceful indolence, so wildly exciting because of that white round throat stretched back like a victim's, those proffered breasts, lifted and taut beneath the lace. But today the lace was soiled and torn, the breasts hung tired under their own weight, the victim throat was no more a smooth column of white flesh, but withered, wrinkled, hollow between starting tendons.
>
> She opened her eyes, and, with a start, he recognized the look she gave him as the same, identically the same look, at once swooning and cynical, humorous and languidly abandoned, as had invited him, irresistibly then, in Paris fifteen years ago. It was the look of 1913 in the face of 1928 – painfully out of its context. He stared at her for a second or two, appalled; then managed to break the silence.

It becomes clear that Anthony's conversion is merely negatively and passively motivated. He has not sought reality and truth, but evaded them, until at last reality has found him and chased him – the analogy is his own – from his bolt-hole:

> Even in the deepest sensual burrow, Anthony reflected as he walked back to his rooms, even in the snuggest of intellectual other-worlds, fate could find one out. And suddenly he perceived that, having spent all his life trying to react away from the stan-

dards of his father's universe, he had succeeded only in becoming precisely what his father was – a man in a burrow. With this small difference, that in his case the burrow happened to be intermittently adulterous instead of connubial all the time; and that the ideas were about societies and not words. For the moment, he was out of his burrow – had been chased out, as though by ferrets. But it would be easy and was already a temptation to return.

Anthony is in fact seeking some way of *escape* from the conditions of human life rather than some way of positively transforming those conditions. And the spirituality which he is indicated as making his own towards the end of the book does actually fortify him, though with a shift of emphasis, in that very detachment and impersonality from which the incident of the dog and his emotional crisis has momentarily jolted him.

'God may or may not exist,' he writes in his diary. 'But there is the empirical fact that contemplation of the divinity – of goodness in its most unqualified form – is a method of realizing that goodness to some slight degree in one's life. . . .' His form of belief seems quite unashamedly chosen to conform to his own ingrained life-attitude:

God – a person or not a person? *Quien sabe?* Only revelation can decide such metaphysical questions. And revelation isn't playing the game – is equivalent to pulling three aces of trumps from up your sleeve.

Of more significance is the practical question. Which gives a man more power to realize goodness – belief in a personal or an impersonal God? Answer: it depends. Some minds work one way, some another. Mine, as it happens, finds no need, indeed, finds it impossible to think of the world in terms of personality.

And, appropriate to this central laxity, his new-found 'spirituality', so far from attending upon the wind that blows where it lists, resolves into the cataloguing of technicalities:

The fundamental problem is practical – to work out systems of psychological exercises for all types of men and women. Catholicism has many systems of mental power – Ignatian, Franciscan, Liguorian, Carmelite and so on. Hinduism, Northern, Southern and Zen Buddhism also have a variety of practices. There is a great work to be done here. Collecting and collating information from all these sources. Consulting books and, more important, people who have actually practised what is in the books, have had the experience of teaching novices. In time it might be possible to establish a complete and definite *Ars Contemplativa*. A series of techniques, adapted to every type of mind. Techniques for meditating on, communicating with and contemplating goodness. Ends in themselves and at the same time means for realizing some of that goodness in practice. . . .

What better comment could be made on this than that which Anthony himself commits to his diary at one candid stage of his reflections:

Reflect that we all have our Poonas, bolt-holes from unpleasant reality. The danger, as Miller is always insisting, of meditation becoming such a bolt-hole. Quietism can be mere self-indulgence. Charismata like masturbations. Masturbations, however, that are dignified, by the amateur mystics who practise them, with all the most sacred names of religion and philosophy. 'The contemplative life.' It can be made a kind of high-brow substitute for Marlene Dietrich: a subject for erotic musings in the twilight.

IV

'MAN', wrote Søren Kierkegaard in a famous definition, 'is spirit. But what is spirit? Spirit is the self'; and, further, 'eternity is essential continuity'. 'Selfness or personality,' according to Aldous Huxley in his last, mystical-didactic phase, is a ' "stinking lump" . . . which has to be passionately repented of and completely died to before there can be any "true knowing of God in purity of spirit." '

The mind-body carries with it the ineradicable smell of all that has been thought and done, desired and felt, throughout its radical and personal past. . . . The world is what (in our eyes) it is, because of all the consciously or unconsciously and physiologically remembered habits formed by our ancestors or by ourselves, either in our present life or in previous existences. These remembered bad habits cause us to believe that multiplicity is the sole reality and that the idea of 'I', 'me', 'mine', represents the ultimate truth. *Nirvana* consists in 'seeing into the abode of reality as it is', and not reality *quoad nos*, as it seems to us. Obviously, this cannot be achieved so long as there is an 'us', to which reality can be relative. Hence the need, stressed by every exponent of the Perennial Philosophy, for mortification, for dying to self. And this must be a mortification not only of the appetites, the feelings and the will, but also of the reasoning powers, of consciousness itself and of that which makes our consciousness what it is – our personal memory and our inherited habit-energies. To achieve complete deliverance, conversion from sin is not enough; there must must also be a conversion of the mind, a *paravritti*, as the Mahayanists call it, or revulsion in the very depths of consciousness. As the result of this revulsion, the habit-energies of accumulated memory are destroyed, and, along with them, the sense of being a separate ego. Reality is no longer perceived *quoad nos* (for the good reason that there is no longer a *nos* to perceive it), but as it is in itself.

Sin, for Huxley, is selfness. For Kierkegaard, as a Christian believer, sin is despair, and despair is precisely the dissociation, the dislocation of the self in its refusal to 'choose itself' – to put itself into inward motion and go forward to claim its unique destiny as a messenger of meaning to the world.

'When did the ego begin to stink?' asks a recent aesthetic sage, in a phrase which seems to have captured the public ear. Answer: *When it began to decompose.*

The later work of Aldous Huxley must be interpreted as a bitter diatribe against personality, which he sees as synonymous with selfness – selfness *when it begins to decompose.*

The word 'personality' is derived from the Latin, and its upper partials are in the highest degree respectable. For some odd philological reason, the Saxon equivalent of 'personality' is hardly ever used. Which is a pity. For if it were used – used as currently as 'belch' is used for 'eructation' – would people make such a reverential fuss about the thing connoted as certain English-speaking philosophers, moralists and theologians have recently done? For 'selfness', though it means precisely the same, carries none of the high-class overtones that go with 'personality'. On the contrary, its primary meaning comes to us embedded, as it were, in discords, like the note of a cracked bell. For, as all exponents of the Perennial Philosophy have constantly insisted, man's obsessive consciousness of, and insistence of being, a separate self is the final and most formidable obstacle to the unitive knowledge of God. To be a self is, for them, the original sin, and to die to self, in feeling, will and intellect, is the final and all-inclusive virtue. . . .

That this God-eclipsing and anti-spiritual selfness should have been given the same name as is applied to the God who is a

Spirit, is, to say the least of it, unfortunate. Like all such mistakes, it is probably, in some obscure and subconscious way, voluntary and purposeful. We love our selfness; we want to be justified in our love; therefore we christen it with the same name as is applied by theologians to Father, Son and Holy Spirit.

A man who has never gone forward to claim his self, and achieve personality, can obviously never comprehend the meaning of personality, just as he can never understand the nature of communion and love. For him, personality *is* selfness, that dissolute conglomeration of appetites, volitions and perceptions which are functions of the body he is given by nature. And when the natural ego begins to disintegrate and to 'stink' beyond endurance there is only one course left – to get rid of it.

Not only must the sufferer withdraw from his offending self – he must withdraw from the world, from other persons, and finally from God. Huxley's mysticism is therefore a-historical, anti-personal and atheistic. The whole cosmic order is, in its eyes, a pointless and inexplicable escapade of an inert and irresponsible deity, or non-deity – an escapade from which we are called to 'liberate' ourselves with all possible speed, in order to turn to 'the pure One, the absolute not-God in whom we must sink from nothingness to nothingness [and who] is called in Mahayana Buddhism the Clear Light of the Void'. (*The Perennial Philosophy*.)

How is the novelist, the portraitist of human life and character, to work within this scheme? ' . . . On the strictly human level, there was nothing that deserved to be taken seriously except the suffering men inflicted upon themselves by their crimes and follies . . .' reflects Huxley's Mr. Propter in the next novel, *After Many a Summer* (1939). 'No, a good satire was much more deeply truthful and, of course, much more profitable than a good tragedy. The trouble was that so few good satires existed, because so few satirists were prepared to carry their criticism of human values far enough.' A defect Huxley undertakes to remedy, for here criticism of human values is carried to the point of their complete abolition.

Huxley's basic dualism is here made unconditional. As a result we have on the one hand the group of puppet-characters – Jo Stoyte, the millionaire, whose palatial Californian residence is the scene of the novel, Dr. Obispo, the ruthless, scientific-minded sensualist, Jeremy Pordage, the ineffectual, flute-voiced litterateur from Oxford, Virginia Maunciple, the innocent-depraved little chorus-girl – puppets whose thoughts and actions bespeak their utter worthlessness and futility – and on the other the more than human, withdrawn, contemplative-practical sage, Mr. Propter, the essentially static mouthpiece of Huxley's teachings on the futility of life on the 'strictly human level' and the necessity for a withdrawal from human life to 'the level of eternity'. Between the two poles significant movement is quite precluded. Life is a dance of puppets, grimly, savagely pointless.

The anti-personal bias of the novel is pronounced; thus Mr. Propter:

> Bondage is the life of personality, and for bondage the personal self will fight with tireless resourcefulness and the most stubborn cunning. . . . The spirit is always willing; but the person, who is a mind as well as a body, is always unwilling – and the person, incidentally, is not weak but extremely strong.

This strange hatred of 'the stinking slough of our personality' is carried to the point of absurdity –

> 'Turn round, please.'
> Mr. Stoyte obeyed. The back, Dr. Obispo reflected, was perceptibly less revolting than the front. Perhaps because it was less personal.

The dislocation of being is expressed in the counterposing of a neutral, arid and abstract 'mysticism' on the one hand by a grossly material sensualism: life is separated into two mutually exclusive compartments. On the one hand –

> 'What is man?' he whispered to himself. . . . 'A nothingness surrounded by God, indigent and capable of God, filled by God if he so desires.' And what is this God of which men are capable? Mr. Propter answered with the definition given by John Tauler in the first paragraph of his *Following of Christ*. 'God is a being withdrawn from creatures, a free power, a pure working.' Man, then, is a nothingness surrounded by, and indigent of, a being withdrawn from creatures, a nothingness capable of free power, filled with a pure working if he so desires.

And on the other:

> Through his dark glasses, Mr. Stoyte looked up at her with an

expression of possessiveness at once gluttonous and paternal. Virginia was his baby, not only figuratively and colloquially, but also in the literal sense of the word. His sentiments were simultaneously those of the purest father-love and the most violent eroticism. . . .

Delicious creature! The hand that had lain inert, hitherto, upon her knee, slowly contracted. Between the broad spatulate thumb and the strong fingers, what smoothness, what a sumptuous and substantial resilience!

'Jinny,' he said. 'My Baby!' . . .

Mr. Propter's peculiarly arid and abstract mysticism has its end in 'a non-personal experience of timeless peace. Accordingly, non-personality, timelessness and peace are what it means. . . .' And it involves, centrally, a repudiation of, and an escape from, time:

' . . . potential evil is *in* time; potential good isn't. The longer you live, the more evil you automatically come into contact with. Nobody comes automatically into contact with good. Men don't find more good merely by existing longer. . . . The solution is very simple and profoundly unacceptable. Actual good is outside time. . . . Time is potential evil, and craving converts the potentiality into actual evil. Whereas a temporal act can never be more than potentially good, with a potentiality, what's more, that can't be actualized except out of time.'

Time as evil, once more, manifests in human life as age, physical decreptitude, death. Thus the thread of narrative depends primarily from Jo Stoyte's haunting fear of the grave, which causes him to employ Dr. Obispo upon researches into the possibilities of artificial longevity. Wound with this principal thread is the intermittent commentary on the human characters provided by the baboons in their enclosure outside the Stoyte mansion:

To the right, on another shelf of rock, a formidable old male, leather-snouted, with the grey bobbed hair of a seventeenth-century Anglican divine, stood guard over his submissive female. . . . The coast was clear. The young male who had been looking for dandruff suddenly saw his opportunity. Chattering with excitement, he bounded down to the shelf on which, too frightened to follow her master, the little female was still squatting. Within ten seconds they had begun to copulate.

Virginia clapped her hands with pleasure. 'Aren't they cute?' she cried. 'Aren't they *human!*'

These threads wind together as the researches of Dr. Obispo coincide with Jeremy Pordage's discovery, among the ancient papers he is cataloguing for Jo Stoyte, that the eighteenth-century fifth earl of the all but extinct line of Gonister has in his old age been similarly experimenting with a diet of raw carps' guts, and has mysteriously arranged for his own counterfeit funeral. On the insistence of the millionaire in his terror of death, the fifth Earl is eventually located in his stinking underground cave:

> Beyond the bars, the light of the lanterns had scooped out of the darkness a narrow world of forms and colours. On the edge of a low bed, at the centre of this world, a man was sitting, staring, as though fascinated, into the light. His legs, thickly covered with coarse reddish hair, were bare. The shirt, which was his only garment, was torn and filthy. Knotted diagonally across the powerful chest was a broad silk ribbon that had evidently once been blue. From a piece of string tied round his neck was suspended a little image of St. George and the Dragon in gold and enamel. He sat hunched up, his head thrust forward and at the same time sunk between his shoulders. With one of his huge and strangely clumsy hands he was scratching a sore place that showed red between the hairs of his left leg.
>
> 'A foetal ape that's had time to grow up,' Dr. Obispo managed to say at last. 'It's *too* good!' Laughter overtook him again. 'Just look at his face!' he gasped, and pointed through the bars. Above the matted hair that concealed the jaws and cheeks, blue eyes stared out of cavernous sockets. There were no eyebrows; but under the dirty, wrinkled skin of the forehead a great ridge of bone projected like a shelf.
>
> . . . 'But what's happened to them?'
>
> 'Just time,' said Dr. Obispo airily.
>
> 'Time?'
>
> 'I don't know how old the female is,' Dr. Obispo went on. 'But the Earl there – let me see, he was two hundred and one last January.'

The novel closes, bitingly acidulous, with Jo Stoyte's mentally preparing himself to accept the identical regime undergone by the fifth Earl.

That Huxley, driven by self-hatred and disgust with life, has reached a dead-end is finally demonstrated by his last, most tasteless production, *Time Must Have a Stop* (1945). Here the puppets, fixed in their unbreakable abstracts of human qualities, and offset by the static and detached figure of a pharisaical 'saint', exist at a remove from reality which gives the novel an air of complete futility to human experience. The 'saved' Bruno Rontini, like Mr. Propter a mere mouthpiece for Huxley's renunciatory gospel, is deprived of inward movement no less than the 'damned' puppet-characters immobilized in their habit of selfhood. In the previous novel, the only character not quite immune from 'the contagion of goodness' is the naïve and inarticulate Pete. It is no accident that for his hero this time Huxley should have chosen an adolescent (Sebastian Barnack is seventeen), that he should have involved him to his undoing for twenty-nine chapters in the depraved realm of 'the flesh' and then, by means of an abrupt hiatus, presented us, with the briefest of explanations, in the final chapter with a reformed and 'saintly' character, complete with copious extracts from those now all-too-familiar notebooks. For Huxley, as we have seen before, is for some reason at which one can only guess – we might label it 'arrested development' – at ease only with the immature. Incapable as he is of revealing the inner processes by which human beings come to inward maturity, even his supposedly adult characters remain adolescents upon whose juvenile responses has been superimposed arbitrarily the veneer of a quasi-adult sophistication and intellectuality.

Sensual depravity or an unreal 'spirituality' – down goes one scale heavily weighted with 'the flesh', and up goes the other with its insubstantial featherweight of spirit. The falsity to human experience of his naïve dislocation of being is paralleled in the novel both by the failure of its action to carry conviction and the air of unreality in which that action takes place. We can believe in the authenticity of Uncle Eustace's Italian villa, located, in accordance with Huxley's now pronounced retreat from history, in a dream-like nineteen-twenties, no more than we can accept the authenticity of Uncle Eustace himself or for that matter any of the book's characters. The vision, distorted for the satire of *After Many a Summer*, is here quite out of focus.

The adult reader is utterly unable to make the required connection between Uncle Eustace's trivial sensualities – his cheerful over-indulgence in wine, women and cigars – and the bathetic solemnities of his post-mortem experiences in the spirit world when, after an evening of luxury, he dies on the seat of the toilet. And the anti-climax of the disembodied Uncle Eustace's eventual choice of reincarnation out of the 'living uterine darkness', the 'vegetative heaven' of Mme. Weyle, should serve, at least, in the mind of no uncommonly penetrating reader, to put Huxley's 'mysticism' in its proper, very humble place.

With this final novel, we may safely conclude, Huxley's career as a significant novelist of the modern plight has come to an end. It is an end implicit, like so many, in its beginning. The novelist of futility, undergoing in mid-career a period in which the potentiality of meaning seemed for a time to offer itself – a potentiality accompanied by a realization of love and the value of human personality – has crossed over into a positive accentuation of futility accompanied by a positive doctrine of non-attachment and impersonality. No hope of development here! And, necessarily, this positive acceptance of the meaninglessness of human life, the worthlessness of personality, has its implications for art. When human life is seen as intrinsically meaningless and evil, then the work of the novelist, whose task is to present a picture of that life in terms of its significance and value, is deprived of all justification. Art and life must be thrown overboard together.

JAMES JOYCE

OR many years understanding of Joyce has been obscured by an approach concentrating upon the technical aspect of his work without relating the technical innovations to the inward necessity which has determined them. This is as much as to say that, more than a quarter-century after the first appearance of *Ulysses*, we are still without a thoroughgoing and fully satisfactory account of the significance of Joyce's work. Now, it is obvious that only charlatans indulge in technical experiment for its own sake, and equally obvious that Joyce was not a charlatan. The form of his work cannot be considered and fully understood without its proper relation to the content. And it is precisely the content of Joyce's work which critics have shrunk from dealing with. They have taken it curiously for granted. As a result, their dealings with its form have been, inevitably, inconsequent and superficial. Yet such a book as *Ulysses* does not obtain its powerful hold upon men's minds by virtue of its technical excellence alone, and one is forced to conclude that the technical approach is a mental sleight adopted in order to maintain a show of capability in the face of a fundamentally unmanageable situation. There is more, a great deal more, in *Ulysses* than meets the eye; it has an exoteric and an esoteric significance, and it is disturbing to think that while its hundreds of thousands of readers are concerned with its overt structure, its inward presuppositions are being quietly assimilated into their consciousness.

Three main strands run through all of Joyce's work; these are: Solitude ('the soul's incurable loneliness'), Religion (in reverse – the repudiation of a Roman Catholic upbringing) and Art (the artist's lonely vocation). These are closely linked. Joyce's work has both an inherent and a representative significance. The biggest question raised by Joyce is that of the entirely self-subsistent work of art. The repudiation of belief implies the surrender of an active, personal task in the realm of existence. The question then arises, can there be a uniquely artistic vocation in separation from and in independence of a primary, existential orientation towards purpose? Joyce's entire work was an attempt to answer this question in the affirmative. It was, in other words, the work of an aesthete, and in Joyce aestheticism itself is under trial.

It will be agreed that Joyce's history is quintessentially that of the artist; and of the artist as aesthete. That is to say, he is an artist *in vacuo*, an artist for the sake of art. But to say this raises once more the whole angry question of the relation of art to life. Aestheticism I interpret as a malady of the spirit in which the poverty of a meaningless and static life is compensated by the transposition into living of properties borrowed from the artistic sphere. When the aesthete is also a practising artist, his work re-echoes the echo made by art in his life – thus Joyce's first book, *Chamber Music*. But the artist-aesthete who is not content to make his work the echo of an echo is faced with a dilemma. Despite all efforts, art cannot be severed from its relation to experience, and the material of the artist-aesthete who rejects the echo and the dream cannot be other than his own intrinsically meaningless and impoverished experience. Joyce accepted this position, and, transferring the meaning and purpose which he repudiated in life to the realm of art, he brought art and life together in a relationship of unparalleled immediacy: it was, so to speak, a symbiotic relationship, in which art fed upon and incorporated life into itself.

There is a story by Edgar Poe in which an artist transfers to canvas the life, health and beauty of his sitter, so that as the painting comes to life the subject undergoes a corresponding depletion of vitality. This parable of the morbid transposition of intrinsic meaning and value from life to art is echoed in *The Picture of Dorian Gray* of Oscar Wilde – another Irishman and aesthete. In Joyce we are able to see such transposition, of which there is an element in all artistic creation, carried to an extreme. Ultimately, such a procedure is a magical one: another aesthete, also an Irishman, W. B. Yeats, was a conscious dabbler in magical practices. The mastery which cannot be exercised in the face of existence is exercised over the material of art, and, by transposing raw life immediately into art, the artist becomes the creator of a magical super-life the validity of which lies in its own self-subsistent structure. *Ulysses* is nothing less than a paradigm of human existence, a microcosmical transliteration of typical experience into magical, verbal form. In the process of transubstantiating life into art, Joyce was forced to make unprecedented artistic inroads into the sordid, the insipid and the obscene, and as a result *Ulysses* has a proto-philosophical character which is not usually associated with aesthetical works. Joyce was not a philosopher, of course, but *Ulysses* contains in concrete, non-conceptual form the raw material of a philosophical system. In reality, no work of art is self-subsistent: every poem draws its meaning from a relation to the truth which is a reality beyond itself. What we witness in *Ulysses*, then, is not the creation of an artistic structure arising out of an orientation towards truth, nor yet a structure un-related to truth (which would be an impossibility) but an account of the relinquishment of meaning through the abandon-ment of truth. Meaning implies selectivity, discrimination, which in turn are dependent upon an initial act of faith. By the abandonment of faith, discrimination is rendered impossible, and there must ensure a surrender to the indifferentiated flux of being: it is this which is presented in *Ulysses*. In *Finnegans Wake*, the abandonment of discrimination is carried from the objective world to the realm where object and subject are primitively confused: from the particular and microcosmic, Joyce moves to the macrocosmical, the universal, and corrupt mythological archetypes lumber through his pages. In this last work we see the autotelic work of art beginning to crumble from within: we see consciousness claimed by the aboriginal unconscious and the word inwardly disintegrated by the pressure of contradictory meanings let loose by the relapse from all discriminations of values.

The most imperceptive comment ever made on Joyce was perpetrated by T. S. Eliot, when in his book on literary heresy he wrote that of the eminent writers of his time Joyce was the most orthodox. Joyce's orthodoxy was limited to the Catholic indoctrination which he suffered in his youth, and from which all his subsequent life was an effort to free himself. Actually, the psychic quality of Joyce's work is astonishingly primitive; it shows marked leanings towards plain animism. This is clearly connected with the magical conception of art which Joyce shared with all aesthetes; *Finnegans Wake* is the most magical of Joyce's works and the most primitive. All the innovations which Joyce made resulted from the magical need to overcome the disparity between life and art: all were in the direction of the greater immediacy, concreteness and self-subsistence of the thing said. As his biographer, Herbert Gorman, truly says of the writing of the final work – 'An attempt would be made to break the bounds of formal speech and achieve that plane where the word, no longer a much-handled and partially-defaced token to arouse in the reader's mind an approximation of the thing meant, became the thing meant itself.' Where, in other words, life became transubstantiated magically into art.

Elsewhere in his biography, Gorman describes Joyce's superstitious awe when confronted with extraordinary natural phenomena. This is what Frazer has to say on the subject:

> Unable to discriminate clearly between words and things, the savage commonly fancies that the link between a name and the person or thing denominated by it is not a mere arbitrary and ideal association, but a real and substantial bond which unites the two in such a way that magic may be wrought on a man as easily through his name as through his hair, his nails, or any other material part of his person. In fact, primitive man regards his name as a vital portion of himself and takes care of it accordingly.

Many readers, I have no doubt, will regard this as a most unwarranted imputation to level at the foremost representative of modern literary culture. I wish it were. But consider: the modern man shares with the primitive all the fundamental traits of human nature; inasmuch as he had emancipated himself from the primitive bondage it is through the spiritual movements hypostasized in the forms of religious cult and dogma. With the abandonment of his religion, and all that it represents, there is nothing to prevent his relapse into psychic domination by cosmic forces. In Joyce we see precisely such an abandonment and precisely such a relapse, preserved for us only by the operation of the civilized techniques of detached and devoted artistic conscience.

I

'BY revising his own account of his early attitudes toward life and art,' writes Harry Levin in his critical monograph, 'Joyce has obscured the fact that they stem naïvely out of the naturalist movement.' The observation is just. The first prose work, *Dubliners*, is entirely naturalist in conception.

This naturalism is artistic passivity: the artist's mind is a sensitive film merely, carefully and impersonally recording the impressions of the external world. As with the photographer, the art consists in arrangement and selection. Nevertheless, the subjective element cannot be entirely overlooked, and this particular camera clicked its shutter only when the external setting synchronized with a fixed internal pattern. The passivity of technique has its counterpart in the mood of passivity and defeat in the face of external necessity which permeates the stories and determines the method of composition. The concluding lines of *Araby* are typical:

> Gazing up into the darkness I saw myself as a creature driven and derided by vanity; and my eyes burned with anguish and anger.

And so are those of *Eveline*:

> She set her white face to him, passive, like a helpless animal. Her eyes gave him no sign of love or farewell or recognition.

The purely aesthetic qualities of *A Portrait of the Artist as a Young Man* – its aromatic evocation of the moods and impressions of childhood, adolescence and immaturity – have tended to obscure the psychological pattern which underlies it. As the portrayal of the making of an artist it has features curious enough to incite comment. An inward passivity and recessiveness distinguish Stephen Dedalus's character from the beginning: passively he takes the impress of his environment, and passively he suffers the temporal necessity which estranges him first from childhood and then from boyhood and leaves him, at the last, a self-aware and self-willed aesthete on the threshold of maturity. It is never explicitly stated what is the force which urges him so irresistibly to the artist's destiny. But the recognition of it as something fatal and immutable follows immediately

upon his explicit rejection of the Jesuit director's call to ordina-
tion and the religious life. 'The voice of the director . . .
repeated itself idly in his memory. . . . His destiny was to be
elusive of social or religious orders.' And to reject the life of
sacerdotal sanctity is, for Stephen – there is no middle course –
to embrace the profane. 'He was destined to learn his own
wisdom apart from others or to learn the wisdom of others
himself wandering among the snares of the world. . . . The
snares of the world were its ways of sin. He would fall.' It is
hard on the heels of this rejection that his call to the artistic
vocation is imperatively sounded, during the seaside walk in
which the exalting banter of some schoolfellows concerning his
strange name, which 'seemed to him a prophecy . . . of the
end he had been born to serve and had been following through
the mists of childhood and boyhood', leads on to the ecstatic
vision of the paddling girl, which provokes his soul to an 'outburst of profane joy'. The vision is recorded at the close of the
fourth chapter. In the fifth and last Stephen the artist emerges,
composing a villanelle, formulating a static, non-kinetic theory
of art, and preparing himself for the artistic life of 'silence,
exile and cunning' in exotic Paris.

To ask what sort of an artist Stephen-Joyce developed into is
to find the answer ready-made. He ventured into literature with
the ebb-tide of the 'decadent' movement of the *fin de siècle*, when
the naturalist and the symbolist movements held joint hege-
mony over the advance guard of the arts: at a time when *The
Yellow Book* was a vivid memory and a still potent influence. On
his first visit to England Joyce was taken under the wing of
Arthur Symons, who arranged the publication of *Chamber Music*
with the decadents' publisher, Elkin Matthews. Returning from
Paris (in *Ulysses*) Stephen is made to wear, appropriately, a
Latin Quarter hat. As Eliot has pointed out, Joyce's early prose
shows the deep impression of Pater and Newman. The association of these two names should give us pause. For they serve to
bring potently to mind the odd relationship which then existed
between the aestheticism of the decadents and the Roman
Catholic religion.

This relationship has only to be stated to be recognized. It is
a simple fact that both in France and England a dispropor-

tionately large number of decadents were pilgrims either from or towards the Roman Church. Curiously, there is a definite link in this respect even between Pater and Newman, for in his youth Pater had come profoundly under the influence of Keble, and had seriously considered taking holy orders – Keble himself being, of course, Newman's closest associate, prior to the latter's secession, in the Oxford movement. There would seem to be a close kinship between the static structure of the Roman Church, its ritual and theology, and the static quality of aestheticism. 'One of Stephen's central ideas', writes Theodore Spencer in his Introduction to the early manuscript, *Stephen Hero*, 'is that only improper art is "kinetic"; it moves us to do something, which true art should not do; on the contrary, the true "aesthetic emotion" is static, and the true artist is essentially impersonal.' That the impersonal element is strong in Roman Catholicism is also a possibly significant fact. It is certainly not accidental that the aesthetic movement was strongly tinged with a temper of diablerie, that it dabbled in strange sins and elaborate vices, in yellow prose and purple passion. It was, self-consciously, a profane literature, and it gloried, rather naïvely, in its daring paganism.

Stephen-Joyce was just such an aesthete. The poem which Stephen composes in the fifth chapter of the *Portrait*, the *Villanelle of the Temptress*, bears all the marks of this sort of yellow decadence. It has the authentic note of aesthetic world-weariness ('Are you not weary of ardent ways') and of abandon ('Lure of the fallen seraphim'). The young poet's 'broken cries and mournful lays rise in one *eucharistic* hymn', thus characteristically confusing the profane Eros with the sacred and Catholic Agape: and the lines of the final stanza:

> And still you hold our longing gaze
> With languorous look and lavish limb,

have the effect almost of parody: which they assuredly are not. In fact, in the book's fifth chapter, subject and treatment combine to reveal the aesthetic at its most lavish and languorous. Stephen's mind, 'when wearied of its search for the essence of beauty amid the spectral words of Aristotle or Aquinas turned often for its pleasures to the dainty songs of the Elizabethans'.

His thinking was 'lit up at moments by . . . lightings of so clear a splendour that in those moments the world perished about his feet as if it had been fire consumed: and thereafter his tongue grew heavy and he met the eyes of others with unanswering eyes for he felt that the spirit of beauty had folded him round like a mantle and that in reverie at least he had been acquainted with nobility.' Waking one morning to compose his villanelle, 'His soul was all dewy wet. Over his limbs in sleep pale cool waves of light had passed. . . . The night had been enchanted. In a dream or vision he had known the ecstasy of seraphic life.' And the initial stages of composition are described in terms appropriate to a Hollywood producer's notion of the Vision Beautiful:

> The instant flashed forth like a point of light and now from cloud on cloud of vague circumstance confused form was veiling softly its afterglow. Oh! In the virgin womb of the imagination the word was made flesh. Gabriel the seraph had come to the virgin's chamber. An afterglow deepened within his spirit, whence the white flame had passed, deepening to a rose and ardent light. That rose and ardent light was her strange wilful heart, strange that no man had known or would know, wilful from before the beginning of the world: and lured by that ardent roselike glow the choirs of the seraphim were falling from heaven.

Stephen the embryo artist, however, appears only towards the end of the fourth chapter. Before that there is nothing to indicate a specifically artistic destiny – or so it would superficially appear. And it is only when we come to understand that for Joyce the artistic vocation stands in antithetical relationship to the religious, and that it is directly connected with 'the snares of the world [which] were its ways of sin', that we can apprehend the relevance of the autobiographical material of the first four chapters. For the substance of those chapters is the conflict in Stephen's lonely, immature and over-indoctrinated soul between his Catholic religiosity and his implication in the realm of natural necessity which comes to an agonizing crisis with the onset of adolescent sexuality.

The Stephen of Chapter Two is 'a boy . . . proud and sensitive and suspicious, battling against the squalor of his life and against the riot of his mind'. With the money gained by an

exhibition and essay prize he attempts vainly to stem the squalid
tide which threatens to submerge the socially declining family.

How foolish his aim had been! . . . He saw clearly . . . his
own futile isolation. He had not gone one step nearer the lives he
had sought to approach nor bridged the restless shame and rancour that had divided him from mother and brother and sister.

Baulked, he 'turned to appease the fierce longings of his heart
before which everything else was idle and alien'. And his
sexual fantasies and solitary orgies have their culmination in
his initiation into the mysteries of profane love.

The phrase is appropriate: for although Joyce describes with
realism how in the throes of his lust, wandering the mean
streets, Stephen 'moaned to himself like some baffled prowling
beast', and writes of his 'wail of despair' as 'a wail of furious
entreaty, a cry for an iniquitous abandonment, a cry which was
but the echo of an obscene scrawl which he had read on the
oozing wall of a urinal', the encounter with the prostitute to
which these prowlings eventually lead reveals itself as an initial
phase in the discovery of a veritable profane mystery, of which
the life of the artist and the practice of art are stages of continuation. But let the narrative – with my italics – speak for itself:

He had wandered into a maze of narrow and dirty streets. From
the foul laneway he heard bursts of hoarse riot and wrangling and
the drawling of drunken singers. He walked onward, undismayed,
wondering *whether he had strayed into the quarter of the Jews*. Women
and girls dressed in long vivid gowns traversed the streets from
house to house. They were leisurely and perfumed. A trembling
seized him and his eyes grew dim. The yellow gasflames arose
before his troubled vision against the vapoury sky, *burning as if
before an altar*. Before the doors and in the lighted halls groups
were gathered *arrayed as for some rite*. He was in another world: he
had awakened from a slumber of centuries.

There follows the description of Stephen's encounter with the
harlot, his entry to her room and his ecstatic abandonment to
her embraces. Her room 'was warm and lightsome'; as she dis-
robes he notes 'the proud conscious movements' of her 'perfumed head': she embraces him 'gaily and gravely . . . her
face lifted to him in serious calm' while her lips 'pressed upon

his brain as upon his lips as though they were the vehicle of a vague speech'.

It is of great interest to discern that Stephen's initiation has a cosmic significance of which he is but half aware, but which Joyce subtly delineates. He has, indeed, entered into the mystery of whoredom, which is the mystery of impersonal cosmic continuance – the procession of natural, physical necessity divorced from the integrating power of spirit. So that the third chapter begins with an account of Stephen's haunting of the brothel quarter, 'calmly waiting for a sudden movement of his own will or a sudden call from his sin-loving soul from their [the whores'] soft perfumed flesh', and passes straightway to the reflections which occupy his brooding mind during his hours of study.

> The equation on the page of his scribbler began to spread out a widening tail, eyed and starred like a peacock's; and, when the eyes and stars of its indices had been eliminated, began slowly to fold itself together again. The indices appearing and disappearing were eyes opening and closing; the eyes opening and closing were stars being born and being quenched. The vast cycle of starry life bore his weary mind onward to its verge and inward to its centre, a distant music accompanying him outward and inward. What music? The music came nearer, and he recalled the words, the words of Shelley's fragment upon the moon wandering companionless, pale for weariness. The stars began to crumble and a cloud of fine stardust fell through space.
>
> The dull light fell more faintly upon the page whereon another equation began to unfold itself slowly and to spread abroad its widening tail. It was his own soul going forth to experience, unfolding itself sin by sin, spreading abroad the balefire of its burning stars and folding back upon itself, fading slowly, quenching its own lights and fires. They were quenched, and the cold darkness filled chaos.

The significance of this frightening passage must not be minimized. It reveals an objective understanding of the process of depersonalization to which Stephen has submitted himself: the simile of the peacock's tail is a covert reference to the isolated, self-regarding ego, which moves with one step from isolation to universality – 'The chaos in which his ardour

extinguished itself was a cold indifferent knowledge of himself.'
His isolate and frigid condition, permeated with the consciousness of sin which, with his Jesuitical upbringing, he cannot
evade, is broken into by the rector's announcement of the
retreat. It is this retreat, with the preacher's elaborate and
harrowing sermon on the pains of eternal damnation awaiting
the confirmed and unrepentant sinner, which composes the
entire third chapter, the sermon itself being the largest single
block of consecutive prose in the entire book. Stephen's indifference is annihilated, and in agony of contrition he is driven to
make his confession and resolution of amendment.

There follows the account of Stephen's subsequent phase of
religiosity, which has at once an aesthetic and a pantheistic or
pancosmic character.

> Every part of his day, divided by what he regarded now as the
> duties of his station in life, circled about its own centre of spiritual
> energy. His life seemed to have drawn near to eternity; every
> thought, word and deed, every instance of consciousness could be
> made to revibrate radiantly in heaven: and at times his sense of
> such immediate repercussion was so lively that he seemed to feel
> his soul in devotion pressing like fingers on the keyboard of a great
> cash register and to see the amount of his purchase start forth
> immediately in heaven, not as a number but as a frail column of
> incense or as a slender flower.

Although his soul (the *Portrait* is an exceedingly soulful book)
is still unable to comprehend the passions of love and hate–'the
only love and . . . the only hate his soul would harbour' being
'a subtle, dark and murmurous presence' which would 'penetrate his being and fire him with a brief iniquitous lust',
nevertheless –

> . . . he could no longer disbelieve in the reality of love since
> God himself had loved his individual soul with divine love from
> all eternity. Gradually, as his soul was enriched with spiritual
> knowledge, he saw the whole world forming one vast symmetrical
> expression of God's power and love. Life became a divine gift for
> every moment and sensation of which, were it even the sight of a
> leaf hanging on the twig of a tree, his soul should praise and thank
> the giver. The world for all its solid substance and complexity no
> longer existed for his soul save as a theorem of divine power and
> love and universality. So entire and unquestionable was this sense

of the divine meaning in all nature granted to his soul that he could scarcely understand why it was in any way necessary that he should continue to live.

His devotion leads him to the practice of continual mortification of all five senses – to mortify his sense of smell, for instance, he seeks out and subjects himself to 'the only odour against which his sense of smell revolted [which] was a certain stale stink like that of longstanding urine'. With all this, however, he finds no inner power to surmount the petty trials of daily living. 'His prayers and fasts availed him little for the suppression of anger at hearing his mother sneeze or at being disturbed at his devotions.' At last, a 'sensation of spiritual dryness together with a growth of doubts and scruples' results from his inability 'to merge his life in the common tide of other lives'. His devotional phase concludes with the reflection that 'perhaps that first hasty confession wrung from him by the fear of hell had not been good?' and he asks himself, dubiously; 'I have amended my life, have I not?'

.   .   .

It is at this point that there occurs the interview at which Stephen's vocation for the priesthood is deliberated. And it is subsequent to this that Stephen takes his momentous seaside walk culminating in the vision of the bird-girl. Two threads may here be drawn together – Stephen's static and aesthetic religiosity and the association of art with the plunge into profane life. They are united in his priest-like devotion to the artist's work and his essential solitariness. The 'instinct, subtle and hostile', which 'armed him against acquiescence' to the director's proposal, is that of solitude.

He saw himself sitting at dinner with the community of a college. What, then, had become of that deep-rooted shyness of his which had made him loth to eat or drink under a strange roof? What had come of the pride of his spirit which had always made him conceive himself as a being apart in every order?

It is precisely the aesthetic aspect of the priest's life which attracts Stephen, and which Joyce puts into words which might have come from the pen of Baron Corvo:

He longed for the minor sacred offices, to be vested with the tunicle of subdeacon at high mass, to stand aloof from the altar, forgotten by the people, his shoulders covered with a humeral veil, holding the paten within its folds or, when the sacrifice had been accomplished, to stand as deacon in a dalmatic cloth of gold on the step below the celebrant, his hands joined and his face towards the people, and sing the chant, *Ite missa est.* If ever he had seen himself celebrant it was as in the pictures of the mass in his child's massbook, in a church without worshippers, save for the angel of the sacrifice, at a bare altar and served by an acolyte scarcely more boyish than himself.

And now, in his portentous walk, his profane experience combines in his solitary soul with his aesthetic religiosity, to bring forth the nascent artist. 'Now, as never before, his strange name seemed to him a prophecy. . . . This was the call of life to his soul . . . not the inhuman voice that had called him to the pale service of the altar. . . . He would create proudly out of the freedom and power of his soul, as the great artificer whose name he bore, a living thing, new and soaring and beautiful, impalpable, imperishable.' It is then that he encounters the girl who 'seemed like one whom magic had changed into the likeness of a strange and beautiful sea-bird', and their wordless communion sets Stephen 'singing wildly to the sea, crying to greet the advent of the life that had cried to him.'

> Her image had passed into his soul for ever and no word had broken the holy silence of his ecstasy. Her eyes had called him and his soul had leaped at the call. To live, to err, to fall, to triumph, to recreate life out of life! A wild angel had appeared to him, the angel of mortal youth and beauty, an envoy from the fair courts of life, to throw open before him in an instant of ecstasy the gates of all the ways of error and glory. On and on and on and on!

It is interesting to observe that this revelation, again, has cosmic overtones:

> He felt above him the vast indifferent dome and the calm processes of the heavenly bodies: and the earth beneath him, the earth that had borne him, had taken him to her breast. . . . His eyelids trembled as if they felt the vast cyclic movement of the earth and her watchers, trembled as if they felt the strange light of some new world. His soul was swooning into some new world, fantastic, dim, uncertain as under sea, traversed by cloudy shapes and beings.

That passage looks forward to *Ulysses*: and the final sentence might be an anticipation of *Finnegans Wake*.

II

BETWEEN the *Portrait* and *Ulysses* there is a vast difference in scope, mood and style. From the new epical work the strain of ninetyish decadence is eliminated, while the 'soulful' sentimentality has been replaced by a determined physicality indicated by the attribution to each part of *Ulysses*, not only of its Homeric parallel but also its physiological keynote. In method, *Ulysses* is a compound of photographic, statistical realism and of poetic allegory. From its pages emerges a factual picture of Dublin life and a paradigm of human existence.

The isolation which was characteristic both of Joyce as a man and of his view of existence presented him with certain problems as a writer. In *Dubliners* he had overcome his difficulties by writing objectively about the people he saw around him. In the *Portrait* he had evaded them by turning his artist's eye towards his reflection in the mirror. Now a casual scrutiny of *Ulysses* reveals that nearly half of its supernumerary characters have been lifted bodily from *Dubliners*, while Stephen Dedalus, who shares the principal role with Leopold Bloom, steps straight from the final page of the *Portrait*. In fact, *Ulysses* is a synthesis, as it were, of the two earlier books. It is both externally realistic and inwardly autobiographical, and furthermore, it is a parable. A parable of solipsism.

There is a sentimental element in nearly all aestheticism, which may be attributed to the aesthetic attempt to enjoy beauty in separation from truth. It is exactly this false striving after an isolated beauty which is responsible for the many tasteless passages in the *Portrait*. Since *Ulysses* is patently not without its direct relation to the *Portrait*, one may pertinently enquire what has happened to the sentimentality of the earlier book.

Sentimentality carries with it its own penality: brutality. Consider Joyce's first work, the slight, wistful lyrics contained in the volume entitled *Chamber Music*. We have Herbert Gorman's assurance that this book's title does in fact carry the lubricious *double entente* which might be expected. That is entirely comprehensible and fitting. A sentimental devotion to beauty leads the mind unavoidably into a compensatory movement towards the brutality of the squalid.

Ulysses itself represents just such a movement: it is among other things a rubbing of the aesthetic nose in the mean, the banal, the sordid. The sentimentality is still there, but Joyce has disowned it. It is now a part of the external human world which he describes. The nearest he allows himself to approach it is through parody.

So far as Joyce may be said to have had a personal style, it was a compound of the scrupulously commonplace and the pompous affectation of the decadent aesthete. The stilted, priggish quality in the prose of *Stephen Hero* is retained right through to the period just preceding *Ulysses*. Despite the verbal craftsmanship which it everywhere displays, it cannot be said that even in *Ulysses* Joyce had found a distinctively personal style. He was essentially an imitator. With consummate skill he mimics the speech and mannerisms of the Dublin citizens under his observation, and with the same skill, lacking the provocation of the outward scene, he turns his talent for mimicry upon literature in order to produce the great blocks of parody with which *Ulysses* is intercalated.

Turning from the soulfulness which marks the *Portrait*, Joyce plunged into the densely physical world of the banal and commonplace. The themes which dominate *Ulysses* are Unbelief, Nature and Necessity, Physicality, Promiscuity, the Commonplace and the Universal, or General, all of which, needless to say, relate to a common centre. 16th June 1904, the date on which the action takes place, is, as Gorman says, 'a day like all others and yet . . . all days in one'.

It cannot be denied that the spiritless universe depicted in *Ulysses* does exist – that multitudes of human lives are plunged miserably into its meaningless banality. Yet, as Joyce well shows, even this banal world has its relation to spirituality, and he is consummately successful in diverting his aesthetic sentimentality to the realm of the commonplace and in mimicking the mediocre life-style of his Dubliners.

The curious rancid sweetness of debased popular 'art' derives directly from this very sentimentality which is the inevitable result of the attempt to separate beauty from truth and to utilize its cosmetic qualities to cover the grossness of the life of appetite. The art of the Dublin citizens is, characteristically, singing – a physical art connected, as Joyce makes clear, with sexuality. *Ulysses* is saturated – it is part of the book's achievement – with this special quality, the mushy, sickly-sweet art of the 'bad infinity', a temporal effusion containing no eternal element. The mawkish, hypocritical quality it produces is represented in speech by the cant religious phrase never far from the Dubliner's lips, while in art it is the insipid charm of the nymph from *Photo Bits* which hangs over Molly Bloom's bed, of 'Love's Old Sweet Song' which Molly is preparing to sing for the adulterous Blazes Boylan, and the stylized lubricity of the pornographic novels which Bloom turns over on the bookstall. All this, however, is but an aspect of the total movement towards immersion in the undifferentiated realm of the general and universal which is portrayed in the course of *Ulysses*, and which I now proceed to delineate.

The interpretation of *Ulysses* which I am here proposing will be deprived of much of its apparent oddity by a citation of the words of a recognized authority. In his book, *James Joyce's Ulysses*, written in consultation with Joyce, Stuart Gilbert emphasizes the *mystical foundations* of the work.

'The fabric of *Ulysses*', bluntly announces Gilbert, 'is woven on strands of mystical religion, and, for readers who would explore the maze . . . and appreciate the subtleties of its pattern, some acquaintance with the cosmology on which it is based seems indispensable.' Gilbert then goes on to cite authorities on Buddhist mysticism. From Sinnett's *The Growth of the Soul* he quotes the following passage.

'There is no line to be drawn in Nature between important things that it is worth while for her laws to pay attention to, and others which are insignificant and fit to be left to chance. The earth's attraction operates equally on a microbe and a mastodon, and the chemical affinity that holds together the elements of the ocean is not permitted to neglect those of the smallest drop of dew.' 'Human affairs are so intensely entangled that it looks as if we must say – all or nothing; either every act, to the smallest, must be automatic and inevitable, or there is no prearranged course of events and no regular working out of Karma at all.'

Gilbert elaborates the implications of that in his own words as
follows:

> The law of destiny, an application of the law of causation, is
> an axiom of esoteric doctrine. Similarly the associated law of the
> conservation of energy on the physical plane has its counterpart
> in a law of the conservation of spiritual forces or personalities. For
> soul, like matter, is indestructible. All that exists has already
> existed and will always exist; creation and destruction are both
> impossible; a flux of transformation pervades the universe but
> nothing can ever be added to it or taken away from it. Admitting,
> then, that human personality, the soul, exists, since *ex nihilo nihil
> fit*, it must have always existed, it can never cease to exist. As
> Stephen Dedalus remarks . . . 'From before the ages He willed
> me and now may not will me away for ever. A *lex eterna* stays
> about Him.' This *lex eterna* is, for esoteric thinkers, the law of
> Karma.

'The structure of *Ulysses*', Gilbert further remarks, 'indicates
that Joyce aspires to outsoar the category of time and see a
simultaneous universe – to take, so to speak, a God's eye view
of the cosmos' – of a necessitarian cosmos, that is, into the
mechanism of which every moment, word, action, is 'ineluctably' integrated.

> Nothing in creation [*sic*] is irrelevant – our 'errors' are more
> than the automatic gestures of some instinctive desire; they are
> part of the scheme of things, incidents on the long way round
> which we must travel to meet ourselves; they are – to use one of
> Stephen's favourite words – ineluctable. . . . For no passage, no
> phrase in *Ulysses* is irrelevant; in this grain of sand, this banal day
> in the life of an inglorious Dubliner, we may discover an entire
> synthesis of the macrocosm and a compelling symbol of the
> history of the race.

In this system, it is clear, there is no room for freedom: it has
been ousted by necessity, as spirit has been ousted by the flesh,
as love by sexuality, faith by promiscuity. There remains, at
most, chance; chance being, for Bloom in the brothel, what
moly – 'a white flower springing from a dark root' – is for
Odysseus in the hall of Circe; even so –

> To omniscience and to such mortal men as are good delvers
> both the flower and its hidden roots are apprehensible. Even the

winning number at the roulette table could be predicted by one
who could discern all the dark roots of the event.

Now, when Gilbert asserts that *Ulysses* is woven on strands of
mystical religion, we can accept this only in the negative sense
that through his repudiation of the Catholicism of his early
years, Joyce was being drawn compulsively towards that view
of the world which is prior and basic to the monistic and
pantheistic religio-philosophical systems of the East, and which
is the outcome of the primal immersion of the soul in the undifferentiated phenomenal flux. The view that 'all that exists
has already existed and will always exist', that 'a flux of transformation pervades the universe but nothing can ever be added
to it or taken away from it', is clearly the result of an immersion
in the world-whirlpool which obviates the possibility of the
concept of Creation, and which, therefore, when the concept of
spirit is introduced, can make no distinction between God and
the world, seeing the world as itself immanently permeated with
the divine essence. Since according to this view the temporal
flux is an endless cycle of indestructible substances, the freedom
of the spirit must consist in liberation from the cosmic chains.
The law of Karma is not educed from the mere contemplation
of the cycle, but is the result of an attempt to introduce rational
and ethical considerations into the contemplation of the otherwise meaningless and evil vital process. According to Buddhist
teachings, it is the force of desire which binds together and
perpetuates physical existence and liberation must come from
the negation of its compulsive action. Since, however, Joyce is
not a philosopher or ethical teacher but an aesthete, we find
Hindu and Buddhist terms employed in his work not for their
doctrinal significance but merely because of their evocation of
the fundamental perception of the undifferentiated phenomenal
flux towards which he is moving: the perception which wanders
through the mind of the distracted Hamlet when, after de-
spatching Polonius, he replied to the King's questions with the
gnomic reflection that 'a man may fish with the worm that hath
eat of a king, and eat of the fish that hath fed of that worm',
meaning nothing by this but to show 'how a king may go a
progress through the guts of a beggar'.

The 'strands of mystical religion', then, draw the possibility of their existence at the expense of the Catholic Christianity with the form of which Joyce's mind was penetrated. In order that the monistic, necessitarian cosmos may emerge, with its ineluctable laws, grinding remorselessly towards a final stasis, all those vestiges of spirit, love and freedom which still glimmer through the hypostasized forms of systematic Catholicism must be discredited and eliminated.

*   *   *   *

The Stephen Dedalus whom we meet in the first pages of *Ulysses*, 'wearily', 'quietly', 'gloomily', 'coldly', conversing with the blithe and blasphemous Buck Mulligan is a young man immersed in the melancholy of that despair which is, according to Kierkegaard, the obverse of *faith*. His position is defined in conversation with the philistine Englishman, Haines.

> Haines, who had been laughing guardedly, walked on beside Stephen and said:
> – We oughtn't to laugh, I suppose. He's rather blasphemous. I'm not a believer myself, that is to say. Still his gaiety takes the harm out of it somehow, doesn't it? What did he call it? Joseph the Joiner?
> – The ballad of Joking Jesus, Stephen answered.
> – O, Haines said, you have heard it before?
> – You're not a believer, are you? Haines asked. I mean, a believer in the narrow sense of the word. Creation from nothing and miracles and a personal God.
> – There's only one sense of the word, it seems to me, Stephen said. . . .
> – Yes, of course [Haines] said as they went on again. Either you believe or you don't, isn't it? Personally I couldn't stomach that idea of a personal God. You don't stand for that, I suppose?
> – You behold in me, Stephen said with grim displeasure, a horrible example of free thought.

To read these opening chapters of *Ulysses* is to experience the persistent, uneasy feeling that one has met this melancholy young man, clad in sombre mourning, before: and that it is not alone his inky cloak nor customary suits of solemn black, but that indeed he has that within which passes show. There is a death, certainly; and a question of guilt.

– The aunt thinks you killed your mother, he said. That's why she won't let me have anything to do with you.

– Someone killed her, Stephen said gloomily.

– You could have knelt down, damn it, Kinch, when your dying mother asked you, Buck Mulligan said. I'm hyperborean as much as you. But to think of your mother begging you with her last breath to kneel down and pray for her. And you refused. There is something sinister in you. . . .

That is on the third page. And on the same page there is a ghost.

Silently, in a dream she had come to him after her death, her wasted body within its loose brown graveclothes giving off an odour of wax and rosewood, her breath, that had bent upon him, mute, reproachful, a faint odour of wetted ashes. . . .

In Buck Mulligan, furthermore, we glimpse a more famous prototype, another usurper. There is a familiar ring to his sentiments on death.

– And what is death, he asked, your mother's or yours or my own? You saw only your mother die. I see them pop off every day in the Mater and Richmond and cut into tripes in the dissecting room. It's a beastly thing and nothing else. It simply doesn't matter. . . .

Indeed, we have to wait only a few pages for an open reference to that which is to be one of the dominating themes of the book, an integral component of Stephen's consciousness. 'Wait till you hear him on *Hamlet*, Haines,' jests Buck Mulligan on Stephen's pet theory: 'He proves by algebra that Hamlet's grandson is Shakespeare's grandfather and that he himself is the ghost of his own father.'

– I mean to say, Haines explained to Stephen as they followed, this tower and these cliffs here remind me somehow of Elsinore *That beetles o'er his base into the sea*, isn't it? . . .

– I read a theological interpretation of it somehow, he said bemused. The Father and the Son idea. The Son striving to be atoned with the Father.

In these brief passages we have set out the ingredients for the entire Hamlet motif which subterraneously pervades *Ulysses*. And it is at this point, significantly, that Mulligan begins to chant his scurrilous 'Ballad of Joking Jesus', at the close of which there occurs the discussion of belief already alluded to.

I have set out in another place the reasons, which seem to me overwhelming, for regarding *Hamlet* as pre-eminently a parable of unbelief. Like Hamlet Stephen is, in Arnold's words, 'wandering between two worlds, one dead – The other powerless to be born' – the dislocated worlds of nature and spirit. But Stephen's orientation differs from Hamlet's in that he has turned his face from the realities hypostasized in the dogmatic religion of his childhood and youth and is moving irresistibly towards undifferentiated nature. The article of belief which still exercised the greatest fascination over his mind is that of the consubstantiality of the Son with the Father, and this he associates curiously with the problem of Shakespeare and *Hamlet*. This train of thought culminates in the long disquisition which Stephen embarks upon in the ninth chapter, to the assembled literati in the Dublin public library, in which the two threads are woven into a single strand.

References to and quotations from the play litter the path of Stephen throughout *Ulysses*. There are seven casual and incidental *Hamlet* references in the short 'Proteus' section (Chap. III) in which Stephen walks alone across the strand towards the city. His Latin Quarter hat of the first chapter becomes 'my Hamlet hat'. And the sense of dread, powerfully suggested throughout the play, appears in the reiterated phrase about the beetling cliff. ('Jesus!' ejaculates Stephen on the beach, 'If I fell over a cliff that beetles o'er his base, fell through the nebeneinander ineluctably.') In the 'Wandering Rocks' episode, as he passes the power-station, there is a clear association of religious *dread*, with the Hamlet motif:

> The whirr of flapping leathern bands and hum of dynamos from the powerhouse urged Stephen to be on. Beingless beings. Stop! Throb always without you and the throb always within. Your heart you sing of. I between you. Where? Between two roaring worlds where they swirl. I. Shatter them, one and both. But stun myself too in the blow. Shatter me you who can. Bawd and butcher, were the words. I say! Not yet awhile. A look around.
>
> Yes, quite true. Very large and wonderful and keeps famous time. You say right, sir. A Monday morning, 'twas so, indeed.

Here the naked animistic power of the dynamos leads by direct transition to dread of the cosmic energies which threaten the divided being 'swirling . . . between two roaring worlds'. The exclamation 'Bawd and butcher' is a repetition of Stephen's words in the library, when he refers to 'The playwright who wrote the folio of this world and wrote it badly' as '*dio-boia*, hangman god'. The repetition of the blasphemy awakening a superstitious fear, however, the automatic response is a repetition of Hamlet's quick change of subject at the approach of Polonius, whom he has been ridiculing to Rosencranz in Act II, Scene ii, of the play.

It is difficult to believe that Joyce's employment of this theme was deliberate. It would seem that while consciously he paid minute attention to the intricate Homeric parallel, the Hamlet theme intruded itself semiconsciously, to work as an obscure leaven through the great mass of the novel. If this theme had been kept consciously in mind, nothing could have kept it from dominating the entire material and bringing about a greater inner unity and intensity of the whole book. As it is, no reader can have failed to remark that after the ninth of the eighteen episodes Joyce's creative impulsiveness seems to flag. The rest of the book is decidedly stiffer reading. In the 'Circe' episode interest quickens, but it is not until we reach the unpunctuated spate of Molly Bloom's bed-monologue which rounds off the book that we feel a full emotional pressure rising unmistakably through the surface of the prose.

Walking alone on the strand after leaving Mr. Deasy's school, ruffled by 'nipping and eager airs', Hamlet-Stephen reflects on his origins.

> Wombed in sin darkness I was too, made not begotten. By them, the man with my voice and my eyes and a ghostwoman with ashes on her breath. They clasped and sundered, did the coupler's will. From before the ages He willed me and now may not will me away or ever. A *lex eterna* stays about Him. Is that then the divine substance wherein Father and Son are consubstantial?
> . . .

Consubstantiality of Father and Son, the remnant of Catholic dogma which so nags at Stephen's mind, is queried here in terms of Necessity. It is by necessity (sexuality) that man is

M

born into the world, but behind the particular sexual act Stephen sees the operation of an eternal necessitarian principle, that of the *dio-boia*, hangman god. The *lex eterna* – we have Gilbert's word for it – is the law of Karma. So that what Stephen is asking is whether it is in the law of Karma, the irreversible process of cosmic necessity, that Father and Son, God and Man, are mutually subsumed. We must turn to the Hamlet disquisition in the library for the further pursuit of these threads.

This literary curiosity rests significantly upon an unquestioned identification of biographical with literary data, and in itself would justify a partially biographical approach to Joyce's own work. In fact, Joyce is clearly identifying himself with Shakespeare in the whole exposition. 'Elizabethan London', we are told, 'lay as far from Stratford as corrupt Paris lies from virgin Dublin.' Whether or not, as Stephen Dedalus asserts, Shakespeare's name was dear to him, that is abundantly true of Stephen himself. And likewise the note of banishment, 'banishment from the heart, banishment from home', which Stephen finds ubiquitous in Shakespeare, aptly characterizes his own work. And the Shakespeare whom, at last, Stephen sketches returning to that spot of earth where he was born, is 'Hamlet *père* and Hamlet *fils*. Dane or Dubliner'. More than that, to stray into the area of biography, Joyce was, at the time of the writing of *Ulysses*, like the author of *Hamlet*, 'a greying man . . . with thirty-five years of life, *nel mezzo del cammin di nostra vita.*'

In brief, Stephen's thesis runs as follows. At an early age Shakespeare had been seduced by Anne Hathaway, 'a bold-faced Stratford wench who tumbles in a cornfield a lover younger than herself'. Belief in himself has been untimely killed; Shakespeare is the fated cuckold. In London he lives loosely, but meanwhile Anne is betraying him with his brother. The theme of the false brother continually recurs in the plays, where also the names of two of the poet's brothers, Edmund and Richard, appear with villainous connotation, and where, furthermore, Shakespeare has hidden here and there his own name, 'as a painter in old Italy set his face in a dark corner of the canvas'. In the play of *Hamlet*, then, Shakespeare is not to be identified with the Prince, but with the betrayed and cuckolded ghost of the King, whose role he is popularly credited with having taken himself upon the stage.

Is it possible that that player Shakespeare, a ghost by absence, and in the vesture of buried Denmark, a ghost by death, speaking his own words to his own son's name (had Hamlet Shakespeare lived he would have been prince Hamlet's twin) is it possible, I want to know, or probable that he did not draw or foresee the logical conclusion of those premises: you are the dispossessed son; I am the murdered father; your mother is the guilty queen, Ann Shakespeare, born Hathaway?

A father, says Stephen, is a necessary evil. Shakespeare wrote *Hamlet* hard upon the death of his own father, and if you hold that he, a greying man with two marriageable daughters, is the youthful Hamlet, then you must hold that his ancient mother is the lustful queen. 'No. The corpse of John Shakespeare does not walk the night. . . . He rests, disarmed of fatherhood, having devised that mystical estate upon his son.' Fatherhood, Stephen continues, is not a biological but 'a mystical estate, an apostolic succession, from only begetter to only begotten'.

– Sabellius, the African, subtlest heresiarch of all the beasts of the field, held that the Father was Himself His own Son. . . . Well: if the father who has not a son be not a father can the son who has not a father be a son? When Rutlandbaconsouthampton-shakespeare . . . wrote *Hamlet* he was not the father of his own son merely but, being no more a son, he was and felt himself the father of all his race, the father of his own grandfather, the father of his unborn grandson. . . . [He is the ghost and the prince . . . He is all in all.]
. . . The boy of act one is the mature man of act five. All in all. In Cymbeline, in Othello he is bawd and cuckold. He acts and is acted on. Lover of an ideal or a perversion, like Jose he kills the real Carmen. His unremitting intellect is the hornmad Iago ceaselessly willing that the moor in him shall suffer.

Since Stephen Dedalus is in the Hamlet role, his interpretation of the play cannot be other than that of his own situation. He interprets it, accordingly, not in the appropriate terms of the disparity between nature and spirit but in the light of his obsession with the problem of consubstantiality. His interpretation is in effect an affirmative answer to the question which he has already raised as to whether natural necessity, the *lex eterna*, is the 'divine substance wherein Father and Son are consubstantial'.

At the beginning of his disquisition, Stephen interjects this reflection:

– As we, or mother Dana, weave and unweave our bodies . . . from day to day, their molecules shuttled to and fro, so does the artist weave and unweave his image. And as the mole on my right breast is where it was when I was born, though all my body has been woven of new stuff time after time, so through the ghost of the unquiet father the image of the unliving son looks forth. In the intense instant of imagination, when the mind, Shelley says, is a fading coal that which I was is that which I am and that which in possibility I may come to be. So in the future, the sister of the past, I may see myself as I sit here now but by reflection from that which then I shall be.

And he continues a little later:

– His own image to a man with that queer thing genius is the standard of all experience, material and moral. . . . The image of other males of his blood will repel him. He will see in them grotesque attempts of nature to foretell or repeat himself.

In the course of the exposition, Stephen refers to incest as 'an avarice of the emotions', in which 'the love so given to one near in blood is covetously withheld from some stranger'. Father and son, however, are 'sundered by a bodily shame so steadfast that the criminal annals of the world, stained with all other incests and bestialities, hardly record its breach'.

Yet, 'Fatherhood, in the sense of conscious begetting, is unknown to man. It is a mystical estate, an apostolic succession, from only begetter to only begotten.' In these curious and obscure speculations Stephen is evidently indicating the possibility, or the necessity, of some kind of spiritual incest of son with father. Continuing this obsession, there runs through his mind a blasphemous parody of the Creed – 'He Who Himself begot, middler the Holy Ghost, and Himself sent Himself, Agenbuyer, between Himself and others, who, put upon by His fiends, stripped and whipped, was nailed like bat to barndoor, starved on crosstree, who let Him bury, stood up, harrowed hell, fared into heaven and there these nineteen hundred years sitteth on the right hand of His Own Self.'

It is plain that everything relates to solipsism. The man 'with that queer thing genius' relates everything to the perfection of his own image. More, he is himself, his own (spiritual) father. The image of himself as the unliving son (in the past) looks through the ghost of the unquiet father (the future): it is the process of time which unites father with son: so that time, cosmic necessity, is the *lex eterna* in which Father and Son are consubstantial. Spirit and freedom are eliminated, and only the monistic necessitarian cosmic mechanism remains. Stephen's entire disquisition on Hamlet-Shakespeare concludes as follows:

– He found in the world without as actual what was in his world within as possible. Maeterlinck says: *If Socrates leave his house today he will find the sage seated on his doorsteps. If Judas go forth tonight it is to Judas his steps will tend.* Every life is many days, day after day. We walk through ourselves, meeting robbers, ghosts, giants, old men, young men, wives, widows, brothers-in-love. But always meeting ourselves. The playwright who wrote the folio of this world and wrote it badly (He gave us light first and the sun two days later), the lord of things as they are whom the most Roman of Catholics call *dio boia*, hangman god, is doubtless all in all in all of us, ostler and butcher, and would be bawd and cuckold too, but that in the economy of heaven, foretold by Hamlet, there are no more marriages, glorified man, an androgynous angel, being a wife unto himself.

Stephen is a self-portrait of Joyce in his immediately post-graduate days. Who then is Bloom? In the meeting of the rootless aesthete with the shrewd, resigned, middle-aged sensual man, Leopold Bloom – himself seeking a counterpart of his dead child, Rudy – there is presented a parable, Gilbert declares, of a universal quest.

Human life is a process of adjustment, a striving after 'atonement' with a sublime father; achieved adjustment would involve personal extinction, yet it is the end to which all creation moves. There is a perpetual levelling in the universe, a crumbling of individualities, which, like mountains, are slowly eroded, silted down, towards the plain of uniformity, towards amalgamation in a 'perfect round'. 'But where are we going?' Novalis asks, and answers: 'Always home.' That return is symbolized in the tale of

Odysseus, in a thousand and one legends of all races, and its biblical paradigm is the homecoming of the prodigal son.

In the Hamlet digression, the overt Homeric theme sometimes overlaps the covert Shakespearian one. Anne Hathaway is referred to as 'poor Penelope in Stratford', while Shakespeare, projecting his image into the late play, *Pericles*, is a man tried 'like another Ulysses'. To follow further Joyce's example of indulgence in biographical criticism, we are justified in arranging a complex syllogism after this pattern. Joyce is Stephen Dedalus, and Stephen in turn is identified with Prince Hamlet. Hamlet in turn is a projection of Shakespeare (identified with Joyce), who also projects himself as the King; he is 'all in all' and therefore is also Pericles-Ulysses. Ulysses is, of course, Bloom, as Penelope is Marion Bloom. So that all are 'consubstantial' one with another. Bloom-Ulysses-Pericles-Shakespeare-Joyce meets at the centre with Joyce-Shakespeare-Hamlet-Telemachus-Stephen. Joyce is both Stephen Dedalus and Leopold Bloom, and the divine substance wherein Father and Son are consubstantial is the process of time which separates his youthful from his mature self. Throughout *Ulysses*, Bloom is the point towards which Stephen is moving. He is, in fact, Stephen's other self. In this day which is 'all days in one', sixteen years are annihilated, and Joyce's former image meets and is atoned with his future self; to repeat the phrase, *he is himself his own father*. Through union with Bloom, the solitary aesthete emerges into the realm of the banal, the commonplace, and the universal. Stephen's solution of the Hamlet problem disposes of the inner drama of doubt which it presents; spirit is theoretically eliminated, and he is prepared for the immersion in nature which is to follow; from the library to the brothel and from the brothel to Eccles Street and Marion Bloom.

Through the entire Hamlet sequence, the subconscious pressure is very great. The reference to Judas in the culminating passage of Stephen's discourse is especially revealing: it was Judas who betrayed his Lord – for thirty pieces of silver. A repudiation of spirit and a movement towards the total embracing of necessity cannot but be felt as a betrayal. 'Do you *believe* your own theory?' asks John Eglinton, and Stephen replies promptly, 'No.'

I believe, O Lord, help my unbelief. That is help me to believe
or help me to unbelieve? Who helps to believe? *Egomen.* Who to
unbelieve? Other chap.

So runs Stephen's inner monologue. It is again suggestive that
precisely at this point John Eglinton remarks to Stephen, who
will allow his theory to appear in print only if he is to be paid
for it, 'You are the only contributor to *Dana* who asks for
pieces of silver.' As if to hammer home the subterranean infer-
ences, the episode closes with Buck Mulligan's trilling of a
bawdy song concerning masturbation, 'the solitary vice', and
his reading of a mock scenario on the subject, while Stephen,
hardly aware of the passing presence of Bloom, who is just then
leaving the library, reflects, ' . . . if Judas go forth tonight.
Why? That lies in space which I in time must come to, ineluctably.' He is moving forward to his meeting with his paternal
alter ego, foretold in his dream of the previous night, in the
'street of harlots'. Bloom and Stephen will be atoned in the
realm of solitary and at the same time universal sexuality.

III

OMITTING the thirty-odd pages devoted to Stephen's discourse,
there must be close upon half a hundred Hamlet references
scattered throughout *Ulysses.* The greater number of these are
associated with Stephen; Bloom, who is beyond the reach of the
inner division which afflicts Stephen (he is too well adjusted to
the world of mediocrity), has a motif of his own – that of Don
Giovanni; an air from Mozart's opera haunts him intermittently
throughout the day, while in the brothel he is referred to openly
as 'a plebeian Don Juan'. Yet Joyce is not consistent in his attribution of the Hamlet motif to Stephen, and the unity of the
two characters is underlined by Bloom's partial participation
in the Hamlet theme. The burial episode, which cannot but
offer itself as a parallel to Act V, scene 1, of *Hamlet,* is given not
to Stephen but to Bloom, whose reflections assume a cast part
clownish, part Hamletesque. ('Gravediggers in *Hamlet,*' Bloom
reflects; 'shows the profound knowledge of the human heart,'
and, snubbed by John Henry Menton at the cemetery gates,

Bloom, like Yorick, is 'chapfallen'.) Indeed, the fatuous, com-
placent indignity of Bloom's *weltanschauung* is well shown in
his graveside meditations:

Mr. Kernan said with solemnity:
– *I am the resurrection and the life.* That touches a man's inmost
heart.
– It does, Mr. Bloom said.
Your heart perhaps but what price the fellow in the six feet by
two with his toes to the daisies? No touching that. Seat of the
affections. Broken heart. A pump after all, pumping thousands
of gallons of blood every day. One fine day it gets bunged up and
there you are. Lots of them lying around here; lungs, hearts,
livers. Old rusty pumps: damn the thing else. That last day idea.
Knocking them all up out of their graves. Come forth, Lazarus!
And he came fifth and lost the job. Get up! Last day! Then every
fellow mousing around for his liver and his lights and the rest of
his traps. Find damn all of himself that morning. Pennyweight of
powder in a skull. Twelve grammes one pennyweight. Troy
measure.

Don Juan is the embodiment of promiscuity, and promiscuity is the point of meeting for all the characteristic themes in
Ulysses. Promiscuity at once presumes solitariness and impersonality, together with universality or generality. The universal-
general is the undifferentiated commonplace, the sordid, the
banal. Consequently it is towards all of these that Stephen is
moving, and the final episodes are permeated with these
qualities. Now Don Juan, ravisher of a thousand maidenheads,
is, as we know from Coleridge and Kierkegaard, a daemonic
personification of an elemental force, uncomplicated by the
intrusion of spirit. In the Don Juan plays, as in Hamlet, there
is indeed an intrusion of the supernatural – in the form of the
statue which appears to conduct the libertine to the fires of hell;
but Don Juan's attitude to the supernatural powers thus
objectified is, unlike Hamlet's, undaunted and contemptuous
throughout. In *Ulysses* the ghost is not masculine but feminine:
it is that of Stephen's mother, for whose sake he would not, at
her deathbed, kneel down to pray. The witches' sabbath in the
brothel is brought to a conclusion by the final uprising of this
apparition. In his desperate repudiation Stephen raises his ashplant and smashes the chandelier: and it is only after this that

Bloom decisively takes him under his protection, settles for the damage, and conducts him away to Eccles Street and Marion Bloom.

'Stephen's mother,' runs the text, 'emaciated, rises stark through the floor in leper grey with a wreath of faded orange blossoms and a torn bridal veil, her face worn and noseless, green with grave mould. . . .' To her uttered 'Beware' Stephen responds with an obscene word and the declaration, '*Non serviam!*'

THE MOTHER

(*Wrings her hands slowly, moaning desperately.*) O Sacred Heart of Jesus, have mercy on him! Save him from hell, O divine Sacred Heart!

STEPHEN

No! No! No! Break my spirit all of you if you can! I'll bring you all to heel.

THE MOTHER

(*In the agony of her deathrattle.*) Have mercy on Stephen, Lord, for my sake! Inexpressible was my anguish when expiring with love, grief and agony on Mount Calvary.

STEPHEN

Nothung! (*He lifts his ashplant high with both hands and smashes the chandelier. Time's livid final flame leaps and, in the following darkness, ruin of allspace, shattered glass and toppling masonry.*)

In that apocalyptic instant of denial Stephen's world has come to an end: his possibilities are exhausted, and he hands over the principal part to Bloom. So far as relations between the two are concerned, the world of Bloom begins, psychologically, at this point. It is the world which we have already encountered in the previous wanderings of Odysseus in which Stephen as Telemachus has no part, and it is characterized by a predominance of the sensual, the commonplace. The style of the two following episodes, 'Eumaeus' and 'Ithaca', is scrupulously banal, empirical, dispassionately impersonal. Only in the final episode, the 'Penelope', which is, however, substantially banal, is there the equable, physiological-erotic fervour of the All-Mother, nature personified, in whom all vestiges of spirit have been obliterated, and who is as free from conflict as from discrimination.

The negative spiritual core of *Ulysses* is the drama of unfaith. The inner process which the book reveals is the movement from meaning towards the meaningless. Supernatural faith is the total transcendent act which raises the self above the phenomenal flux in anticipation of the divine. Faith is the precondition of all discrimination: unfaith is indiscriminate, promiscuous: in the prophetic language of Ezekiel and *Revelation* it is 'fornication'. When the apparition of Stephen's mother arises in the brothel, it is in a wreath of faded orange blossoms and a torn bridal veil. Why? The mystery of whoredom is the desecration of marriage. The apparition symbolizes not only spirit, but faith, both in the divine and in the human aspects: that it is the apparition of a corpse reveals symbolically the inner spiritual condition of Stephen. Marriage is the sacrament of personal communion in which isolation is overcome and spirit and nature atoned through love; whoredom, which isolates the personality and then disintegrates it in the bad universal, is the profane rite of impersonal faithlessness.

Promiscuity is not merely taken for granted in *Ulysses*: it is fundamental to its psychic structure. Yet Joyce was raised a strict Roman Catholic, and the Roman teachings on marriage are hard and irrefragable. It is hardly possible for a Catholic to rid himself so easily of so basic an article of belief, reaching so intimately into the individual life as this. There is here, patently, some gap in Joyce's inner history; a gap which, if it could be filled, might help greatly to explain the disparity between the soulfulness of much of Joyce's earlier work and the brute materiality of *Ulysses*.

Fortunately, the gap can be filled. During the period between the completion of the *Portrait* and the commencement of *Ulysses*, Joyce wrote with unusual speed the little-considered three-act play, *Exiles*, which, in the words of Harry Levin, 'is an attempt to externalize the situation of domestic estrangement in "The Dead" ' – a story in *Dubliners*. In 'The Dead' there is a conflict between flesh and spirit, presented in terms of the contrast between the writer Gabriel Conroy's physical desire for his wife on their return from a Christmas party and the ideal, 'spiritual' devotion of a boy who had loved her in her youth, and who had died as a result of a romantic, clandestine visit to her window in a night of rain. Made aware of the comparison, Gabriel is deflated: 'He saw himself as a ludicrous figure . . . a nervous, well-meaning sentimentalist, orating to vulgarians and idealising his own clownish lusts.' *Exiles* presents the struggle in the mind of an isolated and self-absorbed writer, Richard Rowan, between faithfulness and promiscuity. Playing with resolution the role of the detached onlooker, he permits his wife Bertha to encourage the advances of an old friend, Robert Hand, journalist and man of the world, refusing despite her pleas to influence her one way or another. 'You are a stranger to me,' she cries. 'You do not understand anything in me – not one thing in my heart or soul. A stranger! I am living with a stranger!' When Robert Hand becomes aware of Richard's knowledge of his adulterous intentions, his initial discomfiture passes, when he grasps Richard's inner uncertainty, into challenge. 'I believe that on the last day,' he declares, '(if it ever comes), when we are all assembled together, that the Almighty will speak to us like this. We will say that we lived chastely with one other creature. . . .' – ('Lie to Him?' interjects Richard) – 'Or that we tried to. And he will say to us: Fools! Who told you that you were to give yourselves to one being only? You were made to give yourselves to many freely. I wrote that law with my finger on your hearts.' To this specious argument, Richard succumbs. 'Reach it [i.e. bodily union with Bertha] if you can,' he allows. 'I will use no arm against you that the world puts in my hand. If the law which God's finger has written on our hearts is the law you say I too am God's creature.' Richard then leaves wife and friend together, writes all night in his study, and refuses ever to know what has occurred between them.

That Richard's negative attitude towards his marriage is directly related to his inner isolation and his impotence in the central matter of faith is clear. The confusion between spirit and nature perpetrated in Robert Hand's argument of the divine law reflects Richard's own perplexity. In resigning himself to the cuckold's role, he is resigning himself nominally to divine law, but the divine law of the *dio boia*, or demiurge of

nature, whose realm is that of necessity. It is a drama of unbelief, as Richard's final words make abundantly plain. 'I am
wounded, Bertha . . . I have a deep, deep wound of doubt in
my soul . . . I have wounded my soul for you – a deep wound
of doubt which can never be healed. I can never know, never
in this world. I do not wish to know or to believe. I do not care.
It is not in the darkness of belief that I desire you. But in restless
living wounding doubt. To hold you by no bonds, even of love,
to be united with you in body and soul in utter nakedness. . . .'
It is a far remove from the highly-charged emotional crisis
which is presented in this play to the unconcerned acceptance
of promiscuity throughout *Ulysses*: but the one is a necessary
preliminary to the other. In *Ulysses*, Bloom is the cuckold who
acquiesces phlegmatically and even with a perverse satisfaction
in his wife's successive infidelities. It does not in the least
disturb him to think of her as a whore. 'Suppose he gave her
money,' he reflects of the adulterous Boylan. 'Why not? All a
prejudice. She's worth ten, fifteen, more a pound. What? I
think so. All that for nothing.'

From solitude to universality is but a single step; but in that
step the realm of personal communion represented by marriage is overpassed. There is no contradiction between the
structure of *Ulysses* as a parable of solipsism and its typical and
universal qualities. In terms of sexuality, Stephen's onanistic
isolation leads directly to the promiscuity, the profane universality, of the brothel. We find a parallel in those Eastern doctrines
which assume the complete isolation of the individual soul from
incarnation to incarnation, which can be overcome only by
liberation from the cycle of rebirth and reabsorption in the
universality of the divine oversoul.

As early as the second episode of *Ulysses* we find Stephen
asserting his pantheistic or pancosmical outlook to Mr. Deasy:

> – History, Stephen said, is a nightmare from which I am trying
> to awake.
> From the playfield the boys raised a shout. A whirring: goal.
> What if that nightmare gave you a back kick?
> – The ways of the Creator are not our ways, Mr. Deasy said.
> All history moves towards one great goal, the manifestation of
> God.

Stephen jerked his thumb towards the window, saying:

– That is God.

Hooray! Ay! Whrrwhee!

– What? Mr. Deasy aske d.

– A shout in the street, Stephen answered, shrugging his shoulders.

And *Ulysses*, indeed, as it moves gradually from morning towards night, moves out of history into the cosmic embrace of nature. It begins with Stephen, continues with Bloom and terminates in the bed of Marion Bloom.

Everyone is aware of the meaning of Molly Bloom, whose long, unpunctuated monologue at the close of *Ulysses* in a sense sums up and includes all that had gone before, and whose erotic memories and ruminations end with a reiterated 'Yes' to the blind biological impulse which she transmits and embodies. To quote Gilbert:

. . . Molly Bloom acts as the paradigm or *Massstab* of all the characters (or nearly all) in *Ulysses*. She sums them up in her monologue and in the light of her natural understanding we see their proportions reduced to a real scale of magnitudes. She takes their measure according to an ancient wisdom, the warmblooded yet unsentimental exigence of the life-force. . . . Gaea-Tellus is 'timeless' and 'artless'. . . . She begins small, a very ordinary woman, the *petite bourgeoise* of Eccles Street, a humbler Madame Bovary, to end as the Great Mother of gods, giants and mankind, a personification of the infinite variety of Nature as she had developed by gradual differentiation from the formless plasma of her beginning.

It is towards Molly as Gaea-Tellus that Stephen, through Bloom, is moving. It is she in whom Father and Son are resolved and identified – in the indiscriminate spate of vital being. And it is in relation to her that the note of reincarnation, or metempsychosis, is continuously sounded. Lying abed in the 'Calypso' episode, she connects it with the profane-erotic; the word 'metempsychosis' occurring in a novel by Paul de Kock ('Nice name he has'), she asks her cuckold-husband to explain it to her; and transmogrified to 'met him pike hoses' it echoes throughout Bloom's day with an erotic connotation – for instance, it recurs in connection with a passage from the novel Bloom inspects entitled *Sweets of Sin*.

Reincarnation signifies the relapse of the soul into the undifferentiated phenomenal flux: in another aspect, the relapse is signified by the prevalence of the commonplace. In the solid blocks of verbiage which constitute the last three sections of *Ulysses*, the sovereignty of the mediocre and the commonplace is established. Both matter and style in the fifty pages of the cabmen's shelter episode are designed to immerse the mind in the dreary minutiae of purposeless mundane existence. Boredom is the motif, and the pompous-facetious tone of the writing exactly conveys the desiccated being of the cultural proletarian.

This calculated drabness of submergence is carried further towards impersonality in the penultimate section – 'Ithaca' – by the treatment of the intimate details in Bloom's life, his domestic environment and his marital concerns in the distant and frigid tone of the courtroom and the laboratory. Bloom's simple, irrelevant action in turning on the tap occasions a detailed account of the Dublin municipal water supply; and after the tabulation of data which includes an exact catalogue of the kitchen utensils and a pointless calculation, on the assumption of a constant ratio, of the relative ages of Bloom and Stephen, Bloom's meditations move to the contemplation of interstellar space and the aeons of geological periods: he feels 'The cold of interstellar space, thousands of degrees below freezing point or the absolute zero of Fahrenheit, Centigrade or Reaumur.'

Bloom is resigned to his existence as a fragment of vital substance in a purposeless world motivated by crude appetite. Retiring, with the unavoidable reminder of his wife's marital defections, he composes his mind to equanimity.

> Equanimity?
> As natural as any and every natural act of a nature expressed or understood executed in natured nature by natural creatures in accordance with his, her and their natured natures, or dissimilar similarity. As not as calamitous as a cataclysmic annihilation of the planet in consequence of collision with a dark sun. As less reprehensible than theft, highway robbery. . . . As not more abnormal than all other altered processes of adaptation to altered

condition of existence, resulting in a reciprocal equilibrium between the bodily organism and its attendant circumstances, foods, beverages, acquired habits, indulged inclinations, significant disease. As more than inevitable, irreparable.

He justifies to himself his sentiments by 'The preordained frangibility of the hymen . . . the continued product of seminators by generation: the continual production of semen by distillation: the futility of triumph or protest or vindication: the inanity of extolled virtue: the lethargy of nescient matter: the apathy of the stars', while his antagonistic sentiments converge in a final mood of acquiescent satisfaction:

> . . . at the ubiquity in eastern and western terrestrial hemispheres . . . of adipose posterior female hemispheres, redolent of milk and honey and of excretory sanguine and seminal warmth, reminiscent of secular families of curves of amplitude, insusceptible of moods of impression or of contrarieties of expression, expressive of mute immutable mature animality.

Gaea-Tellus sustains the theme.

IV

THE dilemma in which the aesthete-artist finds himself is that which results from the inevitable discovery that ultimately every work of art, however refined or dreamlike or fantastic, necessarily draws its reality from its commerce with the world beyond itself. No artist has the power to create in an absolute vacuum an artistic entity which shall have about it no taint of lived experience. Aestheticism, in fact, is not logically or practically a tenable position: even the most extreme exponent of art for art's sake implicitly requires of the art-work the quality of formal meaning, and in no conceivable work of art is meaning an inherent, self-enclosed quality existing in independence of meaning beyond itself; and, by the same token, neither can meaning reside with magical intrinsicality in the word. The life which, despite his intention, still nourishes his art, the aesthete must perforce regard as a scandal, like the dollmaker's child in Yeats's poem. How to get rid of it?

Joyce's way of getting rid of life was by expanding the work of art so far that it provided, in intention in least, a verbal counterpart to experienced actuality which could be taken as a substitute for that experience. All of his work from the *Portrait* onwards draws its special quality of concreteness and intensity from the unprecedented attempt to obviate the conventional circumlocutions of fictional narrative and to transpose the raw stuff of experience into the magical immediacy of verbal expression. This explains the ventures into obscenity of this personally rather prudish writer. While this method led, in *Ulysses*, to the scrupulous cataloguing of the minutiae of daily living, in *Finnegans Wake* it resulted in the endeavour, which can only be regarded as magical, to create an all-inclusive cosmos in which the word was equivalent to the fact. Thus, paradoxically, it is the aesthete, who, in his retreat from life, effects the closest possible integration of literature with experience. Nevertheless, the misconception of the role of art remains, and is linked to the prior misconception of the task in relation to experience.

If life is inherently meaningless, how is that meaninglessness to be brought within the meaningful boundaries of art? We know how Joyce dealt with this in *Ulysses*: by an implicitly meaningful depiction of the process of the relinquishment of meaning. In *Finnegans Wake*, however, meaning has reached a further stage of dissolution, and there is nothing for it but to pack the cosmos into the work, entire. Only in relation to this endeavour can Joyce's multiple disruption and recombination of language be explained: language had to be packed so full that it contained everything possible, short of its total disruption into incoherence. In this respect, Joyce was not logical: he did not overstep the bounds of articulation. *Finnegans Wake* is a living contradiction of itself.

There can be no doubt that Joyce is a writer of outstanding quality, and that his work is of the greatest significance. At the same time, respect for his constructive achievement, and for his purely artistic integrity, must not be permitted to blind us to the inner meaning of his work, the self-contradiction which it embodies, and above all the direction to which it points. Joyce has received a great deal of uncomprehending adulation from the sort of culture-snob who is always found around the pedestal of the innovator, just as he has suffered equally the senseless abuse of the philistine. *Finnegans Wake* still occupies an equi-vocal position in current esteem, receiving much ill-considered lip-service from those who have not examined all the implica-tions of the work. Now, either the prose in which *Finnegans Wake* is composed represents an enormously potent advance in the manipulation of language, an advance of which any subse-quent literary work of a creative order must perforce take full account, or it reveals a corruption of language which requires to be exposed and traced to its source. My own view should be patent.

I regard aestheticism as itself fundamentally mistaken, and persisted in, perverse and destructive in its effects. Language is not isolate, is not magical. It is the vehicle of communication and is related intrinsically to meaning, and through meaning, to truth – which is a transcendent value. Language is healthy when it is related directly to meaning, and it can be so related only when the mind itself aspires vertically to truth as an absolute centre. It is corrupt when divorced from meaning, or when through the absence of primary orientation to truth the relation is shifting and confused. This is so even with poetic ambiguity, which must be a unification of multiple meanings and never a dissipation of meaning. Yet, if my analysis is correct, Joyce's entire work is founded upon an initial relinquishment of the possibility of meaning.

A writer in *The Times Literary Supplement* has drawn atten-tion to the disruption of language in *Finnegans Wake* under the pressure of unrelated and contradictory references. Taking the sentence, 'Not yet, though venissoon after, had a kidscad buttended a bland old isaac', he correctly points out that the word 'venissoon' suggests not only 'very soon' and 'venison' but also Swift's Vanessa: this multiplication of reference, characteristic of Joyce's method, being sometimes carried to bewildering lengths.

> The intention of the word 'venissoon' is to provide a chord, three different literal meanings, three different complexes of association, striking harmoniously and simultaneously on the reader's mind. But the analogy is false and harmony is precisely the essential effect which is missed.

N

The associations of notes in a chord are mathematically expli-cable, but the associations of Jacob's venison and Swift's Vanessa are wholly arbitrary. . . . Unless we treat Joyce as God and believe that the whole subconscious mind of humanity is clearly visible to him, we must protest that there is no pre-existent con-nection in our minds between venison and Vanessa, still less between the venison of Esau and the Vanessa of Swift. Nor can Swift's elision create any such connection for us, since even in the text the connection is purely structural. Still more destructive of any harmonious effect are the unintended sound-associations which these portmanteau words may contain.

Even this writer, however, supposes that 'for all these ruinous faults a great and magnificent building lies somewhere concealed under the jungle of accretions, the fantastical surface of architectural superfluities', adding that 'perversely Joyce covered his structure with thick layers of loam'. But this was hardly the case. The distortion, the disintegration of language is a reflection of interior disintegration of a psychic world deprived of the possibility of meaning and of form.

Even the meaninglessness of *Finnegans Wake* (which is, of course, not total) stands in an oblique relationship to meaning. But the meaning is beyond the book. *Finnegans Wake* is not nonsense, or not much more so than *Alice in Wonderland*, which it curiously resembles, is nonsense: it is an articulation of meaning-lessness. As such it is even a considerable work of art: with wonderful finesse it expresses a malady of the spirit through a corruption of language. It is like the utterance of a corpse. Although the morbid coalescence and distortion of language express the disrelation of meaning, the very imprecision of language by which Joyce gains his effects depends upon the tacit assumption of the existence elsewhere of a precise denotation.

What of the book's essential quality, of which the language is the expression? 'The concluding pages,' writes Stuart Gilbert of *Ulysses*, ' . . . are at once intensely personal and symbolic of the divine love of Nature for her children, a springsong of the Earth; it is significant for those who see in Joyce's philosophy nothing beyond a blank pessimism, an evangel of denial, that *Ulysses* ends on a triple paean of affirmation.' That is rather to

sentimentalize the concupiscent meanderings of the blowsy trol-
lop of Eccles Street, I fancy: but I forbear quotation. That
Ulysses ends on an affirmative note is true enough, but affirmation of itself is not necessarily important or interesting: something
depends on the quality of that which is affirmed. Molly Bloom
certainly does not affirm beauty, goodness or truth. What she
affirms is the indiscriminate and total acceptance of a world
devoid of every trace of those values. Reduced to its central
point, she affirms the ubiquity and all-importance of sexual
excitation; she is the woman who says 'Yes' indeed – to the
indiscriminate advances of everything in trousers. The description of her stream of muddy reflections as 'intensely personal'
and symbolic of 'divine love' can hardly be regarded as other
than an abuse of language. That she is intended to embody the
diffuse flux of Nature, is, however, a point nobody could
quarrel with. The bogey of affirmation or denial on Joyce's part
arises to trouble the consciences of the enthusiastic and ingenious commentators, Joseph Campbell and Henry Morton
Robinson. 'Here', they comment, half-way through their monu-
mental *Skeleton Key to Finnegans Wake*, 'is Joyce's world-affirma-
tion, for those who require to see it in so many words.' And the
indicated passage runs as follows:

> . . . For as Anna was at the beginning lives yet and will return
> after great deap sleap rerising and a white night high with a
> cows of Drommhiem as shower as there's a wet enclouded in
> Westwicklow or a little black rose a truant in a thorntree. We
> drames our dreams tell Bappy returns. And Sein annews. We will
> not say it shall not be, this passing of order and order's coming,
> but in the herbest country and in the country around Blath as in
> that city self of legionds they look for its being ever yet. So shuttle
> the pipers done. Eric aboy! And it's time that all paid tribute to
> this massive mortiality, the pink of punk perfection as photo-
> graphy in mud. Some may seek to dodge the gobbet for its
> quantity of quality but who wants to cheat the choker's got to
> learn to chew the cud.

As a footnote to that passage, we find the following altogether
typical sentence, in which a statement and its negation are
simultaneously present: 'Gosem pher, gezumpher, greeze a
jarry grim felon! Good bloke him!'

'We have to had them whether we'll like it or not,' writes Joyce, destroying the temporal sequence, of the aboriginal parent figures:

> They'll have to have us now then we're here on theirspot. Scant hope theirs or ours to escape life's high carnage of semperidentity by subsisting peasmeal upon variables. Bloody certainly have we got to see to it ere smellful demise surprends us on this concrete that down the gullies of the eras we may catch ourselves looking forward to what will in no time be staring you larrikins on the postface in that multimirror megaron of returningties, whirled without end to end.

On the quality of the 'affirmation' it seems hardly necessary to comment. 'Young man, you'd better,' said Carlyle grimly to the fledgeling who largely informed him: 'I accept the universe.' The affirmation is meaningless in itself, and the element of compulsion renders it valueless in any case.

Finnegans Wake begins in every respect where *Ulysses* left off. In location, it begins in bed: and further, it remains there. The immersion in undifferentiated being towards which the course of the earlier book was flowing is here almost complete. The solipsistical character of Joyce's universe is even more clearly brought out. In *Ulysses* the reader is plunged into the world of undifferentiated external phenomena: here, however, the border between the objective and the subjective is in dissolution and we peer through a murky and wavering twilight of looming, muttering figures which confuse with each other and re-emerge in the 'ineluctable' movement of the unending cosmic cycle. The characters from *Ulysses*, themselves figments of solipsism, are here present in universalized force. Bloom, who in the 'Ithaca' episode had already been dubbed 'Everyman or noman', is here blown up to monstrous dimensions as the mythological tavern-keeper of Chapelizod, Humphrey Chimpden Earwicker, who in turn merges indistinguishably into the earth-presence of the animistic father-figure, Here Comes Everybody, universal man. Marion Bloom becomes, in Anna Livia Plurabelle, incarnate femininity metamorphosed into the chattering stream, running towards dissolution in the sea. Stephen Dedalus and Buck Mulligan, antitypes even in *Ulysses*, are here, as Shem and Shaun, elevated to twin sons of the universal father.

The entire cycle is played out through the action and interaction of these type-figures drawn from the inchoate depths of isloated subjectivity and fixed in the endless motion of cosmic necessity. There is nothing here which is not potentially present in the earlier book. On examination, *Finnegans Wake* proves to be commonplace from end to end: despite its pretensions to mythological profundity, it is thoroughly banal; and despite the attempt, as in *Ulysses*, to impose an external structure (Viconian philosophy and the rest) it is formless and monotonous.

Like *Ulysses*, however, the book does rest upon a psychic pattern, and it is this which gives it what organic form it possesses. In *Ulysses* the pattern arises from the repudiation of meaning; here it is produced by the disintegration of being. The father-figure who looms large in the first part of the book, preyed upon by the agenbite of some obscure felony, gives place at length to his twin sons, each of whom represents an aspect of his divided self, aesthete-introvert and extrovert-libertine. In the third book, in which the extrovert-figure, Shaun, attempts to play the hero role in place of the superseded H.C.E., he appears first in character, delivering a masterful harangue to the people, then as Jaun (Don Juan) delivering a salacious sermon to a group of young girls, and finally as Yawn, in which condition he is himself the subject of a ruthless inquest in the course of which he dissolves murmurously back into the landscape from which all of the characters draw their origin. Having run her course, at the end of the book Anna Livia, universal mother, runs back into the parent ocean, and the final sentence turns to meet the first word on page one.

It had been widely recognized that *Finnegans Wake* is a comic conception. But what is the quality of its humour? Comedy is polar to tragedy, and can hardly be understood without reference to it. Now tragedy is bound up intrinsically with the concept of human dignity, of which indeed it is an assertion. And man's principal claim to dignity is precisely that he is spirit. Humour is the outcome of the ludicrous disparity between the possibility of spirit and its absence in actuality. Falstaff, for example, is (like Don Juan) a force of nature; he is also –

lecherous, bawdy, and oblivious of all except that pertaining to fleshly appetite – the epitome of human indignity. And *Finnegans Wake*, founded upon the raffish popular ballad of the hod-carrier Finnegan who dies by a fall from his ladder and revives at the wake when a drop of whiskey is splashed on his face, is unrelievedly Falstaffian throughout. It is no exaggeration to say that the book has a daemoniacal character. Just as it is erected upon utter spiritlessness and total immersion in the whirlpool of nature (the book is a great deal more obscene than *Ulysses*), the cosmic chuckle which is articulated through its pages is founded upon indignity – and desecration.

'Religion,' wrote Swift, 'supposes Heaven and Hell, the word of God and Sacraments and twenty other Circumstances, which taken seriously, are a wonderful check to Wit and Humour, and such as a true Poet cannot possibly give into with a saving to his Poetical License; but yet it is necessary for him, that others shou'd believe those things seriously, that his Wit may be exercised on their *Wisdom*, for so doing: For tho' a Wit need not have Religion, Religion is necessary to a Wit, as an Instrument is to the Hand that plays upon it.' In this case, however, wit has its say, not at the readers' expense, so much as at that of the residual catholicism still operative in Joyce's mind. This is particularly to be seen in its scurrilous treatment of symbols for the holy – for instance, the transformation of the Four Evangelists with their Gospel into the four old men leading their ass, and the reference to Jesus in the Church as 'the tout that pumped the stout'. Another psychotic compulsion is towards the transformation of the sacred into the erotic: e.g., 'Behose our handmades for the lured!' 'Let us pry,' and so forth. Joyce certainly worked hard to extirpate the Catholic in him, but the whole procedure, to the reader not involved in the situation, becomes excessively tedious when carried through seven hundred obsessed pages.

Not only *Finnegans Wake*, then, but the whole of Joyce's work is a symptom of the disintegration of the self-subsistent ego, turned in upon itself through the rejection of meaning consequent upon the initial failure of belief. Joyce puts this humorous self-accusation in the part of the book which concerns the activities of the autobiographical caricature, Shem the Penman:'You were bred, fed, fostered and fattened from holy childhood up in this two easter island on the piejaw of hilarious heaven and roaring the other place (plunders to night of you, blunders what's left of you, flash as flash can!) and now, forsooth, a nogger among the blankards of this dastard century, you have become of twosome twiminds forenenst gods, hidden and discovered, nay, condemned fool, anarch, egoarch, hiresiarch, you have reared your disunited kingdom on the vacuum of your own most intensely doubtful soul.' True enough, Joyce's history is that of the ingrowing, isolated ego, forced by the repudiation of faith and meaning into narrower circles of introversion and self-division, into further endeavours to overcome meaninglessness in terms of an impossible larger meaning which always receded. The disintegration of the isolated ego was countered by the devoted artistic labour of integration which itself was, nevertheless, inevitably subject to the same inner collapse. That Joyce was to some degree aware of the progress of the malady is shown in his account of the activities of Shem, in which the symbiotic character of his art-aestheticism is put into words more revealing than my comments could ever be:

Then, pious Eneas, conformant to the fulminant firman which enjoins on the tremylose terrian that, when the call comes, he shall produce nichthemerically from his unheavenly body a no uncertain quantity of obscene matter not protected by copriright in the United Stars of Ourania or bedeed and bedood and bedang and bedung to him, with this double dye, brought to blood heat, gallic acid on iron ore, through the bowels of his misery, flashly, faithly, nastily, appropriately, this Esuan Menschavik and the first till last alshemist wrote over every square inch of the only foolscap available, his own body, till by its corrosive sublimation one continuous present tense integument slowly unfolded all marryvoising moodmoulded cyclewheeling history (thereby, he said, reflecting from his own individual person life unlivable, transaccidentated through the slow fires of consciousness into a dividual chaos, perilous, potent, common to allflesh, human only, mortal) but with each word that would not pass away the squidself which he had squirtscreened from the crystalline world waned chagreenold and doriangrayer in its dudhud.

NOTES

P. 11. *Technique as Discovery* . . . by Mark Schorer. *The Hudson Review*, New York, Vol. 1, No. 1, Spring 1948. It is significant that Schorer arrives at the terms *form* and *content* by way of a descent from *beauty* and *truth*. 'Modern criticism, through its exacting scrutiny of literary texts, has demonstrated with finality that in art beauty and truth are indivisible and one,' he writes. 'The Keatsian overtones of these terms are mitigated and an old dilemma solved if for beauty we substitute form, and for truth, content. We may, without risk of loss, narrow them even more, and speak of technique and subject matter.' It is this inadmissible reduction of *truth* to *content* which is the root of Schorer's error.

Schorer's essay is selected for special commendation by Cleanth Brooks in his Foreword to the compendious collection, *Critiques and Essays in Criticism, 1920–1948*, edited by R. W. Stallman (New York, 1948), ' . . . a selection of the best critical writings of those who created, promoted, or followed in the development of the critical movement inaugurated by T. S. Eliot in *The Sacred Wood* (1920) and by I. A. Richards in *The Principles of Literary Criticism* (1924),' as the editor describes it. 'The purpose of this book,' Mr. Stallman also declares, 'is to consolidate and to make accessible the contemporary achievement in criticism.' Quoting Schorer's remarks on technique, Professor Brooks writes: 'I subscribe to all that is said here. It is an admirable summary of what modern criticism has achieved.' If that were so, one would have a serious quarrel with that amorphous entity, 'modern criticism'. But all that has in reality happened is that the academic mind has caught up with the earlier writings of Richards and Eliot and is engaged in consolidating and systematizing some of their ideas at second-hand, and with its customary bleak rigidity.

P. 32. *Heroic Ages of the Past* . . . Hemingway invites comparison with the Icelandic Sagas. Here is a characteristic passage from *The Story of Burnt Njal*:

Kol Egil's son said: 'Let me get at Kolskegg,' and turning to Kolskegg he said: 'This I have often said, that we two would be just about an even match in fight.'

'That we can soon prove,' says Kolskegg.

Kol thrust at him with his spear; Kolskegg had just slain a man and had his hands full, and so he could not throw his shield before the blow, and the thrust came upon his thigh, on the outside of the limb and went through it.

Kolskegg turned sharp round, and strode towards him, and smote him with his short sword on the thigh, and cut off his leg, and said: 'Did it touch thee or not?'

'Now,' says Kol, 'I pay for being bare of my shield.'

So he stood a while on his other leg and looked at the stump.

'Thou needest not to look at it,' said Kolskegg; ' 'tis even as thou seest, the leg is off.'

Then Kol fell down dead.

P. 33. *The Sun Also Rises*. In England, entitled *Fiesta*.

P. 38. *Transposition of emotional attitudes* . . . it must be remembered that in Italy Hemingway had been a serving soldier; in Spain he was that very different character, a war correspondent.

P. 41. *The primary emotional focal point of the novel*. . . . The strength of *For Whom the Bell Tolls* arises from the unconscious origin of its unifying symbols – exotic Spain, the filial Maria and the paternal Pablo, the war (conflict), the mountains, the bridged chasm. These identical symbols are employed by a lesser novelist, Victor Canning, in *The Chasm*, in exactly the same way. In this novel, however, it is a war-worn English architect instead of an American professor who is isolated in an Italian mountain village instead of a Spanish mountain cave, with a group of peasants; but he, too, falls intensely in love with the girl of the place, makes an enemy of his primitive rival in manhood, and, likewise in a tight corner, meets death in circumstances strikingly similar to Robert Jordan's – the breaking of a bridge across a chasm. This novel appeared in 1947, six years after Hemingway's book, but I do not suspect its author of plagiarism.

P. 52. *Sensitive and charming style*. . . . On this question of Forster's celebrated charm, I am reminded of Laura Riding's remarks concerning *A Room with a View*. 'Before reading this book I had met Mr. Forster and found him charming; the book was recommended to me by my friends as a charming book. I read it. I could not deny that it was charming. Yet it was to me unpleasantly painful to read. It was too charming. I do not mean to be flippant, or to disgust, or to alter my original conviction of Mr. Forster's personal charm. . . . But the truth is that it affected me in the same way as would the sight of a tenderly and exquisitely ripe pimple. I longed to squeeze it and have done with it.' – *Anarchism is not Enough* (1928).

P. 57. *Nature and Convention*. . . . An early story, 'The Machine Stops', is a Wellsian fantasy of the future, when the surface of the earth is derelict and mankind lives in luxurious subterranean cells 'serviced' by a perfected mechanical system. But at last the machine gradually breaks down, and two characters in revolt against its tyranny regain the earth's surface.

They wept for humanity, those two, not for themselves. They could not bear that this should be the end. Ere silence was completed their hearts were opened, and they knew what had been important on the earth. Man, the flower of all flesh, the noblest of all creatures visible, man who had once made god in his image, and had mirrored his strength on the constellations, beautiful naked man was dying, strangled in the garments that he had woven. Century after century had he toiled, and here was his reward. Truly the garment had seemed heavenly at first, shot with the colours of culture, sewn with the threads of self-denial. And heavenly it had been so long as it was a garment and no more, so long as man could shed it at will and live by the essence that is his soul, and the essence, equally divine, that is his body. The sin against the body – it was for that they wept in chief: the centuries of wrong against the muscles and the nerves, and those five portals by which we can alone apprehend – glozing it over with talk of evolution, until the body was white pap, the home of ideas as colourless, last sloshy stirrings of a spirit that had grasped the stars.

Bad writing, false feeling and loose thinking reinforce each other in this typical passage; it is, to borrow a word, sloshy. The early muddle between 'the essence that is soul' and 'the essence, equally divine, that is body' is a foreshadowing of the muddle in *Howards End* between culture and the practical life. Note the poetical bits about the stars.

P. 58. *The character of Leonard Bast.* . . . So mild a critic as Frank Swinnerton, in his *Georgian Literary Scene*, has precisely this objection to make. ' . . . I have been a clerk.' So has the present writer.

P. 87. *Sentimentality.* . . . That brilliant critic of the 'twenties, J. F. Holms, reviewing *Mrs. Dalloway* on its first appearance, in *The Calendar of Modern Letters* for July 1925, wrote that ' . . . most of the book, despite its pure and brilliant impressionism, is sentimental in conception and texture, and is accordingly æsthetically worthless. Such judgments, as is evident in this review, cannot be expressed in terms of purely literary criticism, which, indeed, is an instrument not applicable to the valuation of contemporary literature, as should be clear from experience and history.'

P. 101. *F. R. Leavis.* . . . Review of *Between the Acts* in *Scrutiny*, Vol. X, No. 3, January 1942.

P. 106. *Fullest enjoyment . . . irresponsibility of old age . . .* Quotations from *The Art of Growing Old*, 1944.

P. 107. *D. H. Lawrence.* . . . I elected to write on Margiad Evans.

rather than take the more obvious choice of subject, partly because I have already dealt in outline with Lawrence in a study which forms part of an earlier book of criticism.

P. 149. *A recent æsthetic sage* . . . none other than 'Palinurus', or Mr. Cyril Connolly, in *The Unquiet Grave*.

P. 155. *This final novel.* . . . Written in 1946. Since then Mr. Huxley has produced a further work, *Ape and Essence*, of which all I can say is that it abundantly confirms my analysis of his artistic decline. In this further projection of a Brave New World where a degraded human community is ruled by an 'enlightened' corps of eunuch priests enforcing an absolute repression of sexuality except at a periodic Saturnalia; where graves are desecrated and corpses systematically looted by seductive females with the words 'No, No' printed large on buttocks and breasts, and where all is in the power of a remote, inhuman, evil God whose hatred must be appeased by human sacrifice, one has an overwhelming sensation of encountering a strictly private universe. The book is a cruel self-parody.

P. 158. *Imperceptive comment on Joyce.* . . . The book is Mr. Eliot's *After Strange Gods* (1934).

P. 159. *His biographer, Herbert Gorman.* . . . In *James Joyce, a Definitive Biography* (1941).

P. 160. *Harry Levin.* . . . In *James Joyce* (1944).

P. 176. *Hamlet a parable of unbelief* . . . see my *Underground Man*.

P. 191. *The dollmaker's child.* . . . This poem, 'The Dolls', is in *Responsibilities* (1914). Afraid that her husband has heard the doll's outcry against the 'noisy and filthy thing' in the cradle, the doll-maker's wife –

> . . . murmurs into his ear,
> Head upon shoulder leant:
> 'My dear, my dear, oh dear,
> It was an accident.'

P. 196. *The quality of the affirmation.* . . . Compare with the 'Yea-saying' of Nietzsche's Zarathustra.

INDEX

A Case of
Need

A Case of
Need

A NOVEL BY
JEFFERY HUDSON

AN  Book

The World Publishing Company

New York   Cleveland

I will prescribe regimen for the good of my patients, according to my judgment and ability, and never do harm to anyone. To please no one will I prescribe a deadly drug, nor give advice which may cause his death. Nor will I give a woman a pessary to procure abortion. But I will preserve the purity of my life and my art. . . .

FROM THE HIPPOCRATIC OATH DEMANDED OF THE YOUNG PHYSICIAN ABOUT TO ENTER UPON THE PRACTICE OF HIS PROFESSION.

There is no moral obligation to conserve DNA.

GARRETT HARDIN

CONTENTS

CONTENTS

EMW

CONTINUATION SHEET

best described as a plus four (4+) hypersensitivity reaction, with expiration at
4:23 am. Patient discharged at 4:34.

Discharge diagnosis:

1. hemorrhage $2°$ to spontaneous miscarriage.
2. systemic anaphylaxis following
   penicillin G administration i.m.

DISPOSITION-
DISCHARGE TO Ward 8
date 11/15/
sign John B Williamson, MD

John B. Williamson, M.D.

JB/ka

October 10

ONE

ALL HEART SURGEONS ARE BASTARDS, and Conway is no exception. He came storming into the path lab at 8:30 in the morning, still wearing his green surgical gown and cap, and he was furious. When Conway is mad he clenches his teeth and speaks through them in a flat monotone. His face turns red, with purple blotches at the temples.

"Morons," Conway hissed, "goddamned morons." He pounded the wall with his fist; bottles in the cabinets rattled.

We all knew what was happening. Conway does two open-heart procedures a day, beginning the first at 6:30. When he shows up in the path lab two hours later, there's only one reason.

"Stupid clumsy bastard," Conway said. He kicked over a wastebasket. It rolled noisily across the floor.

"Beat his brains in, his goddamned brains," Conway said, grimacing and staring up at the ceiling as if addressing God. God, like the rest of us, had heard it before. The same anger, the same clenched teeth and pounding and profanity. Conway always ran true to form, like the rerun of a movie.

Sometimes his anger was directed against the thoracic man, sometimes against the nurses, sometimes against the pump technicians. But oddly enough, never against Conway.

"If I live to be a hundred," Conway hissed through his teeth, "I'll never find a decent anes man. Never. They don't exist. Stupid, shit-eating bastards, all of them."

We glanced at each other: this time it was Herbie. About four times a year the blame fell on Herbie. The rest of the time he and Conway were good friends. Conway would praise him to the sky, call him the finest anesthesiologist in the country, better than Sonderick at the Brigham, better than Lewis at the Mayo, better than anyone.

But four times a year, Herbert Landsman was responsible for a DOT, the surgical slang for a death on the table. In cardiac surgery, it happened a lot: fifteen percent for most surgeons, eight percent for a man like Conway.

Because Frank Conway was good, because he was an eight-percenter, a man with lucky hands, a man with the touch, everyone put up with his temper tantrums, his moments of anger and destructiveness. Once he kicked over a path microscope and did a hundred dollars' worth of damage. Nobody blinked, because Conway was an eight-percenter.

Of course, there was scuttlebutt in Boston about how he kept his percentage, known privately among surgeons as the "Kill rate," down. They said Conway avoided cases with complications. They said Conway avoided jerry cases.[1] They said Conway never innovated, never tried a new and dangerous procedure. The arguments were, of course, wholly untrue. Conway kept his kill rate low because he was a superb surgeon. It was as simple as that.

The fact that he was also a miserable person was considered superfluous.

"Stupid, stinking bastard," Conway said. He looked angrily around the room. "Who's on today?"

"I am," I said. I was the senior pathology staff member in charge for the day. Everything had to be cleared through me. "You want a table?"

"Yeah. Shit."

"When?"

"Tonight."

It was a habit of Conway's. He always did his autopsies on the dead cases in the evening, often going long into the night. It was as if he wanted to punish himself. He never allowed anyone, not even his residents, to be present. Some said he cried while he did them. Others said he giggled. The fact was that nobody really knew. Except Conway.

"I'll tell the desk," I said. "They'll hold a locker for you."

"Yeah. Shit." He pounded the table. "Mother of four, that's what she was."

"I'll tell the desk to arrange everything."

"Arrested before we got into the ventricle. Cold. We massaged for thirty-five minutes, but nothing. *Nothing*."

"What's the name?" I said. The desk would need the name.

"McPherson," Conway said, "Mrs. McPherson."

He turned to go and paused by the door. He seemed to falter, his body sagging, his shoulders slumping.

"Jesus," he said, "a mother of four. What the hell am I going to tell him?"

[1] Geriatrics.

He held his hands up, surgeon-style, palms facing him, and stared at his fingers accusingly, as if they had betrayed him. I suppose in a sense they had.

"Jesus," Conway said. "I should have been a dermatologist. Nobody ever dies on a dermatologist."

Then he kicked the door open and left the lab.

WHEN WE WERE ALONE, one of the first-year residents, looking very pale, said to me, "Is he always like that?"

"Yes," I said. "Always."

I turned away, looking out at the rush-hour traffic moving slowly through the October drizzle. It would have been easier to feel sympathy for Conway if I didn't know that his act was purely for himself, a kind of ritual angry deceleration that he went through every time he lost a patient. I guess he needed it, but still most of us in the lab wished he could be like Delong in Dallas, who did crossword puzzles in French, or Archer in Chicago, who went out and had a haircut whenever he lost someone.

Not only did Conway disrupt the lab, he put us behind. In the mornings, that was particularly bad, because we had to do the surgical specimens and we were usually behind schedule anyway.

I turned my back to the window and picked up the next specimen. We have a high-speed technique in the lab: the pathologists stand before waist-high benches and examine the biopsies. A microphone hangs from the ceiling before each of us, and it's controlled by a foot pedal. This leaves your hands free; whenever you have something to say, you step on the pedal and speak into the mike, recording your comments on tape. The secretaries type it up later for the charts.[2]

I've been trying to stop smoking for the past week, and this specimen helped me: it was a white lump imbedded in a slice of lung. The pink tag attached gave the name of the patient; he was down in the OR now with his chest cut open. The surgeons were waiting for the path dx[3] before proceeding further with the operation. If this was a benign tumor, they'd simply remove one lobe of his lung. If it was malignant, they'd take the whole lung and all his lymph nodes.

I stepped on the floor pedal.

"Patient AO–four-five-two-three-three-six. Joseph Magnuson. The speci-

---

[2] The files containing the history of treatment of patients in the hospital. Called a "chart" because the bulk of the file consists of daily charts of temperature, blood pressure, pulse and respiration, the so-called "vital signs."
[3] Diagnosis.

men is a section of right lung, upper lobe, measuring"—I took my foot off the pedal and measured it—"five centimeters by seven point five centimeters. The lung tissue is pale pink in color and crepitant.[4] The pleural surface is smooth and glistening, with no evidence of fibrous material or adhesions. There is some hemorrhage. Within the parenchyma is an irregular mass, white in color, measuring"—

I measured the lump—"approximately two centimeters in diameter. On cut surface, it appears whitish and hard. There is no apparent fibrous capsule, and there is some distortion of surrounding tissue structure. Gross impression . . . cancer of the lung, suggestive of malignancy, question-mark metastatic. Period, signed, John Berry."

I cut a slice of the white lump and quick-froze it. There was only one way to be certain if the mass was benign or malignant, and that was to check it under the microscope. Quick-freezing the tissue allowed a thin section to be rapidly prepared. Normally, to make a microscope slide, you had to dunk your stuff into six or seven baths; it took at least six hours, sometimes days. The surgeons couldn't wait.

When the tissue was frozen hard, I cranked out a section with the microtome, stained the slice, and took it to the microscope. I didn't even need to go to high dry: under the low-power objective, I could see the lacy network of lung tissue formed into delicate alveolar sacs for exchange of gas between blood and air. The white mass was something else again.

I stepped on the floor button.

"Micro examination, frozen section. The whitish mass appears composed of undifferentiated parenchyma cells which have invaded the normal surrounding tissue. The cells show many irregular, hyperchromatic nuclei and large numbers of mitoses. There are some multinucleate giant cells. There is no clearly defined capsule. Impression is primary malignant cancer of the lung. Note marked degree of anthracosis in surrounding tissue."

Anthracosis is accumulation of carbon particles in the lung. Once you gulp carbon down, either as cigarette smoke or city dirt, your body never gets rid of it. It just stays in your lungs.

The telephone rang. I knew it would be Scanlon down in the OR, wetting his pants because we hadn't gotten back to him in thirty seconds flat. Scanlon is like all surgeons. If he's not cutting, he's not happy. He hates to stand around and look at the big hole he's chopped in the guy while he waits for the path report. He never stops to think that after he takes a biopsy and drops it into a steel dish, an orderly has to bring it all

---

[4] Crepitant means it is crackly and filled with air. This is normal.

the way from the surgical wing to the path labs before we can look at it. Scanlon also doesn't figure that there are eleven other operating rooms in the hospital, all going like hell between seven and eleven in the morning. We have four residents and pathologists at work during those hours, but biopsies get backed up. There's nothing we can do about it—unless they want to risk a misdiagnosis by us.

And they don't. They just want to bitch, like Conway. It gives them something to do. All surgeons have persecution complexes anyway. Ask the psychiatrists.

As I went to the phone, I stripped off one rubber glove. My hand was sweaty; I wiped it on the seat of my pants, then picked up the receiver. We are careful about the phone, but just to be safe it gets swabbed with alcohol and Formalin at the end of each day.

"Berry speaking."

"Berry, what's going on up there?"

After Conway, I felt like taking him on, but I didn't. I just said, "You've got a malignancy."

"I thought so," Scanlon said as if the whole path work-up had been a waste of time.

"Yeah," I said and hung up.

I wanted a cigarette badly. I'd only had one at breakfast, and I usually have two.

Returning to my table, I saw three specimens were waiting: a kidney, a gallbladder, and an appendix. I started to pull my glove back on when the intercom clicked.

"Dr. Berry?"

"Yes?"

The intercom has a high pickup. You can speak in a normal voice anywhere in the room, and the girl will hear you. They mount the microphone high up, near the ceiling, because the new residents usually rush over and shout into it, not knowing how sensitive it is. That blasts the ears off the girl at the other end.

"Dr. Berry, your wife is on the telephone."

I paused. Judith and I have an understanding: no calls in the morning. I'm always busy from seven to eleven, six days a week, sometimes seven if one of the staff gets sick. She's usually very good about it. She didn't even call when Johnny drove his tricycle into the back of a truck and had to have fifteen stitches in his forehead.

"All right," I said, "I'll take it." I looked down at my hand. The glove was half on. I stripped it off and went back to the phone.

"Hello?"

"John?" Her voice was trembling. I hadn't heard her sound that way in years. Not since her father died.

"What is it?"

"John, Arthur Lee just called."

Art Lee was an obstetrician friend of ours; he had been best man at our wedding.

"What's the problem?"

"He called here asking for you. He's in trouble."

"What kind of trouble?" As I spoke, I waved to a resident to take my place at the table. We had to keep those surgical specimens moving.

"I don't know," Judith said, "but he's in jail."

My first thought was that it was some kind of mistake. "Are you sure?"

"Yes. He just called. John, is it something about——?"

"I don't know," I said. "I don't know any more than you do." I cradled the phone in my shoulder and stripped away my other glove. I threw them both in the vinyl-lined wastebasket. "I'll go see him now," I said. "You sit tight and don't worry. It's probably a minor thing. Maybe he was drinking again."

"All right," she said in a low voice.

"Don't worry," I repeated.

"All right."

"I'll speak to you soon."

I hung up, untied my apron, and placed it on the peg by the door. Then I went down the hall to Sanderson's office. Sanderson was chief of the path labs. He was very dignified looking; at forty-eight, his hair was just turning gray at the temples. He had a jowly, thoughtful face. He also had as much to fear as I did.

"Art's in jail," I said.

He was in the middle of reviewing an autopsy case. He shut the file. "Why?"

"I don't know. I'm going to see him."

"Do you want me to come with you?"

"No," I said. "It's better if I go alone."

"Call me," Sanderson said, peering over his half frames, "when you know."

"I will."

He nodded. When I left him, he had opened the file again, and was reading the case. If he had been upset by the news, he wasn't showing it. But then Sanderson never did.

In the hospital lobby I reached into my pocket for my car keys, then realized I didn't know where they were holding Art, so I went to the information desk to call Judith and ask her. The girl at the desk was Sally Planck, a good-natured blonde whose name was the subject of endless jokes among the residents. I phoned Judith and asked where Art was; she didn't know. It hadn't occurred to her to ask. So I called Arthur's wife, Betty, a beautiful and efficient girl with a Ph.D. in biochem from Stanford. Until a few years ago, Betty had done research at Harvard, but she stopped when she had her third child. She was usually very calm. The only time I had seen her upset was when George Kovacs had gotten drunk and urinated all over her patio.

Betty answered the phone in a state of stony shock. She told me they had Arthur downtown, on Charles Street. He had been arrested in his home that morning, just as he was leaving for the office. The kids were very upset, and she had kept them home from school that day, and now what did she do with them? What was she supposed to tell them, for Pete's sake?

I told her to say it was all a mistake and hung up.

I DROVE MY VOLKSWAGEN out of the doctors' parking lot, past all the shiny Cadillacs. The big cars are all owned by practicing physicians; pathologists are paid by the hospital and can't afford all those glistening horses.

It was 8:45, right in the middle of rush-hour traffic, which in Boston means a life-and-death proposition. Boston has the highest accident rate in the U.S., even higher than Los Angeles, as any EW[5] intern can tell you. Or pathologists: we see a lot of automobile trauma at autopsy. They drive like maniacs; like sitting in the EW as the bodies come in, you think there's a war going on. Judith says it's because they're repressed. Art has always said it was because they're Catholic and think God will look after them as they wander across the double stripe, but Art is a cynic. Once, at a medical party, a surgeon explained how many eye injuries occur from plastic dashboard figurines. People get into accidents, pitch forward, and have their eyes put out by the six-inch Madonna. It happens a lot; Art thought it was the funniest thing he had ever heard.

He laughed until he was crying. "Blinded by religion," he kept saying, doubled over in laughter. "Blinded by religion."

The surgeon did plastic stuff, and he didn't see the humor. I guess because he'd repaired too many punched-out eyesockets. But Art was convulsed.

Most people at the party were surprised by his laughter; they thought

[5] Emergency ward.

it was excessive and in rather poor taste. I suppose of all the people there I was the only one who understood the significance of this joke to Art. I was also the only one who knew the great strains under which he worked.

Art is my friend, and he has been ever since we went to medical school together. He's a bright guy and a skilled doctor, and he believes in what he's doing. Like most practicing doctors, he tends to be a little too authoritarian, a little too autocratic. He thinks he knows what's best, and nobody can know that all the time. Maybe he goes overboard, but I can't really knock him. He serves a very important function. After all, somebody around here has to do the abortions.

I don't know exactly when he started. I guess it was right after he finished his gynecology residency. It's not a particularly difficult operation—a well-trained nurse can do it with no problem. There's only one small catch.

It's illegal.

I remember very well when I first found out about it. There was some talk among some of the path residents about Lee; they were getting a lot of D & C's that were positive. The D & C's had been ordered for a variety of complaints—menstrual irregularity, pain, mid-period bleeding—but quite a few were showing evidence of pregnancy in the scrapings. I got concerned because the residents were young and loose-mouthed. I told them right there in the lab that it wasn't funny, that they could seriously damage a doctor's reputation by such jokes. They sobered up quickly. Then I went to see Arthur. I found him in the hospital cafeteria.

"Art," I said, "something's bothering me."

He was in a jovial mood, eating a doughnut and coffee. "Not a gynecological problem, I hope." He laughed.

"Not exactly. I overheard some of the residents say that you had a half-dozen pregnancy-positive scrapings in the last month. Have you been notified?"

Immediately, the hearty manner was gone. "Yes," he said, "I have."

"I just wanted you to know. There might be trouble in the tissue committee when these things come up, and——"

He shook his head. "No trouble."

"Well, you know how it looks."

"Yes," he said. "It looks like I'm performing abortions."

His voice was low, almost dead calm. He was looking directly at me. It gave me a strange feeling.

"We'd better have a talk," he said. "Are you free for a drink about six tonight?"

"I guess so."

"Then meet me in the parking lot. And if you get some free time this afternoon, why don't you have a look at a case of mine?"

"All right," I said, frowning.

"The name is Suzanne Black. The number is AO–two-two-one-three-six-five."

I scribbled the number on a napkin, wondering why he should have remembered it. Doctors remember a lot about their patients, but rarely the hospital number.

"Take a good look at this case," Art said, "and don't mention it to anyone until you talk to me."

Puzzled, I went back to work in the lab. I was up for an autopsy that day, so I wasn't free until four in the afternoon. Then I went to the record room and pulled the chart for Suzanne Black. I read it right there —it wasn't very long. She was Dr. Lee's patient, first admitted at age twenty. She was a junior at a local Boston college. Her CC[6] was menstrual irregularity. Upon questioning, it was revealed that she had recently suffered a bout of German measles, had been very tired afterward, and had been examined by her college doctor for possible mononucleosis. She reported irregular spotting approximately every seven to ten days, but no normal flow. This had been going on for the last two months. She was still tired and lethargic.

Physical examination was essentially normal, except that she had a mild fever. Blood tests were normal, though hematocrit[7] was somewhat low.

Dr. Lee ordered a D & C to correct her irregularity. This was in 1956, before the advent of estrogen therapy. The D & C was normal; no evidence of tumors or pregnancy. The girl seemed to respond well to this treatment. She was followed for the next three months and had normal periods.

It looked like a straightforward case. Illness or emotional stress can disrupt a woman's biological clock, and throw off her menses; the D & C reset that clock. I couldn't understand why Art had wanted me to look at it. I checked the path report on the tissue. It had been done by Dr. Sanderson. The write-up was brief and simple: gross appearance normal, micro examination normal.

I returned the chart and went back to the lab. When I got there, I still couldn't imagine what the point of the case was. I wandered around, doing odds and ends, and finally began the work-up on my autopsy.

[6] Chief complaint, the term for the medical disorder that brings the patient to seek treatment.
[7] A test of the amount of hemoglobin, or red cells, in the blood.

I don't know what made me think of the slide.

Like most hospitals, the Lincoln keeps path slides on file. We save them all; it is possible to go back twenty or thirty years and reexamine the microscopic slides from a patient. They're stored in long boxes arranged like card catalogs in a library. We had a whole room full of such boxes.

I went to the appropriate box and found slide 1365. The label gave the case number and Dr. Sanderson's initials. It also said in large letters, "D & C."

I took the slide back to the micro room, where we have ten microscopes in a long row. One was free; I slipped the slide onto the stage and had a look.

I saw it immediately.

The tissue was a uterine scraping, all right. It showed a rather normal endometrium in the proliferative phase, but the stain stopped me. This slide had been stained with Zenker-Formalin stain, giving everything a brilliant blue or green color. It was a rather unusual stain, employed for special diagnostic problems.

For routine work, the Hematoxylin-Eosin stain is used, producing pink and purple colors. Almost every tissue slice is stained with H & E, and if this is not the case, the reasons for the unusual stain are noted in the pathological summary.

But Dr. Sanderson had not mentioned that the slide was Zenker-Formalin.

The obvious conclusion was that the slides had been switched. I looked at the handwriting on the label. It was Sanderson's, no doubt about it. What had happened?

Almost immediately, other possibilities came to mind. Sanderson had forgotten to note in his report that an unusual stain was used. Or two sections were made, one H & E, the other Zenker-Formalin, and only the Zenker was saved. Or that there had been some legitimate mixup.

None of these alternatives was particularly convincing. I thought about it and waited impatiently until six that evening, when I met Art in the parking lot and got into his car. He wanted to go someplace away from the hospital to talk. As he drove, he said, "Read the case?"

"Yes," I said. "Very interesting."

"You checked the section?"

"Yes. Was it the original?"

"You mean, was it a scraping from Suzanne Black? No."

"You should have been more careful. The stain was different. That kind of thing can get you into trouble. Where did the slide come from?"

Art smiled thinly. "A biological supply house. 'Slide of normal endometrial scraping.' "

"And who made the switch?"

"Sanderson. We were new to the game, in those days. It was his idea to put in a phony slide and write it up as normal. Now, of course, we're much more refined. Every time Sanderson gets a normal scraping, he makes up a few extra slides and keeps them around."

"I don't understand," I said. "You mean Sanderson is in this with you?"

"Yes," Art said. "He has been for several years."

Sanderson was a very wise, very kind, and very proper man.

"You see," Art said, "that whole chart is a lie. The girl was twenty, all right. And she had German measles. And she had menstrual irregularity, too, but the reason was she was pregnant. She had been knocked up on a football weekend by a guy she said she loved and was going to marry, but she wanted to finish college first, and a baby would get in the way. Furthermore, she managed to get measles during the first trimester. She wasn't a terribly bright girl, but she was bright enough to know what it meant when you got measles. She was very worried when she came to see me. She hemmed and hawed for a while, and then blurted it all out and asked for an abortion.

"I was pretty horrified. I was fresh from my residency, and I still had a little starry idealism in me. She was in a terrible fix; she was a wreck and acted as if the world had collapsed around her. I guess in a way it had. All she could see was her problem as a college dropout, the unwed mother of a possibly deformed child. She was a nice enough girl, and I felt sorry for her, but I said no. I sympathized with her, feeling rotten inside, but I explained that my hands were tied.

"So then she asked me if it was a dangerous operation, to have an abortion. At first I thought she was planning to try it on herself, so I said it was. Then she said she knew of a man in the North End who would do it for two hundred dollars. He had been a medical orderly in the Marines, or something. And she said that if I wouldn't do it for her, she'd go to this man. And she walked out of my office."

He sighed and shook his head as he drove.

"I went home that night feeling like hell. I hated her: I hated her for intruding on my new practice, for intruding on my neatly planned life. I hated her for the pressure she was putting on me. I couldn't sleep; I kept thinking all night. I had a vision of her going to a smelly back room somewhere and meeting a leering little guy who would letch her and maybe even manage to kill her. I thought about my own wife and our year-old baby, and how happy it could all be. I thought about the amateur abortions I'd seen as an intern, when the girls came in bleeding and foaming at three in the morning. And let's face it, I thought about the sweats I'd had in college. Once with Betty, we sat around for six weeks waiting for her period. I knew perfectly well that anybody can get pregnant by accident. It's not hard, and it shouldn't be a crime."

I smoked a cigarette and said nothing.

"So I got up in the middle of the night and fought it out with six cups of coffee, staring at the kitchen wall. By morning I had decided that the law was unfair. I had decided that a doctor could play God in a lot of crappy ways, but this was a good way. I had seen a patient in trouble and I had refused to help her when it was within my power. That was what bothered me—I had denied her treatment. It was just as bad as denying penicillin to a sick man, just as cruel and just as foolish. The next morning, I went to see Sanderson. I knew he had liberal ideas about a lot of things. I explained the whole situation and told him I wanted to do a D & C. He said he would arrange to do the path examination himself, and he did. That was how it all started."

"And you've been doing abortions ever since?"

"Yes," Art said. "When I've felt that they were warranted."

After that, we went to a bar in the North End, a simple place, filled with Italian and German laborers. Art was in a talkative, almost confessional mood.

"I often wonder," he said, "about what medicine would be like if the predominant religious feeling in this country were Christian Scientist. For most of history, of course, it wouldn't have mattered; medicine was pretty primitive and ineffective. But supposing Christian Science was strong in the age of penicillin and antibiotics. Suppose there were pressure groups militating against the administration of these drugs. Suppose there were sick people in such a society who *knew* perfectly well that they didn't have to die from their illness, that a simple drug existed which would cure them. Wouldn't there be a roaring black market in these drugs? Wouldn't people die from home administration of overdoses, from impure, smuggled drugs? Wouldn't everything be an unholy mess?"

"I see your analogy," I said, "but I don't buy it."

"Listen," he said. "Morality must keep up with technology, because if a person is faced with the choice of being moral and dead or immoral and alive, they'll choose life every time. People today know that abortions are safe and easy. They know it isn't a long tedious, dangerous operation. They know it's simple and they want the personal happiness it can give them. They demand it. And one way or another they get it. If they're rich, they go to Japan or Puerto Rico; if they're poor, they go to the Marine orderly. But one way or another, they get that abortion."

"Art," I said. "It's illegal."

He smiled. "I never thought you had so much respect for the law."

That was a reference to my career. After college, I entered law school and stuck it out for a year and a half. Then I decided I hated it and quit to try medicine. In between, I did some army time.

"But this is different," I said. "If they catch you, they'll toss you in the clink and take away your license. You know that."

"I'm doing what I have to do."

"Don't be an ass."

"I believe," he said, "that what I'm doing is right."

Looking at his face, I saw he meant it. And as time went on, I personally encountered several cases where an abortion was the obvious, humane answer. Art handled them. I joined Dr. Sanderson in covering up in the path department. We fixed things so that the tissue committee never knew. That was necessary because the tissue committee of the Lincoln was composed of all the chiefs of service, as well as a rotating group of six doctors. The average age of the men on the tissue committee was sixty-one, and, at any given time, at least a third were Catholic.

Of course it was not a well-kept secret. Many of the younger doctors knew what Art was doing, and most agreed with him, because he exercised careful judgment in deciding his cases. Most would have performed abortions too, if they had dared.

A few didn't agree with Art and would have been tempted to turn him in if they'd had the guts. Anal retentives like Whipple and Gluck, men whose religion precluded compassion and common sense.

For a long time, I worried about the Whipples and the Glucks. Later on I ignored them, turning away from their nasty knowing glances and pinched, disapproving faces. Perhaps that was a mistake.

Because now Art was down, and if his head rolled, so would Sanderson's. And so would mine.

THERE WAS NO PLACE TO PARK near the police station. Finally I came to a lot four blocks away and walked quickly back to find out why Arthur Lee was in jail.

TWO

WHEN I WAS IN THE ARMY a few years back, I served as an MP in Tokyo, and the experience taught me a lot. MP's were the most unpopular people in the city in those days, during the last phases of the occupation. In our white helmets and uniforms, we represented the final reminders of a tiresome military authority to the Japanese. To the Americans on the Ginza, drunk with sake or whiskey if they could afford it, we represented all that was frustrating or constricting about rigid military life. We were therefore a challenge to anyone who saw us, and more than one of my friends ran into trouble. One was blinded by a knife in the eye. Another was killed.

Of course, we were armed. I remember when we were first issued our guns, a hard-nosed captain said to us: "You have your weapons, now take my advice: never use the gun. You shoot a rowdy drunk, even in self-defense, and you'll find out later his uncle is a congressman or a general. Keep the gun in sight, but keep it in your holster. Period."

In effect we were ordered to bluff our way through everything. We learned to do it. All cops learn to do it.

I remembered this as I faced the surly police sergeant in the Charles Street Station. He looked up at me as if he'd enjoy breaking my skull.

"Yeah? What is it?"

"I'm here to see Dr. Lee," I said.

He smiled. "The little chink's up tight, is he? Too bad."

"I'm here to see him," I repeated.

"Can't."

He looked back at his desk and shuffled the papers on it in a busy, irritable dismissal.

"Would you care to explain that?"

"No," he said. "I wouldn't care to explain that."

I took out my pen and notebook. "I'd like your badge number, please."

"What are you, a funny guy? Beat it. You can't see him."

"You are required by law to give your badge number upon request."

"That's nice."

I looked at his shirt and pretended to write down the number. Then I started for the door.

He said casually, "Going somewhere?"

"There's a phone booth right outside."

"So?"

"It's a shame. I'll bet your wife spent hours sewing those stripes on your shoulder. It takes them ten seconds to get them off. They use a razor blade: doesn't even damage the uniform."

He stood up heavily behind the desk. "What's your business here?"

"I've come to see Dr. Lee."

He looked at me evenly. He didn't know if I could have him busted, but he knew it could be done.

"You his lawyer?"

"That's right."

"Well, for Christ's sake, you should have said so before." He took a set of keys from his desk drawer. "Come on." He smiled at me, but his eyes were still hostile.

I followed him back through the station. He said nothing, but grunted a couple of times. Finally he said over his shoulder, "You can't blame me for being careful. Murder is murder, you know."

"Yes," I said.

ART WAS LOCKED IN A NICE CELL. It was tidy and didn't smell much. Actually, Boston has some of the nicest cells in America. They have to: lots of famous people have spent time in those cells. Mayors, public officials, people like that. You can't expect a man to run a decent campaign for re-election if he's in a lousy cell, can you?

It just wouldn't look right.

Art was sitting on his bed, staring at a cigarette between his fingers. The stone floor was littered with butts and ash. He looked up as we came down the hallway.

"John!"

"You have him for ten minutes," the sergeant said.

I entered the cell. The sergeant locked the door behind me and stood there, leaning against the bars.

"Thank you," I said. "You can go now."

He gave me a mean look and sauntered off, rattling the keys.

When we were alone, I said to Art, "You all right?"

"I think so."

Art is a small, precise man, a fastidious dresser. Originally he's from San Francisco from a large family of doctors and lawyers. Apparently his mother was American: he doesn't look very Chinese. His skin is more olive than yellow, his eyes lack epicanthic folds, and his hair is light brown. He is very nervous, constantly moving his hands in fluttering movements, and the total effect is more Latin than anything else.

He was pale now and tense. When he got up to pace the cell, his movements were quick and abrupt.

"It was good of you to come."

"In case there's any question, I'm the representative of your lawyer. That's how I got in here." I took out my notebook. "Have you called your lawyer?"

"No, not yet."

"Why not?"

"I don't know." He rubbed his forehead and massaged his eyes with his fingers. "I'm not thinking straight. Nothing seems to make sense. . . ."

"Tell me your lawyer's name."

He told me, and I wrote it in the notebook. Art had a good lawyer. I guess he figured he'd need one, sometime.

"Okay," I said. "I'll call him when I leave. Now what's going on?"

"I've been arrested," Art said. "For murder."

"So I gathered. Why did you call me?"

"Because you know about these things."

"About murder? I don't know anything."

"You went to law school."

"For a year," I said. "That was ten years ago. I almost flunked out, and I don't remember a thing I learned."

"John," he said, "this is a medical problem and a legal problem. Both. I need your help."

"You'd better start from the beginning."

"John, I didn't do it. I swear I didn't. I never touched that girl."

He was pacing faster and faster. I gripped his arm and stopped him. "Sit down," I said, "and start from the beginning. Very slowly."

He shook his head and stubbed out his cigarette. Immediately he lit another, then said, "They picked me up at home this morning, about seven. Brought me in and started questioning me. At first they said it was routine, whatever that means. Then they turned nasty."

"How many were there?"

"Two. Sometimes three."

"Did they get rough? Slap you around? Bright lights?"

"No, nothing like that."

"Did they say you could call a lawyer?"

"Yes. But that was later. When they advised me of my constitutional rights." He smiled that sad, cynical smile of his. "At first, you see, it was just for routine questioning, so it never occurred to me to call one. I had done nothing wrong. They talked to me for an hour before they even mentioned the girl."

"What girl?"

"Karen Randall."

"You don't mean *the* Karen——"

He nodded. "J. D. Randall's daughter."

"Jesus."

"They began by asking me what I knew about her, and whether I'd ever seen her as a patient. Things like that. I said yes, that she had come to me a week ago for consultation. Chief complaint of amenorrhea."

"What duration?"

"Four months."

"Did you tell them the duration?"

"No, they didn't ask me."

"Good," I said.

"They wanted to know other details about her visit. They wanted to know if that was her only problem, they wanted to know how she had acted. I wouldn't tell them. I said that the patient had spoken in confidence. So then they switched tacks: they wanted to know where I was last night. I told them I had made evening rounds at the Lincoln and then taken a walk in the park. They asked me if I had gone back to my office. I said no. They asked me if anyone had seen me in the park that night. I said I couldn't remember anyone, certainly nobody I knew."

Art sucked deeply on his cigarette. His hands were trembling. "Then they started to hammer at me. Was I sure I hadn't returned to my office? What had I done after making rounds? Was I sure I hadn't seen Karen since last week? I didn't understand the point of the questions."

"And what was the point?"

"Karen Randall was brought to the Mem EW at four this morning by her mother. She was bleeding profusely—exsanguinating actually—and was in a state of hemorrhagic shock when she arrived. I don't know what treatment they gave her, but anyway she died. The police think I aborted her last night."

I frowned. It just didn't make sense. "How can they be so sure?"

"They wouldn't say. I kept asking. Maybe the kid was delirious and mentioned my name at the Mem. I don't know."

I shook my head. "Art, cops fear false arrest like they fear the plague. If they arrest you and can't make it stick, a lot of people are going to lose their jobs. You're a respected member of the professional community, not some drunken bum without a penny or a friend in the world. You have recourse to good legal advice, and they know you'll get it. They wouldn't dare charge you unless they had a strong case."

Art waved his hand irritably. "Maybe they're just stupid."

"Of course they're stupid, but not that stupid."

"Well," he said, "I don't know what they've got on me."

"You must know."

"I don't," he said, resuming his pacing. "I can't even begin to guess."

I watched him for a moment, wondering when to ask the question, knowing that I would have to, sooner or later. He noticed I was staring.

"No," he said.

"No what?"

"No, I didn't do it. And stop looking at me that way." He sat down again and drummed his fingers on the bunk. "Christ, I wish I had a drink."

"You'd better forget that," I said.

"Oh, for Christ's sake—"

"You only drink socially," I said, "and in moderation."

"Am I on trial for my character and personal habits, or for——"

"You're not on trial at all," I said, "and you don't want to be."

He snorted.

"Tell me about Karen's visit," I said.

"There's nothing much to tell. She came asking for an abortion, but I wouldn't do it because she was four months pregnant. I explained to her why I couldn't do it, that she was too far along, and that an abortion would now require abdominal section."

"And she accepted that?"

"She seemed to."

"What did you put in your records?"

"Nothing. I didn't open a file on her."

I sighed. "That," I said, "could be bad. Why didn't you?"

"Because she wasn't coming to me for treatment, she wasn't becoming my patient. I knew I'd never see her again, so I didn't open a file."

"How are you going to explain that to the police?"

"Look," he said, "if I'd known that she was going to get me arrested, I might have done lots of things differently."

I lit a cigarette and leaned back, feeling the cold stone against my neck. I could already see that it was a messy situation. And the small details, innocent in another context, could now assume great weight and importance.

"Who referred her to you?"

"Karen? I assumed Peter."

"Peter Randall?"

"Yes. He was her personal physician."

"You didn't ask her who referred her?" Art was usually careful about that.

"No. She arrived late in the day, and I was tired. Besides, she came right to the point; she was a very direct young lady, no foolishness about her. When I heard the story, I assumed Peter had sent her to me to explain the situation, since it was obviously too late to arrange an abortion."

"Why did you assume that?"

He shrugged. "I just did."

It wasn't making sense. I was sure he wasn't telling me everything. "Have other members of the Randall family been referred to you?"

"What do you mean?"

"Just what I said."

"I don't think it's relevant," he said.

"It might be."

"I assure you," he said. "It's not."

I sighed and smoked the cigarette. I knew Art could be stubborn when he wanted to. "O.K.," I said. "Then tell me more about the girl."

"What do you want to know?"

"Had you ever seen her before?"

"No."

"Ever met her socially?"

"No."

"Ever helped any of her friends?"

"No."

"How can you be sure?"

"Oh, hell," he said, "I can't be sure, but I doubt it very much. She was only eighteen."

"O.K.," I said. Art was probably right. I knew he usually aborted only married women, in their late twenties and thirties. He had often said he didn't want to get involved with the younger ones, though he did on occasion. Older women and married women were much safer, more close mouthed and realistic. But I also knew that he had recently been doing more young girls, calling them "teeny-bopper scrapes," because he said to do only married women was discrimination. He meant that partly as a joke, and partly not.

"How was she," I said, "when she came to your office? How would you describe her?"

"She seemed like a nice girl," Art said. "She's pretty and intelligent and well poised. Very direct, as I said before. She came into my office, sat down, folded her hands in her lap, and reeled it all off. She used medical terms too, like amenorrhea. I suppose that comes from being in a family of doctors."

"Was she nervous?"

"Yes," he said, "but then they all are. That's why the differential is so hard."

The differential diagnosis of amenorrhea, particularly in young girls, must consider nervousness as a strong etiologic possibility. Women often delay or miss their menstrual periods for psychological reasons.

"But four months?"

"Well, not likely. And she'd also had a weight gain."

"How much?"

"Fifteen pounds."

"Not diagnostic," I said.

"No," he said, "but suggestive."

"Did you examine her?"

"No. I offered to, but she refused. She had come to me for an abortion, and when I said no, she left."

"Did she say what her plans were?"

"Yes," Art said. "She gave a little shrug and said, 'Well, I guess I'll just have to tell them and have the kid.'"

"So you thought she would not seek an abortion elsewhere?"

"Exactly. She seemed very intelligent and perceptive, and she seemed to follow my explanation of the situation. That's what I try to do in these cases—explain to a woman why it is impossible for her to have a safe abortion, and why she must reconcile herself to having the child."

"Obviously she changed her mind."

"Obviously."

"I wonder why."

He laughed. "Ever met her parents?"

"No," I said, and then seeing my chance, "have you?"

But Art was quick. He gave me a slow, appreciative grin, a kind of subtle salute, and said, "No. Never. But I've heard about them."

"What have you heard?"

At that moment, the sergeant came back and began clanking the key into the lock.

"Time's up," he said.

"Five more minutes," I said.

"Time's up."

Art said, "Have you spoken to Betty?"

"Yes," I said. "She's fine. I'll call her when I leave here and tell her you're all right."

"She's going to be worried," Art said.

"Judith will stay with her. It'll be O.K."

Art grinned ruefully. "Sorry to cause all this trouble."

"No trouble." I glanced at the sergeant, standing with the door open, waiting. "The police can't hold you. You'll be out by the afternoon."

The sergeant spit on the floor.

I shook hands with Art. "By the way," I said, "where's the body now?"

"Perhaps at the Mem. But it's probably gone to the City by now."

"I'll check," I said. "Don't worry about a thing." I stepped out of the cell and the sergeant locked up behind me. He said nothing as he led me out, but when we reached the lobby, he said, "Captain wants to see you."

"All right."

"Captain's very interested in having a little talk."

"Just lead the way," I said.

THREE

THE SIGN ON THE FLAKING GREEN DOOR SAID HOMICIDE, and underneath, on a hand-printed name card, "Captain Peterson." He turned out to be a stiff, burly man with close-cropped gray hair and a terse manner. He came around the desk to shake hands with me, and I noticed he had a limp in his right leg. He made no effort to hide it; if anything, he exaggerated it, allowing his toe to scrape loudly over the floor. Cops, like soldiers, can be proud of their infirmities. You knew Peterson hadn't received his in an auto accident.

I was trying to determine the cause of Peterson's injury and had decided that it was probably a bullet wound—rarely does anyone get cut with a knife in the calf—when he stuck out his hand and said, "I'm Captain Peterson."

"John Berry."

His handshake was hearty, but his eyes were cold and inquiring. He waved me to a chair.

"The sergeant said he hadn't seen you around before and I thought

I ought to meet you. We know most of the criminal lawyers in Boston."

"Don't you mean trial lawyers."

"Of course," he said easily. "Trial lawyers." He looked at me expectantly.

I said nothing at all. A short silence passed, then Peterson said, "Which firm do you represent?"

"Firm?"

"Yes."

"I'm not a lawyer," I said, "and I don't know what makes you think I am."

He pretended to be surprised. "That's not the impression you gave the sergeant."

"No?"

"No. You told him you were a lawyer."

"I did?"

"Yes," Peterson said, placing his hands flat on his desk.

"Who says so?"

"He says so."

"Then he's wrong."

Peterson leaned back in his chair and smiled at me, a very pleasant, let's-not-get-all-excited smile.

"If we had known you weren't a lawyer, you'd never have been allowed to see Lee."

"That's possible. On the other hand, I was not asked for my name or my occupation. Nor was I asked to sign in as a visitor."

"The sergeant was probably confused."

"That's logical," I said, "considering the sergeant."

Peterson smiled blankly. I recognized his type: he was a successful cop, a guy who had learned when to take it and when to dish it out. A very diplomatic and polite cop, until he got the upper hand.

"Well?" he said at last.

"I'm a colleague of Dr. Lee."

If he was surprised, he didn't show it. "A doctor?"

"That's right."

"You doctors certainly stick together," he said, still smiling. He had probably smiled more in the last two minutes than he had in the last two years.

"Not really," I said.

The smile began to fall, probably from fatigue of unused muscles. "If you are a doctor," Peterson said, "my advice to you is to stay the hell away from Lee. The publicity could kill your practice."

"What publicity?"

"The publicity from the trial."

"There's going to be a trial?"

"Yes," Peterson said. "And the publicity could kill your practice."

"I don't have a practice," I said.

"You're in research?"

"No," I said. "I'm a pathologist."

He reacted to that. He started to sit forward, caught himself, and leaned back again. "A pathologist," he repeated.

"That's right. I work in hospitals, doing autopsies and things."

Peterson was silent for some time. He frowned, scratched the back of his hand, and looked at his desk. Finally he said, "I don't know what you're trying to prove, Doctor. But we don't need your help, and Lee is too far gone to——"

"That remains to be seen."

Peterson shook his head. "You know better than that."

"I'm not sure I do."

"Do you know," Peterson said, "what a doctor could claim in a false-arrest suit?"

"A million dollars," I said.

"Well, let's say five hundred thousand. It doesn't matter much. The point is essentially the same."

"You think you have a case."

"We have a case." Peterson smiled again. "Oh, Dr. Lee can call you as a witness. We know that. And you can talk up a storm using the big words, trying to fool the jury, to impress them with your weighty scientific evidence. But you can't get past the central fact. You just can't get past it."

"And what fact is that?"

"A young girl bled to death in the Boston Memorial Hospital this morning, from an illegal abortion. That fact, straight and simple."

"And you allege Dr. Lee did it?"

"There is some evidence," Peterson said mildly.

"It had better be good," I said, "because Dr. Lee is an established and respected——"

"Listen," Peterson said, showing impatience for the first time, "what do you think this girl was, a ten-dollar doxy? This was a nice girl, a hell of a nice girl, from a good family. She was young and pretty and sweet, and she got butchered. But she didn't go to some Roxbury midwife or some North End quack. She had too much sense and too much money for that."

"What makes you think Dr. Lee did it?"

"That's none of your business."

I shrugged. "Dr. Lee's lawyer will ask the same question, and then it will be his business. And if you don't have an answer——"

"We have an answer."

I waited. In a sense, I was curious to see just how good, just how diplomatic Peterson was. He didn't have to tell me anything; he didn't have to say another word. If he did say more, it would be a mistake.

Peterson said, "We have a witness who heard the girl implicate Dr. Lee."

"The girl arrived at the hospital in a state of shock, delirious and precomatose. Anything she said will constitute weak evidence."

"At the time she said it, she wasn't in a state of shock. She said it much earlier."

"To whom?"

"To her mother," Peterson said, with a grin of satisfaction. "She told her mother that Lee did it. As they were leaving for the hospital. And her mother will swear to that."

FOUR

I TRIED TO PLAY IT PETERSON'S WAY. I tried to keep my face blank. Fortunately you have a lot of practice at that in medicine; you are trained to show no surprise if a patient tells you they make love ten times a night, or have dreams of stabbing their children, or drink a gallon of vodka daily. It is part of the mystique of the doctor that nothing surprises him.

"I see," I said.

Peterson nodded. "A reliable witness," he said. "A mature woman, stable, careful in her judgments. And very attractive. She will make an excellent impression on the jury."

"Perhaps."

"And now that I have been so frank," Peterson said, "perhaps you would tell me your special interest in Dr. Lee."

"I have no special interest. He is my friend."

"He called you before he called his lawyer."

"He is allowed two telephone calls."

"Yes," Peterson said, "but most people use them to call their lawyer and their wife."

"He wanted to talk to me."

"Yes," he said. "But the question is why."

"I have had some legal training," I said, "as well as my medical experience."

"You have an LL.B.?"

"No," I said.

Peterson ran his fingers across the edge of his desk. "I don't think I understand."

"I'm not convinced," I said, "that it is important that you do."

"Could it be you are involved in this business in some way?"

"Anything is possible," I said.

"Does that mean yes?"

"That means anything is possible."

He regarded me for a moment. "You take a very tough line, Dr. Berry."

"Skeptical."

"If you are so skeptical, why are you convinced Dr. Lee didn't do it?"

"I'm not the defense attorney."

"You know," Peterson said, "anyone can make a mistake. Even a doctor."

WHEN I GOT OUTSIDE into the October drizzle, I decided this was a hell of a time to quit smoking. Peterson had unnerved me; I smoked two cigarettes as I walked to the drugstore to buy another pack. I had expected him to be stupid and pointlessly tough. He was neither of those things. If what he had said was true, then he had a case. It might not work, but it was strong enough to protect his job.

Peterson was caught in a quandary. On the one hand, it was dangerous to arrest Dr. Lee; on the other, it was dangerous not to arrest him, if the case seemed strong enough. Peterson was forced into a decision, and he had made it. Now he would stick by it as long as he could. And he had an escape: if things began to go bad, he could blame it all on Mrs. Randall. He could use the familiar line so famous among surgeons and internists that it was abbreviated DHJ: doing his job. That meant that if the evidence was strong enough, you acted and did not care whether you were right or not; you were justified in acting on the evidence.[1] In that

---

[1] This happens a lot in medicine. For example, a patient presents with fever, leukocytosis—increased numbers of white cells—and pain in the right lower quadrant of the abdomen. The obvious diagnosis is appendicitis. The surgeon may perform an appendectomy only to find that the appendix is normal. But he is vindicated, so long as he is not overhasty, because the evidence is consistent with appendicitis, and delay may be fatal.

sense, Peterson's position was strengthened. He was taking no gambles: if Art was convicted, Peterson would receive no accolades. But if Art was acquitted, Peterson was covered. Because he was doing his job.

I went into the drugstore, bought two packs of cigarettes, and made some phone calls from a pay phone. First I called my lab and told them I'd be gone the rest of the day. Then I called Judith and asked her to go over to the Lees' house and stay with Betty. She wanted to know if I'd seen Art, and I said I had. She asked if he was all right, and I said everything was fine, that he'd be out in an hour or so.

I don't usually keep things from my wife. Just one or two small things, like what Cameron Jackson did at the conference of the American Society of Surgeons a few years back. I knew she'd be upset for Cameron's wife, as she was when they got divorced last spring. The divorce was what is known locally as an MD, a medical divorce, and it had nothing to do with conventions. Cameron is a busy and dedicated orthopedist, and he began missing meals at home, spending his life in the hospital. His wife couldn't take it after a while. She began by resenting orthopedics and ended by resenting Cameron. She got the two kids and three hundred dollars a week, but she's not happy. What she really wants is Cameron —without medicine.

Cameron's not very happy, either. I saw him last week and he spoke vaguely of marrying a nurse he'd met. He knew people would talk if he did, but you could see he was thinking, "At least this one will understand—"

I often think of Cameron Jackson and the dozen people I know like him. Usually, I think of him late at night, when I've been held up at the lab or when I've been so busy I haven't had time to call home and say I'll be late.

Art Lee and I once talked about it, and he had the last word, in his own cynical way. "I'm beginning to understand," he said, "why priests don't marry."

Art's own marriage has an almost stifling sort of stability. I suppose it comes from his being Chinese, though that can't be the whole answer. Both Art and his wife are highly educated, and not visibly tied to tradition, but I think they have both found it difficult to shake off. Art is always guilt ridden about the little time he spends with his family, and lavishes gifts on his three children; they are all spoiled silly. He adores them, and it's often hard to stop him once he begins talking about them. His attitude toward his wife is more complex and ambiguous. At times he seems to expect her to revolve around him like a trusting dog, and at times she seems to want this as much as he does. At other times she is more independent.

Betty Lee is one of the most beautiful women I've ever seen. She is soft-spoken, gracious, and slender; next to her Judith seems big, loud, and almost masculine.

Judith and I have been married eight years. We met while I was in medical school and she was a senior at Smith. Judith was raised on a farm in Vermont, and is hard headed, as pretty girls go.

I said, "Take care of Betty."

"I will."

"Keep her calm."

"All right."

"And keep the reporters away."

"Will there be reporters?"

"I don't know. But if there are, keep them away."

She said she would and hung up.

I then called George Bradford, Art's lawyer. Bradford was a solid lawyer and a man with the proper connections; he was senior partner of Bradford, Stone and Whitlaw. He wasn't in the office when I called, so I left a message.

Finally I called Lewis Carr, who was clinical professor of medicine at the Boston Memorial Hospital. It took a while for the switchboard to page him, and as usual he came on briskly.

"Carr speaking."

"Lew, this is John Berry."

"Hi, John. What's on your mind?"

That was typical of Carr. Most doctors, when they receive calls from other doctors, follow a kind of ritual pattern: first they ask how you are, then how your work is, then how your family is. But Carr had broken this pattern, as he had broken other patterns.

I said, "I'm calling about Karen Randall."

"What about her?" His voice turned cautious. Obviously it was a hot potato at the Mem these days.

"Anything you can tell me. Anything you've heard."

"Listen, John," he said, "her father is a big man in this hospital. I've heard everything and I've heard nothing. Who wants to know?"

"I do."

"Personally?"

"That's right."

"Why?"

"I'm a friend of Art Lee."

"They got him on this? I heard that, but I didn't believe it. I always thought Lee was too smart—"

"Lew, what happened last night?"

Carr sighed. "Christ, it's a mess. A real stinking hell of a mess. They blew it in outpatient."

"What do you mean?"

"I can't talk about this now," Carr said. "You'd better come over and see me."

"All right," I said. "Where is the body now? Do your people have it?"

"No, it's gone to the City."

"Have they performed the post yet?"

"I haven't any idea."

"O.K.," I said. "I'll stop by in a few hours. Any chance of getting her chart?"

"I doubt it," Carr said. "The old man has it now."

"Can't spring it free?"

"I doubt it," he said.

"O.K.," I said. "I'll see you later."

I hung up, put in another dime, and called the morgue at the City. The secretary confirmed that they had received the body. The secretary, Alice, was a hypothyroid; she had a voice as if she had swallowed a bass fiddle.

"Done the post yet?" I said.

"They're just starting."

"Will they hold it? I'd like to be there."

"I don't think it's possible," Alice said, in her rumbling voice. "We have an eager beaver from the Mem."

She advised me to hurry down. I said I would.

FIVE

IT IS WIDELY BELIEVED IN BOSTON that the best medical care in the world is found here. It is so universally acknowledged among the citizens of the city that there is hardly any debate.

The best hospital in Boston is, however, a question subject to hot and passionate debate. There are three major contenders: the General, the

Brigham, and the Mem. Defenders of the Mem will tell you that the General is too large and the Brigham too small; and the General is too coldly clinical and the Brigham too coldly scientific; that the General neglects surgery at the expense of medicine and the Brigham the reverse. And finally, you will be told solemnly that the house staffs of the General and the Brigham are simply inferior in training and intelligence to those of the Mem.

But on anybody's list of hospitals, the Boston City comes near the bottom. I drove toward it, passing the Prudential Center, the proudest monument to what the politicians call the New Boston. It is a vast complex of skyscrapers, hotels, shops, and plazas, with lots of fountains and wasted space, giving it a modern look. It stands within a few minutes' lustful walk of the red-light district, which is neither modern nor new, but like the Prudential Center, functional in its way.

The red-light district lies on the outskirts of the Negro slums of Roxbury, as does the Boston City. I bounced along from one pothole to another and thought that I was far from Randall territory.

It was natural that the Randalls would practice at the Mem. In Boston the Randalls were known as an old family, which meant that they could claim at least one seasick Pilgrim, straight off the Mayflower, contributing to the gene pool. They had been a family of doctors for hundreds of years: in 1776, Wilson Randall had died on Bunker Hill.

In more recent history, they had produced a long line of eminent physicians. Joshua Randall had been a famous brain surgeon early in the century, a man who had done as much as anyone, even Cushing, to advance neurosurgery in America. He was a stern, dogmatic man; a famous, though apocryphal story had passed into medical tradition.

Joshua Randall, like many surgeons of his period, had a rule that no resident working under him could marry. One resident sneaked off and did; a few months later, Randall discovered what had happened and called a meeting of all his residents. He lined them up in a row and said, "Dr. Jones, please take one step forward."

The guilty doctor did, trembling slightly.

Randall said, "I understand you have gotten married." He made it sound like a disease.

"Yes, sir."

"Before I discharge you from the staff, do you have anything to say in your defense?"

The young doctor thought for a moment, then said, "Yes, sir. I promise I'll never do it again."

Randall, according to the story, was so amused by this reply that he kept the resident after all.

After Joshua Randall came Winthrop Randall, the thoracic surgeon. J. D. Randall, Karen's father, was a heart surgeon, specializing in valvular replacements. I had never met him, but I'd seen him once or twice—a fierce, patriarchal man, with thick white hair and a commanding manner. He was the terror of the surgical residents, who flocked to him for training, but hated him.

His brother, Peter, was an internist with his offices just off the Commons. He was very fashionable, very exclusive, and supposedly quite good, though I had no way of knowing.

J. D. had a son, Karen's brother, who was in medical school at Harvard. A year ago, there was a rumor that the kid was practically flunking out, but nothing recently.

In another town, at another time, it might seem odd that a young boy with such a distinguished medical tradition would choose to try and live it down. But not Boston: in Boston the wealthy old families had long felt only two professions were worthy of one's attention. One was medicine and the other was law; exceptions were made for the academic life, which was honorable enough so long as one became a professor at Harvard.

But the Randalls were not an academic family, or a legal family. They were a medical family, and any Randall who could, contrived to get himself through medical school and into a house officership[1] at the Mem. Both the medical school and the Mem had, in the past, made allowances for poor grades when it came to the Randalls, but over the years, the family had more than repaid the trust. In medicine, a Randall was a good gamble.

And that was about all I knew about the family, except that they were very wealthy, firmly Episcopal, determinedly public spirited, widely respected, and very powerful.

I would have to find out more.

THREE BLOCKS FROM THE HOSPITAL, I passed through the Combat Zone at the corner of Mass and Columbus avenues. At night it teems with whores, pimps, addicts, and pushers; it got its name because doctors at the

---

[1] Position as an intern or resident, where one is an M.D. but not licensed to practice, and still completing education.

City see so many stabbings and shootings from this area they regard it as the location of a limited war.[2]

The Boston City itself is an immense complex of buildings sprawling over three city blocks. It has more than 1,350 beds, mostly filled with alcoholics and derelicts. Within the Boston medical establishment, the City is known as the Boston Shitty because of its clientele. But it is considered a good teaching hospital for residents and interns, because one sees there many medical problems one would never see in a more affluent hospital. A good example is scurvy. Few people in modern America contract scurvy. To do so requires general malnutrition and a complete abstinence from fruit for five months. This is so rare that most hospitals see a case every three years; at the Boston City there are a half-dozen each year, usually in the spring months, the "scurvy season."

There are other examples: severe tuberculosis, tertiary syphilis, gunshot wounds, stabbings, accidents, self-abuse, and personal misfortune. Whatever the category, the City sees more of it, in a more advanced state, than any other hospital in Boston.[3]

THE INTERIOR OF THE CITY HOSPITAL is a maze built by a madman. Endless corridors, above ground and below, connect the dozen separate buildings of the hospital. At every corner, there are large green signs pointing directions, but they don't help much; it is still hopelessly confusing.

As I cut through the corridors and buildings, I remembered my rotation through the hospital as a resident. Small details came back. The soap: a strange, cheap, peculiar-smelling soap that was used everywhere. The paper bags hung by each sink, one for paper towels, the other for rectal gloves. As an economy, the hospital saved used gloves, cleaned them, and used them again. The little plastic nametags edged in black, blue, and red depending on your service. I had spent a year in this hospital, and during that time I had done several autopsies for the medical examiner.

[2] Formerly the most violent area in Boston was Scollay Square, but it was demolished five years ago to make way for government buildings. Some consider that an improvement; some a step backward.
[3] The frequently bizarre cases means that every doctor and surgeon has a backlog of strange stories. One surgeon is fond of telling how he was on the Accident Floor—the City's EW—when two victims of an auto accident were brought in. One man had lost his leg at the knee. The other had massive crush injury to the chest, so bad that the degree of damage could not at first be ascertained from the heavy bleeding. On an X ray of the chest, however, it was seen that one man's foot and lower leg had been rammed into the second man's chest, where it was lodged at the time of admission.

THERE ARE FOUR MEDICAL SITUATIONS in which the coroner claims juris-
diction and an autopsy is required by law. Every pathology resident knows
the list cold:

If the patient dies under violent or unusual circumstances.

If the patient is DOA.[4]

If he dies within twenty-four hours of admission.

If a patient dies outside the hospital while not under a doctor's care.

Under any of these circumstances, an autopsy is performed at the City.
Like many cities, Boston has no separate police morgue. The second floor
of the Mallory Building, the pathology section of the hospital, is given
over to the medical examiner's offices. In routine cases, most of the autopsies are performed by first-year residents from the hospital in which the
patient died. For the residents, new to the game and still nervous, a
coroner's autopsy can be a tense business.

You don't know what poisoning or electrocution looks like, for instance, and you're worried about missing something important. The solution, passed down from resident to resident, is to do a meticulous PM, to
take lots of pictures and notes as you go, and to "save everything," meaning to keep pieces of tissue from all the gross organs in case there is a
court action that requires reexamination of the autopsy findings. Saving
everything is, of course, an expensive business. It requires extra jars, extra
preservative, and more storage space in the freezers. But it is done without
question in police cases.

Yet even with the precautions, you worry. As you do the post, there is
always that fear, that dreadful thought at the back of your mind that the
prosecution or the defense will demand some piece of information,
some crucial bit of evidence either positive or negative, that you cannot
supply because you did not consider all the possibilities, all the variables,
all the differentials.

FOR SOME LONG-FORGOTTEN REASON, there are two small stone sphinxes just
inside the doors of Mallory. Each time I see them, they bother me; somehow sphinxes in a pathology building smack of Egyptian embalming
chambers. Or something.

I went up to the second floor to talk to Alice. She was grumpy; the
post hadn't been started because of some delay; everything was going to

---

[4] Dead on arrival at hospital.

hell in a wheelbarrow these days; did I know that a flu epidemic was expected this winter?

I said I did, and then asked, "Who's doing the post on Karen Randall?"

Alice gave a disapproving frown. "They sent someone over from the Mem. His name, I believe, is Hendricks."

I was surprised. I had expected someone big to do this case.

"He inside?" I asked, nodding toward the end of the hall.

"Umm," Alice said.

I walked down toward the two swinging doors, past the freezers on the right which stored the bodies, and past the neatly labeled sign: AUTHORIZED PERSONNEL ONLY BEYOND THIS POINT. The doors were wood, without windows, marked IN and OUT. I pushed through into the autopsy room. Two men were talking in a far corner.

The room was large, painted a dull, institutional green. The ceiling was low, the floor was concrete, and the pipes overhead were exposed; they don't spend much on interior decoration here. In a neat row were five stainless-steel tables, each six feet long. They were tilted slightly and made with a lip. Water flowed constantly down the table in a thin sheet and emptied into a sink at the lower end. The water was kept running all during the autopsy, to carry away blood and bits of organic matter. The huge exhaust fan, three feet across and built into one frosted-glass window, was also kept on. So was the small chemical unit that blew scented ersatz air-freshener into the room, giving it a phony pinewoods odor.

Off to one side was a changing room where pathologists could remove their street clothes and put on surgical greens and an apron. There were four large sinks in a row, the farthest with a sign that said THIS SINK FOR WASHING HANDS ONLY. The others were used to clean instruments and specimens. Along one wall was a row of simple cabinets containing gloves, bottles for specimens, preservatives, reagents, and a camera. Unusual specimens were often photographed in place before removal.

As I entered the room, the two men looked over at me. They had been discussing a case, a body on the far table. I recognized one of the men, a resident named Gaffen. I knew him slightly. He was very clever and rather mean. The other man I did not know at all; I assumed he was Hendricks.

"Hello, John," Gaffen said. "What brings you here?"

"Post on Karen Randall."

"They'll start in a minute. Want to change?"

"No, thanks," I said. "I'll just watch."

Actually I would have liked to change, but it seemed like a bad idea. The only way I could be certain of preserving my observer's role would be to remain in street clothes. The last thing I wanted to do was to be considered an active participant in the autopsy, and therefore possibly influencing the findings.

I said to Hendricks, "I don't think we've met. I'm John Berry."

"Jack Hendricks." He smiled, but did not offer to shake hands. He was wearing gloves, and had been touching the autopsy body before them.

"I've just been showing Hendricks a few physical findings," Gaffen said, nodding to the body. He stepped back so I could see. It was a young Negro girl. She had been an attractive girl before somebody put three round holes in her chest and stomach.

"Hendricks here has been spending all his time at the Mem," Gaffen said. "He hasn't seen much of this sort of thing. For instance, we were just discussing what these little marks might represent."

Gaffen pointed to several flesh tears on the body. They were on the arms and lower legs.

Hendricks said, "I thought perhaps they were scratches from barbed wire."

Gaffen smiled sadly. "Barbed wire," he repeated.

I said nothing. I knew what they were, but I also knew that an inexperienced man would never be able to guess.

"When was she brought in?" I said.

Gaffen glanced at Hendricks, then said, "Five A.M. But the time of death seems to be around midnight." To Hendricks he said, "Does that suggest anything?"

Hendricks shook his head and bit his lip. Gaffen was giving him the business. I would have objected but this was standard procedure. Browbeating often passes for teaching in medicine. Hendricks knew it. I knew it. Gaffen knew it.

"Where," Gaffen said, "do you suppose she was for those five hours after death?"

"I don't know," Hendricks said miserably.

"Guess."

"Lying in bed."

"Impossible. Look at the lividity.[5] She wasn't lying *flat* anywhere. She was half seated, half rolled over on her side."

Hendricks looked at the body again, then shook his head again.

"They found her in the gutter," Gaffen said. "On Charleston Street, two blocks from the Combat Zone. In the gutter."

---

[5] The seeping of blood to the lowest portions of the body after death. It often helps establish the position of the body.

"Oh."

"So," Gaffen said, "what would you call those marks now?"

Hendricks shook his head. I knew this could go on forever; Gaffen could play it for all it was worth. I cleared my throat and said, "Actually, Hendricks, they're rat bites. Very characteristic: an initial puncture, and then a wedge-shaped tear."

"Rat bites," he said in a low voice.

"Live and learn," Gaffen said. He checked his watch. "I have a CPC now. Good to see you again, John." He stripped off his gloves and washed his hands, then came back to Hendricks.

Hendricks was still looking at the bullet holes and the bites.

"She was in the gutter for five hours?"

"Yes."

"Did the police find her?"

"Yes, eventually."

"Who did it to her?"

Gaffen snorted. "You tell me. She has a history of a primary luetic oral lesion, treated at this hospital, and five episodes of hot tubes, treated at this hospital."

"Hot tubes?"

"P.I.D."[6]

"When they found her," Gaffen said, "she had forty dollars in cash in her bra."

He looked at Hendricks, shook his head, and left the room. When we were alone, Hendricks said to me, "I still don't get it. Does that mean she was a prostitute?"

"Yes," I said. "She was shot to death and lay in the gutter for five hours, being chewed by sewer rats."

"Oh."

"It happens," I said. "A lot."

The swinging door opened, and a man wheeled in a white-shrouded body. He looked at us and said, "Randall?"

"Yes," Hendricks said.

"Which table you want?"

"The middle."

"All right." He moved the cart close, then swung the body over onto the stainless-steel table, shifting the head first, then the feet. It was already

[6] Pelvic Inflammatory Disease, usually infection of the fallopian tubes by Neisseria gonococcus, the agent of gonorrhea. Gonorrhea is considered to be the most common infectious disease of mankind. Twenty percent of prostitutes are thought to be infected.

quite stiff. He removed the shroud quickly, folded it, and set it on the cart.

"You gotta sign," he said to Hendricks, holding out a form.

Hendricks signed.

"I'm not very good at this," Hendricks said to me. "This legal stuff. I've only done one before, and that was an industrial thing. Man hit on the head at work and killed. But nothing like this . . ."

I said, "How did you get chosen for this one?"

He said, "Just lucky, I guess. I heard that Weston was going to do it, but apparently not."

"Leland Weston?"

"Yes."

Weston was the chief pathologist of the City hospital, a great old man and probably the best pathologist in Boston, bar none.

"Well," Hendricks said. "We might as well get started."

He went to the sink and began a long and thorough scrub. Pathologists who scrub for a post always annoy me. It makes them too much like parodies of surgeons: the idiotic reverse of the coin, a man dressed in a surgical uniform—baggy pants, V-neck shortsleeve blouse—cleaning his hands before operating on a patient who was past caring whether he received sterile treatment or not.

But in Hendricks' case, I knew he was just stalling.

AUTOPSIES ARE NEVER VERY PRETTY. They are particularly depressing when the deceased is as young and as attractive as Karen Randall was. She lay nude on her back, her blonde hair streaming down in the water. Her clear blue eyes stared up at the ceiling. While Hendricks finished scrubbing, I looked at the body and touched the skin. It was cold and smooth, the color gray-white. Just what you'd expect for a girl who had bled to death.

Hendricks checked to see that there was film in the camera, then waved me aside while he took three pictures from different angles.

I said, "Have you got her chart?"

"No. The old man has that. All I've got is a summary of the OPD discharge."

"Which was?"

"Clinical diagnosis of death secondary to vaginal hemorrhage complicated by systemic anaphylaxis."

"Systemic anaphylaxis? Why?"

"Beats me," Hendricks said. "Something happened in the OPD, but I couldn't find out."

"That's interesting," I said.

Hendricks finished with his pictures and went to the blackboard. Most labs have a blackboard, on which the pathologist can write his findings as he makes them—surface markings of the body, weight and appearance of organs, that sort of thing. He went to the board and wrote, "Randall, K." and the case number.

At that moment, another man entered the room. I recognized the bald, stooping figure of Leland Weston. He was in his sixties, about to retire, and despite his stoop he had a kind of energy and vigorousness. He shook hands with me briskly, then with Hendricks, who seemed very relieved to see him.

Weston took over the autopsy himself. He began, as I remembered he always did, by walking around the body a half-dozen times, staring at it intently, and muttering to himself. Finally he stopped and glanced at me.

"Observed her, John?"

"Yes."

"What do you make of it?"

"Recent weight gain," I said. "There are striation marks on her hips and breasts. She is also overweight."

"Good," Weston said. "Anything else?"

"Yes," I said. "She has an interesting hair distribution. She has blonde hair, but there is a thin line of dark hair on her upper lip, and some more on her forearms. It looks sparse and fine to me, new looking."

"Good," Weston said, nodding. He gave me a slight, crooked grin, the grin of my old teacher. For that matter, Weston had trained most of the pathologists in Boston at one time or another. "But," he said, "you've missed the most important finding."

He pointed to the pubic area, which was cleanly shaven. "That," he said.

"But she's had an abortion," Hendricks said. "We all know that."

"Nobody," Weston said sternly, "knows anything until the post is completed. We can't afford to prediagnose." He smiled. "That is a recreation reserved for the clinicians." He pulled on a pair of gloves and said, "This autopsy report is going to be the best and most accurate we can make. Because J. D. Randall will be going over it with a fine comb. Now then." He examined the pubic area closely. "The differential of a shaved groin is difficult. It may imply an operation, but many patients do it for purely personal reasons. In this case, we might note that it was carefully done, with no nicks or small cuts at all. That is significant: there isn't a nurse in the world who can do a pre-op shave on a fleshy region like this without making at least one small slip. Nurses are in a hurry and small cuts don't matter. So . . ."

"She shaved herself," Hendricks said.

"Probably," Weston nodded. "Of course, that doesn't rule in or out an operation. But it should be kept in mind."

He proceeded with the autopsy, working smoothly and quickly. He measured the girl at five-four and weighed her at one-forty. Considering the fluid she had lost, that was pretty heavy. Weston wrote it on the blackboard and made his first cut.

The standard autopsy incision is a Y-shaped cut running down from each shoulder, meeting at the midline of the body at the bottom of the ribs, and then continuing as a single incision to the pubic bone. The skin and muscle is then peeled away in three flaps; the ribs are cut open, exposing the lungs and heart; the abdomen is widely incised. Then the carotid arteries are tied and cut, the colon is tied and cut, the trachea and pharynx are cut—and the entire viscera, heart, lungs, stomach, liver, spleen, kidneys, and intestine are removed in a single motion.

After that, the eviscerated body is sewn shut. The isolated organs can then be examined at leisure, and sections cut for microscopic examination. While the pathologist is doing this, the deaner cuts the scalp open, removes the skullcap, and takes out the brain if permission for brain removal has been obtained.

Then I realized: there was no deaner here.[7] I mentioned this to Weston.

"That's right," he said. "We're doing this one by ourselves. Completely."

I watched as Weston made his cut. His hands trembled slightly, but his touch was still remarkably swift and efficient. As he opened the abdomen, blood welled out.

"Quick," he said. "Suction."

Hendricks brought a bottle attached to a suction hose. The abdominal fluid—dark red-black, mostly blood—was removed and measured in the bottle. Altogether, nearly three liters were withdrawn.

"I wish we had the chart," Weston said. "I'd like to know how many units they gave her in the EW."

I nodded. The normal blood volume in an average person was only

[7] Deaner is a traditional term for the man who takes care of the dissecting room. It is an ancient term, dating back to the days when anatomy dissections were done by horse gelders and butchers. The deaner keeps the rooms clean, cares for the corpses, and aids in the dissection.

about five quarts. To have so much in the abdomen implied a perforation somewhere.

When the fluid was drained, Weston continued the dissection, removing the organs and placing them in a stainless-steel pan. He carried them to the sink and washed them, then examined them one by one, beginning at the top, with the thyroid.

"Peculiar," he said, holding it in his hand. "It feels like fifteen grams or so."

The normal thyroid weighed between twenty and thirty.

"But probably a normal variation," Weston said. He cut it open and examined the cut surface. We could see nothing unusual.

Then he incised the trachea, opening it down to the bifurcation into the lungs, which were expanded and pale white, instead of their normal pink-purple.

"Anaphylaxis," Weston said. "Systemic. Any idea what she was hypersensitive to?"

"No," I said.

Hendricks was taking notes. Weston deftly followed the bronchi down into the lungs, then opened the pulmonary arteries and veins.

He moved on to the heart, which he opened by making two looping incisions into the right and left sides, exposing all four chambers. "Perfectly normal." Then he opened the coronary arteries. They were normal too, patent with little atherosclerosis.

Everything else was normal until we got to the uterus. It was purplish with hemorrhagic blood, and not very large, about the size and shape of a light bulb, with the ovaries and fallopian tubes leading into it. As Weston turned it in his hands, we saw the slice through the endometrium and muscle. That explained the bleeding into the peritoneal cavity.

But I was bothered by the size. It just didn't look like a pregnant uterus to me, particularly if the girl was four months' pregnant. At four months, the fetus was six inches long, with a pumping heart, developing eye and face, and forming bones. The uterus would be markedly enlarged.

Weston thought the same thing. "Of course," he said, "she probably got some oxytocin[8] at the EW, but still, it's damned peculiar."

He cut through the uterine wall and opened it up. The inside had been scraped quite well and carefully; the perforation was obviously a late development. Now, the inside of the uterus was filled with blood and numerous translucent, yellowish clots.

[8] A drug to contract the uterus, useful for initiating birth and for stopping uterine bleeding.

"Chicken-fat clots,"[9] Weston said. That meant it was post-mortem.

He cleaned away the blood and clots and examined the scraped endometrial surface carefully.

"This wasn't done by a total amateur," Weston said. "Somebody knew at least the basic principles of curettage."

"Except for the perforation."

"Yes," he said. "Except for that."

"Well," he said, "at least we already know one thing. She didn't do it to herself."

That was an important point. A large proportion of acute vaginal hemorrhages are the result of women attempting self-abortion, with drugs, or salt solutions, or soaps, or knitting needles and other devices. But Karen couldn't have done this kind of scraping on herself. This required a general anesthetic for the patient.

I said, "Does this look like a pregnant uterus to you?"

"Questionable," Weston said. "Very questionable. Let's check the ovaries."

Weston incised the ovaries, looking for the corpus luteum, the yellow spot that persists after the ovum has been released. He didn't find one. In itself, that proved nothing; the corpus luteum began to degenerate after three months, and this girl was supposedly in her fourth month.

The deaner came in and said to Weston, "Shall I close up now?"

"Yes," Weston said. "You might as well."

The deaner began to suture the incision and wrap the body in a clean shroud. I turned to Weston. "Aren't you going to examine the brain?"

"No permission," Weston said.

The medical examiner, though he demanded an autopsy, usually did not insist on brain examination unless the situation suggested possible neuropathy.

"But I would have thought a family like the Randalls, medically oriented . . ."

"Oh, J. D. is all for it. It's Mrs. Randall. She just refuses to have the brain removed, absolutely refuses. Ever met her?"

I shook my head.

"Quite a woman," Weston said dryly.

He turned back to the organs, working down the GI tract from esophagus to anus. It was completely normal. I left before he finished everything; I had seen what I wanted to see and knew that the final report

[9] See Appendix I: Delicatessen Pathologists.

would be equivocal. At least on the basis of the gross organs, they would be unable to say that Karen Randall was definitely pregnant.

That was peculiar.

SIX

I HAVE TROUBLE BUYING LIFE INSURANCE. Most pathologists do: the companies take one look at you and shudder—constant exposure to tuberculosis, malignancies, and lethal infectious disease makes you a very poor risk. The only person I know who has more trouble getting insured is a biochemist named Jim Murphy.

When he was younger, Murphy played halfback for Yale and was named to the All-East team. That in itself is an accomplishment, but it is amazing if you know Murphy and have seen his eyes. Murphy is practically blind. He wears lenses an inch thick and walks with his head drooping, as if the weight of the glass burdened him down. His vision is barely adequate under most circumstances, but when he gets excited or tight, he walks into things.

On the surface it would not seem that Murphy had the makings of a halfback, even at Yale. To know his secret, you have to see him move. Murphy is fast. He also has the best balance of anyone I know. When he was playing football, his teammates devised a series of plays especially designed to allow the quarterback to point Murphy in the proper direction and send him on his way. This usually worked, though on several occasions Murphy made brilliant runs in the wrong direction, twice charging over the goal line for a safety.

He has always been drawn to unlikely sports. At the age of thirty, he decided to take up mountain climbing. He found it very agreeable, but he couldn't get insured. So he switched to sports-car racing and was doing very well until he drove a Lotus off the track, rolled it four times, and broke both clavicles in several places. After that, he decided he'd rather be insured than active, so he gave it all up.

Murphy is so fast he even speaks in a kind of shorthand, as if he can't be bothered putting all the articles and pronouns into his sentences. He drives his secretaries and technicians mad, not only because of his speech, but also because of the windows. Murphy keeps them wide open, even in winter, and he is an unrelenting opponent of what he calls "bad air."

When I walked into his lab in one wing of the BLI[1] I found it filled with apples. There were apples in the refrigerators, on the reagent benches, on desks as paperweights. His two technicians, wearing heavy sweaters under their lab coats, were both eating apples as I entered.

"Wife," Murphy said, shaking hand with me. "Makes a specialty. Want one? I have Delicious and Cortland today."

"No, thanks," I said.

He took a bite from one after polishing it briskly on his sleeve. "Good. Really."

"I haven't got time," I said.

"Always in a rush," Murph said. "Jesus Christ, always in a rush. Haven't seen you or Judith for months. What've you been up to? Terry's playing guard on the Belmont first eleven."

He lifted a picture from his desk and held it under my nose. It showed his son in a football uniform, growling into the camera, looking like Murph: small, but tough.

"We'll have to get together soon," I said to him, "and talk about families."

"Ummmm." Murph devoured his apple with remarkable speed. "Let's do that. How's bridge game? Wife and I had an absolutely devastating time last weekend. Two weekends ago. Playing with——"

"Murph," I said. "I have a problem."

"Probably an ulcer," Murph said, selecting another apple from a row along his desk. "Nervous guy I know. Always in a rush."

"Actually," I said, "this is right up your alley."

He grinned in sudden interest. "Steroids? First time in history a pathologist's interested in steroids, I bet." He sat down behind his desk and propped his feet up. "Ready and waiting. Shoot."

Murphy's work concerned steroid production in pregnant women and fetuses. He was located in the BLI for a practical, if somewhat grisly reason—he needed to be near the source of supply, which in his case was clinic mothers and the occasional stillbirths[2] assigned to him.

"Can you do a hormone test for pregnancy at autopsy?" I asked.

He scratched his head in swift, nervous fluttery movements. "Hell. Suppose so. But who'd want to?"

"I want to."

---

[1] Boston Lying-In Hospital.

[2] Stillbirths, abortuses and placentas are in hot demand at the BLI for the dozen or so groups doing hormone research. Sometimes rather bitter arguments break out over who needs the next dead baby most for their studies.

"What I mean is, can't you tell at autopsy if she's pregnant or not?"

"Actually, no, in this case. It's very confused."

"Well. No accepted test, but I imagine it could be done. How far along?"

"Four months, supposedly."

"Four months? And you can't tell from the uterus?"

"Murph—"

"Yeah, sure, it could be done at four months," he said. "Won't stand up in a courtroom or anything, but yeah. Could be done."

"Can you do it?"

"That's all we do in this lab," he said. "Steroid assays. What've you got?"

I didn't understand; I shook my head.

"Blood or urine. Which?"

"Oh. Blood." I reached into my pocket and drew out a test tube of blood I had collected at the autopsy. I'd asked Weston if it was O.K., and he said he didn't care.

Murph took the tube and held it to the light. He flicked it with his finger. "Need two cc's," he said. "Plenty here. No problem."

"When will you let me know?"

"Two days. Assay takes forty-eight hours. This is post blood?"

"Yes. I was afraid the hormones might be denatured or something . . ."

Murph sighed. "How little we remember. Only proteins can be denatured, and steroids are not proteins, right? This'll be easy. See, the normal rabbit test is chorionic gonadotrophin in urine. But in this lab we're geared to measure that, or progesterone, or any of a number of other eleven-beta hydroxylated compounds. In pregnancy, progesterone levels increase ten times. Estriol levels increase a thousand times. We can measure a jump like that, no sweat." He glanced at his technicians. "Even in *this* lab."

One of the technicians took up the challenge. "I used to be accurate," she said, "before I got frostbite on my fingers."

"Excuses, excuses," Murphy grinned. He turned back to me and picked up the tube of blood. "This'll be easy. We'll just pop it onto the old fractionating column and let it perk through," he said. "Maybe we'll do two independent aliquots, just in case one gets fouled up. Who's it from?"

"What?"

He waved the test tube in front of me impatiently. "Whose blood?"

"Oh. Just a case," I said, shrugging.

"A four-month pregnancy and you can't be sure? John boy, not leveling with your old buddy, your old bridge opponent."

"It might be better," I said, "if I told you afterward."

"O.K., O.K. Far from me to pry. Your own way, but you *will* tell me?"

"Promise."

"A pathologist's promise," he said, standing up, "rings of the eternal."

SEVEN

THE LAST TIME ANYONE COUNTED, there were 25,000 named diseases of man, and cures for 5,000 of them. Yet it remains the dream of every young doctor to discover a new disease. That is the fastest and surest way to gain prominence within the medical profession. Practically speaking, it is much better to discover a new disease than to find a cure for an old one; your cure will be tested, disputed, and argued over for years, while a new disease is readily and rapidly accepted.

Lewis Carr, while still an intern, hit the jackpot: he found a new disease. It was pretty rare—a hereditary dysgammaglobulinemia affecting the beta-fraction which he found in a family of four—but that was not important. The important thing was that Lewis discovered it, described it, and published his results in the *New England Journal of Medicine*.

Six years later he was made clinical professor at the Mem. There was never any question he would be; simply a matter of waiting until somebody on the staff retired and vacated an office.

Carr had a good office in terms of status at the Mem; it was perfect for a young hot shot internist. For one thing, it was cramped and made even worse by the stacks of journals, texts, and research papers scattered all around. For another, it was dirty and old, tucked away in an obscure corner of the Calder Building, near the kidney research unit. And for the finishing touch, amid the squalor and mess sat a beautiful secretary, looking sexy, efficient, and wholly unapproachable: a nonfunctional beauty to contrast with the functional ugliness of the office.

"Dr. Carr is making rounds," she said without smiling. "He asked for you to wait inside."

I went in and took a seat, after removing a stack of back issues of the *American Journal of Experimental Biology* from the chair. A few moments later, Carr arrived. He wore a white lab coat, open at the front (a clinical professor would never button his lab coat) and a stethoscope around his neck. His shirt collar was frayed (clinical professors aren't paid much), but his black shoes gleamed (clinical professors are careful about things that really count). As usual, his manner was very cool, very collected, very political.

Unkind souls said Carr was more than political, that he shamelessly sucked up to the senior staff men. But many people resented his swift success and his confident manner. Carr had a round and childlike face; his cheeks were smooth and ruddy. He had an engaging boyish grin that went over very well with the female patients. He gave me that grin now.

"Hi, John." He shut the door to his outer office and sat down behind his desk. I could barely see him over the stacked journals. He removed the stethoscope from his neck, folded it, and slipped it into his pocket. Then he looked at me.

I guess it's inevitable. Any practicing doctor who faces you from behind a desk gets a certain manner, a thoughtful-probing-inquisitive air which is unsettling if there's nothing wrong with you. Lewis Carr got that way now.

"You want to know about Karen Randall," he said, as if reporting a serious finding.

"Right."

"For personal reasons."

"Right."

"And anything I tell you goes no further?"

"Right."

"O.K.," he said. "I'll tell you. I wasn't present, but I have followed things closely."

I knew that he would have. Lewis Carr followed everything at the Mem closely; he knew more local gossip than any of the nurses. He gathered his knowledge reflexively, the way some other people breathed air.

"The girl presented in the outpatient ward at four this morning. She was moribund on arrival; when they sent a stretcher out to the car she was delirious. Her trouble was frank vaginal hemorrhage. She had a temperature of 102, dry skin with decreased turgor, shortness of breath, a racing pulse, and low blood pressure. She complained of thirst."[1]

Carr took a deep breath. "The intern looked at her and ordered a cross match so they could start a transfusion. He drew a syringe for a count and crit[2] and rapidly injected a liter of D 5.[3] He also attempted to locate the source of the hemorrhage but he could not, so he gave her oxytocin

---

[1] Thirst is an important symptom in shock. For unknown reasons, it appears only in severe shock due to fluid loss, and is regarded as an ominous sign.

[2] White count and hematocrit.

[3] Five percent dextrose in water, used to replace lost fluid volume.

to clamp down the uterus and slow bleeding, and packed the vagina as a temporary measure. Then he found out who the girl was from the mother and shit in his pants. He panicked. He called in the resident. He started the blood. And he gave her a good dose of prophylactic penicillin. Unfortunately, he did this without consulting her chart or asking the mother about allergic reactions."

"She was hypersensitive."[4]

"Severely," Carr said. "Ten minutes after giving the penicillin i.m.[5] the girl went into choking spasms and appeared unable to breathe despite a patent airway. By now the chart was down from the record room, and the intern realized what he had done. So he administered a milligram of epinephrine i.m. When there was no response, he went to a slow IV, benadryl, cortisone, and aminophylline. They put her on positive pressure oxygen. But she became cyanotic,[6] convulsive, and died within twenty minutes."

I lit a cigarette and thought to myself that I wouldn't like to be that intern now.

"Probably," Carr said, "the girl would have died anyway. We don't know that for sure, but there's every reason to think that at admission her blood loss already approached fifty percent. That seems to be the cutoff, as you know—the shock is usually irreversible. So we probably couldn't have kept her. Of course, that doesn't change anything."

I said, "Why'd the intern give penicillin in the first place?"

"That's a peculiarity of hospital procedure," Carr said. "It's a kind of routine around here for certain presenting symptoms. Normally when we get a girl with evidence of a vaginal bleed and a high fever—possible infection—we give the girl a D & C, put her to bed, and stick her a shot of antibiotic. Send her home the next day, usually. And it goes down on the charts as miscarriage."

"Is that the final diagnosis on Karen Randall's record? Miscarriage?"

Carr nodded. "Spontaneous. We always put it down that way, because if we do that, we don't have to fool with the police. We see quite a few self-induced or illegally induced abortions here. Sometimes the girls come in with so much vaginal soap they foam like overloaded dishwashers. Other times, it's bleeding. In every case, the girl is hysterical and full of wild lies. We just take care of it quietly and send her on her way."

---

[4] Penicillin reactions occur in 9–10% of normal patients.
[5] Intramuscularly.
[6] Blue.

"And never report it to the police?"[7]

"We're doctors, not law-enforcement officers. We see about a hundred girls a year this way. If we reported every one, we'd all spend our time in court testifying and not practicing medicine."

"But doesn't the law require——"

"Of course," Carr said quickly. "The law requires that we report it. The law also requires that we report assaults, but if we reported every drunk who got into a bar brawl, we'd never hear the end of it. No emergency ward reports everything it should. You just can't operate on that basis."

"But if there's been an abortion——"

"Look at it logically," Carr said. "A significant number of these cases are spontaneous miscarriages. A significant number aren't, but it doesn't make sense for us to treat it any other way. Suppose you know that the butcher of Barcelona worked on a girl; suppose you call in the police. They show up the next day and the girl tells them it was spontaneous. Or she tells them she tried it on herself. But either way she won't talk, so the police are annoyed. Mostly, with you, because you called them in."

"Does this happen?"

"Yes," Carr said, "I've seen it happen twice myself. Both times, the girl showed up crazy with fear, convinced she was going to die. She wanted to nail the abortionist, so she demanded the police be called in. But by morning, she was feeling fine, she'd had a nice hospital D & C, and she realized her problems were over. She didn't want to fool with the police; she didn't want to get involved. So when the cops came, she pretended it was all a big mistake."

"Are you content to clean up after the abortionists and let it go?"

"We are trying to restore people to health. That's all. A doctor can't make value judgments. We clean up after a lot of bad drivers and mean drunks, too. But it isn't our job to slap anybody's hand and give them a lecture on driving or alcohol. We just try to make them well again."

I wasn't going to argue with him; I knew it wouldn't do any good. So I changed the subject.

"What about the charges against Lee? What happened there?"

"When the girl died," Carr said, "Mrs. Randall became hysterical. She started to scream, so they gave her a tranquilizer and sedative. After that, she settled down, but she continued to claim that her daughter had named Lee as the abortionist. So she called the police."

"Mrs. Randall did?"

[7] See Appendix II: Cops and Doctors.

"That's right."

"What about the hospital diagnosis?"

"It remains miscarriage. That is a legitimate medical interpretation. The change to illegal abortion is made on nonclinical grounds, so far as we are concerned. The autopsy will show whether an abortion was performed."

"The autopsy showed it," I said. "Quite a good abortion, too, except for a single laceration of the endometrium. It was done by someone with skill—but not quite enough skill."

"Have you talked with Lee?"

"This morning," I said. "He claims he didn't do it. On the basis of that autopsy, I believe him."

"A mistake—"

"I don't think so. Art's too good, too capable."

Carr removed the stethoscope from his pocket and played with it, looked uncomfortable. "This is a very messy thing," he said. "Very messy."

"It has to be cleared up," I said. "We can't hide our heads in the sand and let Lee go to hell."

"No, of course not," Carr said. "But J. D. was very upset."

"I imagine so."

"He practically killed that poor intern when he saw what treatment had been given. I was there, and I thought he was going to strangle the kid with his bare hands."

"Who was the intern?"

"Kid named Roger Whiting. Nice kid, even though he went to P & S."

"Where is he now?"

"At home, probably. He went off at eight this morning." Carr frowned and fiddled once more with his stethoscope. "John," he said, "are you sure you want to get involved in this?"

"I don't want anything to do with it," I said. "If I had my choice, I'd be back in my lab now. But I don't see any choice."

"The trouble is," Carr said slowly, "that this thing has gotten out of control. J. D. is very upset."

"You said that before."

"I'm just trying to help you understand how things are." Carr rearranged things on his desk and did not look at me. Finally he said, "The case is in the proper hands. And I understand Lee has a good lawyer."

"There are a lot of dangling questions. I want to be sure they're all cleaned up."

"It's in the proper hands," Carr said again.

"Whose hands? The Randalls? The goons I saw down at the police station?"

"We have an excellent police force in Boston," Carr said.

"Bullshit."

He sighed patiently and said, "What can you hope to prove?"

"That Lee didn't do it."

Carr shook his head. "That's not the point."

"It seems to me that's precisely the point."

"No," Carr said. "The point is that the daughter of J. D. Randall was killed by an abortionist, and somebody has to pay. Lee's an abortionist—that won't be hard to prove in court. In a Boston court, the jury is likely to be more than half Catholic. They'll convict him on general principles."

"On general principles?"

"You know what I mean," Carr said, shifting in his chair.

"You mean Lee's the goat."

"That's right. Lee's the goat."

"Is that the official word?"

"More or less," Carr said.

"And what are your feelings about it?"

"A man who performs abortions puts himself in danger. He's breaking the law. When he aborts the daughter of a famous Boston physician—"

"Lee says he didn't do it."

Carr gave a sad smile. "Does it matter?"

EIGHT

IT TAKES THIRTEEN YEARS from the time you leave college to the time you become a cardiac surgeon. You have four years of medical school, a year of internship, three of general surgery, two of thoracic surgery, two of cardiac surgery. Somewhere along the line, you spend two years working for Uncle Sam.[1]

It takes a certain kind of man to assume this burden, to set his sights on such a distant goal. By the time he is ready to begin surgery on his own, he has become another person, almost a new breed, estranged by

[1] See Appendix III: Battlefields and Barberpoles.

his experience and his dedication from other men. In a sense, that is part of the training: surgeons are lonely men.

I thought of this as I looked down through the glass overhead viewing-booth into OR 9. The booth was built into the ceiling, allowing you a good view of the entire room, the staff, and the procedure. Students and residents often sat up here and watched. There was a microphone in the OR, so that you heard everything—the clink of instruments, the rhythmic hiss of the respirator, the quiet voices—and there was a button you could press to talk to the people below. Otherwise they could not hear you.

I had come to this room after going to J. D. Randall's office. I had wanted to see the chart on Karen, but Randall's secretary said she didn't have it. J. D. had it, and J. D. was in surgery now. That had surprised me. I had thought he would have taken the day off, considering. But apparently it had not entered his mind.

The secretary said the operation was probably almost over, but one look through the glass told me it was not. The chest of the patient was still open and the heart was still incised; they had not even begun suturing. There I was not going to interrupt them; I'd have to come back later to try and get the chart.

But I stayed a moment to watch. There is something compelling about open-heart surgery, something fantastic and fabulous, a mixture of dream and nightmare, all come true. There were sixteen people in the room below me, including four surgeons. Everyone was moving, working, checking in smooth, coordinated movements, like a kind of ballet, like a surrealistic ballet. The patient, draped in green, was dwarfed by the heart-lung machine alongside him, a giant complex as large as an automobile, shining steel, with smoothly moving cylinders and wheels.

At the head of the patient was the anesthetist, surrounded by equipment. There were several nurses, two pump technicians who monitored the dials and gauges on the machine, nurses, orderlies, and the surgeons. I tried to tell which was Randall, but I could not; in their gowns and masks, they all looked the same, impersonal, interchangeable. That was not true, of course. One of those four men had responsibility for everything, for the conduct of all sixteen workers present. And responsibility for the seventeenth person in that room, the man whose heart was stopped.

In one corner, displayed on a television, was the electrocardiogram. The normal EKG is a briskly bouncing line, with spikes for every heartbeat, every wave of electrical energy that fires the heart muscle. This one was flat: just a meaningless squiggle. That meant that according to one major criterion of medicine, the patient was dead. I looked at the pink lungs through the open chest; they were not moving. The patient was not breathing.

The machine did all that for him. It pumped his blood, oxygenated it, removed the carbon dioxide. In its present form, the machine had been in use for about ten years.

The people below me did not seem in awe of the machine or the surgical procedure. They worked matter-of-factly at their jobs. I suppose that was one reason why it all seemed so fantastic.

I watched for five minutes without realizing the time. Then I left. Outside, in the corridor, two residents slouched in a doorway, still wearing their caps with their masks hanging loosely around their necks. They were eating doughnuts and coffee, and laughing about a blind date.

NINE

ROGER WHITING, M.D., lived near the hospital in a third-floor walkup on the sleazy side of Beacon Hill, where they dump the garbage from Louisburg Square. His wife answered the door. She was a plain girl, about seven months' pregnant. She looked worried.

"What do you want?"

"I'd like to talk to your husband. My name's Berry. I'm a pathologist at the Lincoln."

She gave me a hard suspicious glance. "My husband is trying to sleep. He's been on call for the last two days, and he's tired. He's trying to sleep."

"It's very important."

A slim young man in white ducks appeared behind her. He looked more than tired; he looked exhausted and afraid. He said, "What is it?"

"I'd like to talk to you about Karen Randall."

"I've been over it," he said, "a dozen times. Talk to Dr. Carr about it."

"I did."

Whiting ran his hands through his hair, then said to his wife, "It's O.K., honey. Get me some coffee, would you?" He turned to me. "Want some coffee?"

"Please," I said.

We sat in the living room. The apartment was small, the furniture cheap and rickety. But I felt at home: it had been only a few years since

I had done my own internship. I knew all about the money problems, the stresses, the hellish hours, and the slop work you had to do. I knew about the irritating calls from nurses in the middle of the night, asking you to okay another aspirin for patient Jones. I knew how you could drag yourself out of bed to see a patient and how you could, in the small hours of the morning, make a mistake. I had nearly killed an old man with heart failure when I was an intern. With three hours of sleep during the last two days, you could do anything and not give a damn.

"I know you're tired," I said. "I won't stay long."

"No, no," he said very earnestly. "Anything I can do to help. I mean, now . . ."

The wife came in with two cups of coffee. She looked at me angrily. The coffee was weak.

"My questions," I said, "have to do with the girl when she first arrived. Were you in the ward?"

"No. I was trying to sleep. They called me."

"What time was this?"

"Almost exactly four."

"Describe what happened."

"I was sleeping in my clothes, in that little room just off the OPD. I wasn't asleep long when they called me; I'd just gotten through putting another IV into a lady who pulls them out. She says she doesn't, but she does." He sighed. "Anyway, when they called me, I was bleary as hell. I got up and dunked my head in cold water, then toweled off. When I got to the ward, they were bringing the girl in on a stretcher."

"Was she conscious?"

"Yes, but disoriented. She was pale, and she'd lost a lot of blood. She was feverish and delirious. We couldn't get a good temperature because she kept gnashing her teeth, so we figured it was about 102 and got to work on the cross-matching."

"What else was done?"

"The nurses got a blanket over her and propped her feet up with shock blocks.[1] Then I examined the lesion. It was very clearly vaginal hemorrhage and we diagnosed it as miscarriage."

"About the bleeding," I said, "was there any discharge accompanying it?" He shook his head. "Just blood."

"No tissue? No signs of a placenta?"

"No. But she'd been bleeding for a long time. Her clothes . . ." He

---

[1] Shock blocks are simply wooden blocks used to elevate the legs in cases of shock, helping to get blood to the head.

looked across the room, seeing it again in his mind. "Her clothes were very heavy. The nurses had trouble getting them off."

"During this time, did the girl say anything coherent?"

"Not really. She was mumbling every once in a while. Something about an old man, I think. Her old man, or an old man. But it wasn't clear, and nobody was really paying any attention."

"Did she say anything else?"

He shook his head. "Just when they were cutting her clothes off her. She would try to pull them back. Once she said, 'You can't do this to me.' And then later she said, 'Where am I?' But that was just delirious talk. She wasn't really coherent."

"What did you do about the bleeding?"

"I tried to localize it. It was hard, and things were pretty rushed. And we couldn't angle the lights down properly. Finally I decided to pack it with gauze pads and concentrate on getting her blood volume back up."

"Where was Mrs. Randall during all this?"

"She waited by the door. She seemed all right until we had to tell her what had happened. Then she went to pieces. Just went to pieces."

"What about Karen's records? Had she ever been admitted to the hospital before?"

"I didn't see her chart," he said, "until . . . later. They had to be pulled from the record room. But she had been in before. Pap smears every year since she was fifteen. Usual blood tests from her twice-yearly physicals. She was well looked after medically, as you might expect."

"Was there anything unusual in her past history? Besides the hypersensitivity, I mean."

He gave a sad smile. "Isn't that enough?"

For a fleeting moment I was angry with him. He was soaking in self-pity, despite his natural fright. But I wanted to tell him he'd better get used to the idea of people dying in front of him, lots of people. And he'd better get used to the idea that he could make a mistake, because they happened. Sometimes the mistakes were balder than others, but it was just degree. I wanted to tell him if he'd asked Mrs. Randall about Karen's hypersensitivity, and she'd said the girl was O.K., that Whiting would have been free and clear. The girl would still have died, of course, but Whiting would be clear. His mistake was not killing Karen Randall; it was not asking permission first.

I thought about saying this, but I didn't.

"Any indication in the chart of psychiatric problems?" I asked.

"No."

"Nothing unusual at all?"

"No." Then he frowned. "Wait a minute. There was one strange thing. A complete set of skull films were ordered about six months ago."

"Did you see the films?"

"No. I just read the radiologist's dx."

"And what was that?"

"Normal. No pathology."

"Why were the films taken?"

"It didn't say."

"Was she in an accident of some kind? A fall, or an auto accident?"

"Not that I know of."

"Who ordered the films?"

"Probably Dr. Randall. Peter Randall, that is. He was her doctor."

"And you don't know why the X rays were taken?"

"No."

"But there must be a reason," I said.

"Yes," he said, but he didn't seem very interested. He stared moodily at his coffee, then sipped it. Finally he said, "I hope they take that abortionist and screw him to the wall. Whatever he gets, he deserves worse."

I stood. The boy was under stress and almost on the verge of tears. All he could see was a promising medical career jeopardized because he had made a mistake with the daughter of a prominent physician. In his anger and frustration and self-pity, he, too, was looking for a goat. And he needed one worse than most.

"Are you planning to settle in Boston?" I asked.

"I was," he said with a wry look.

WHEN I LEFT THE INTERN I called Lewis Carr. I wanted to see Karen Randall's chart more than ever. I had to find out about those X rays.

"Lew," I said. "I'm going to need your help again."

"Oh?" He sounded thrilled by the prospect.

"Yes. I've got to get her chart. It's imperative."

"I thought we went over that."

"Yes, but something new has come up. This thing is getting crazier by the minute. Why were X rays ordered——"

"I'm sorry," Carr said. "I can't help you."

"Lew, even if Randall does have the chart, he can't keep——"

"I'm sorry, John. I'm going to be tied up here for the rest of the day and most of tomorrow. I'm just not going to have time."

He was speaking formally, a man counting his words, repeating the sentences over to himself before speaking them aloud.

"What happened? Randall get to you and button your mouth?"

"I feel," Carr said, "that the case should be left in the hands of those best equipped to deal with it. I'm not, and I don't think other doctors are, either."

I knew what he was saying and what he meant. Art Lee used to laugh about the elaborate way doctors backed out of things, leaving behind a spoor of double-talk. Art called it The Pilate Maneuver.

"O.K.," I said, "if that's the way you feel."

I hung up.

In a way, I should have expected it. Lewis Carr always played the game, following all the rules, just like a good boy. That was the way he always had been, and the way he always would be.

TEN

MY ROUTE FROM WHITING to the medical school took me past the Lincoln Hospital. Standing out in front near the taxi stand was Frank Conway, hunched over, his hands in his pockets, looking down at the pavement. Something about his stance conveyed sadness and a deep, dulling fatigue. I pulled over to the curb.

"Need a ride?"

"I'm going to Children's," he said. He seemed surprised that I had stopped. Conway and I aren't close friends. He is a fine doctor but not pleasant as a man. His first two wives had divorced him, the second after only six months.

"Children's is on the way," I said.

It wasn't, but I'd take him anyway. I wanted to talk to him. He got in and I pulled out into traffic.

"What takes you to Children's?" I said.

"Conference. They have a congenital CPC once a week. You?"

"Just a visit," I said. "Lunch with a friend."

He nodded and sat back. Conway was young, only thirty-five. He had breezed through his residencies, working under the best men in the country. Now he was better than any of them, or so it was said. You couldn't be sure about a man like Conway: he was one of the few doctors who become so famous so fast that they take on some aspects of politicians and

movie stars; they acquire blindly loyal fans and blindly antagonistic critics; one either loves them or loathes them. Physically, Conway was a commanding presence, a stocky, powerful man with gray-flecked hair and
deep, piercing blue eyes.

"I wanted to apologize," Conway said, "about this morning. I didn't
mean to blow up that way."

"It's O.K."

"I have to apologize to Herbie. I said some things. . . ."

"He'll understand."

"I feel like hell," Conway said. "But when you watch a patient just collapse under you, just fall apart before your very eyes. . . . You don't know
how it is."

"I don't," I admitted.

We drove for a while in silence, then I said, "Can I ask you a favor?"

"Sure."

"Tell me about J. D. Randall."

He paused. "Why?"

"Just curious."

"Bullshit."

"All right," I said.

"They got Lee, didn't they?" Conway said.

"Yes."

"Did he do it?"

"No."

"Are you sure?"

"I believe what he tells me," I said.

Conway sighed. "John," he said, "you're not a fool. Suppose somebody
hung this thing on you. Wouldn't you deny it?"

"That's not the question."

"Sure it is. Anybody'd deny it."

"Isn't it possible Art didn't do it?"

"It's not merely possible. It's likely."

"Well then?"

Conway shook his head. "You're forgetting the way it works. J. D. is a
big man. J. D. lost a daughter. There happens to be a convenient Chinaman in the neighborhood, who is known to do the nasty deed. A perfect
situation."

"I've heard that theory before. I don't buy it."

"Then you don't know J. D. Randall."

"That's true."

"J. D. Randall," Conway said, "is the arch-prick of the universe. He has money and power and prestige. He can have whatever he wants—even a little Chinaman's head."

I said, "But why should he want it?"

Conway laughed. "Brother, where have you been?"

I must have looked puzzled.

"Don't you know about . . ." He paused, seeing that I did not. Then he very deliberately folded his arms across his chest and and said nothing. He stared straight ahead.

"Well?" I said.

"Better ask Art."

"I'm asking you," I said.

"Ask Lew Carr," Conway said. "Maybe he'll tell you. I won't."

"Well then," I said, "tell me about Randall."

"As a surgeon."

"All right, as a surgeon."

Conway nodded. "As a surgeon," he said, "he isn't worth shit. He's mediocre. He loses people he shouldn't lose. Young people. Strong people."

I nodded.

"And he's mean as hell. He chews out his residents, puts them through all sorts of crap, keeps them miserable. He has a lot of good young men working under him, and that's how he controls them. I know; I did two years of thoracic under Randall before I did my cardiac at Houston. I was twenty-nine when I first met Randall, and he was forty-nine. He comes on very strong with his busy manner and his Bond Street suits and his friends with châteaux in France. None of it means he's a good surgeon, of course, but it carries over. It throws a halo around him. It makes him look good."

I said nothing. Conway was warming to his subject, raising his voice, moving his strong hands. I didn't want him to stop.

"The trouble," Conway said, "is that J. D. is in the old line. He started surgery in the forties and fifties, with Gross and Chartriss and Shackleford and the boys. Surgery was different then; manual skill was important and science didn't really count. Nobody knew about electrolytes or chemistry, and Randall's never felt comfortable with it. The new boys are; they've been weaned on enzymes and serum sodium. But it's all a troublesome puzzle to Randall."

"He has a good reputation," I said.

"So did John Wilkes Booth," Conway said. "For a while."

"Do I sense a professional jealousy?"

"I can cut circles around him with my left hand," Conway said. "Blindfolded."

I smiled.

"And hung over," he added. "On a Sunday."

"What's he like personally?"

"A prick. Just a prick. The residents say he walks around with a hammer in his pocket and a half-dozen nails, just in case he sees the opportunity to crucify somebody."

"He can't be that unpleasant."

"No," Conway admitted. "Not unless he's in especially good form. Like all of us, he has his off days."

"You make him sound very grim."

"No worse than the average bastard," he said. "You know, the residents say something else, too."

"Oh?"

"Yes. They say J. D. Randall likes cutting hearts because he never had one of his own."

ELEVEN

NO ENGLISHMAN IN HIS RIGHT MIND would ever go to Boston, particularly in 1630. To embark on a long sea journey to a hostile wilderness took more than courage, more than fortitude—it required desperation and fanaticism. Above all it required a deep and irreconcilable break with English society.

Fortunately, history judges men by their actions, not their motivations. It is for that reason that Bostonians can comfortably think of their ancestors as proponents of democracy and freedom, Revolutionary heroes, liberal artists and writers. It is the city of Adams and Revere, a city that still cherishes the Old North Church and Bunker Hill.

But there is another face to Boston, a darker face, which lies hidden in the pillory, the stocks, the dunking stool, and the witch hunts. Hardly a man now alive can look at these devices of torture for what they are: evidences of obsession, neurosis, and perverse cruelty. They are proofs of a society encircled by fear of sin, damnation, hellfire, disease, and Indians—in roughly that order. A tense, fearful, suspicious society. In short, a society of reactionary religious fanatics.

There is also a geographical factor, for Boston was once a swamp. Some say this accounts for its outstandingly bad weather and uniformly humid climate; others say it is unimportant.

Bostonians are inclined to overlook much of the past. Like a slum kid who makes good, the city has swung far from its origins, and attempted to conceal them. As a colony of common men, it has established an untitled aristocracy to rival the most ancient and rigid of Europe. As a city of religion, it has developed a scientific community unrivaled in the East. It is also strongly narcissistic—a trait it shares with another city of questionable origin, San Francisco.

Unfortunately for both these cities, they can never quite escape their past. San Francisco cannot quite shake off its booming, crude, gold-rush spirit to become a genteel Eastern town. And Boston, no matter how hard it tries, cannot quite elude Puritanism and become English again.

We are all tied to the past, individually and collectively. The past shows through in the very structure of our bones, the distribution of our hair, and the coloring of our skin, as well as the way we walk, stand, eat, dress —and think.

I was reminded of this as I went to meet William Harvey Shattuck Randall, student of medicine.

ANYONE NAMED AFTER WILLIAM HARVEY[1] to say nothing of William Shattuck, must feel like a damned fool. Like being named after Napoleon or Cary Grant, it places too great a burden on a child, too much of a challenge. Many things in life are difficult to live down, but nothing is more difficult than a name.

George Gall is a perfect example. After medical school, where he suffered through countless jokes and puns, he became a surgeon, specializing in liver and gallbladder disease. It was the worst possible thing he could do with a name like that, but he went into it with a strange, quiet certainty, as if it had all been foreordained. In a sense perhaps it had. Years later, when the jokes began to wear very thin, he wished he could change his name, but that was impossible.[2]

I doubted that William Harvey Shattuck Randall would ever change his own name. Though a liability, it was also an asset, particularly if he remained in Boston; besides, he seemed to be bearing up well. He was husky and blond and open-faced in a pleasant way. There was an All-

---

[1] The English court physician who, in 1628, discovered that blood circulated in a closed loop.

[2] A doctor cannot change his name after receiving his M.D. degree without invalidating that degree. This means that there is a great rush in the final weeks of med school among doctors flocking into court to change their names before they receive their diplomas.

American wholesomeness about him which made his room incongruous and faintly ridiculous.

William Harvey Shattuck Randall lived on the first floor of Sheraton Hall, the medical-school dormitory. Like most rooms in the dorm, his was a single, though rather more spacious than most. Certainly more spacious than the fourth-floor pigeonhole I had occupied when I was a student. The top-floor rooms are cheaper.

They'd changed the paint color since my day. It was dinosaur-egg gray, then; now it was vomit green. But it was still the same old dorm—the same bleak corridors, the same dirty stairs, the same stale odor of sweat socks, textbooks, and hexachlorophene.

Randall had fixed his room up nicely. The decor was antique; the furniture looked as if it had been bought at a Versailles auction. There was a faded, nostalgic splendor about it, with its tattered red velvet and chipped gilded wood.

Randall stood back from the door. "Come in," he said. He didn't ask who I was. He had taken one look and smelled doctor. You get so you can do it, when you've been around them long enough.

I came into the room and sat down.

"Is it about Karen?" He seemed more preoccupied than sad, as if he had just returned from something important or were about to leave.

"Yes," I said. "I know this is a bad time . . ."

"No, go ahead."

I lit a cigarette and dropped the match into a gilded Venetian-glass ashtray. It was ugly but expensive.

"I wanted to talk to you about her."

"Sure."

I kept waiting for him to ask who I was, but he didn't really seem to care. He sat down in an armchair across from me, crossed his legs, and said, "What do you want to know?"

"When did you see her last?"

"Saturday. She came in from Northampton on the bus, and I picked her up at the terminal after lunch. I had a couple of hours free. I drove her out to the house."

"How did she seem?"

He shrugged. "Fine. There was nothing wrong with her, she seemed very happy. Talked all about Smith and her roommate. Apparently she had this wild roommate. And she talked about clothes, that sort of thing."

"Was she depressed? Nervous?"

"No. Not at all. She acted the same as always. Maybe a little excited about coming home after being away. I think she was a little worried about Smith. My parents treat her as the baby of the family, and she thought they didn't have confidence in her ability to make it. She was a little . . . defiant, I guess you'd say."

"When did you see her before last Saturday?"

"I don't know. Not since late August, I guess."

"So this was a reunion."

"Yes," he said. "I was always glad to see her. She was very bubbly, with a lot of energy, and she was a good mimic. She could give you an imitation of a professor or a boyfriend and she was hysterical. In fact, that was how she got the car."

"The car?"

"Saturday night," he said. "We were all at dinner. Karen, myself, Ev, and Uncle Peter."

"Ev?"

"My stepmother," he said. "We all call her Ev."

"So there were five of you?"

"No, four."

"What about your father?"

"He was busy at the hospital."

He said it very matter-of-factly, and I let it drop.

"Anyway," William said, "Karen wanted a car for the weekend and Ev refused, saying she didn't want her to be out all night. So Karen turned to Uncle Peter, who is a softer touch, and asked if she could borrow his car. He was reluctant, so she threatened to imitate him, and he immediately loaned her the car."

"What did Peter do for transportation?"

"I dropped him off at his place that night, on my way back here."

"So you spent several hours with Karen on Saturday."

"Yes. From around one o'clock to nine or ten."

"Then you left with your uncle?"

"Yes."

"And Karen?"

"She stayed with Ev."

"Did she go out that night?"

"I imagine so. That was why she wanted the car."

"Did she say where she was going?"

"Over to Harvard. She had some friends in the college."

"Did you see her Sunday?"

"No. Just Saturday."

"Tell me," I said, "when you were with her—did she look any different to you?"

He shook his head. "No. Just the same. Of course, she'd put on a little weight, but I guess all girls do that when they go to college. She was very active in the summer, playing tennis and swimming. She stopped that when she got to school, and I guess she put on a few pounds." He smiled slowly. "We kidded her about it. She complained about the lousy food, and we kidded her about eating so much of it that she still gained weight."

"Had she always had a weight problem?"

"Karen? No. She was always a skinny little kid, a real tomboy. Then she filled out in a real hurry. It was like a caterpillar, you know, and the cocoon."

"Then this was the first time she'd ever been overweight?"

He shrugged. "I don't know. To tell you the truth, I never paid that much attention."

"Was there anything else you noticed?"

"No, nothing else."

I looked around the room. On his desk, next to copies of Robbins' *Pathology and Surgical Anatomy,* was a photograph of the two of them. They both looked tanned and healthy. He saw me looking and said, "That was last spring, in the Bahamas. For once the whole family managed to get a week off together. We had a great time."

I got up and took a closer look. It was a flattering picture of her. Her skin was darkly tanned, contrasting nicely with her blue eyes and blonde hair.

"I know it's a peculiar question," I said, "but has your sister always had dark hair on her lips and arms?"

"That was funny," he said, in a slow voice. "Now that you mention it. She had just a little bit there, on Saturday, Peter told her she'd better bleach it or wax it. She got mad for a couple of minutes, and then she laughed."

"So it was new?"

"I guess so. She might have had it all along, but I never noticed it until then. Why?"

"I don't know," I said.

He stood and came over to the picture. "You'd never think she would be the type for an abortion," he said. "She was such a great girl, funny and happy and full of energy. She had a real heart of gold. I know that sounds stupid, but she did. She was kind of the family mascot, being the youngest. Everybody loved her."

I said, "Where was she this summer?"

He shook his head. "I don't know."

"You don't know?"

"Well, not exactly. In theory, Karen was on the Cape, working in an art gallery in Provincetown." He paused. "But I don't think she was there much. I think she spent most of her time on the Hill. She had some kooky friends there; she collected oddball types."

"Men friends? Women friends?"

"Both." He shrugged. "But I don't really know. She only mentioned it to me once or twice, in casual references. Whenever I tried to ask her about it, she'd laugh and change the subject. She was very clever about discussing only what she wanted to."

"Did she mention any names?"

"Probably, but I don't remember. She could be maddening about names, talking about people casually as if you knew them intimately. Using just their first names. It was no good reminding her that you'd never heard of Herbie and Su-su and Allie before." He laughed. "I do remember she once did an imitation of a girl who blew bubbles."

"But you can't remember any names?"

He shook his head. "Sorry."

I stood to go. "Well," I said, "you must be very tired. What are you on these days?"

"Surgery. We just finished OB-GYN."

"Like it?"

"It's O.K.," he said blandly.

As I was leaving, I said, "Where did you do your OB?"

"At the BLI." He looked at me for a moment and frowned. "And to answer your question, I assisted on several. I know how to do one. But I was on duty at the hospital Sunday night. All night long. So there it is."

"Thanks for your time," I said.

"Sure," he said.

AS I LEFT THE DORMITORY, I saw a tall, lean, silver-haired man walking toward me. Of course I recognized him, even from a distance.

J. D. Randall was, if nothing else, distinctive.

TWELVE

THE SUN WAS SETTING, and the light on the quadrangle was turning yellow-gold. I lit a cigarette and walked up to Randall. His eyes widened slightly as he saw me, and then he smiled.

"Dr. Berry."

Very friendly. He held out his hand. I shook it: dry, clean, scrubbed to two inches above the elbow for ten minutes. A surgeon's hand.

"How do you do, Dr. Randall."

He said, "You wanted to see me?"

I frowned.

"My secretary," he said, "told me you had stopped by my office. About the chart."

"Oh, yes," I said, "the chart."

He smiled benignly. He was half a head taller than I. "I think we had better clear up a few things."

"All right."

"Come with me."

He didn't intend it as a command, but it came out that way. I was reminded that surgeons were the last autocrats in society, the last class of men who were given total control over a situation. Surgeons assumed the responsibility for the welfare of the patient, the staff, everything.

We walked back toward the parking lot. I had the feeling that he had come especially to see me. I had no idea how he knew I was there, but the feeling was very strong. As he walked, he swung his arms loosely at his sides. For some reason, I watched them; I remembered the neurologist's law of swinging arms.[1] I saw his hands, which were huge, all out of proportion to the rest of his body, huge hands, thick and hairy and red. His nails were trimmed to the required one-millimeter surgical length. His hair was cut short and his eyes were cold, gray, and businesslike.

"Several people have mentioned your name to me lately," he said.

"Oh?"

"Yes."

We came into the parking lot. His car was a silver Porsche; he stopped beside it and leaned casually against the polished fender. Some-

[1] A paralyzed man will swing a paralyzed arm less than a good arm.

thing about his manner told me I was not invited to do the same. He looked at me for a moment in silence, his eyes flicking over my face, and then he said, "They speak highly of you."

"I'm glad to hear that."

"A man of good judgment and good sense."

I shrugged. He smiled at me again, then said, "Busy day?"

"Busier than some days."

"You're at the Lincoln, is that right?"

"Yes."

"You're well thought of there."

"I try to do a good job."

"I'm told your work is excellent."

"Thank you." His approach was throwing me off; I didn't see where he was going. I didn't have to wait long.

"Did you ever think of changing hospitals?"

"What do you mean?"

"There may be other . . . possibilities. Openings."

"Oh?"

"Indeed."

"I'm quite happy where I am."

"For the present," he said.

"Yes, for the present."

"Do you know William Sewall?"

William Sewall was chief pathologist of the Mem. He was sixty-one and would shortly retire. I found myself disappointed in J. D. Randall. The last thing I had expected him to be was obvious.

"Yes, I know Sewall," I said. "Slightly."

"He will soon retire—"

"Timothy Stone is second man there, and he's excellent."

"I suppose," Randall said. He stared up at the sky. "I suppose. But many of us are not happy with him."

"I hadn't heard that."

He smiled thinly. "It isn't widely known."

"And many of you would be happier with me?"

"Many of us," Randall said carefully, "are looking for a new man. Perhaps someone from the outside, to bring a new viewpoint to the hospital. Change things around a bit; shake things up."

"Oh?"

"That is our thinking," Randall said.

"Timothy Stone is a close friend," I said.

"I don't see the relevance of that."

"The relevance," I said, "is that I wouldn't screw him."

"I would never suggest that you do."

"Really?"

"No," Randall said.

"Then maybe I'm missing the point," I said.

He gave his pleasant smile. "Maybe you are."

"Why don't you explain?"

He scratched the back of his head reflectively. I could see he was about to change tactics, to try a different approach. He frowned.

"I'm not a pathologist, Dr. Berry," he said, "but I have some friends who are."

"Not Tim Stone, I'll bet."

"Sometimes I think pathologists work harder than surgeons, harder than anyone. Being a pathologist seems to be a full-time job."

"That may be right," I said.

"I'm surprised you have so much free time," he said.

"Well, you know how it is," I said. I was beginning to be angry. First the bribe, then the threat. Buy him off or scare him off. But along with my anger, I had a strange curiosity: Randall was not a fool, and I knew he wouldn't be talking this way to me unless he was afraid of something. I wondered for a moment whether he had done the abortion himself, and then he said, "You have a family?"

"Yes," I said.

"Been in Boston some time?"

"I can always leave," I said, "if I find the pathological specimens too distasteful."

He took that very well. He didn't move, didn't shift his weight on the fender of the car. He just looked at me with those gray eyes and said, "I see."

"Maybe you'd better come right out and tell me what's on your mind."

"It's quite simple," he said. "I'm concerned about your motives. I can understand the ties of friendship, and I can even see how personal affection can be blinding. I admire your loyalty to Dr. Lee, though I would admire it more if you chose a less reprehensible subject. However, your actions seem to extend beyond loyalty. What *are* your motives, Dr. Berry?"

"Curiosity, Dr. Randall. Pure curiosity. I want to know why everybody's out to screw an innocent guy. I want to know why a profession dedicated to the objective examination of facts has chosen to be biased and uninterested."

He reached into his suit pocket and took out a cigar case. He opened it and withdrew a single slim cigar, clipped off the end, and lit it.

"Let's be sure," he said, "that we know what we're talking about. Dr. Lee is an abortionist. Is that correct?"

"You're talking," I said. "I'm listening."

"Abortion is illegal. Furthermore, like every surgical procedure, it carries with it a finite risk to the patient—even if practiced by a competent person, and not a drunken . . ."

"Foreigner?" I suggested.

He smiled. "Dr. Lee," he said, "is an abortionist, operating illegally, and his personal habits are questionable. As a doctor, his ethics are questionable. As a citizen of the state, his actions are punishable in a court of law. That's what's on my mind, Dr. Berry. I want to know why you are snooping around, molesting members of my family—"

"I hardly think that's the word for it."

"—and making a general nuisance of yourself in this matter when you have better things to do, things for which the Lincoln Hospital pays you a salary. Like every other doctor, you have duties and responsibilities. You are not fulfilling those duties. Instead you are interfering in a family matter, creating a disturbance, and attempting to throw a smoke screen around a reprehensible individual, a man who has violated all the codes of medicine, a man who has chosen to live beyond the limits of the law, to thumb his nose at the dictates of the framework of society—"

"Doctor," I said. "Looking at this as purely a family matter: what would you have done if your daughter had come to you with the news that she was pregnant? What if she had consulted you instead of going directly to an abortionist? What would you have done?"

"There is no point in mindless conjecture," he said.

"Surely you have an answer."

He was turning a bright crimson. The veins in his neck stood out above his starched collar. He pursed his lips, then said, "Is this your intention? To slander my family in the wild hope of helping your so-called friend?"

I shrugged. "It strikes me as a legitimate question," I said, "and there are several possibilities." I ticked them off on my fingers. "Tokyo, Switzerland, Los Angeles, San Jaun. Or perhaps you have a good friend in New York or Washington. That would be much more convenient. And cheaper."

He turned on his heel and unlocked the door to his car.

"Think about it," I said. "Think hard about what you would have done for that family name."

He started the engine and glared at me.

"While you're at it," I said, "think about why she didn't come to you for help."

"My daughter," he said, his voice trembling with rage, "my daughter is a wonderful girl. She is sweet and beautiful. She doesn't have a malicious or dirty thought in her head. How dare you drag her down to your——"

"If she was so sweet and pure," I said, "how did she get pregnant?"

He slammed the door shut, put the car in gear, and roared off in a cloud of angry blue exhaust.

THIRTEEN

WHEN I RETURNED HOME, the house was dark and empty. A note in the kitchen told me that Judith was still over at the Lees with the kids. I walked around the kitchen and looked into the refrigerator; I was hungry but restless, unwilling to sit down and make a sandwich. Finally I settled for a glass of milk and some leftover cole slaw, but the silence of the house depressed me. I finished and went over to the Lees; they live just a block away.

From the outside, the Lee house is brick, massive, New England, and old, like all the other houses on the street. It has absolutely no distinguishing characteristics. I had always wondered about the house; it didn't seem suited to Art.

Inside, things were grim. In the kitchen, Betty sat with a rigid smile on her face as she fed the year-old baby; she looked tired and ragged; normally she was immaculately dressed with an unwilting, indefatigable manner. Judith was with her and Jane, our youngest, was holding on to Judith's skirt. She had begun that just a few weeks earlier.

From the living room, I heard the sound of the boys playing cops and robbers with cap pistols. With every bang, Betty shuddered. "I wish they'd stop," she said, "but I haven't the heart. . . ."

I went into the living room. All the furniture was overturned. From behind an easy chair Johnny, our four-year-old, saw me and waved, then fired his gun. Across the room the two Lee boys were huddled behind the couch. The air was acrid with smoke and the floor littered with rolls of paper caps.

Johnny fired, then called, "I got you."

"Did not," said Andy Lee, who was six.

"I did too. You're dead."

"I'm not dead," Andy said and fanned his gun. He was out of caps, though, and made only a clicking noise. He ducked down and said to Henry Lee, "Cover me while I reload."

"O.K., partner."

Andy reloaded, but his fingers were slow, and he grew impatient. Halfway through he stopped, aimed his gun, and shouted "Bang! Bang!" Then he continued.

"No fair," Johnny called, from behind the chair. "You're dead."

"So are you," Henry said. "I just got you."

"Oh, yeah?" Johnny said and fired three more caps. "You only winged me."

"Oh, yeah?" Henry said. "Take that."

The shooting continued. I walked back to the kitchen, where Judith was standing with Betty. Betty said, "How is it?"

I smiled. "They're arguing over who got whom."

"What did you find out today?"

"Everything's going to be all right," I said. "Don't worry."

She gave me a wry smile. Art's smile. "Yes, Doctor."

"I'm serious."

"I hope you're right," she said, putting a spoon of apple sauce into the baby's mouth. It dribbled out over her chin; Betty scooped it up and tried again.

"We just had some bad news," Judith said.

"Oh?"

"Bradford called. Art's lawyer. He won't take the case."

"Bradford?"

"Yes," Betty said. "He called half an hour ago."

"What did he say?"

"Nothing. Just that he couldn't take it at this time."

I lit a cigarette and tried to be calm. "I'd better call him," I said.

Judith looked at her watch. "It's five-thirty. He probably won't be——"

"I'll try anyway," I said. I went into Art's study. Judith came with me. I shut the door, closing off the sounds of gunfire.

Judith said, "What's really happening?"

I shook my head.

"Bad?"

"It's too early to say," I said. I sat down behind Art's desk and started to call Bradford.

"Are you hungry? Did you get anything to eat?"

"I stopped for a bite," I said, "on my way over."

"You look tired."

"I'm O.K.," I said. She leaned over the desk and I kissed her cheek.

"By the way," she said, "Fritz Werner has been calling. He wants to talk to you."

I might have expected that. Count on Fritz to know everything. Still, he might have something important; he might be very helpful. "I'll call him later."

"And before I forget," she said, "there's that party tomorrow."

"I don't want to go."

"We have to," she said. "It's George Morris."

I had forgotten. "All right," I said. "What time?"

"Six. We can leave early."

"All right," I said.

She went back to the kitchen as the secretary answered the phone and said, "Bradford, Wilson and Sturges."

"Mr. Bradford, please."

"I'm sorry," the secretary said. "Mr. Bradford has gone for the day."

"How can I reach him?"

"Mr. Bradford will be in the office at nine tomorrow morning."

"I can't wait that long."

"I'm sorry, sir."

"Don't be sorry," I said. "Just find him for me. This is Dr. Berry calling." I didn't know if the name would mean anything, but I suspected it might.

Her tone changed immediately. "Hold the line please, Doctor."

There was a pause of several seconds while I waited in the mechanical humming silence of the "Hold" button. Being on the "Hold" button is the technological equivalent of purgatory. That was what Art used to say. He hates telephones and never uses them unless he has to.

The secretary came back on. "Mr. Bradford is just leaving, but he will speak to you now."

"Thank you."

A mechanical click.

"George Bradford speaking."

"Mr. Bradford, this is John Berry."

"Yes, Dr. Berry. What can I do for you?"

"I'd like to speak to you about Art Lee."

"Dr. Berry, I'm just leaving—"

"Your secretary told me. Perhaps we could meet somewhere."

He hesitated and sighed into the phone. It sounded like a hissing, impatient serpent. "That won't serve any purpose. I'm afraid my decision is quite firm. The matter is out of my hands."

"Just a short meeting."

He paused again. "All right. I'll meet you at my club in twenty minutes. The Trafalgar. See you then."

I hung up. The bastard: his club was downtown. I would have to run like hell to make it in time. I straightened my tie and hurried off to my car.

THE TRAFALGAR CLUB is located in a small, dilapidated house on Beacon Street, just down from the Hill. Unlike the professional clubs of larger cities, the Trafalgar is so quiet that few Bostonians even know of its existence.

I had never been there before, but I could have predicted the decor. The rooms were paneled in mahogany; the ceilings were high and dusty; the chairs heavy, padded tan leather, comfortable and wrinkled; the carpets were worn Orientals. In atmosphere, it reflected its members—stiff, aging, and masculine. As I checked my coat, I saw a sign which stated crisply, FEMALE GUESTS MAY BE ENTERTAINED BETWEEN THE HOURS OF 4 AND 5:30 O'CLOCK ON THURSDAYS ONLY. Bradford met me in the lobby.

He was a short, compact man, impeccably dressed. His black chalk-stripe suit was unwrinkled after a day of work, his shoes gleamed, and his cuffs protruded the proper length beyond his jacket sleeves. He wore a pocket watch on a silver chain, and his Phi Beta Kappa key contrasted nicely with the dark material of his vest. I didn't have to look him up in Who's Who to know that he lived someplace like Beverly Farms, that he had attended Harvard College and Harvard Law School, that his wife had gone to Vassar and still wore pleated skirts, cashmere sweaters, and pearls, or that his children attended Groton and Concord. Bradford wore it all, quietly and confidently.

"I'm ready for a drink," he said as we shook hands. "How about you?"

"Fine."

The bar was on the second floor, a large room with high windows looking out on Beacon Street and the Commons. It was a subdued room, smelling faintly of cigar smoke. Men spoke in low voices and talked in small groups. The bartender knew what everyone drank without being told: everyone, that is, except me. We sat in two comfortable chairs by the window and I ordered a vodka Gibson. Bradford just nodded to the bartender. While we waited for the drinks, he said, "I am sure you must be disappointed in my decision, but frankly——"

"I'm not disappointed," I said, "because I'm not on trial."

Bradford reached into his pocket, looked at his watch, and put it back. "No one," he said crisply, "is on trial at this moment."

"I disagree. I think a great many people are on trial."

He rapped the table irritably and frowned across the room at the bartender. The psychiatrists call that displacement.

"And what," he said, "is that supposed to mean?"

"Everybody in this town is dropping Art Lee as if he had bubonic plague."

"And you suspect a dark conspiracy?"

"No," I said. "I'm just surprised."

"I have a friend," Bradford said, "who claims that all doctors are essentially naïve. You don't strike me as naïve."

"Is that a compliment?"

"That's an observation."

"I try," I said.

"Well, there's really no mystery and no conspiracy here. In my case, you must realize that I have many clients, of whom Mr. Lee is just one."

"Dr. Lee."

"Quite right. Dr. Lee. He is just one of my clients, and I have obligations to all of them which I discharge as I am best able. It happens that I spoke with the district attorney's office this afternoon, to determine when Dr. Lee's case would come up for hearing. It seems that Dr. Lee's case will conflict with another I have previously accepted. I cannot be in two courtrooms at once. I explained this to Dr. Lee."

The drinks came. Bradford raised his glass. "Cheers."

"Cheers."

He sipped his drink and looked at the glass. "When I explained my position to him, Dr. Lee accepted it. I also told him that my firm would make every effort to see that he had excellent legal counsel. We have four senior partners, and it is quite likely that one of them will be able to——"

"But not certain?"

He shrugged. "Nothing is certain in this world."

I sipped the drink. It was lousy, mostly vermouth with a touch of vodka.

"Are you a good friend of the Randalls?" I asked.

"I know them, yes."

"Does that have anything to do with your decision?"

"Certainly not." He sat up quite stiffly. "A lawyer learns very early to separate clients and friends. It's frequently necessary."

"Especially in a small town."

He smiled. "Objection, Your Honor."

He sipped his drink again. "Off the record, Dr. Berry, you should know that I am in complete sympathy with Lee. We both recognize that abortion is a fact of life. It happens all the time. The last figures I saw listed American abortions at a million yearly; it's very common. Speaking practically, it is necessary. Our laws relating to abortion are hazy, ill-defined, and absurdly strict. But I must remind you that the doctors are much more strict than the law itself. The abortion committees in hospitals are overcautious. They refuse to perform abortions under circumstances where the law would never intervene. In my opinion, before you can change the abortion laws, you must change the prevailing climate of medical opinion."

I said nothing. The Passing of the Buck is a time-honored ceremony, to be observed in silence. Bradford looked at me and said, "You don't agree?"

"Of course," I said. "But it strikes me as an interesting defense for an accused man."

"I wasn't proposing it as a defense."

"Then perhaps I misunderstood you."

"I wouldn't be surprised," he said dryly.

"Neither would I," I said, "because you haven't been making much sense. I always thought lawyers got right to the problem, instead of running circles around it."

"I am trying to clarify my position."

"Your position is quite clear," I said. "I'm worried about Dr. Lee."

"Very well. Let's talk about Dr. Lee. He has been indicted under a seventy-eight-year-old Massachusetts law which makes any abortion a felony punishable by fines and imprisonment up to five years. If the abortion results in death, the sentence may be from seven to twenty years."

"Is it second-degree murder or manslaughter?"

"Neither, technically. In terms of——"

"Then the charge is bailable?"

"Conceivably so. But in this case not, because the prosecution will attempt a murder charge under a common law act which says any death resulting from a felony is murder."

"I see."

"In terms of the progress of the case, the prosecution will bring forth evidence—good evidence, I'm sure—that Dr. Lee is an abortionist. They will show that the girl, Karen Randall, previously visited Dr. Lee and that he inexplicably kept no records of her visit. They will show that he cannot account for several crucial hours during Sunday evening. And they will present Mrs. Randall's testimony that the girl told her Lee performed the abortion.

"In the end, it will come down to a conflict of testimony. Lee, a proven abortionist, will say he didn't do it; Mrs. Randall will say he did. If you were the jury, whom would you believe?"

"There is no proof that Dr. Lee aborted that girl. The evidence is wholly circumstantial."

"The trial will be held in Boston."

"Then hold it elsewhere," I said.

"On what grounds? That the moral climate here is unfavorable?"

"You're talking technicalities. I'm talking about saving a man."

"In the technicalities lies the strength of the law."

"And the weaknesses."

He gave me a thoughtful look. "The only way to 'save' Dr. Lee, as you say, is to demonstrate that he did not perform the operation. That means the real abortionist must be found. I think the chances of doing so are slim."

"Why?"

"Because, when I talked to Lee today, I came away convinced he was lying through his teeth. I think he did it, Berry. I think he killed her."

FOURTEEN

WHEN I RETURNED TO THE HOUSE, I found that Judith and the kids were still at Betty's. I made myself another drink—a strong one, this time—and sat in the living room, dead tired but unable to relax.

I have a bad temper. I know that, and I try to control it, but the truth is I am clumsy and abrupt with people. I guess I don't like people much; maybe that's why I became a pathologist in the first place. Looking back over the day, I realized I had lost my temper too often. That was stupid; there was no percentage in it; no gain, and potentially a great deal of loss.

The telephone rang. It was Sanderson, head of the path labs at the Lincoln. The first thing he said was, "I'm calling from the hospital phone."

"O.K.," I said.

The hospital phone had at least six extensions. In the evening, anyone could listen in.

"How was your day?" Sanderson said.

"Interesting," I said. "How was yours?"

"It had its moments," Sanderson said.

I could imagine. Anyone who wanted me out of his hair would put the squeeze on Sanderson. It was the most logical thing to do, and it could be managed quite subtly. A few jokes: "Say, I hear you're shorthanded these days." A few earnest inquiries: "What's this I hear about Berry being sick? Oh? I heard that he was. But he hasn't been in, has he?" Then a few choice words from the chiefs of service: "Sanderson, how the hell do you expect me to keep my medical staff in line when you're letting your path people take off all the time?" And finally someone from the administration: "We run a shipshape hospital here, everybody has his job and everybody does it, no deadwood on board."

The net effect would be an intense pressure to get me back in the lab or find a new man.

"Tell them I've got tertiary syphilis," I said. "That should hold them."

Sanderson laughed. "There's no problem," he said. "Yet. I've got a pretty tough old neck. I can keep it stuck out a while longer."

Then he paused, and said, "How much longer do you think it will be?"

"I don't know," I said. "It's complicated."

"Come by and see me tomorrow," he said. "We can discuss it."

"Good," I said. "Maybe by then I'll know more. Right now, it's just as bad as the Peru case."

"I see," Sanderson said. "Tomorrow, then."

"Right."

I hung up, certain he knew what I was talking about. I had meant that there was something wrong with the Karen Randall business, something out of place. It was like a case we had three months ago, a rare thing called agranulocytosis, the complete absence of white cells in the blood. It's a serious condition because without white cells, you can't fight infection. Most people are carrying disease organisms around in their mouth or body normally—staph or strep, sometimes diphtheria and pneumococcus—and if your bodily defenses go down, you infect yourself.

Anyhow, the patient was American, a doctor working for the Public Health Service in Peru. He was taking a Peruvian drug for asthma, and one day he began to get sick. He had sores in his mouth and a temperature, and he felt lousy. He went to a doctor in Lima and had a blood test. His white count was 600.[1] The next day it was down to 100, and the next

---

[1] Normal white count is 4–9,000 cells/cubic centimeter. With infection, this may double or triple.

day it was zero. He got a plane to Boston and checked into our hospital.

They did a bone-marrow biopsy, sticking a hollow needle into his sternum[2] and drawing out some marrow. I looked at it microscopically and was puzzled. He had lots of immature cells of the granulocyte series in his marrow, and while it was abnormal, it was not terribly bad. I thought, "Hell, something is wrong here," so I went to see his doctor.

His doctor had been tracing the Peruvian drug the patient was taking. It turned out to contain a substance removed from the American market in 1942 because it suppressed white-cell formation. The doctor figured this was what was wrong with his patient—he had suppressed his own white cells, and now he was infecting himself. The treatment was simple: take him off the drug, do nothing, and wait for his marrow to recover.

I told the doctor that the marrow didn't look so bad on the slide. We went to see the patient and found he was still sick. He had ulcers in his mouth, and staph infections on his legs and back. He had a high fever, was lethargic, and answered questions slowly.

We couldn't understand why his marrow should seem so basically normal when he was so damned sick; we puzzled over this for most of the afternoon. Finally, about four, I asked the doctor if there had been any infection at the site of biopsy, where they had made the puncture to draw marrow. The doctor said he hadn't checked. We went to the patient and examined his chest.

Surprise: unpunctured. The marrow biopsy hadn't been taken from this patient. One of the nurses or residents had screwed up the tags, mislabeling a marrow sample from a man with suspected leukemia. We immediately drew a sample from our patient and found a very suppressed marrow indeed.

The patient later recovered, but I would never forget our puzzling over the lab results.

I HAD THE SAME FEELING NOW—something was wrong, something was out of place. I couldn't put my finger on it, but I had the suspicion that people were working at cross-purposes, almost as if we were talking about different things. My own position was clear: Art was innocent until proven guilty, and that wasn't proven yet.

Nobody else seemed to care whether Art was guilty or not. The issue that was crucial to me was irrelevant to them.

Now why was that?

2 Breastbone.

TUESDAY

October
11

ONE

WHEN I AWOKE IT FELT LIKE A NORMAL DAY. I was exhausted and it was drizzling outside, cold, gray, and uninviting. I pulled off my pajamas and took a hot shower. While I was shaving, Judith came in and kissed me, then went to the kitchen to make breakfast. I smiled into the mirror and caught myself wondering what the surgical schedule would be like.

Then I remembered: I wasn't going to the hospital today. The whole business came back to me.

It was not a normal day.

I went to the window and stared at the drizzle on the glass. I wondered then for the first time whether I ought to drop everything and go back to work. The prospect of driving to the lab, parking in the lot, hanging up my coat, and putting on my apron and gloves—all the familiar details of routine—seemed suddenly very appealing, almost enticing. It was my job; I was comfortable at it; there were no stresses or strains; it was what I was trained to do. I had no business playing amateur detective. In the cold morning light, the idea seemed ludicrous.

Then I began to remember the faces I had seen. Art's face, and the face of J. D. Randall, and Bradford's smug confidence. And I knew that if I didn't help Art, nobody would.

In one sense, it was a frightening, almost terrifying thought.

JUDITH SAT WITH ME AT BREAKFAST. The kids were still asleep; we were alone.

"What are you planning today?" she said.

"I'm not sure."

I had been asking myself that very question. I had to find out more, lots more. About Karen, and Mrs. Randall particularly. I still didn't know very much about either of them.

"I'll start with the girl," I said.

"Why?"

"From what I've been told, she was all sweetness and light. Everybody loved her; she was a wonderful girl."

"Maybe she was."

"Yes," I said, "but it might be good to get the opinion of someone besides her brother and her father."

"How?"

"I'll begin," I said, "with Smith College."

SMITH COLLEGE, Northampton, Massachusetts, 2,200 girls getting an exclusive education in the middle of nowhere. It was two hours on the turnpike to the Holyoke exit; another half-hour on small roads until I passed under the train tracks and came into the town. I've never liked Northampton. It has a peculiarly repressed atmosphere for a college town; you can almost smell irritation and frustration in the air, the heavy combined frustration of 2,200 pretty girls consigned to the wilderness for four years, and the combined irritation of the natives who are forced to put up with them for that time.

The campus is beautiful, particularly in autumn, when the leaves are turning. Even in the rain, it's beautiful. I went directly to the college information office and looked up Karen Randall in the paperback directory of students and faculty. I was given a map of the campus and set out for her dorm, Henley Hall.

It turned out to be a white frame house on Wilbur Street. There were forty girls living inside. On the ground floor was a living room done in bright, small-print fabric, rather foolishly feminine. Girls wandered around in dungarees and long, ironed hair. There was a bell desk by the door.

"I'd like to see Karen Randall," I said to the girl.

She gave me a startled look, as if she thought I might be a middle-aged rapist.

"I'm her uncle," I said. "Dr. Berry."

"I've been away all weekend," the girl said. "I haven't seen Karen since I got back. She went to Boston this weekend."

I was in luck: this girl apparently didn't know. I wondered whether the other girls did; it was impossible to tell. It seemed likely that her housemother would know, or would find out soon. I wanted to avoid the housemother.

"Oh," said the girl behind the desk. "There's Ginnie. Ginnie's her roommate."

A dark-haired girl was walking out the door. She wore tight dungarees and a tight poor-boy sweater, but the overall effect remained oddly prim. Something about her face disowned the rest of her body.

The desk girl waved Ginnie over and said, "This is Dr. Berry. He's looking for Karen."

Ginnie gave me a shocked look. She knew. I quickly took her and steered her to the living room, and sat her down.

"But Karen's——"

"I know," I said. "But I want to talk to you."

"I think I'd better check with Miss Peters," Ginnie said. She started to get up. I pushed her gently back down.

"Before you do," I said, "I'd better tell you that I attended Karen's autopsy yesterday."

Her hand went to her mouth.

"I'm sorry to be so blunt, but there are serious questions that only you can answer. We both know what Miss Peters would say."

"She'd say I can't talk to you," Ginnie said. She was looking at me suspiciously, but I could see I had caught her curiosity.

"Let's go some place private," I said.

"I don't know . . ."

"I'll only keep you a few minutes."

She got up and nodded toward the hall. "Men aren't normally allowed in our rooms," she said, "but you're a relative, aren't you?"

"Yes," I said.

Ginnie and Karen shared a room on the ground floor, at the back of the building. It was small and cramped, cluttered with feminine mementos—pictures of boys, letters, joke birthday cards, programs from Ivy football games, bits of ribbon, schedules of classes, bottles of perfume, stuffed toy animals. Ginnie sat on one bed and waved me to a desk chair.

"Miss Peters told me last night," Ginnie said, "that Karen had . . . died in an accident. She asked me not to mention it to anyone for a while. It's funny. I never knew anybody who died—I mean, my age, that kind of thing—and it's funny. I mean peculiar, I didn't feel anything, I couldn't get very worked up. I guess I don't really believe it yet."

"Did you know Karen before you were roommates?"

"No. The college assigned us."

"Did you get along?"

She shrugged. Somehow, she had learned to make every bodily gesture a wiggle. But it was unreal, like a practiced gesture perfected before the mirror.

"I guess we got along. Karen wasn't your typical freshman. She wasn't scared of the place, and she was always going away for a day or the weekend. She practically never went to class, and she always talked about how she hated it here. That's the thing to say, you know, but she meant it, she really did. I think she really *did* hate it."

"Why do you think so?"

"Because of the way she acted. Not going to class, always leaving campus. She'd sign out for weekends, saying she was going to visit her parents. But she never did, she told me. She hated her parents."

Ginnie got up and opened a closet door. Inside, tacked to the door, was a large glossy photograph of J. D. Randall. The picture was covered with minute punctures.

"You know what she used to do? She used to throw darts at this picture. That's her father, he's a surgeon or something; she threw darts at him every night, before going to sleep."

Ginnie closed the door.

"What about her mother?"

"Oh, she liked her mother. Her real mother; she died. There's a step-mother now. Karen never liked her very much."

"What else did Karen talk about?"

"Boys," Ginnie said, sitting on the bed again. "That's all any of us talk about. Boys. Karen went to private school around here someplace, and she knew a lot of boys. Yalies were always coming to see her."

"Did she date anyone in particular?"

"I don't think so. She had lots of guys. They were all chasing her."

"Popular?"

"Or something," Ginnie said, wrinkling her nose. "Listen, it isn't nice to say things about her now, you know? And I have no reason to think it's true. Maybe it's all a big story."

"What's that?"

"Well, you get here as a freshman and nobody knows you, nobody's ever *heard* of you before, and you can tell people anything you like and get away with it. I used to tell people I was a high-school cheerleader, just for the fun of it. Actually I went to private school, but I always wanted to be a high-school cheerleader."

"I see."

"They're so wholesome, you know?"

"What kind of stories did Karen tell you?"

"I don't know. They weren't exactly stories. Just sort of implications. She liked people to believe that she was wild, and all her friends were wild. Actually, that was her favorite word: *wild*. And she knew how to make something sound real. She never just told you straight out, in a whole long thing. It was little comments here and there. About her abortions and all."

"Her abortions?"

"She said she had had two before she ever got to college. Now that's pretty incredible, don't you think? Two abortions? She was only seventeen, after all. I told her I didn't believe it, so she went into this explanation of how it was done, the complete explanation. Then I wasn't so sure."

A girl from a medical family could easily acquire a knowledge of the mechanics of a D & C. That didn't prove she'd had an abortion herself.

"Did she tell you anything specific about them? Where they were done?"

"No. She just said she'd had them. And she kept saying things like that. She wanted to shock me, I know that, but she could be pretty crude when she wanted. I remember the first—no, the second weekend we were here, she went out Saturday night, and she got back late. I went to a mixer. Karen came in all a mess, crawled into bed with the lights out, and said, 'Jesus, I love black meat.' Just like that. I didn't know what to say, I mean, I didn't know her well then, so I didn't say anything. I just thought she was trying to shock me."

"What else did she say to you?"

Ginnie shrugged. "I can't remember. It was always little things. One night, as she's getting ready to go out for the weekend, and she's whistling in front of the mirror, she says to me, 'I'm really going to get it this weekend.' Or something like that, I don't remember the exact words."

"And what did you say?"

"I said, 'Enjoy yourself.' What *can* you say when you get out of the shower and somebody says that to you? So she said, 'I will, I will.' She was always coming up with shocking little comments."

"Did you ever believe her?"

"After a couple of months, I was beginning to."

"Did you ever have reason to think she was pregnant?"

"While she was here? At school? No."

"You're sure?"

"She never said anything. Besides, she was on the pill."

"Are you certain of that?"

"Yeah, I think so. At least, she made this big ceremony of it every morning. The pills are right there."

"Where?"

Ginnie pointed. "Right there on her desk. In that little bottle."

I got up and went to the desk, and picked up the plastic bottle. The label was from Beacon Pharmacy; there were no typed directions. I took out my notebook and wrote down the prescription number and the name of the doctor. Then I opened the bottle and shook out a pill. There were four left.

"She took these every day?"

"Every single day," Ginnie said.

I was no gynecologist and no pharmacologist, but I knew several things. First, that most birth-control pills were now sold in a dispenser to help a woman keep track of the days. Second, that the initial hormone dosage had been cut from ten milligrams a day to two milligrams. That meant the pills were small.

These pills were huge in comparison. There were no surface markings of any kind; they were chalky white and rather crumbly to the touch. I slipped one into my pocket and replaced the others in the bottle. Even without checking, I had a pretty good idea what the pills were.

"Did you ever meet any of Karen's boyfriends?" I asked.

Ginnie shook her head.

"Did Karen ever talk about them? Talk about her dates?"

"Not really. Not personally, if you know what I mean. She'd talk about how they'd been in bed, but it was usually just gross stuff. She was always trying to gross you out. You know, the earthy bit. Wait a minute."

She got up and went to Karen's dresser. There was a mirror over the dresser; stuck into the frame were several pictures of boys. She plucked out two and handed them to me.

"This guy was one she talked about, but I don't think she was seeing him anymore. She used to date him over the summer or something. He goes to Harvard."

The picture was a standard publicity pose of a boy in a football uniform. He had the number 71, and was crouched down in a three-point stance, snarling into the camera.

"What's his name?"

"I don't know."

I picked up a Harvard-Columbia football program and looked up the roster. Number 71 was a right guard, Alan Zenner. I wrote the name in my notebook and gave the picture back to Ginnie.

"This other one," she said, handing me the second picture, "is a newer guy. I think she was seeing him. Some nights, she'd come back and kiss the picture before she went to bed. His name was Ralph, I think. Ralph or Roger."

The picture showed a young Negro standing in a tight, shiny suit with an electric guitar in one hand. He was smiling rather stiffly.

"You think she was seeing him?"

"Yes, I think so. He's part of a group that plays in Boston."

"And you think his name is Ralph?"

"Something like that."

"You know the name of the group?"

Ginnie frowned. "She told me once. Probably more than once, but I don't remember. Karen sort of liked to keep her boys a mystery. It wasn't like some girl sitting down and telling you every little thing about her boyfriend. Karen never did that, it was always bits and snatches."

"You think she was meeting this fellow when she went away for weekends?"

Ginnie nodded.

"Where did she go on weekends? Boston?"

"I imagine. Boston or New Haven."

I turned the picture over in my hands. On the back it said, "Photo by Curzin, Washington Street."

"Can I take this picture with me?"

"Sure," she said. "I don't care."

I slipped it into my pocket, then sat down again.

"Did you ever met any of these people? Any of the boys?"

"No. I never met any of her friends. Oh—wait a minute. I did, once. A girl."

"A girl?"

"Yes. Karen told me one day that this good friend of hers was coming up for a day. She told me all about how cool this girl was, how wild. This big build-up. I was really waiting for something spectacular. Then when she showed up . . ."

"Yes?"

"Really strange," Ginnie said. "Very tall, with real long legs, and all the time Karen kept saying how she wished she had long legs like that, and the girl just sort of sat there and didn't say anything. She was pretty, I guess. But really strange. She acted like she was asleep. Maybe she was up on something; I don't know. Finally she began to talk, after about an hour of just sitting there, and she said these weird things."

"Like what?"

"I don't know. Weird things. 'The rain in Spain is mainly down the drain.' And she made up poetry about people running in spaghetti fields. It was pretty dull, I mean, not what you'd call good."

"What was this girl's name?"

"I don't remember. Angie, I think."

"Was she in college?"

"No. She was young, but she wasn't in college. She worked. I think Karen said she was a nurse."

"Try to remember her name," I said.

Ginnie frowned and stared at the floor, then shook her head. "I can't," she said. "I didn't pay that much attention."

I didn't want to let it go, but it was getting late. I said, "What else can you tell me about Karen? Was she nervous? Jittery?"

"No. She was always very calm. Everybody else in the house was nervous, especially around hourly time, when we have our exams, but she didn't seem to care."

"Did she have a lot of energy? Was she bouncy and talkative?"

"Karen? Are you kidding? Listen, she was always half dead, except for her dates, when she'd perk up, but otherwise she was always tired and always complaining about how tired she was."

"She slept a lot?"

"Yes. She slept through most of her classes."

"Did she eat a lot?"

"Not particularly. She slept through most of her meals, too."

"She must have lost weight, then."

"Actually, it went up," Ginnie said. "Not too much, but enough. She couldn't get into most of her dresses, after six weeks. She had to buy some more."

"Did you notice any other changes?"

"Well, only one, but I'm not sure it really matters. I mean, it mattered to Karen, but nobody else cared."

"What was that?"

"Well, she had the idea that she was getting hairy. You know, arms and legs and on her lip. She complained that she was shaving her legs all the time."

I looked at my watch and saw that it was nearly noon. "Well, I don't want to keep you from your classes."

"Doesn't matter," Ginnie said. "This is interesting."

"How do you mean?"

"Watching you work, and all."

"You must have talked with a doctor before."

She sighed. "You must think I'm stupid," she said, in a petulant voice. "I wasn't born yesterday."

"I think you're very intelligent," I said.

"Will you want me to testify?"

"Testify? Why?"

"In court, at the trial."

Looking at her, I had the feeling she was practicing before the mirror once again. Her face had a secretly wise expression, like a movie heroine.

"I'm not sure I follow you."

"You can admit it to me," she said. "I know you're a lawyer."

"Oh."

"I figured it out ten minutes after you arrived. You want to know how?"

"How?"

"When you picked up those pills and looked at them. You did it very carefully, not like a doctor at all. Frankly, I think you'd make a terrible doctor."

"You're probably right," I said.

"Good luck with your case," she said as I was leaving.

"Thanks."

Then she winked at me.

TWO

THE X-RAY ROOM on the second floor of the Mem had a fancy name: Radiological Diagnosis. It didn't matter what they called it, it was the same inside as every other X-ray room anywhere. The walls were sheets of white frosted glass, and there were little jam-clips for the films. It was quite a large room, with sufficient space for a half-dozen radiologists to work at once.

I came in with Hughes. He was a radiologist at the Mem that I'd known for a long time; he and his wife sometimes played bridge with Judith and me. They were good players, blood players, but I didn't mind. Sometimes I get that way myself.

I hadn't called Lewis Carr because I knew he wouldn't help me. Hughes was low on the General totem pole and didn't give a damn whether I wanted to look at films from Karen Randall or the Aga Khan, who had come here for a kidney operation some years ago. He took me right up to the X-ray room.

On the way I said, "How's your sex life?"

That's a standard rib for a radiologist. It's well known that radiologists have the shortest lifespan of any medical specialist. The exact reasons are unknown, but the natural assumption is that the X rays get to them.

In the old days, radiologists used to stand in the same room as the patient when the films were taken. A few years of that, and they'd soak up enough gamma to finish them. Then, too, in the old days the film was less sensitive, and it took a whopping big dose to get a decent contrast exposure.

But even now, with modern techniques and better knowledge, a ribald tradition remains, and radiologists are condemned to suffer through a lifetime of jokes about their lead-lined jockstraps and their shriveled gonads. The jokes, like the X rays, are an occupational hazard. Hughes took it well.

"My sex life," he said, "is a damn sight better than my bridge game."

As we came into the room, three or four radiologists were at work. They were each seated in front of an envelope full of films and a tape recorder; they took out films individually and read off the patient's name and unit number, and the kind of film it was—AP or LAO, IVP, or thorax, and so forth—and then they slapped it up against the frosted glass and dictated their diagnosis.[1]

One wall of the room was given over to the intensive care patients. These were seriously ill people, and their films were not stored in manila envelopes. Instead they were hung on revolving racks. You pressed a button and waited until the rack came around to the films of the patient you wanted to see. It meant you could get to a critically ill patient's films rapidly.

The film storeroom was adjacent to the X-ray room. Hughes went in and pulled Karen Randall's films, and brought them back. We sat down in front of a sheet of glass, and Hughes clipped up the first picture.

"Lateral skull film," he said, peering at it. "Know why it was ordered?"

"No," I said.

I, too, looked at the plate, but I could make little of it. Skull films —X rays of the head—are difficult to interpret. The cranium is a complex piece of bone, producing a confusing interlocking pattern of light and dark. Hughes examined it for some time, occasionally tracing lines with the cap of his fountain pen.

"Seems normal," he said at last. "No fractures, no abnormal calcification, no evidence of air or hematoma. Of course, it'd be nice to have an arteriogram or a PEG."[2]

---

[1] AP is anteroposterior, indicating that the X rays penetrated from front to back, where they struck the plate. LAO is left anterior oblique and IVP is contrast media in the genitourinary tract, a film showing kidneys, ureters, and bladder.
[2] These are ways of making skull films easier to interpret. An arteriogram is an X ray taken after the cerebral arteries have been filled with radio opaque liquid. A PEG, or pneumoencephalogram, consists of draining all the cerebrospinal fluid and

"Let's have a look at the other views," he said. He pulled down the lateral view and put up the face-on, AP film. "This looks normal, too," he said. "I wonder why they were taken—was she in an auto accident?"

"Not that I know of."

He rummaged in the file. "No," he said. "Obviously. They didn't do face films. Only skull films."

Face films were a separate series of angles, utilized to check for fractures of the facial bones.

Hughes continued to examine the AP film, then put the lateral back up. He still could find nothing abnormal.

"Damned if I can figure it," he said, tapping the plate. "Nothing. Not a goddamned thing there, for my money."

"All right," I said, standing up. "Thanks for your help."

As I left I wondered whether the X rays had helped clear things up or just made everything worse.

THREE

I STEPPED INTO A PHONE BOOTH near the hospital lobby. I got out my notebook and found the pharmacy number and the prescription number. I also found the pill I had taken from Karen's room.

I chipped off a flake with my thumbnail and ground it into the palm of my hand. It crushed easily into a soft powder. I was pretty sure what it was, but to be certain I touched the tip of my tongue to the powder.

There was no mistaking the taste. Crushed aspirin on your tongue tastes terrible.

I dialed the pharmacy.

"Beacon Pharmacy."

"This is Dr. Berry at the Lincoln. I'd like to know a drug as follows—"

"Just a minute while I get a pencil."

A short pause.

"Go ahead, Doctor."

---

pumping in air to increase contrast in the ventricles. It is a painful procedure which cannot be done under anesthesia. Both techniques are considered minor surgery, and are not done unless there is a good evidence for their necessity.

"The name is Karen Randall. The number is one-four-seven-six-six-seven-three. Prescribing doctor Peter Randall."

"I'll check that for you."

The phone was put down. I heard whistling and pages flipping, then: "Yes, here it is. Darvon, twenty capsules, 75 milligram. Orders—'Once every four hours as needed for pain.' It was refilled twice. Do you want the dates?"

"No," I said. "That's fine."

"Is there anything else?"

"No, thanks. You've been very helpful."

"Any time."

I replace the receiver slowly. Things were getting more and more screwy. What kind of girl pretended to take birth-control pills but actually took aspirin, which she stored in an empty bottle that once contained pills for menstrual cramps?

FOUR

DEATH FROM ABORTION is a relatively rare event. This basic fact tends to be obscured in all the fanfare and statistics. The statistics, like the fanfare, are emotional and imprecise. Estimates vary widely, but most people agree that about a million illegal abortions are performed each year, and about 5,000 women die as a result of them. This means that the operative mortality is about 500/100,000.

This is a very high figure, especially in the light of mortality in hospital abortions. Death in hospital abortions ranges from 0–18/100,000, which makes it, at worst, about as dangerous as a tonsillectomy (17/100,000).

All this means is that illegal abortions are about twenty-five times as deadly as they have to be. Most people are horrified by this. But Art, who thought clearly and carefully about such things, was impressed by the statistic. And he said something very interesting: that one reason abortion remained illegal was because it was so safe.

"You have to look at the volume of business," he once said. "A million women is a meaningless number. What it comes down to is one illegal abortion every thirty seconds, day in, day out, year after year. That makes it a very common operation, and for better or worse, it's safe."

In his cynical way, he talked about the Death Threshold, as he called it.

He defined the Death Threshold as the number of people who must die each year of needless, accidental causes before anyone gets excited about it. In numerical terms, the Death Threshold was set at about 30,000 a year—the number of Americans who died of automobile accidents.

"There they are," Art said, "dying on the highways at the rate of about eighty a day. Everybody accepts it as a fact of life. So who's going to care about the fourteen women who die every day of abortions?"

He argued that in order to force doctors and lawyers into action, the abortion death figures would have to approach 50,000 a year, and perhaps more. At the current mortality rates, that meant ten million abortions a year.

"In a way, you see," he said, "I'm doing a disservice to society. I haven't lost anybody in abortion, so I'm keeping those death figures down. That's good for my patients, of course, but bad for society as a whole. Society will only act out of fear and gross guilt. We are attuned to large figures; small statistics don't impress us. Who'd give a damn if Hitler had only killed ten thousand Jews?"

He went on to argue that by doing safe abortions he was preserving the status quo, keeping the pressure off legislators to change the laws. And then he said something else.

"The trouble with this country," he said, "is that the women have no guts. They'd rather slink off and have a dangerous, illegal operation performed than change the laws. The legislators are all men, and men don't bear the babies; they can afford to be moralistic. So can the priests: if you had women priests, you'd see a hell of a quick change in religion. But politics and religion are dominated by the men, and the women are reluctant to push too hard. Which is bad, because abortion is their business —their infants, their bodies, their risk. If a million women a year wrote letters to their congressmen, you might see a little action. Probably not, but you might. Only the women won't do it."

I think that thought depressed him more than anything else. It came back to me as I drove to meet a woman who, from all reports, had plenty of guts: Mrs. Randall.

NORTH OF COHASSET, about half an hour from downtown Boston, is an exclusive residential community built along a stretch of rocky coast. It is rather reminiscent of Newport—old frame houses with elegant lawns, looking out at the sea.

The Randall house was enormous, a four-story Gothic white frame building with elaborate balconies and turrets. The lawn sloped down to the water; altogether there was probably five acres of land surrounding the house. I drove up the long gravel drive and parked in the turnabout next to two Porsches, one black, the other canary-yellow. Apparently the whole family drove Porsches. There was a garage tucked back to the left of the house with a gray Mercedes sedan. That was probably for the servants.

I got out and was wondering how I would ever get past the butler when a woman came out of the front door and walked down the steps. She was pulling on her gloves as she went, and seemed in a great hurry. She stopped when she saw me.

"Mrs. Randall?"

"Yes," she said.

I don't know what I was expecting, but certainly nothing like her. She was tall, and dressed in a beige Chanel suit. Her hair was jet black and glossy, her legs long, her eyes very large and dark. She couldn't have been older than thirty. You could have cracked ice-cubes on her cheekbones, she was so hard.

I stared at her in dumb silence for several moments, feeling like a fool but unable to help myself. She frowned at me impatiently. "What do you want? I haven't got all day."

Her voice was husky and her lips were sensual. She had the proper accent, too: flattened inflection and the slightly British intonation.

"Come on, come on," she said. "Speak up."

"I'd like to talk to you," I said, "about your daughter."

"My stepdaughter," she said quickly. She was sweeping past me, moving toward the black Porsche.

"Yes, your stepdaughter."

"I've told everything to the police," she said. "And I happen to be late for an appointment, so if you will excuse me . . ." She unlocked the door to her car and opened it.

I said, "My name is——"

"I know who you are," she said. "Joshua was talking about you last night. He told me you might try to see me."

"And?"

"And he told me, Dr. Berry, to suggest that you go to hell."

She was doing her best to be angry, but I could see she was not. There was something else showing in her face, something that might have been curiosity or might have been fear. It struck me as odd.

She started the engine. "Good day, Doctor."

I leaned over toward her. "Following your husband's orders?"

"I usually do."

"But not always," I said.

She was about to put the car in gear, but she stopped, her hand resting on the shift. "I beg your pardon," she said.

"What I mean is that your husband doesn't quite understand everything," I said.

"I think he does."

"You know he doesn't, Mrs. Randall."

She turned off the engine and looked at me. "I'll give you thirty seconds to get off this property," she said, "before I call the police." But her voice was trembling, and her face was pale.

"Call the police? I don't think that's wise."

She was faltering; her self-confidence draining away from her.

"Why did you come here?"

"I want you to tell me about the night you took Karen to the hospial. Sunday night."

"If you want to know about that night," she said, "go look at the car." She pointed to the yellow Porsche.

I went over and looked inside.

It was like a bad dream.

The upholstery had once been tan, but now it was red. Everything was red. The driver's seat was red. The passenger seat was deep red. The dashboard knobs were red. The steering wheel was red in places. The floor carpet was crusty and red.

Quarts of blood had been lost in that car.

"Open the door," Mrs. Randall said. "Feel the seat."

I did. The seat was damp.

"Three days later," she said. "It still hasn't dried out. That's how much blood Karen lost. That's what he did to her."

I shut the door. "Is this her car?"

"No. Karen didn't have a car. Joshua won't let her have one until she is twenty-one."

"Then whose car is it?"

"It's mine," Mrs. Randall said.

I nodded to the black car she was sitting in. "And this?"

"It's new. We just bought it yesterday."

"We?"

"I did. Joshua agreed."

"And the yellow car?"

"We have been advised by the police to keep it, in case it is needed as evidence. But as soon as we can . . ."

I said, "What exactly happened Sunday night?"

"I don't have to tell you anything," she said, tightening her lips.

"Of course not." I smiled politely. I knew I had her; the fear was still in her eyes.

She looked away from me, staring straight forward through the glass of the windshield.

"I was alone in the house," she said. "Joshua was at the hospital with an emergency. William was at medical school. It was about three-thirty at night and Karen was out on a date. I heard the horn blowing on the car. It kept blowing. I got out of bed and put on a bathrobe and went downstairs. My car was there, the motor running and the lights on. The horn was still blowing. I went outside . . . and saw her. She had fainted and fallen forward onto the horn button. There was blood everywhere."

She took a deep breath and fumbled in her purse for cigarettes. She brought out a pack of French ones. I lit one for her.

"Go on."

"There isn't any more to tell. I got her into the other seat and drove to the hospital." She smoked the cigarette with a swift, nervous movement. "On the way, I tried to find out what had happened. I knew where she was bleeding from, because her skirt was all wet but her other clothes weren't. And she said, 'Lee did it.' She said it three times. I'll never forget it. That pathetic, weak little voice . . ."

"She was awake? Able to talk to you?"

"Yes," Mrs. Randall said. "She passed out again just as we got to the hospital."

"How do you know it was an abortion?" I said. "How do you know it wasn't a miscarriage?"

"I'll tell you," Mrs. Randall said. "Because when I looked at Karen's purse, I found her checkbook. The last check she had made out was to 'cash.' And it was for three hundred dollars. Dated Sunday. *That's* how I know it was an abortion."

"Was the check ever cashed? Have you inquired?"

"Of course it wasn't cashed," she said. "The man who has that check is now in jail."

"I see," I said thoughtfully.

"That's good," she said. "And now you must excuse me."

She got out of the car and hurried back up the steps to the house.

"I thought you were late for an appointment," I said.

She paused and looked back at me. "Go to hell," she said, and then slammed the door behind her.

I walked back to my car, considering her performance. It was very convincing. There were only two flaws that I could spot. One was the amount of blood in the yellow car. I was bothered that there was more blood on the passenger seat.

Then too, apparently Mrs. Randall didn't know that Art's fee for an abortion was $25—just enough to cover the lab costs. Art never charged more. It was a way, in his own mind, of keeping himself honest.

FIVE

THE SIGN WAS BATTERED: CURZIN PHOTOS. Underneath, in small, yellowing print, "Photos for all Purposes. Passports, Publicity, Friends. One-Hour Service."

The shop stood on a corner at the north end of Washington Street, away from the lights of the movie houses and the big department stores. I went inside and found a little old man and a little old woman, standing side by side.

"Yes?" said the man. He had a gentle manner, almost timid.

"I have a peculiar problem," I said.

"Passport? No problem at all. We can have the pictures for you in an hour. Less, if you're in a rush. We've done it thousands of times."

"That's right," said the woman, nodding primly. "More than thousands."

"My problem is different," I said. "You see, my daughter is having her sweet-sixteen party, and——"

"We don't do engagements," said the man. "Sorry."

"No indeed," the woman said.

"It's not an engagement, it's a sweet-sixteen party."

"We don't do them," the man said. "Out of the question."

"We used to," explained the woman. "In the old days. But they were such a fright."

I took a deep breath. "What I need," I said, "is some information. My daughter is mad about a rock-'n'-roll group, and you took their picture. I want this to be a surprise, so I thought that I'd——"

"Your daughter is sixteen?" He seemed suspicious.

"That's right. Next week."

"And we took a picture of a group?"

"Yes," I said. I handed him the photograph.

He looked at it for a long time.

"This isn't a group, this is one man," he said finally.

"I know, but he's part of a group."

"It's just one man."

"You took the picture, so I thought that perhaps——"

By now the man had turned the picture over in his hand.

"We took this picture," he announced to me. "Here, you can see our stamp on the back. Curzin Photos, that's us. Been here since 1931. My father had it before I did, God rest his soul."

"Yes," said the woman.

"You say this is a group?" the man asked, waving the picture at me.

"One member of a group."

"Possibly," he said. He handed the picture to the woman. "Did we do any groups like that?"

"Possibly," she said. "I can never keep them clear."

"I think it was a publicity picture," I offered.

"What's the name of this group?"

"I don't know. That's why I came to you. The picture had your stamp——"

"I saw it, I'm not blind," the man snapped. He bent over and looked under the counter. "Have to check the files," he said. "We keep everything on file."

He began producing sheafs of pictures. I was surprised; he really had photographed dozens of groups.

He shuffled through them very fast. "My wife can never remember them, but I can. If I can see them all, I remember them. You know? That's Jimmy and the Do-Dahs." He flipped through rapidly. "The Warblers. The Coffins. The Cliques. The Skunks. The names stick with you. Funny thing. The Lice. The Switchblades. Willy and the Willies. The Jaguars."

I tried to glance at the faces as he went, but he was going very fast.

"Wait a minute," I said, pointing to one picture. "I think that's it."

The man frowned. "The Zephyrs," he said, his tone disapproving. "That's what they are, the Zephyrs."

I looked at the five men, all Negro. They were dressed in the same shiny suits that I'd seen in the single photo. They were all smiling uneasily, as if they disliked having their picture taken.

"You know the names?" I said.

He turned the picture over. The names were scrawled there. "Zeke, Zach, Roman, George, and Happy. That's them."

"O.K.," I said. I took out my notebook and wrote the name down. "Do you know how I can reach them?"

"Listen, you sure you want them for your girl's party?"

"Why not?"

The man shrugged. "They're a little tough."

"Well, I think they'll be O.K. for one night."

"I don't know," he said doubtfully. "They're pretty tough."

"Know where I can find them?"

"Sure," the man said. He jerked his thumb down the street. "They work nights at the Electric Grape. All the niggers hang out there."

"O.K.," I said. I went to the door.

"You be careful," the woman advised me.

"I will."

"Have a nice party," the man said.

I nodded and shut the door.

ALAN ZENNER WAS A HUGE MOUNTAIN OF A KID. He wasn't as big as a Big Ten tackle, but he was plenty large. I guessed he was about six-one and two-twenty.

Give or take.

I found him as he was leaving the Dillon Field House at the end of practice. It was late afternoon; the sun was low, casting a golden glow over Soldiers' Field stadium and the buildings nearby—the Field House, the Hockey Rink, the indoor tennis courts. On a side field, the freshman squad was still scrimmaging, raising a cloud of yellow-brown dust in the fading light.

Zenner had just finished showering; his short black hair was still damp and he was rubbing it, as if remembering the coach's admonition not to go out with wet hair.

He said he was in a hurry to eat dinner and start studying, so we talked as we crossed over the Lars Anderson bridge toward the Harvard houses. For a while I made small talk. He was a senior in Leverett House, the Towers, and he was majoring in history. He didn't like his thesis topic. He was worried about getting into law school; the law school didn't give athletes a break. All they cared about were grades. Maybe he would go to Yale law instead. That was supposed to be more fun.

We cut through Winthrop House and walked up toward the Varsity Club. Alan said he was eating two meals a day there, lunch and dinner, during the season. The food was O.K. Better than the regular crap anyway.

Finally, I shifted the conversation to Karen.

"What, you, too?"

"I don't understand."

"You're the second one today. Foggy was here earlier."

"Foggy?"

"The old man. That's what she used to call him."

"Why?"

"I don't know. It was her name for him, that's all. She had lots of names for him."

"You talked with him?"

Zenner said carefully, "He came to see me."

"And?"

Zenner shrugged. "I told him to go away."

"Why is that?"

We came to Massachusetts Avenue. The traffic was heavy. "Because," he said, "I didn't want to get involved."

"But you already are involved."

"Like hell I am." He started across the street, deftly maneuvering among the cars.

I said, "Do you know what happened to her?"

"Listen," he said, "I know more about it than anybody. Even her parents. Anybody."

"But you don't want to get involved."

"That's the picture."

I said, "This is very serious. A man has been charged with murdering her. You have to tell me what you know."

"Look," he said. "She was a nice girl, but she had problems. We had problems together. For a while it was O.K., and then the problems got too big, and it was over. That's all. Now get off my back."

I shrugged. "During the trial," I said, "the defense will call you. They can make you testify under oath."

"I'm not testifying in any trial."

"You won't have a choice," I said. "Unless, perhaps, there never is a trial."

"Meaning what?"

"Meaning we'd better have a talk."

Two blocks down Massachusetts Avenue toward Central Square was a dirty little tavern with an out-of-focus color TV over the bar. We ordered two beers and watched the weather report while we waited. The forecaster was a cheerful little pudgy fellow who smiled as he predicted rain tomorrow, and the next day.

Zenner said, "What's your interest in all this?"

"I think Lee is innocent."

He laughed. "You're the only one who does."

The beers came. I paid. He sipped his and licked the foam off his lip.

"O.K.," he said, settling back in the booth. "I'll tell you how it was. I met her at a party last spring, around April. We got along well, right off. It seemed just great. I didn't know anything about her when I met her, she was just a good-looking girl. I knew she was young. I didn't know how young until the next morning when I practically flipped. I mean, Christ, sixteen. . . . But I liked her. She wasn't cheap."

He drank half the glass in a single gulp.

"So, we started seeing each other. And little by little, I found out about her. She had a way of explaining things in bits and snatches. It was very tantalizing, like the old movie serials. Come back next Saturday for the next installment, that kind of thing. She was good at it."

"When did you stop seeing her?"

"June, early June. She was graduating from Concord, and I said I'd come out to see the graduation. She didn't want that. I said why. And then the whole thing came out about her parents and how I wouldn't get along. You see," he said, "my name was Zemnick before, and I grew up in Brooklyn. It's that way. She made her point, and I kissed her off. I was really pissed at the time. Now, I don't care anymore."

"You never saw her again?"

"Once. It must have been late July. I had a construction job on the Cape, a real soft one, and a lot of my friends were out there. I'd heard some things about her, things I hadn't heard when I was dating her. And how she collects jocks. About her problems with her parents and how she hated her old man. Things began to make sense when they hadn't made sense before. And I heard that she'd had an abortion and was telling people it was my kid."

He finished his beer and motioned to the bartender. I had another with him.

"One day I run into her out by Scusset. She's in a gas station getting her car filled and I happen to pull in. So we have a little talk. I ask her if it was true about the abortion, and she says yes. I ask her if it was my kid, and she says in a real steady voice that she doesn't know who the father is. So I tell her to go to hell and walk off. Then she comes running up and says she's sorry, can't we be friends again and see each other. I say no we can't. So she starts to cry. Well, hell, that's awful to have a girl crying in a gas station. So I said I'd take her out that night."

"Did you?"

"Yeah. It was terrible. Alan, do this; Alan, do that; faster, Alan, now slower. Alan, you sweat so much. She never shut up."

"Was she living on the Cape last summer?"

"She said she was. Working in an art gallery or something. But I heard she spent most of her time in Beacon Hill. She had some crazy friends."

"What friends?"

"I don't know. Friends."

"Did you ever meet any of them?"

"Only one. At a party one time on the Cape. Somebody introduced me to a girl named Angela who was supposed to be a friend of Karen's. Angela Harley or Hardy, something like that. Damned good-looking girl, but strange."

"How do you mean?"

"Just strange. Far out. When I met her, she was high on something. She kept saying strange things like 'The nose of God has the power of sour.' You couldn't talk to her; she was out of it. Too bad, she was damned good-looking."

"Did you ever meet her parents?"

"Yeah," he said. "Once. Quite a pair. Old stiff upper lip and warm lower lips. No wonder she hated them."

"How do you know she hated them?"

"What do you think she talked about? Her parents. Hour after hour. She hated Foggy. She sometimes called him Good Old Dad, because of the initials. She had names for her stepmother, too, but you wouldn't believe them. The funny thing is, though, that she was very close to her mother. Her real mother. She died when Karen was about fourteen or fifteen. I think that was when it all started."

"What started?"

"The wild stuff. All the drugs and the action. She wanted people to think she was wild. She wanted to be shocking. As if she had to prove it. She was very big on drugs and always took them in public. Some people said she was addicted to amphetamines, but I don't know if that was true. A lot of people on the Cape had been stung by her, and there were lots of nasty stories. They used to say that Karen Randall would go up on anything, and down on everything." He grimaced slightly as he said it.

"You liked her," I said.

"Yeah," he said, "as long as I could."

"That time on the Cape, was it the last time you saw her?"

"Yeah."

The next beer came. He looked at his glass and twisted it around in his hands for a few seconds.

"No," he said, "that's not true."

"You saw her again?"

He hesitated. "Yes."

"When?"

"Sunday," he said, "last Sunday."

SIX

"IT WAS ALMOST LUNCHTIME," Zenner said. "I was hung over from a party after the game. Really hung. Too hung. I was worried about looking good at practice Monday, because I had missed a few plays on Saturday. The same play: an end sweep. I wasn't pulling fast enough, it kept happening. So I was a little worried.

"Anyway, I was in my room trying to get dressed for lunch. Tying my tie. I had to do it three times, because I kept getting it crooked. I was really hung. And I had a bad headache; and in she walks, right into the room, just like I was expecting her."

"Were you?"

"I never wanted to see anyone less in my life. I had finally gotten over her, you know, worked it all out of my system. Then she shows up again, looking better than ever. A little heavy, but still good. My roommates had all gone to lunch, so I was the only one there. She asked me if I would take her to lunch."

"What did you say?"

"I said no."

"Why?"

"Because I didn't want to see her. She was like the plague, she infected you. I didn't want her around. So I asked her to please leave, but she didn't. She sat down and lit a cigarette and said she knew it was all over with us, but she needed somebody to talk to. Well, I'd heard that one before, and I wasn't having any. But she wouldn't leave. She sat there on the couch and wouldn't leave. She said I was the only person she could talk to.

"So finally I just gave up. I sat down and said, 'O.K., talk.' And I kept telling myself that I was a fool and that I'd regret it, just the way I regretted the last time. There are some people you just can't be around."

"What did you talk about?"

"Her. That was all she ever talked about. Herself, her parents, her brother—"

"Was she close to her brother?"

"In a way. But he's kind of straight arrow, like Foggy. Fired for the medical bit. So Karen never told him a lot of things. Like the drugs and stuff. She just never mentioned it to him."

"Go on."

"So I sat there and listened to her talk. She talked about school for a while, and then about some mystical thing she was starting where you meditated twice a day for half an hour. It was supposed to be like washing out your mind, or dipping a cloth in ink, or something. She had just started it but she thought it was great."

"How did she act during this time?"

"Nervous," Zenner said. "She smoked a pack just while she sat there, and she kept fiddling with her hands. She had a Concord Academy ring. She kept pulling it off, and putting it on, and twisting it. The whole damned time."

"Did she say why she had come down from Smith for the weekend?"

"I asked her," Zenner said. "And she told me."

"Told you what?"

"That she was going to have an abortion."

I sat back and lit a cigarette. "What was your reaction?"

He shook his head. "I didn't believe her." He glanced quickly at me, then sipped the beer. "I didn't believe anything about her anymore. That was the trouble. I was just turned off, I wasn't paying attention. I couldn't let myself, because she still . . . had an effect on me."

"Was she aware of that?"

"She was aware of everything," he said. "She didn't miss anything. She was like a cat; she worked by her instincts and they were always right. She could walk into a room and just look around, and she immediately knew everything about everyone. She had this sense for emotions."

"Did you talk to her about the abortion?"

"No. Because I didn't believe her. I just let it drop. Only she came back to it, about an hour later. She said she was scared, that she wanted to be with me. She kept saying she was scared."

"Did you believe that?"

"I didn't know what to believe. No. No, I didn't believe her." He finished his beer in a gulp and put the mug down. "But look," he said, "what the hell was I supposed to do? She was nuts, that girl. Everybody knew it and it was true. She had this thing with her parents and with everybody else, and it pushed her over the brink. She was crazy."

"How long did you talk with her?"

"About an hour and a half. Then I said I had to eat lunch and study and that she'd better go. So she left."

"You don't know where she was going?"

"No. I asked her, and she just laughed. She said she never knew where she was going."

SEVEN

IT WAS LATE IN THE DAY when I left Zenner, but I called Peter Randall's office anyway. He wasn't there. I said it was urgent so his nurse suggested I try his lab. He often worked late in his lab on Tuesday and Thursday nights.

I didn't call. I went right over.

Peter Randall was the only member of the Randall family I had ever met before. I'd run into him once or twice at medical parties. It was impossible to miss him—first, because he was so physically outstanding, and second, because he liked parties and attended every one he heard about.

He was a titanic fat man, jowled and jovial, with a hearty laugh and a flushed face. He smoked continuously, drank exorbitantly, talked amusingly, and was in general the treasure of every hostess. Peter could make a party. He could revive one instantly. Betty Gayle, whose husband was chief of medicine at the Lincoln, had once said, "Isn't he a marvelous social animal?" She was always saying things like that, but for once she was right. Peter Randall was a social animal—gregarious, extroverted, relaxed, good-humored. His wit and his manner gave him a remarkable kind of freedom.

For instance, Peter could successfully tell the most foul and revolting dirty joke, and you would laugh. Inside, you would be thinking, "That's a pretty dirty joke," but you would be laughing despite yourself, and all the wives would be laughing, too. He could also flirt with your wife, spill his drink, insult the hostess, complain, or do anything else. You never minded, never frowned.

I wondered what he would have to say about Karen.

HIS LAB WAS ON THE FIFTH FLOOR of the biochem wing of the medical school. I walked down the corridor, smelling the smell of laboratories—a combination of acetone, bunsen burners, pipette soap, and reagents. A clean, sharp smell. His office was small. A girl behind the desk was typing a letter, wearing a white lab coat. She was strikingly attractive, but I suppose I should have expected that.

"Yes? May I help you?" She had a slight accent.

"I'm looking for Dr. Randall."

"Is he expecting you?"

"I'm not sure," I said. "I called earlier, but he may not have gotten my message."

She looked at me and sized me up for a clinician. There was that slightly supercilious look in her eyes that all researchers get when they are around clinicians. Clinicians don't use their minds, you see. They fool with dirty, unscientific things like patients. A researcher, on the other hand, inhabits a world of pure, satisfying intellectualism.

"Come with me," she said. She got up and walked down the hall. She wore wooden shoes without heels—that explained her accent. Following behind her, I watched her bottom and wished she was not wearing a lab coat.

"He's about to start a new incubation run," she said over her shoulder. "He'll be very busy."

"I can wait."

We entered the lab. It was bare, at a corner of the wing, looking down over the parking lot. So late in the day, most of the cars were gone.

Randall was bent over a white rat. As the girl came in, he said, "Ah, Brigit. You're just in time." Then he saw me. "Well now, what have we here?"

"My name is Berry," I said. "I——"

"Of course, of course. I remember you well." He dropped the rat and shook hands with me. The rat scampered across the table but stopped at the edge, looking down at the floor and sniffing.

"John, isn't it?" Randall said. "Yes, we've met several times." He picked up the rat again and chuckled. "In fact, my brother just called me about you. You've got him quite ruffled—a snot-nosed snoop, I believe his words were."

He seemed to find this very amusing. He laughed again and said, "It's what you get for pestering his dearly beloved. Apparently you upset her."

"I'm sorry about that."

"Don't be," Peter said cheerfully. He turned to Brigit and said, "Call the others, will you? We have to get this thing going."

Brigit wrinkled her nose, and Peter winked at her. When she was gone, he said, "Adorable creature, Brigit. She keeps me in shape."

"In shape?"

"Indeed," he said, patting his stomach. "One of the great pitfalls to modern, easy living is weak eye muscles. Television's to blame; we sit there and don't exercise our eyes. The result is flabby eyes, a terrible tragedy. But Brigit prevents all that. Preventive medicine of the finest sort." He sighed happily. "But what can I do for you? I can't imagine why you'd want to see me. Brigit, yes, but not me."

I said, "You were Karen's physician."

"So I was, so I was."

He took the rat and placed it in a small cage. Then he looked among a row of larger cages for another.

"Those damned girls. I keep telling them dye is cheap, but they never put enough on. There!" His hand darted in and brought out a second rat. "We're taking all the ones with dye on the tail," he explained. He held the rat so I could see the spot of purple color. "They've been injected with parathyroid hormone yesterday morning. Now," he said, "I regret to say they are going to meet their Maker. Know anything about killing rats?"

"A little."

"You wouldn't care to dispatch them for me, would you? I hate to sacrifice them."

"No, thanks."

He sighed. "I thought so. Now, about Karen: yes, I was her physician. What can I tell you?"

He seemed apparently friendly and open.

"Did you treat her in the middle of the summer for an accident?"

"An accident? No."

The girls came in. There were three, including Brigit. They were all attractive, and whether by chance or design, one was blonde, one brunette, and one redhead. They stood in a line in front of him, and Peter smiled benignly at each of them, as if he were about to bestow presents.

"We have six tonight," he said, "and then we can all go home. Is the dissecting equipment set out?"

"Yes," Brigit said. She pointed to a long table with three chairs. In front of each chair was a cork pad, some pins, a pair of forceps, a scalpel, and an ice bath.

"What about the agitation bath? All ready?"

"Yes," said another girl.

"Good," Peter said. "Then let's get started."

The girls took their places at the table. Randall looked at me and said, "I guess I'll have to go through with it. I really hate this. Some day I'll get so worried about the little beasts' last moments that I'll chop off my fingers as well as their heads."

"What do you use?"

"Well, that's a long story." He grinned. "You see before you the squeamish connoisseur of rat-dispatching. I have tried everything—chloroform, neck breaking, squeezing. Even a little guillotine that the British are so fond of. I have a friend in London who sent me one—he swears by it—but it was always getting clogged with fur. So," he said, picking up one rat and examing it thoughtfully, "I went back to basics. I use a meat cleaver."

"You're kidding."

"Oh, I know it sounds bad. It looks bad, too, but it's the best way. You see, we have to get the dissection done quickly. The experimental design demands that."

He took the rat over to the sink. A heavy butcher's block was there, by the rim of the basin. He set the rat on the block and put a wax bag in the sink. Then he went over to the cabinet and brought out a meat cleaver, a heavy, stubby thing with a solid wooden handle.

"They sell these things," he said, "in the chemical supply houses. But they're too delicate and they never stay sharp. I bought this one second-hand from a butcher. It's superb."

He sharpened the edge on a stone briefly, then tested it on a piece of paper. It cut through cleanly.

The telephone rang at that moment, and Brigit jumped up to answer it. The other girls relaxed, obviously glad for a delay. Peter also seemed relieved.

Brigit spoke for a moment, then said, "It's the rental agency. They are going to deliver the car."

"Good," Peter said. "Tell them to leave it in the parking lot and leave the keys over the sun visor."

While Brigit was relaying the instructions, Peter said to me, "Damned nuisance. My car's been stolen."

"Stolen?"

"Yes. Quite annoying. It happened yesterday."

"What kind of a car was it?"

"A little Mercedes sedan. Battered, but I was fond of it. If I had my way," he said with a grin, "I'd see the thieves arrested for kidnapping, not car theft. I was very fond of that car."

"Have you reported it to the police?"

"Yes." He shrugged. "For whatever it's worth."

Brigit hung up and returned to her seat. Peter sighed, picked up the cleaver, and said, "Well, better get on with it."

He held the rat by the tail. The rat tried to pull away, spread-eagling its body on the block. In a swift motion, Peter lifted the cleaver over his head and brought it down. There was a loud *thump!* as the blade struck the block. The girls stared away. I looked back and saw Peter holding the wriggling decapitated body over the sink. The blood drained out for a few moments. Then he carried it over to Brigit and placed it on the cork pad.

"Number one," he said briskly. He returned to the block, pushed the head into the paper bag, and selected a second rat.

I watched Brigit work. With swift, practiced moves she pinned the body on its back to the cork. Then she cut into the legs, clearing away the flesh and muscle around the bones. Next she clipped the bones free of the body and dropped them into the ice bath.

"A minor triumph," Peter said, preparing the next rat on the block. "In this lab, we perfected the first *in vitro* bone cultures. We are able to keep isolated bone tissue alive for as long as three days. The real problem is getting the bone out of the animal and into the bath before the cells die. We've got it down to a fine art now."

"What exactly is your field?"

"Calcium metabolism, particularly as it relates to parathyroid hormone and thyrocalcitonin. I want to know how those hormones work to release calcium from bone."

Parathyroid hormone was a little-understood substance secreted by four small glands attached to the thyroid. Nobody knew much about it, except that the parathyroids seemed to control calcium levels in the blood, and that these levels were strictly regulated—much more so than, say, blood sugar or free fatty acid. Blood calcium was necessary for normal nerve transmission and normal muscle contraction, and it was theorized that calcium was shunted to and from the bone, as occasion demanded. If you had too much calcium in your blood, you deposited it in bone. If you had too little, you drew it out of bone. But nobody knew quite how this was accomplished.

"The time course is crucial," Peter continued. "I once performed an interesting experiment. I took a dog and put in an arterial bypass. I was able to take his blood, treat it with chemicals to remove all calcium, and put it back again. I ran this thing for hours, taking out literally pounds of calcium. Yet the blood levels remained normal, readjusting instantly. That dog was draining large quantities of calcium out of his bone and into his blood at a very rapid rate."

The cleaver swung down again with a heavy sound. The rat wriggled and was still. It was given to the second girl.

"I got interested in all this," Peter said. "The whole problem of calcium storage and release. It's fine to say you can put your calcium into bone, or take it out; but bone is a crystal, it's hard and rigidly structured. We can apparently build it up or tear it down in fractions of a second. I wanted to know how."

He reached into a cage and produced another rat with a purple tail.

"So I decided to set up an *in vitro* system to study bone. Nobody thought I could do it. Bone metabolism was too slow, they said. Impossible to measure. But I succeeded, several hundred rats later." He sighed. "If the rats ever take over the world, I'll be tried for my war crimes."

He positioned the rat on the block.

"You know, I've always wanted to find a girl to do this work for me. I kept looking for a cold-blooded German girl, or a sadist of some sort. Never found one. All of those"—he nodded to the three at the table— "came to work only after I agreed that they would never have to kill the animals."

"How long have you been doing this work?"

"Seven years now. I started very slowly, half a day a week. Then it got to be every Tuesday. Pretty soon it was Tuesdays and Thursdays. Then it was all weekend as well. I've cut down my practice as much as I can. This work is really addicting."

"You like it?"

"I adore it. It's a game, a big wonderful game. A puzzle where nobody knows the answer. If you're not careful, though, you can become obsessed with the answers. Some people in the biochem department work longer hours than any practicing doctor. They drive themselves. But I won't let that happen to me."

"How do you know?"

"Because whenever I feel the symptoms coming on—the urge to work round the clock, to keep going until midnight, or to come in at five in the morning—I say to myself, it's just a game. I repeat that over and over. And it works: I settle down."

The cleaver finished the third rat.

"Ah," Peter said, "halfway there." He scratched his stomach reflectively. "But enough about me. What about you?"

"I'm just interested in Karen."

"Ummm. And you wanted to know about an accident? There was none, that I recall."

"Why were skull films taken last summer?"

"Oh *that*." He stroked the fourth victim soothingly and set it on the block. "That was typical Karen."

"What do you mean?"

"She came into my office and said, 'I'm going blind.' She was very concerned, in her own breathless way. You know how sixteen-year-old girls can be: she was losing her vision, and her tennis game was suffering. She wanted me to do something. So I drew some blood and ordered a few tests. Drawing blood always impresses them. And I checked her blood pressure and listened to her and generally gave the impression I was being very thorough."

"And you ordered skull films."

"Yes. That was part of the cure."

"I don't follow you."

"Karen's problems were purely psychosomatic," he said. "She's like ninety percent of the women I see. Some little thing goes wrong—like your tennis game—and bang! you have a medical problem. You go to see your doctor. He can find nothing physically wrong with you. But does this satisfy you? No: on to another doctor, and still another, until you find one who will pat your hand and say, 'Yes, you're a very sick woman.'" He laughed.

"So you ordered all these tests as a diversion?"

"Largely," he said. "Not entirely. I believe in caution, and when one hears a complaint as serious as vision loss, one must investigate. I checked her fundi. Normal. I did a visual fields. Normal, but she said it came and went. So I took a blood sample and ordered tests of thyroid function and hormone levels. Normal. And the skull films. They were normal, too, or have you already seen them?"

"I saw them," I said. I lit a cigarette as the next rat died. "But I'm still not sure why——"

"Well, put it together. She's young, but it's still possible—vision and headache, slight weight gain, lethargy. That could be pan hypopituitarism with optic nerve involvement."

"You mean a pituitary tumor?"

"It's possible, just possible. I figured the tests would show if she was pan hypopit. The skull films might show something if she was really badly off. But everything came back negative. It was all in her mind."

"Are you sure?"

"Yes."

"The labs might have made a mistake."

"That's true. I would have run a second test, just to be sure."

"Why didn't you?"

"Because she never came back," Peter said. "That's the key to it all. One day she comes in near hysteria because she's going blind. I say come back in a week, and my nurse makes the appointment. A week later, no show. She's out playing tennis, having a fine time. It was all in her mind."

"Was she menstruating when you saw her?"

"She said her periods were normal," he said. "Of course, if she were four months' pregnant at the time of her death, she would just have conceived when I saw her."

"But she never came back to you?"

"No. She was rather scatterbrained, actually."

He killed the last rat. All the girls were now busily working. Peter collected the carcasses and put them into the paper bag, then dropped the bag into a wastebasket. "Ah," he said, "at last." He washed his hands vigorously.

"Well," I said, "thanks for your time."

"Not at all." He dried his hands on a paper towel, then stopped. "I suppose I ought to make some sort of official statement," he said, "since I'm the uncle and so forth."

I waited.

"J. D. would never speak to me again if he knew I'd had this conversation with you. Try to keep that in mind if you talk to anybody else."

"O.K.," I said.

"I don't know what you're doing," Peter said, "and I don't want to know. You've always struck me as pretty level and sensible, and I assume you're not wasting your time."

I didn't know what to say. I couldn't see what he was leading up to, but I knew he was leading up to something.

"My brother, at this moment, is neither level nor sensible. He's paranoid; you can't get anything out of him. But I understand that you were present at the autopsy."

"That's right."

"What's the dx[1] there?"

[1] See Appendix IV: Abbreviations.

"It's uncertain on the basis of the gross," I said. "Nothing clear at all."

"And the slides?"

"I haven't seen them yet."

"What was your impression at autopsy?"

I hesitated, then made my decision. He had been honest with me; I'd be honest with him.

"Not pregnant," I said.

"Hmmm," he said. "Hmmmm."

He scratched his stomach again, then held out his hand.

"That's very interesting," he said.

We shook hands.

EIGHT

WHEN I GOT HOME, a big squad car with a flashing light was waiting at the curb. Captain Peterson, still crew-cut and tough-looking, leaned against the fender and stared at me as I pulled into my driveway.

I got out of my car and looked at the nearby houses. People had noticed the flasher and were staring out of their windows.

"I hope," I said, "that I didn't keep you waiting."

"No," Peterson said with a little smile. "Just arrived. I knocked at the door and your wife said you weren't back yet, so I waited out here."

I could see his bland, smug expression in the alternating flashes of red from the light. I knew he had kept the light on to irritate me.

"Something on your mind?"

He shifted his position on the car. "Well, yes, actually. We've had a complaint about you, Dr. Berry."

"Oh?"

"Yes."

"From whom?"

"Dr. Randall."

I said innocently, "What kind of complaint?"

"Apparently you have been harassing members of his family. His son, his wife, even his daughter's college friends."

"Harassing?"

"That," said Peterson carefully, "was what he said."

"And what did you say?"

"I said I'd see what could be done."

"So here you are."

He nodded and smiled slowly.

The flasher was beginning to get on my nerves. Down the block, one or two kids were standing in the street, watching in silence.

I said, "Have I broken any law?"

"That hasn't been determined yet."

"If I have broken a law," I said, "then Dr. Randall may go to court about it. Or he may go to court if he feels he can show material damage as a result of my alleged actions. He knows that, and so do you." I smiled at him, giving him some of his own. "And so do I."

"Maybe we should go down to the station and talk about it."

I shook my head. "Haven't got time."

"I can take you in for questioning, you know."

"Yes," I said, "but it wouldn't be prudent."

"It might be quite prudent."

"I doubt it," I said. "I am a private citizen acting within my rights as a private citizen. I did not force myself upon anyone, did not threaten anyone. Any person who did not wish to speak with me did not have to."

"You trespassed on private property. The Randall home."

"That was quite inadvertent. I was lost, and I wanted to ask directions. I passed a large building, so large it never occurred to me it might be a private dwelling. I thought it was some kind of institution."

"Institution?"

"Yes. Like an orphanage, you know. Or a nursing home. So I drove in to ask directions. Imagine my surprise when I discovered that by purest chance——"

"Chance?"

"Can you prove otherwise?"

Peterson gave a fair imitation of a good-natured chuckle. "You're being very clever."

"Not really," I said. "Now why don't you turn off that flasher and stop drawing attention? Because otherwise I will file a complaint of harassment by police. And I'll file it with the Chief of Police, the District Attorney's office, and the Mayor's office."

He reached indolently through the window and flicked a switch. The light stopped.

"Someday," he said, "all this may catch up with you."

"Yes," I said. "Me, or somebody else."

He scratched the back of his hand, as he had done in his office. "There are times," he said, "when I think you're either an honest man or a complete fool."

"Maybe both."

He nodded slowly. "Maybe both." He opened the door and swung into the driver's seat.

I went up to the front door and let myself in. As I closed the door, I heard him pull away from the curb.

NINE

I DIDN'T FEEL MUCH LIKE ATTENDING A COCKTAIL PARTY, but Judith insisted. As we drove to Cambridge, she said, "What was it all about?"

"What?"

"The business with the police?"

"It was an attempt to call me off."

"On what grounds?"

"Randall filed a complaint. Harassment."

"Justified?"

"I think so."

I told her quickly about the people I had seen that day. When I was finished, she said, "It sounds complicated."

"I'm sure I've barely scratched the surface."

"Do you think Mrs. Randall was lying about the check for three hundred dollars?"

"She might have been," I admitted.

Her question stopped me. I realized then that things had been happening so fast, I hadn't had time to consider everything I had learned, to sift it out and put it together. I knew there were inconsistencies and trouble spots—several of them—but I hadn't worked on them in any logical way.

"How's Betty?"

"Not good. There was an article in the paper today. . . ."

"Was there? I didn't see it."

"Just a small article. Arrest of physician for abortion. Not many details, except his name. She's gotten a couple of crank calls."

"Bad?"

"Pretty bad. I try to answer the phone, now."

"Good girl."

"She's trying to be very brave about it, trying to go on as if everything was normal. I don't know if that's worse or better. Because she can't. Things aren't normal, and that's all there is to it."

"Going over there tomorrow?"

"Yes."

I parked on a quiet residential block in Cambridge not far from the Cambridge City Hospital. It was a pleasant area of old frame houses and maple trees along the road. Brick-paved sidewalks; the whole Cambridge bit. As I parked Hammond pulled up on his motorcycle.

Norton Francis Hammond III represents the hope of the medical profession. He doesn't know it, and it's just as well; if he did, he'd be insufferable. Hammond comes from San Francisco, from what he calls "a long line of shipping." He looks like a walking advertisement for the California life—tall, blond, tanned, and handsome. He is an excellent doctor, a second-year resident in medicine at the Mem, where he is considered so good that the staff overlooks things like his hair, which reaches almost to his shoulders, and his moustache, which is long, curling, and flamboyant.

What is important about Hammond, and the few other young doctors like him, is that they are breaking old patterns without rebelling against the Establishment. Hammond is not trying to antagonize anyone with his hair, his habits, or his motorcycle; he simply doesn't give a damn what the other doctors think of him. Because he takes this attitude, the other doctors cannot object—he does, after all, know his medicine. Though they find his appearance irritating, they have no ground for complaint.

So Hammond goes his way unmolested. And because he is a resident, he has a teaching function. He influences the younger men. And therein lies the hope of future medicine.

Since World War II, medicine has undergone great change, in two successive waves. The first was an outpouring of knowledge, techniques, and methods, beginning in the immediate postwar period. It was initiated by the introduction of antibiotics, continued with understanding of electrolyte balances, protein structure, and gene function. For the most part, these advances were scientific and technical, but they changed the face of medical practice drastically, until by 1965 three of the four most commonly prescribed drug classes—antibiotics, hormones (mostly The Pill), and tranquilizers—were all postwar innovations.[1]

[1] The fourth class, analgesics, was mostly that old standby, aspirin, synthesized in 1853. Aspirin is as much a wonder drug as any other. It is a pain-killer, a swelling-

The second wave was more recent and involved social, not technical change. Social medicine, and socialized medicine, became real problems to be solved, like cancer and heart disease. Some of the older physicians regarded socialized medicine as a cancer in its own right, and some of the younger ones agreed. But it has become clear that, like it or not, doctors are going to have to produce better medical care for more people than they ever have before.

It is natural to expect innovation from the young, but in medicine this has not been easy, for the old doctors train the young ones, and too often the students become carbon copies of their teachers. Then too, there is a kind of antagonism between generations in medicine, particularly now. The young men are better prepared than the old guard; they know more science, ask deeper questions, demand more complex answers. They are also, like young men everywhere, hustling for the older men's jobs.

That was why Norton Hammond was so remarkable. He was effecting a revolution without a rebellion.

He parked his motorcycle, locked it, patted it fondly, and dusted off his whites.[2] Then he saw us.

"Hiya, kids." As nearly as I could tell, Hammond called everyone kid.

"How are you, Norton?"

"Hanging in." He grinned. "Against all obstacles." He punched my shoulder. "Hey, I hear you've gone to war, John."

"Not exactly."

"Any scars yet?"

"A few bruises," I said.

"Lucky," he said, "taking on old A. R."

Judith said, "A. R.?"

"Anal Retentive: that's what the boys on the third floor call him."

"Randall?"

"None other." He smiled at Judith. "The kid's bitten off quite a chunk."

"I know."

"They say A. R. prowls the third floor like a wounded vulture. Can't believe anybody'd oppose his majestic self."

"I can imagine," I said.

"He's been in a terrible state," Hammond said. "He even chewed out Sam Carlson. You know Sam? He's a resident up there, working under A. R., rooting about in the nether regions of surgical politics. Sam is

---

reducer, a fever-breaker, and an antiallergic drug. None of its actions can be explained.
[2] See Appendix V: Whites.

A. R.'s golden boy. A. R. loves him, and nobody can figure out why. Some say it's because he is stupid, Sam is, blindingly stupid. Crushingly, awesomely stupid."

"Is he?" I said.

"Beyond description," Hammond said. "But Sam got chewed out yesterday. He was in the cafeteria, eating a chicken-salad sandwich—no doubt after asking the serving ladies what a chicken was—when Randall came in, and said, 'What are you doing here?' And Sam said, 'Eating a chicken-salad sandwich.' And A. R. said, 'What the hell for?'"

"What did Sam say?"

Hammond grinned broadly. "I have it on good authority, that Sam said, 'I don't know, sir.' And he put aside the sandwich and walked out of the cafeteria."

"Hungry," I said.

Hammond laughed. "Probably." He shook his head. "But you can't really blame A. R. He's lived in the Mem for a hundred years or so, and never had a problem. Now, with the headhunt, and then his daughter . . ."

"Headhunt?" Judith said.

"My, my, the grapevine is collapsing. The wives are usually the first to know. All hell's broken out at the Mem over the Clinic pharmacy."

I said, "They lose something?"

"You bet."

"What?"

"A gross of morphine ampoules. Hydromorphine hydrochloride. That's three to five times more powerful on a weight basis than morphine sulfate."

"When?"

"Last week. The pharmacist nearly got the ax—he was off hustling a nurse when it happened. It was lunchtime."

"They haven't found the stuff?"

"No. Turned the hospital upside down, but nothing."

"Has this ever happened before?" I said.

"Apparently it has, a few years back. But only a couple of ampoules were taken then. This was a major haul."

I said, "Paramedical?"

Hammond shrugged. "Could be anybody. Personally, I think it must have been a commercial move. They took too much. The risk was too great: can you imagine yourself waltzing into the Mem outpatient clinic and waltzing out with a box of morphine bottles under your arm?"

"Not really."

"Guts."

"But surely that's too much for one person," I said.

"Of course. That's why I think it was commercial. I think it was a robbery, carefully planned."

"By somebody outside?"

"Ah," he said. "Now you get down to the question."

"Well?"

"The thinking is that somebody did it from the inside."

"Any evidence?"

"No. Nothing."

We walked up the stairs to the wooden frame house. I said, "That's very interesting, Norton."

"You bet your ass it's interesting."

"Know anybody who's up?"

"On the staff? No. The word is that one of the girls in cardiac cath used to shoot speeds,[3] but she kicked it a year ago. Anyhow, they went over her pretty hard. Stripped her down, checked for needle marks. She was clean."

I said, "How about——"

"Doctors?"

I nodded. Doctors and drugs are a taboo subject. A reasonable number of doctors are addicts; that's no secret, any more than it's a secret that doctors have a high suicide rate.[4] Less widely known is a classic psychiatric syndrome involving a doctor and his son, in which the son becomes an addict and the doctor supplies his needs, to the mutual satisfaction of both. But nobody talks about these things.

"The doctors are clean," Hammond said, "as far as I know."

"Anybody quit their job? Nurse, secretary, anybody?"

He smiled. "You're really hot on this, aren't you?"

I shrugged.

"Why? Think it's related to the girl?"

"I don't know."

"There's no reason to connect the two," Hammond said. "But it would be interesting."

"Yes."

"Purely speculative."

"Of course."

"I'll call you," Hammond said, "if anything turns up."

---

[3] Injected amphetamines, such as methedrene, intravenously.

[4] Psychiatrists have the highest suicide rate of all, more than ten times that of the GP.

"Do that," I said.

We came to the door. Inside, we could hear party sounds: tinkling glasses, talk, laughter.

"Good luck with your war," Hammond said. "I hope to hell you win."

"So do I."

"You will," Hammond said. "Just don't take any prisoners."

I smiled. "That's against Geneva Conventions."

"This," Hammond said, "is a very limited war."

THE PARTY WAS HELD BY GEORGE MORRIS, chief resident in medicine at the Lincoln. Morris was about to finish his residency and begin private practice, so it was a kind of coming-out party, given for himself.

It was done very well, with an understated comfortability that must have cost him more than he could afford. I was reminded of those lavish parties given by manufacturers to launch a new product, or a new line. In a sense, that was what it was.

George Morris, twenty-eight, with a wife and two children, was deeply in debt: any doctor in his position would be. Now he was about to start burrowing out from under, and to do that he needed patients. Referrals. Consults. In short, he needed the good will and help of established physicians in the area, and that was why he had invited 200 of them to his home and filled them to the neck with the best booze he could buy and the best canapés the caterers could provide.

As a pathologist, I was flattered to have received an invitation. I couldn't do anything for Morris; pathologists deal with corpses and corpses don't need referrals. Morris had invited Judith and me because we were friends.

I think we were his only friends at the party that night.

I looked around the room: the chiefs of service from most of the big hospitals were there. So were the residents, and so were the wives. The wives had clustered in a corner, talking babies; the doctors were clustered into smaller groups, by hospital or by specialty. It was a kind of occupational division, very striking to see.

In one corner, Emery was arguing the therapeutic advantage of lower I^{131} doses in hyperthyroidism; in another, Johnston was talking about hepatic pressures in porto caval shunts; in still another, Lewiston could be heard muttering his usual line about the inhumanity of electroshock therapy for depressives. From the wives, occasional words like "IUD" and "chickenpox" drifted out.

Judith stood next to me, looking sweet and rather young in a blue

A-line. She was drinking her Scotch quickly—she's a gulper—and obviously preparing to plunge into the group of wives.

"I sometimes wish," she said, "that they'd talk about politics or something. Anything but medicine."

I smiled, remembering Art's line about doctors being illpolitical. He meant it the way you used words like illiterate. Art always said doctors not only held no real political views, but also were incapable of them. "It's like the military," he had once said. "Political views are considered unprofessional." As usual, Art was exaggerating, but there was something to what he said.

I think Art likes to overstate his case, to shock and irritate and goad people. It is a characteristic of his. But I think he is also fascinated by the thin line that separates truth from untruth, statement from overstatement. It is a characteristic of his to constantly throw out his comments and see who picks them up and how they react to them. He does this particularly when he is drunk.

Art is the only doctor I know who will get drunk. The others can apparently pour back fantastic quantities of alcohol without really showing it; they get talkative for a while, and then sleepy. Art gets drunk, and when he is drunk he is particularly angry and outrageous.

I have never understood this about him. For a while I thought he was a case of pathological intoxication,[5] but later I decided it was a sort of personal indulgence, a willingness to let himself go when others kept themselves rigidly in control. Perhaps he needs this indulgence; perhaps he can't help it; perhaps he actively seeks it as an excuse to blow off steam.

Certainly he is bitter toward his profession. Many doctors are, for various reasons: Jones because he is hooked on research and can't make as much money as he'd like; Andrews because urology cost him his wife and a happy family life; Telser because he is surrounded in dermatology by patients whom he considers neurotic, not sick. If you talk to any of these men, the resentment shows itself sooner or later. But they are not like Art. Art is resentful against the medical profession itself.

I suppose in any profession you meet men who despise themselves and their colleagues. But Art is an extreme example. It is almost as if he went into medicine to spite himself, to make himself unhappy and angry and sad.

In my blackest moments, I think he does abortions only to jar and ir-

---

[5] Defined as a person who becomes more inebriated than his blood alcohol levels would explain. In the most extreme cases, a single drink may make a man a raving, destructive lunatic.

ritate his colleagues. That is unfair, I think, but I can never be sure. When he is sober, he talks intellectually, unreeling arguments for abortion. When he is drunk, he talks emotions, attitudes, stances, complacency.

I think he feels hostility toward medicine and gets drunk so that he can release his hostility with an excuse—he's drunk. Certainly he has gotten into bitter, almost vicious fights with other doctors when he was drunk; he once told Janis that he'd aborted his wife and Janis, who didn't know, looked as if he'd been kicked in the balls. Janis is Catholic but his wife isn't. Art managed to end a perfectly happy dinner party right on the spot.

I attended that party, and I was annoyed with Art afterward. He apologized to me a few days later, and I told him to apologize to Janis, which he did. For some strange reason, Janis and Art subsequently became close friends, and Janis became a convert to abortion. I don't know what Art said to him or how he convinced him, but whatever it was, it worked.

Because I know Art better than most people, I attach a great importance to his being Chinese. I think his origin and his physical appearance have been a great influence on him. There are a lot of Chinese and Japanese men in medicine, and there are a lot of jokes about them—half-nervous jokes about their energy and their cleverness, their drive to success. It is precisely the kind of jokes one hears about Jews. I think Art, as a Chinese-American, has fought this tradition, and he has also fought his upbringing, which was essentially conservative. He swung the other way, became radical and leftist. One proof of this is his willingness to accept all things new. He has the most modern office equipment of any OB man in Boston. Whenever a new product comes out, he buys it. There are jokes about this, too—the gadget-oriented Orientals—but the motivation is different. Art is fighting tradition, routine, the accepted way.

When you talk to him, he seems bursting with ideas. He has a new method for doing the Pap smear.[6] He wants to abandon the routine, digital pelvic exam as a waste of time. He thinks that basal temperature as an indicator of ovulation is more effective than reported. He thinks forceps should be eliminated from all deliveries, no matter how complicated. He thinks that general anesthesia in deliveries should be abandoned in favor of heavy doses of tranquilizers.

When you first hear these ideas and theories, you are impressed. Only later do you realize that he is compulsively attacking tradition, finding fault whenever and wherever he can.

I suppose it is only natural that he should begin performing abortions. And I suppose that I should question his motives. But I don't usually, be-

[6] The Pap smear is the most accurate diagnostic test in all of medicine.

cause I feel that a man's reasons for doing something are less important than the ultimate value of what he does. It is a historical truth that a man may do the wrong thing for the right reasons. In that case he loses. Or he may do the right thing for the wrong reasons. In that case, he is a hero.

Of all the people at the party, one might be able to help me. That was Fritz Werner, but I didn't see him; I kept looking.

Instead I ran into Blake. Blake is a senior pathologist at the General, but he is principally known for his head, which is enormous, round, and smooth. The features of his face are small and childlike, a tiny jaw and wide-set eyes, so that Blake looks like everybody's vision of future man. He is a coldly, sometimes maddeningly intellectual man, and he is fond of games. He and I have played one game, off and on, for years.

He greeted me with a wave of his martini glass and, "Ready?"

"Sure."

"Moans to Rocky," he said.

It sounded easy. I took out my notebook and pencil and tried it out. At the top of the page I wrote MOANS and at the bottom, ROCKY. Then I tried to fit things together.

MOANS
 LOANS
  LOINS
   LOONS
    BOONS
     BOOKS
      ROOKS
       ROCKS
        ROCKY

It took only a few moments.

"How many?" Blake said.

"Nine."

He smiled. "I'm told it can be done in five. I have seven." He took the pad from me and wrote:

MOANS
 LOANS
  LOONS
   LOOKS
    ROOKS
     ROCKS
      ROCKY

I reached into my pocket and gave him a quarter. He had won the last three in a row, and over the years, he had beaten me consistently. But then Blake beat everybody.

"By the way," he said, "I heard another argument. Do you know the DNA template one?"[7]

"Yes," I said.

He shook his head. "Pity. I enjoy it. Springing it on people, I mean."

I smiled at him, barely able to conceal my pleasure.

"You know the latest on Youth in Asia? The one about the right to refuse medication? You can fit it into the fluoride arguments, very neatly."[8]

I'd heard that one, too, and I told him so. This seemed to depress him. He wandered off to try his luck with someone else.

Blake collects arguments on medical philosophy. He is never happier than when he is logically demonstrating to a surgeon that he has no right to operate, or to an internist that he is ethically bound to kill every patient he can. Blake likes words and tosses around ideas the way small children play softball in the street. It is easy for him, effortless and amusing. He and Art get along well together. Last year the two of them had a four-hour argument over whether an obstetrician was morally responsible for all childen born under his direction, from the time they were born until they died.

In retrospect, all of Blake's arguments seem no more useful or important than watching an athlete exercise in a gym, but at the time they can be fascinating. Blake has a keen sense of the arbitrary, and it stands him in good stead when working with members of the most arbitrary profession on earth.

Wandering around the party, I heard snatches of jokes and conversations; it was, I thought, a typical medical party.

"Did you hear about the French biochemist who had twins. He baptized one and kept the other as a control."

"They all get bacteremia sooner or later, anyway. . . ."

"And he was walking around—*walking around,* mind you, with a blood pH of seven-point-six and a potassium of one. . . ."

"Well, what the hell do you expect of a Hopkins man?"

"So he said, 'I gave up smoking, but I'll be damned if I'll give up drinking.'"

---

[7] See Appendix VI: Arguments on Abortion.
[8] See Appendix VII: Medical Morals.

"Sure, you can correct the blood gases, but it doesn't help the vasculature. . . ."

"She was always a nice girl. Very well dressed. They must have spent a fortune on her clothes. . . ."

". . . course he's pissed. Anybody'd be pissed. . . ."

". . . oliguric my ass. He was *an*uric for five days, and he still survived. . . ."

". . . in a seventy-four-year-old man, we just excised it locally and sent him home. It's slow growing, anyhow. . . ."

". . . liver reached down to his knees, practically. But no hepatic failure. . . ."

"She said she'd sign herself out if we didn't operate, so naturally, we . . ."

". . . but the students are always bitching; it's a nonspecific response. . . ."

"Well, apparently this girl had bitten it off of him. . . ."

"Really? Harry, with that little nurse in Seven? The blonde?"

". . . don't believe it. He publishes more journal articles than most people can read in a lifetime. . . ."

". . . metastases to the *heart* . . ."

"Anyway, it goes like this: there's this desert prison, see, with an old prisoner, resigned to his life, and a young one just arrived. The young one talks constantly of escape, and, after a few months, he makes a break. He's gone a week, and then he's brought back by the guards. He's half dead, crazy with hunger and thirst. He describes how awful it was to the old prisoner. The endless stretches of sand, no oasis, no signs of life anywhere. The old prisoner listens for a while, then says, 'Yep. I know. I tried to escape myself, twenty years ago.' The young prisoner says, 'You did? Why didn't you tell me, all these months I was planning my escape? Why didn't you let me know it was impossible?' And the old prisoner shrugs, and says, 'So who publishes negative results?'"

AT EIGHT, I was beginning to get tired. I saw Fritz Werner come in, waving to everyone and talking gaily. I started over toward him, but Charlie Frank caught me on the way.

Charlie stood half hunched over, with a twisted, painful expression on his face as if he'd just been stabbed in the stomach. His eyes were wide and sad. Altogether, it was quite a dramatic effect, but Charlie always looked that way. He wore an air of impending crisis and imminent tragedy on his shoulders, and it burdened him, crushing him to the floor. I had never seen him smile.

In a tense, half whisper, he said, "How is he?"

"Who?"

"Art Lee."

"He's all right." I didn't want to talk about Lee with Charlie Frank.

"Is it true he's been arrested?"

"Yes."

"Oh, my God." He gave a little gasp.

"I think it will turn out all right in the end," I said.

"Do you?"

"Yes," I said, "I do."

"Oh, my God." He bit his lip. "Is there anything I can do?"

"I don't think so."

He was still holding onto my arm. I looked across the room at Fritz, hoping Charlie'd notice and let go. He didn't.

"Say, John . . ."

"Yes?"

"What's this I hear about you, ah, getting involved?"

"Let's say I'm interested."

"I ought to tell you," Charlie said, leaning close, "that there's talk in the hospitals. People are saying that you're concerned because you're mixed up in it yourself."

"Talk is cheap."

"John, you could make a lot of enemies."

In my mind, I was thinking over Charlie Frank's friends. He was a pediatrician, and very successful: he worried over his young patients more than their mothers and that comforted them.

"Why do you say that?"

"It's just a feeling I get," he said with a sad look.

"What do you suggest I do?"

"Stay away from it, John. It's ugly. Really ugly."

"I'll remember that."

"A lot of people feel very strongly—"

"So do I."

"—that this is something to be left to the courts."

"Thanks for the advice."

His grip on my arm hardened. "I'm saying this as a friend, John."

"O.K., Charlie. I'll remember."

"It's really ugly, John."

"I'll remember."

"These people won't stop at anything," he said.

"What people?"

Quite abruptly, he let go of my arm. He gave an embarrassed little shrug. "Well, you have to do what you think is best, in any case."

And he turned away.

FRITZ WERNER WAS STANDING, as usual, by the bar. He was a tall, painfully thin, almost emaciated man. He kept his hair trimmed short, and this emphasized his large, dark, brooding eyes. He had a birdlike manner, a gawky walk, and a habit of craning his thin neck forward when he was addressed, as if he could not hear well. There was an intensity about him, which might have stemmed from his Austrian ancestry or from his artistic nature. Fritz painted and sketched as a hobby, and his office always had a cluttered, studiolike appearance. But he made his money as a psychiatrist, listening patiently to bored, middle-aged matrons who had decided at a late date that there was something wrong with their minds.

He smiled as we shook hands. "Well, well, if it isn't poison ivy."

"I'm beginning to think so myself."

He looked around the room. "How many lectures so far?"

"Just one. Charlie Frank."

"Yes," Fritz said, "you can always count on him for bad advice."

"And what about you?"

He said, "Your wife is looking very charming tonight. Blue is her color."

"I'll tell her."

"Very charming. How is your family?"

"Good, thanks. Fritz—"

"And your work?"

"Listen, Fritz. I need help."

He laughed softly. "You need more than help. You need rescue."

"Fritz—"

"You've been seeing people," he said. "I imagine you've met them all by now. What did you think of Bubbles?"

"Bubbles?"

"Yes."

I frowned. I had never heard of anyone named Bubbles. "You mean, Bubbles the stripper?"

"No. I mean Bubbles the roommate."

"*Her* roommate?"

"Yes."

"The one at Smith?"

"God, no. The one from last summer, on the Hill. Three of them shared an apartment. Karen, and Bubbles, and a third girl who had some kind of medical connections—nurse, or technician, or something. They made quite a group."

"What's the real name of this girl Bubbles? What does she do?"

Someone came up to the bar for another drink. Fritz looked out at the room and said in a professional voice, "This sounds quite serious. I suggest you send him to see me. As it happens, I have a free hour tmorrow at two-thirty."

"I'll arrange it," I said.

"Good," he said. "Nice to see you again, John."

We shook hands.

JUDITH WAS TALKING TO NORTON HAMMOND, who was leaning against the wall. As I walked up, I thought to myself that Fritz was right: she was looking good. And then I noticed that Hammond was smoking a cigarette. There was nothing wrong with that, of course, except that Hammond didn't smoke.

He didn't have a drink in his hand, and he was smoking rather slowly and deeply.

"Say," I said, "you want to watch that."

He laughed. "My social protest for the night."

Judith said, "I tried to tell him somebody would smell it."

"Nobody here can smell anything," Hammond said. It was probably true; the room was thick with blue smoke. "Besides, remember Goodman and Gilman."[9]

"Still. Be careful."

"Think of it," he said, taking a deep drag. "No bronchogenic carcinoma, no oat-cell carcinoma, no chronic bronchitis and emphysema, no arteriosclerotic heart disease, no cirrhosis, no Wernicke-Korsakoff. It's beautiful."

"It's illegal."

He smiled and pulled at his moustache. "You're up for abortion but not maryjane, is that it?"

"I can only take one crusade at a time."

---

[9] Goodman and Gilman, The Pharmacological Basis of Therapeutics, the definitive text of pharmacology used by doctors. There is a discussion of the effects of marijuana on page 300 which has been widely quoted in recent legal proceedings.

A thought came to me as I watched him suck in a mouthful of smoke and exhale clear air. "Norton, you live on the Hill, don't you?"

"Yes."

"Do you know anybody named Bubbles?"

He laughed. "Everybody knows Bubbles. Bubbles and Superhead. They're always together."

"Superhead?"

"Yeah. That's her bag at the moment. He's an electronic musician. A composer. He likes things that sound like ten dogs howling. They're living together."

"Didn't she live with Karen Randall?"

"I don't know. Maybe. Why?"

"What's her real name? Bubbles."

He shrugged. "I never heard her called anything else. But the guy: his name is Samuel Archer."

"Where does he live?"

"Over behind the State House somewhere. In a basement. They have it fixed up like a womb."

"A womb?"

"You have to see it to believe it," Norton said, and he gave a relaxed, satisfied sigh.

TEN

JUDITH SEEMED TENSE ON THE DRIVE BACK. She sat with her knees together and her hands clasped around them. She was squeezing her hands hard; the knuckles were white.

"Something wrong?"

"No," she said. "Just tired."

I said, "Was it the wives?"

She smiled slightly. "You've become very famous. Mrs. Wheatstone was so upset that she missed a bid at this afternoon's game, I understand."

"What else did you hear?"

"They all asked me why you were doing it, helping Art. They thought it was a marvelous example of a man sticking by his friend. They thought it was heartwarming and humane and wonderful."

"Uh-huh."

"And they kept asking why."

"Well, I hope you told them it's because I'm a nice guy."

She smiled in the darkness. "I wish I'd thought of that."

Her voice was sad, though, and her face in the reflected light of the headlights was drawn. I knew it wasn't easy for her to be with Betty all the time. But somebody had to do it.

For some reason, I remembered my student days and Purple Nell. Purple Nell was a seventy-eight-year-old former alcoholic who had been dead a year before she became our cadaver. We called her Nell, and a lot of other things, small grim jokes to help us get through our work. I remembered my desire to quit, to stop cutting the cold, damp, stinking flesh, to stop peeling away the layers. I dreamed of the day I would be finished with Nell, when I could forget her, and the smells, and the feel of greasy, long-dead flesh. Everyone said it got easier. I wanted to stop, to be finished and done. But I never quit until all the dissections had been completed, all the nerves and arteries traced out and learned.

After my initial harsh experience with cadavers, I was surprised to find I was interested in pathology. I like the work and have learned to push from my mind the smells and the sight of each new corpse, each new postmortem. But somehow autopsies are different, in some strange sense more hopeful. At autopsy you are dealing with a man, newly dead, and you know his story. He is not a faceless, anonymous cadaver but a person who has recently waged a very private battle, the only private battle in life, and lost. Your job is to find out how, and why, he lost, in order to help others who will soon do battle—and yourself. It is a far cry from the dissection cadavers, which exist in a kind of sickening, professional death, as if their only purpose in their twilight, embalmed afterlife is to be thoroughly, inspectably dead.

WHEN WE GOT HOME, Judith went in to check on the kids and call Betty. I took the sitter home. She was a short, pert girl named Sally, a cheerleader at Brookline High. Normally, when I drove her home we talked about neutral, safe things: how she liked school, where she wanted to go to college, things like that. But tonight I was feeling inquisitive, and old, and out of touch, like a man returning to his country after an extended time abroad. Everything was different, even the kids, even youth. They weren't doing what we had done. They had different challenges and different problems. At least, they had different drugs. Perhaps the problems were still the same. At least, that was what you wanted to think.

Finally I decided I had had too much to drink at the party, and had better keep my mouth shut. So I let Sally talk about passing her driver's test, and nothing more. As she talked, I felt both cowardly and relieved. And then I thought that it was foolish, that there was no reason for me to be curious about my babysitter, no reason to get to know her, and that if I tried it might be interpreted wrongly. It was safer to talk about drivers' licenses; solid, respectable, reasonable ground.

Then, for some reason, I thought of Alan Zenner. And something Art had said. "If you want to know about this world, turn on your television to an interview program, and turn off the sound." I did, a few days later. It was bizarre: the faces moving, the tongues going, the expressions and the hands. But no sound. Nothing at all. You had no idea what they were saying.

I FOUND THE ADDRESS in the phone book: Samuel F. Archer, 1334 Langdon Street. I dialed the number. A recorded voice came on.

"I am sorry, sir, the number you have dialed is not in service at this time. If you will hold the line, an operator will give you further information."

I waited. There was a series of rhythmic clicks, like the beat of a telephone heart, and then the operator. "Information. What number are you calling?"

"Seven-four-two-one-four-four-seven."

"That number has been disconnected."

"Do you have another listing?"

"No, sir."

Probably Samuel F. Archer had moved, but perhaps he hadn't. I drove there directly. The apartment was located on a steep hill on the east slope of Beacon Hill, in a battered apartment building. The hallway smelled of cabbage and baby formula. I went down a flight of creaking wooden stairs to the basement, where a green light flashed, illuminating a door painted flat black.

A sign said, GOD GROWS HIS OWN.

I knocked.

From inside, I could hear screeches, whines, warbles, and something that sounded like groans. The door opened and I faced a young man in his twenties with a full beard and long, damp black hair. He wore dungarees, sandals, and a purple polka-dot shirt. He looked at me blandly, showing neither surprise nor interest. "Yes?"

"I am Dr. Berry. Are you Samuel Archer?"

"No."

"Is Mr. Archer in?"

"He's busy right now."

"I'd like to see him."

"You a friend of his?"

He was staring at me with open suspicion. I heard more sounds—a grating, a rumble, and a long, drawn-out whistle.

"I need his help," I said.

He seemed to relax slightly. "This is a bad time."

"It's urgent."

"You're a doctor?"

"Yes."

"You have a car?"

"Yes."

"What kind?"

"Chevrolet. Nineteen-sixty-five."

"What's the license?"

"Two-one-one-five-sixteen."

He nodded. "O.K.," he said. "Sorry, but you know how it is these days. You can't trust anyone.[1] Come in." He stepped back from the door. "But don't say anything, all right? I'll tell him first. He's composing, and he gets pretty wrapped up. It's the seventh hour and it should be O.K. But he does flip out easy. Even late."

We walked through what seemed to be a living room. There were studio couches and a few cheap lamps. The walls were white, and painted in weird, flowing designs in fluorescent colors. An ultraviolet lamp heightened the effect.

"Wild," I said, hoping that was the right thing.

"Yeah, man."

We went into the next room. The lighting was low. A pale, short boy with an immense head of curly blond hair squatted on the floor, surrounded by electronic equipment. Two speakers stood by the far wall. A tape recorder was running. The pale boy was working with his equipment, twirling knobs, producing the sounds. He did not look up at us as we entered. He seemed to be concentrating hard, but his movements were slow.

"Stay here," said the bearded boy. "I'll tell him."

---

[1] The Federal narcotics agents, or "narcs," are known in Boston to favor Chevrolets with licenses beginning with 412 or 414.

I stood by the door. The bearded boy approached the other and said gently, "Sam. Sam."

Sam looked up at him. "Hi," he said.

"Sam, you have a visitor."

Sam seemed puzzled. "I do?" He still had not noticed me.

"Yes. He is a very nice man. A very nice man. Do you understand that? He is very friendly."

"Good," Sam said slowly.

"He needs your help. Will you help him?"

"Sure," Sam said.

The bearded boy beckoned to me. I came over and said to him, "What is it?"

"Acid," he said. "Seventh hour. He should be coming down now. But go easy, right?"

"O.K.," I said.

I squatted down so I was on Sam's level. Sam looked at me with blank eyes.

"I don't know you," he said finally.

"I'm John Berry."

Sam did not move. "You're old, man," he said. "Really *old.*"

"In a way," I said.

"Yeah, man, wow. Hey, Marvin," he said, looking up at his friend, "did you see this guy? He's really *old.*"

"Yes," Marvin said.

"Hey, wow, old."

"Sam," I said, "I'm your friend."

I held out my hand, slowly, so as not to frighten him. He did not shake it; he took it by the fingers and held it to the light. He turned it slowly, looking at the palm, then the back. Then he moved the fingers.

"Hey, man," he said, "you're a doctor."

"Yes," I said.

"You have doctor's hands. I can feel it."

"Yes."

"Hey, man. Wow. Beautiful hands."

He was silent for a time, examining my hands, squeezing them, stroking them, feeling the hairs on the back, the fingernails, the tips of the fingers.

"They shine," he said. "I wish I had hands like that."

"Maybe you do," I said.

He dropped my hands and looked at his own. Finally he said, "No. They're different."

"Is that bad?"

He gave me a puzzled look. "Why did you come here?"

"I need your help."

"Yeah. Hey. O.K."

"I need some information."

I did not realize this was a mistake until Marvin started forward. Sam became agitated; I pushed Marvin back.

"It's O.K., Sam. It's O.K."

"You're a cop," Sam said.

"No. No cop. I'm not a cop, Sam."

"You are, you're lying."

"He often gets paranoid," Marvin said. "It's his bag. He's worried about freaking out."

"You're a cop, a lousy cop."

"No, Sam. I'm not a cop. If you don't want to help me, I'll leave."

"You're a rock, a cop, a sock, a lock."

"No, Sam. No. No."

He settled down then, his body relaxing, his muscles softening.

I took a deep breath. "Sam, you have a friend. Bubbles."

"Yes."

"Sam, she has a friend named Karen."

He was staring off into space. It was a long time before he answered. "Yes. Karen."

"Bubbles lived with Karen. Last summer."

"Yes."

"Did you know Karen?"

"Yes."

He began to breathe rapidly, his chest heaving, and his eyes got wide. I put my hand on his shoulder, gently. "Easy, Sam, Easy. Easy. Is something wrong?"

"Karen," he said, staring off across the room. "She was . . . terrible."

"Sam—"

"She was the worst, man. The worst."

"Sam, where is Bubbles now?"

"Out. She went to visit Angela. Angela . . ."

"Angela Harding," Marvin said. "She and Karen and Bubbles all roomed together in the summer."

"Where is Angela now?" I asked Marvin.

At that moment, Sam jumped up and began to shout "Cop! Cop!" at the top of his lungs. He swung at me, missed, and tried to kick me. I caught his foot, and he fell, striking some of the electronic equipment. A loud, high-pitched whee-whee-whee filled the room.

Marvin said, "I'll get the thorazine."[2]

"Screw the thorazine," I said. "Help me." I grabbed Sam and held him down. He screamed over the howl of the electronic sound.

"Cop! Cop! Cop!"

He kicked and thrashed. Marvin tried to help, but he was ineffectual. Sam was banging his head against the floor.

"Get your foot under his head."

He didn't understand.

"Move!" I said.

He got his foot under, so Sam would not hurt his head. Sam continued to thrash and twist in my grip. Abruptly, I released him. He stopped writhing, looked at his hands, then looked at me.

"Hey, man. What's the matter?"

"You can relax now," I said.

"Hey, man. You let me go."

I nodded to Marvin, who went and unplugged the electronic equipment. The howls stopped. The room became strangely silent.

Sam sat up, staring at me. "Hey, you let me go. You really let me go." He looked at my face.

"Man," he said, touching my cheek, "you're beautiful."

And then he kissed me.

WHEN I GOT HOME, Judith was lying awake in bed.

"What happened?"

As I undressed, I said, "I got kissed."

"By Sally?" She sounded amused.

"No. By Sam Archer."

"The composer?"

"That's right."

"Why?"

"It's a long story," I said.

"I'm not sleepy," she said.

I told her about it, then got into bed and kissed her. "Funny," I said, "I've never been kissed by a man before."

---

[2] Thorazine is a tranquilizer, universally used as an antidote to LSD and employed to end bad trips. However, when other psychedelic compounds such as STP are used, thorazine heightens the drug effect instead of abolishing it. Thus physicians who see LSD psychosis in the EW no longer automatically administer thorazine.

She rubbed my neck. "Like it?"

"Not much."

"That's strange," she said, "I like it fine," and she pulled me down to her.

"I bet you've been kissed by men all your life," I said.

"Some are better than others."

"Who's better than others?"

"You're better than others."

"Is that a promise?"

She licked the tip of my nose with her tongue. "No," she said, "that's a come-on."

WEDNESDAY

October
12

ONE

ONCE A MONTH, the Lord takes pity on the Cradle of Liberty and lets the sun shine on Boston. Today was that day: cool, bright and clear, with an autumn crispness in the air. I awoke feeling good, with the sharp expectation that things would happen.

I had a large breakfast, including two eggs, which I ate with guilty relish, savoring their cholesterol. Then I went into my study to plan the day. I began by drawing up a list of everyone I had seen and trying to determine if any of them were suspects. Nobody really was.

The first person to suspect in any abortion question is the woman herself, since so many are self-induced. The autopsy showed that Karen must have had anesthetic for the operation; therefore she didn't do it.

Her brother knew how to do the procedure, but he was on duty at the time. I could check that, and might, later on, but for the moment, there was no reason to disbelieve him.

Peter Randall and J. D. were both possibilities, technically speaking. But somehow I couldn't imagine either of them doing it.

That left Art, or one of Karen's Beacon Hill friends, or somebody I hadn't met yet and didn't even know existed.

I stared at the list for a while, and then called the Mallory Building at the City. Alice wasn't there; I talked with another secretary.

"Have you got the path diagnosis on Karen Randall?"

"What's the case number?"

"I don't know the case number."

Very irritably, she said, "It would help if you did."

"Please check it anyway," I said.

I knew perfectly well that the secretary had a file-card system right in front of her, with all the finished posts for a month arranged alphabetically and by number. It would be no trouble for her.

After a long pause, she said, "Here it is. Vaginal hemorrhage secondary to uterine perforation and lacerations, following attempted dilation and curettage for three-month pregnancy. The secondary diagnosis is systemic anaphylaxis."

"I see," I said, frowning. "Are you sure?"

"I'm just reading what it says," she said.

"Thanks," I said.

I hung up, feeling odd. Judith gave me a cup of coffee and said, "What happened?"

"The autopsy report says Karen Randall was pregnant."

"Oh?"

"Yes."

"Wasn't she?"

"I never thought so," I said.

I knew I could be wrong. It might have been proven in the micro exam, where the gross had shown nothing. But somehow it didn't seem likely.

I called Murph's lab to see if he had finished with the blood-hormone assay, but he hadn't; it wouldn't be finished until after noon. I said I'd call him back.

Then I opened the phone book and looked up the address of Angela Harding. She was living on Chestnut Street, a very good address.

I went over to see her.

CHESTNUT STREET IS OFF CHARLES, near the bottom of the Hill. It's a very quiet area of townhouses, antique shops, quaint restaurants, and small grocery stores; most of the people who live here are young professionals —doctors and lawyers and bankers—who want a good address but can't yet afford to move out to Newton or Wellesley. The other people who live here are old professionals, men in their fifties and sixties whose children are grown and married, permitting them to move back to the city. If you are going to live anywhere in Boston, you have to live on Beacon Hill.

There were, of course, some students living here, but usually they were stacked three or four deep in small apartments; it was the only way they could afford the rents. Older residents seemed to like the students; they added a little color and youth to the neighborhood. That is, they liked the students so long as the students looked clean and behaved themselves.

Angela Harding lived on the second floor of a walk-up; I knocked on the door. It was answered by a slim, dark-haired girl wearing a mini-skirt and a sweater. She had a flower painted on her cheek, and large, blue-tinted granny glasses.

"Angela Harding?"

"No," said the girl. "You're too late. She's already gone. But maybe she'll call back."

I said, "My name is Dr. Berry. I'm a pathologist."

"Oh."

The girl bit her lip and stared at me uncertainly.

"Are you Bubbles?"

"Yes," she said. "How did you know?" And then she snapped her fingers. "Of course. You were the one with Superhead last night."

"Yes."

"I heard you'd been around."

"Yes."

She stepped back from the door. "Come in."

The apartment had almost no furniture at all. A single couch in the living room, and a couple of pillows on the floor; through an open door, I saw an unmade bed.

"I'm trying to find out about Karen Randall," I said.

"I heard."

"Is this where you all lived last summer?"

"Yeah."

"When did you last see Karen?"

"I haven't seen her for months. Neither has Angela," she said.

"Did Angela tell you that?"

"Yes. Of course."

"When did she say that to you?"

"Last night. We were talking about Karen last night. You see, we'd just found out about her, uh, accident."

"Who told you?"

She shrugged. "The word got around."

"What word?"

"That she got a bad scrape."

"Do you know who did it?"

She said, "They've picked up some doctor. But you know that."

"Yes," I said.

"He probably did it," she said, with a shrug. She brushed her long black hair away from her face. She had very pale skin. "But I don't know."

"How do you mean?"

"Well, Karen was no fool. She knew the score. Like, she'd been through the routine before. Including last summer."

"An abortion?"

"Yeah. That's right. And afterward she was real depressed. She took a couple of down-trips, real freaks, and it shook her up. She had this thing about babies, and she knew it was rotten because it gave her freak trips. We didn't want her to fly for a while after the abortion, but she insisted, and it was bad. Real bad."

I said, "How do you mean?"

"One time she became the knife. She was scraping out the room and screaming the whole time that it was bloody, that all the walls were covered with blood. And she thought the windows were babies and that they were turning black and dying. Really bad news."

"What did you do?"

"We took care of her." Bubbles shrugged. "What else could we do?"

She reached over to a table and picked up a jar and a small wire loop. She swung the loop in the air and a stream of bubbles floated out and drifted gently downward. She watched them. One after another, they fell to the floor and popped.

"Real bad."

"Last summer," I said, "who did the abortion?"

Bubbles laughed. "I don't know."

"What happened?"

"Well, she got knocked up. So she announces that she's going to get rid of it, and she takes off for a day, and then comes back all smiling and happy."

"No problems?"

"None." She swung out another stream of bubbles and watched them. "None at all. Excuse me a minute."

She went into the kitchen, poured a glass of water, and swallowed it with a pill.

"I was coming down," she said, "you know?"

"What was it?"

"Bombs."

"Bombs?"

"Sure. You know." She waved her hand impatiently. "Speed. Lifts. Jets. Bennies."

"Amphetamine?"

"Methedrene."

"You on it all the time?"

"Just like a doctor." She brushed her hair back again. "Always asking questions."

"Where do you get the stuff?"

I had seen the capsule. It was at least five milligrams. Most of the black-market material is one milligram.

"Forget it," she said. "All right? Just forget it."

"If you wanted me to forget it," I said, "why did you let me see you take it?"

"A shrink, too."

"Just curious."

"I was showing off," she said.

"Maybe you were."

"Maybe I was." She laughed.

"Was Karen on speed, too?"

"Karen was on everything." Bubbles sighed. "She used to shoot speed."

I must have looked puzzled, because she made jabbing motions at her elbow with her finger, imitating intravenous injection.

"Nobody else shoots it," Bubbles said. "But Karen went all out."

I said, "Her trips . . ."

"Acid. Once, DMT."

"How did she feel afterward?"

"Like hell. She was really turned off. Wired out. Down, you know, they were really down-trips."

"Did she stay turned off?"

"Yeah. The rest of the summer. Never made it once with a guy for the rest of the summer. Like she was afraid."

"Are you sure about that?"

"Yeah," she said. "Sure."

I looked around the apartment. "Where is Angela?"

"Out."

"Where did she go? I'd like to talk to her."

"She really needs to talk to you, right now."

I said, "Is she in some kind of trouble?"

"No."

"I'd like to talk to her."

Bubbles shrugged. "If you can find her, talk to her."

"Where did she go?"

"I told you. Out."

"I understand she's a nurse," I said.

"That's right," Bubbles said. "You got the——"

At that point, the door opened and a tall girl burst into the room. She said, "That bastard isn't anywhere, he's hiding, the rotten——"

She stopped when she saw me.

"Lo, Ang," Bubbles said. She nodded to me. "You got an oldie but goodie here to see you."

Angela Harding swept into the room and slumped on the couch, and lit a cigarette. She wore a very short black dress, black-net stockings, and patent-leather black boots. She had long dark hair and a hard, classically beautiful face with bones that looked chiseled; the face of a model. I had trouble picturing her as a nurse.

"You're the one who wants to know about Karen?"

I nodded.

"Sit down," she said. "Take a load off."

Bubbles said, "Ang, I didn't tell him—"

"Get me a Coke, would you, Bubbles?" Angela said. Bubbles nodded quietly and went into the kitchen. "You want a Coke?"

"No, thanks."

She shrugged. "Suit yourself." She sucked on the cigarette and stubbed it out. Her movements were quick but she kept her composure, a calm in her face. She lowered her voice. "I didn't want to talk about Karen in front of Bubbles. She's pretty upset about it."

"Karen?"

"Yes. They were close."

"And you?"

"Not so close."

"How's that?"

"She came on strong, in the beginning. Nice girl, a little wild, but fun. Very strong in the beginning. So we decided to share a room, the three of us. Then later Bubbles moves in with Superhead, and I'm stuck with Karen. It wasn't so easy."

"Why?"

"She was a crazy kid. She was nuts."

Bubbles came back with the Coke. "She wasn't."

"Not around you. She had an act for you."

"You're just mad because of——"

"Yeah. Right. Sure." Angela tossed her head and shifted her long legs. She turned to me and said, "She's talking about Jimmy. Jimmy was a resident I knew, in OB."

"That was the service you were on?"

"Yes," she said. "Jimmy and I had a thing, and I thought it was good. It *was* good. Then Karen stepped in."

Angela lit another cigarette and avoided my eyes. I could not really tell whether she was talking to me or to Bubbles. Obviously the two girls did not agree.

"I never thought she'd do it," Angela said. "Not your own roommate. I mean, there are rules. . . ."

"She liked him," Bubbles said.

"She *liked* him. Yeah, I suppose so. For a quick seventy-two hours."

Angela stood and paced up and down the room. Her dress barely reached to mid thigh. She was a strikingly beautiful girl, much more beautiful than Karen.

"You're not fair," Bubbles said.

"I don't *feel* fair."

"You know what you're saying is a lie. You know that Jimmy——"

"I don't know anything," Angela said. "All I know is that Jimmy's in Chicago now finishing his residency, and I'm not with him. Maybe if I was—" She stopped.

"Maybe," Bubbles said.

"Maybe what?" I said.

"Skip it," Angela said.

I said, "When did you last see Karen?"

"I don't know. It must have been August sometime. Before she started school."

"You didn't see her last Sunday?"

"No," she said, still pacing. She didn't even break step. "No."

"That's funny. Alan Zenner saw her last Sunday."

"Who?"

"Alan Zenner. He was a friend of hers."

"Uh-huh."

"He saw her, and she told him she was coming over here."

Angela and Bubbles exchanged looks. Bubbles said, "The dirty little—"

"It's not true?" I asked.

"No," Angela said tightly. "We didn't see her."

"But he was positive—"

"She must have changed her mind. She usually did, you know. Karen changed her mind so often you wondered if she had one."

Bubbles said, "Ang, listen . . ."

"Get me another Coke, will you?"

There was no mistaking the command in the voice. Bubbles got up meekly for another Coke.

"Bubbles is nice," Angela said, "but a little naïve. She likes everything to be sweet and nice in the end. That's why what happened to Karen bothers her so much."

"I see."

She stopped pacing and stood in front of me. Her body took on a rigidity that melted slowly into an icy calm. "Was there anything in particular you wanted to ask me?"

"Just if you'd seen Karen."

"No. The answer is no."

I stood. "Well then, thank you for your time."

Angela nodded. I went to the door. As I left I heard Bubbles say, "Is he leaving?"

And Angela said, "Shut up."

TWO

SHORTLY BEFORE NOON I called Bradford's office and was told that one of the staff was taking Dr. Lee's case. The man was named George Wilson. My call was put through to him. Over the phone he sounded smooth and self-confident; he agreed to meet me for drinks at five, but not at the Trafalgar Club. We would meet at Crusher Thompson's, a bar downtown.

After that, I had lunch in a drive-in and read the morning papers. The story about Art's arrest had finally broken, big, hitting all the front pages, though there was still no link to Karen Randall's death. Along with the story was a picture of Art. There were dark, sadistic circles under his eyes. His mouth drooped in a sinister way and his hair was disheveled. He could have been any cheap hood.

The stories didn't say much, just a bare outline of the facts of his arrest. They didn't have to say much: the picture said it all. In a way it was clever. You couldn't move for a prejudicial pretrial publicity on the basis of an unflattering picture.

After lunch I smoked a cigarette and tried to put it all together. I didn't have much success. The descriptions I had heard of Karen were too conflicting, too uncertain. I had no clear picture of her, or what she might have done. Particularly what she might have done if she arrived in Boston for a weekend, pregnant, and needing an abortion.

At one I called Murphy's lab again. Murph answered the phone. "Hormones Unlimited."

"Hello, Murph. What's the word?"

"On Karen Randall?"

"Murph, you've been doing homework."

"Not exactly," he said. "The City just called. Weston was on the phone. Wanted to know if you'd brought in a blood sample."

"And what did you say?"

"Yes."

"And what did he say?"

"Wanted to know the results. I told him."

"What are the results?"

"All the hormone and excretion metabolite levels are flat low. She wasn't pregnant. Absolutely impossible."

"O.K.," I said. "Thanks."

Murph had just put some life back into my theory. Not much, but some.

"You going to explain all this, John?"

"Not now," I said.

"You promised."

"I know," I said. "But not now."

"I knew you'd do this to me," Murph said. "Sarah will hate me." Sarah was his wife. She thrived on gossip.

"Sorry, but I just can't."

"Hell of a thing to do to an old friend."

"Sorry."

"If she divorces me," Murph said, "I'm naming you as co-defendant."

THREE

I ARRIVED AT THE MALLORY PATH LABS AT THREE. The first man I ran into was Weston, who was looking tired. He gave me a lopsided smile of greeting.

"What did you find out?" I said.

"The findings are negative," he said, "for pregnancy."

"Oh?"

"Yes." He picked up the folder containing the path protocol and thumbed through it. "No question."

"I called here earlier and was told the report was three months' pregnancy."

Weston said carefully, "Whom did you talk with?"

"A secretary."

"There must have been some kind of mistake."

"I guess," I said.

He handed me the folder. "Want to see the slides, too?"

"Yes. I'd like to."

We walked to the pathologists' reading room, a long room divided into individual cubicles, where the pathologists kept their microscopes and slides, and wrote up their autopsies.

We stopped at one booth.

"There it is," Weston said, pointing to a box of slides. "I'll be curious to have your opinion on them when you're through."

He left me, and I sat down in front of the scope, switched on the light, and began work. There were thirty slides in the box, made from all the major organs. Six had been made from different parts of the uterus: I began with them.

It was immediately clear that the girl was not pregnant. The endometrium was not hyperplastic. If anything, it appeared dormant and atrophic, with a thin proliferative layer, few glands, and decreased vascularity. I checked several other slides to be sure. They were all the same. Some contained thromboses from the scraping, but that was the only difference.

As I looked at the slides I considered their meaning. The girl had not been pregnant, yet she had been convinced she was. Therefore her periods must have stopped. That could account for the dormant appearance of the endometrium. But what had caused the periods to stop? I ran through the differential in my mind.

In a girl of this age, neurogenic factors came immediately to mind. The pressures and excitement of beginning school and moving to a new environment might have temporarily suppressed menstruation—but not for three months, and not with the associated signs: obesity, change, in hair distribution, and so on.

Then there were hormonal disorders. Adrenal virilizing syndromes, Stein-Leventhal, irradiation. All of them seemed unlikely for one reason or another, but there was one quick way to find out.

I put the adrenal slide under the stage. There was good evidence of cortical atrophy, particularly in the cells of the zona fascicularis. The zona glomerulosa appeared normal.

Rule out virilizing syndromes and adrenal tumor.

Next I looked at the ovaries. Here the changes were striking. The follicles were small, immature, withered-looking. The whole organ, like the uterine endometrium, had a dormant appearance.

Rule out Stein-Levanthal and ovarian tumor.

Finally, I put the thyroid slide under the stage. Even under the lowest power, the atrophy of the gland was apparent. The follicles were shrunken and the lining cells were low. Clear hypothyroidism.

That meant that the thyroid, adrenals, and ovaries were all atrophic. The diagnosis was clear, though the etiology was not. I opened the folder and read through the official report. Weston had done it; the style was brisk and direct. I came to the micro write-ups. He had noted the endometrium was low and aberrant-looking, but he had considered the other glands to be "of normal appearance, questionmark early atrophic changes."

I shut the folder and went to see him.

HIS OFFICE WAS LARGE, lined with books, and very neat. He sat behind an old, heavy desk smoking a briar pipe, looking scholarly and venerable.

"Something wrong?" he asked.

I hesitated. I had been wondering whether he had covered up, whether he had joined the others who were out to frame Art. But that was ridiculous; Weston couldn't be bought, not at his age, not with his reputation. Nor was he particularly close to the Randall family. He would have no reason to falsify the report.

"Yes," I said. "I wondered about your micro diagnosis."

He puffed the pipe calmly. "Oh?"

"Yes. I've just reviewed the slides, and they seem pretty atrophic to me. I thought perhaps——"

"Well, John," Weston said, chuckling "I know what you're going to say. You thought perhaps I'd want to review them." He smiled at me. "I *have* reviewed them. Twice. This is an important postmortem and I did it as carefully as I know how. The first time I examined the slides, I felt as you did, that they seemed to show pan hypopituitarism affecting all three target organs—thyroid, adrenals, gonads. I felt that very strongly, so I went back to the gross organs. As you yourself saw, the gross organs were not strikingly abnormal."

"It might have been recently acquired," I said.

"Yes," he said, "it might. That's what makes it so difficult. Then, too, we'd like a look at the brain, to check for evidence of neoplasm or infarction. But that's not possible; the body was cremated this morning."

"I see."

He smiled up at me. "Sit down, John. It makes me nervous to have you standing like that." When I was sitting, he said, "Anyway I looked at the gross, and then went back to the slides. This time I was less certain. I wasn't fully convinced. So I checked some old cases of pan hypopit, reviewed the old slides, and finally looked at the Randall slides a third time.

By then I felt I could not be certain of a diagnosis of pituitary dysfunction. The more I looked, the less certain I felt. I wanted some kind of corroboratory evidence—brain pathology, or X rays, or blood hormones. That was why I called Jim Murphy."

"Oh?"

"Yes." His pipe went out; he relit it again. "I suspected you'd taken the blood sample to do estradiol tests, and that you'd get Murphy to do it. I wanted to know if you'd also decided to have other hormone levels checked—TSH, ACTH, T_4, anything that might help."

"Why didn't you just call me?"

"I did, but your lab didn't know where you were."

I nodded. Everything he had said made perfect sense. I felt my body slowly relaxing.

"By the way," Weston said, "I understand some skull films of Karen Randall were taken a while back. Any idea what they showed?"

"Nothing," I said. "They were negative."

Weston sighed. "Pity."

"I'll tell you something interesting though," I said.

"What's that?"

"They were ordered because she complained of blurring vision."

Weston sighed. "John, do you know the most common cause of blurring vision?"

"No."

"Lack of sleep," Weston said. He pushed the pipe to the side of his mouth and held it in his teeth. "What would you do if you were in my position? Make a diagnosis on the basis of a complaint which led to negative X rays?"

"The slides *are* suggestive," I reminded him.

"But only suggestive." He shook his head slowly. "This is already a confused case, John. I'm not going to make it more confused by throwing in a diagnosis I'm not sure about. After all, I may be called into court to defend it. I'd rather not stick my neck out. If the prosecution or the defense wants to find a pathologist to review the material and stick *his* neck out, that's fine. The material is here for anyone to see. But I'm not going to do it. My years in the courtroom have taught me one thing, at least."

"What's that?"

"Never take a position unless you are certain it can be defended against any onslaught. That may sound like good advice to a general," he said, smiling, "but then, a courtroom is nothing more than a very civilized war."

FOUR

I HAD TO SEE SANDERSON. I had promised to see him, and now I needed his advice badly. But as I entered the lobby of the Lincoln Hospital, the first person I saw was Harry Fallon.

He was slinking down a corridor, wearing a raincoat and hat pulled down over his forehead. Harry is an internist with a large suburban practice in Newton; he is also a former actor and something of a clown. I greeted him and he raised the brim of his hat slowly. His eyes were bloodshot and his face sallow.

"I hab a code," Harry said.

"Who are you seeing?"

"Gordon. The cheeb residend." He took out a Kleenex and blew his nose loudly. "Aboud my bat code."

I laughed. "You sound like you've swallowed cotton."

"Thang you bery mugh." He sniffled. "This is no labbing madder."

He was right, of course. All practicing doctors feared getting sick. Even small colds were considered bad for your image, for what is loosely called "patient rapport," and any serious illness became a matter for the utmost secrecy. When old Henley finally developed chronic glomerulo-nephritis, he went to elaborate lengths to be sure his patients never found out; he would visit his doctor in the middle of the night, sneaking about like a thief.

"It doesn't sound like a bad cold," I told Harry.

"Hah. You thingh so? Listen to me." He blew his nose again, a long, honking sound, somewhere between a foghorn and the death rattle of a hippopotamus.

"How long have you had it?"

"Du days. Du miberable, miberable days. My padends are nodicing."

"What are you taking for it?"

"Hod toddies," he said. "Besd thing for a virus. Bud the world is againsd me, John. Today, on tob ov my code, I got a tickud."

"A tickud?"

"Yes. For double-barking."

I laughed, but at the back of my mind, something was bothering me, something I knew I should be remembering and thinking about, something I had forgotten and ignored.

It was a strange and irritating feeling.

I MEET SANDERSON IN THE PATH LIBRARY. It's a square room with lots of chairs, the folding kind, and a projector and screen. Path conferences are held here, in which autopsies are reviewed, and they are so frequent you can practically never get in to use the library books.

On the shelves, in boxes, were autopsy reports for every person done in the Lincoln since 1923, the year we began to keep good records. Prior to that time, nobody had a very good idea of how many people were dying from what diseases, but as knowledge of medicine and the human body increased, that information became vitally important. One proof of increased interest was the number of autopsies performed; in 1923 all the reports filled one slim box; but by 1965, it required half a shelf for all the records. At present, more than seventy percent of all patients who died in the hospital were autopsied, and there was talk of microfilming the reports for the library.

In one corner of the room was a portable electric coffeepot, a bowl of sugar, a stack of paper cups, and a sign that said, "5 cents a cup. Scout's honor." Sanderson was fussing with the pot, trying to get it to work. The pot represented an ancient challenge: it was said nobody was permitted to finish his path residency at the Lincoln until he had mastered its workings.

"Someday," Sanderson muttered, "I'm going to electrocute myself on this damned thing." He plugged it in; crackling sounds were heard. "Me, or some other poor bastard. Cream and sugar?"

"Please," I said.

Sanderson filled two cups, holding the pot at arm's length. Sanderson was notoriously bad with anything mechanical. He had a superb, almost instinctive understanding of the human body and its functions of flesh and bone, but mechanical, steel, and electrical objects were beyond him. He lived in constant fear that his car, or his TV, or his stereo would break down; he regarded them all as potential traitors and deserters.

He was a tall, powerfully built man who had once rowed stroke for the Harvard heavyweights. His forearms and wrists were as thick as most men's calves. He had a solemn, thoughtful face; he might have been a judge, or an excellent poker player.

"Did Weston say anything else?" he asked.

"No."

"You sound unhappy."

"Let's say I'm worried."

Sanderson shook his head. "I think you're barking up the wrong tree here," he said. "Weston wouldn't fake a report for anybody. If he says he was unsure, then he was."

"Maybe you should examine the slides yourself."

"I'd like to," Sanderson said, "but you know that's impossible."

He was right. If he showed up at Mallory and asked to see the slides, it would be taken as a personal insult by Weston. That kind of thing just wasn't done.

I said, "Maybe if he asked you . . ."

"Why should he?"

"I don't know."

"Weston has made his diagnosis and signed his name to it. The matter closes there, unless it comes up again during the trial."

I felt a sinking feeling. Over the past days, I had come to believe very strongly that there must not be a trial. Any trial, even an acquittal, would seriously damage Art's reputation, his standing, and his practice. A trial had to be prevented.

"But you think she was hypopit," Sanderson said.

"Yes."

"Etiology?"

"Neoplasm, I think."

"Adenoma?"[1]

"I imagine. Maybe craniopharyngioma."

"How long?"

"It couldn't be very long," I said. "X rays four months ago were normal. No enlargement or erosion of the sella turcica. But she did complain of vision trouble."

"What about pseudotumor?"

Pseudotumor cerebri is a disorder of women and young children. Patients get all the symptoms of a tumor, but don't actually have one. It is related to withdrawal of steroid therapy; women sometimes get it when taking birth-control pills. But as far as I knew, Karen wasn't taking pills. I told Sanderson.

"Too bad we don't have slides of the brain," he said.

I nodded.

[1] A chromophobe adenoma is the most common tumor of the pituitary. It is slow-growing and relatively benign, but it presses on the optic nerve, causing visual symptoms, and it may create endocrine dysfunction.

"On the other hand," Sanderson said, "an abortion was performed. We can't forget that."

"I know," I said. "But it's just another indicator that Art didn't do it. He wouldn't have aborted her without doing a bunny test first, and such a test would have been negative."

"That's only circumstantial evidence, at best."

"I know," I said, "but it's something. A start."

"There is another possibility," Sanderson said. "Supposing the abortionist was willing to take Karen's word that she was pregnant."

I frowned. "I don't understand. Art didn't know the girl; he had never seen her before. He would never—"

"I'm not thinking of Art," Sanderson said. He was staring at his feet, as if he had something embarrassing on his mind.

"What do you mean?"

"Well, this is all highly speculative. . . ."

I waited for him.

"A lot of muck has been thrown already. I hate to add to it," he said.

I said nothing.

"I never knew it before," Sanderson continued. "I thought I was pretty well-informed about these things, but I never knew it until today. As you can imagine, the whole medical community is buzzing. J. D. Randall's girl dies from an abortion—you can't keep other doctors from talking about *that*." He sighed. "Anyway, it was something one of the wives told my wife. I don't even know if it's true."

I wasn't going to push Sanderson. He could take his time in telling me; I lit a cigarette and waited patiently.

"Oh hell," Sanderson said, "it's probably just a rumor. I can't imagine I'd never heard of it before."

"What?" I said finally.

"Peter Randall. Peter does abortions. Very quiet and exclusive, but he does them."

"Jesus," I said, sitting down in a chair.

"It's hard to believe," Sanderson said.

I smoked a cigarette and thought it over. If Peter did abortions, did J. D. know? Did he think Peter had done it, and was covering up for him? Was that what he meant by "a family matter"? If so, why had Art been dragged into this?

And why would Peter abort the girl in the first place? Peter had evidence that there might be something else wrong with the girl. He was a good enough doctor to think of a pit tumor. If the girl came to him saying she was pregnant, he'd certainly think back to her vision trouble. And he'd run tests.

"Peter didn't do it," I said.

"Maybe she put pressure on him. Maybe she was in a hurry. She only had one weekend."

"No. He wouldn't respond to pressure from her."

"She was family."

"She was a young and hysterical girl," I said, remembering Peter's description.

Sanderson said, "Can you be sure Peter didn't do it?"

"No," I admitted.

"Let's suppose he did. And let's suppose Mrs. Randall knew about the abortion. Or that the girl told her, as she was bleeding to death, that Peter had done it. What would Mrs. Randall do? Turn in her brother-in-law?"

I could see where he was leading me. It certainly provided an explanation for one of the puzzles of the case—why Mrs. Randall had called in the police. But I didn't like it, and I told Sanderson so.

"The reason you don't like it is you're fond of Peter."

"That may be."

"You can't afford to exclude him or anyone else. Do you know where Peter was last Sunday night?"

"No."

"Neither do I," Wes Sanderson said, "but I think it's worth checking."

"No," I said, "it's not. Peter wouldn't do it. And even if he did, he wouldn't have botched it so badly. No professional would have."

"You're prejudging the case," Sanderson said.

"Look, if Peter could have done it—without tests, without anything—then so could Art."

"Yes," Sanderson said mildly. "That has occurred to me."

FIVE

I WAS FEELING IRRITABLE when I left Sanderson. I couldn't decide exactly why. Perhaps he was right; perhaps I was unreasonably and illogically searching for fixed points, for things and people to believe in.

But there was something else. In any court action, there was always the chance that Sanderson and I could be implicated, and our role in fooling the tissue committee brought out. Both Sanderson and I had a large stake in this business, a stake as large as Art's. We hadn't talked about that, but it was there in the back of my mind, and I was sure in the back of his as well. And that put a different interpretation on things.

Sanderson was perfectly correct: we could put the squeeze on Peter Randall. But if we did, we'd never know why we did. We could always say it was because we believed Peter was guilty. Or because it was expedient, to save a falsely accused man.

But we would always wonder whether we did it simply to protect ourselves.

Before I did anything, I would have to get more information. Sanderson's argument made no distinction between Mrs. Randall knowing that Peter had done the abortion and merely suspecting that he had.

And there was another question. If Mrs. Randall suspected that Peter had done the abortion and wished to keep him from being arrested, why had she named Art? What did she know about Art?

Art Lee was a circumspect and cautious man. He was hardly a household word among the pregnant women of Boston. He was known to a few physicians and a relatively small number of patients. His clientele was carefully chosen.

How had Mrs. Randall known he performed abortions? There was one man who might know the answer: Fritz Werner.

FRITZ WERNER lived in a townhouse on Beacon Street. The ground floor was given over to his office—an anteroom and a large, comfortable room with desk, chair, and couch—and to his library. The upper two floors comprised his living quarters. I went directly to the second floor and entered the living room to find it the same as always: a large desk by the window, covered with pens, brushes, sketchbooks, pastels; drawings by Picasso and Miró on the walls; a photograph of T. S. Eliot glowering into the camera; an informal, signed portrait of Marianne Moore talking with her friend Floyd Patterson.

Fritz was sitting in a heavy armchair, wearing slacks and an enormous bulky sweater. He had stereophonic earphones on his head, was smoking a thick cigar, and crying. The tears rolled down his flat, pale cheeks. He wiped his eyes when he saw me, and took off the earphones.

"Ah, John. Do you know any Albinoni?"

"No," I said.

"Then you don't know the adagio."

"I'm afraid not."

"It always makes me sad," he said, dabbing his eyes. "Infernally, infernally sad. So sweet. Do sit down."

I sat. He turned off his record player and took off the record. He dusted it carefully and replaced it in the jacket.

"It was good of you to come. How was your day?"

"Interesting."

"You've looked up Bubbles?"

"Yes, I did."

"How did you find her?"

"Confusing."

"Why do you say that?"

I smiled. "Don't analyze me, Fritz. I never pay my doctor bills."

"No?"

"Tell me about Karen Randall," I said.

"This is very nasty, John."

"Now you sound like Charlie Frank."

"Charlie Frank is not a *complete* fool," Fritz said. "By the way, did I tell you I have a new friend?"

"No," I said.

"I do, a marvelous creature, most amusing. We must talk about him some time."

"Karen Randall," I said, bringing him back to the point.

"Yes indeed." Fritz took a deep breath. "You didn't know the girl, John," he said. "She was not a nice child. Not at all. She was a mean, lying, unpleasant little child with severe neuroses. Bordering on psychosis, if you ask me."

He walked into the bedroom, stripping off his sweater. I followed him in and watched as he put on a clean shirt and a tie.

"Her problems," Fritz said, "were sexual in nature, stemming from a repressed childhood with her parents. Her father is not the most well-adjusted man I know. Marrying that woman is a perfect example. Have you met her?"

"The present Mrs. Randall?"

"Yes. Ghastly, *ghastly* woman."

He shuddered as he knotted his tie and straightened it in the mirror.

"Did you know Karen?" I asked.

"It was my misfortune to do so. I knew her parents as well. We first met at that marvelous, glorious party given by the Baroness de——"

"Just tell me," I said.

Fritz sighed. "This girl, this Karen Randall," he said, "she presented her parents with their own neuroses. In a sense she acted out their fantasies."

"What do you mean?"

"Breaking the mold—being sexually free, not caring what people said, dating the wrong kinds of people, and always with sexual undertones. Athletes. Negroes. That sort of thing."

"Was she ever your patient?"

He sighed. "No, thank God. At one point it was suggested that I take her, but I refused. I had three other adolescent girls at the time, and they were quite enough. Quite enough."

"Who asked you to take her?"

"Peter, of course. He's the only one with any sense in the family."

"What about Karen's abortions?"

"Abortions?"

"Come on, Fritz."

He went to a closet and found a sport coat, pulled it on, and tugged at the lapels. "People never understand," he said. "There is a cycle here, a pattern which is as easily recognizable, as familiar, as an MI.[1] You learn the pattern, the symptoms, the trouble. You see it acted out before you, again and again. A rebellious child chooses the weak point of its parent —with unfailing, uncanny accuracy—and proceeds to exploit it. But then when punishment comes, it must be in terms of the same weak point. It must all fit together: if someone asks you a question in French, you must answer in French."

"I don't understand."

"For a girl like Karen, punishment was important. She wanted to be punished, but her punishment, like her rebellion, had to be sexual in nature. She wanted to suffer the pain of childbirth, so she could compensate for breaking with her family, her society, her morality. . . . Dylan put it beautifully; I have the poem here somewhere." He began rummaging through a bookshelf.

"It's all right," I said.

"No, no, a lovely quotation. You'd enjoy it." He searched for a few more moments, then straightened. "Can't find it. Well, never mind. The point is that she needed suffering, but never experienced it. That was why she kept getting pregnant."

"You talk like a psychiatrist."

"We all do, these days."

"How many times did she get pregnant?"

[1] Myocardial infarction, a heart attack.

"Twice, that I know of. But that is just what I hear from my other patients. A great many women felt threatened by Karen. She impinged upon their system of values, their framework of right and wrong. She challenged them, she implied that they were old and sexless and timid and foolish. A middle-aged woman can't stand such a challenge; it is terrifying. She must respond, must react, must form an opinion which vindicates herself—and therefore condemns Karen."

"So you heard a lot of gossip."

"I heard a lot of fear."

He smoked his cigar. The room was filled with sunlight and blue smoke. He sat on the bed and began pulling on his shoes.

"Frankly," he said, "after a while I began to resent Karen myself. She went overboard, she did too much, she went too far."

"Perhaps she couldn't help it."

"Perhaps," Fritz said, "she needed a good spanking."

"Is that a professional opinion?"

He smiled. "That is just my human irritation showing through. If I could count the number of women who have run out and had affairs— disastrous affairs—just because of Karen. . . ."

"I don't care about the women," I said, "I care about Karen."

"She's dead now," Fritz said.

"That pleases you?"

"Don't be silly. Why do you say that?"

"Fritz . . ."

"Just a question."

"Fritz," I said, "how many abortions did Karen have before last weekend?"

"Two."

"One last summer," I said, "in June. And one before that?"

"Yes."

"And who aborted her?"

"I haven't the slightest," he said, puffing on his cigar.

"It was somebody good," I said, "because Bubbles said that Karen was only gone for an afternoon. It must have been very skillful and nontraumatic."

"Very likely. She was a rich girl, after all."

I looked at him, sitting there on the bed, tying his shoes and smoking the cigar. Somehow, I was convinced he knew.

"Fritz, was it Peter Randall?"

Fritz grunted. "If you know, why ask?"

"I need confirmation."

"You need a strong noose around you neck, if you ask me. But yes: it was Peter."

"Did J. D. know?"

"Heaven help us! Never!"

"Did Mrs. Randall know?"

"Hmmm. There I am not certain. It is possible but somehow I doubt it."

"Did J. D. know that Peter did abortions?"

"Yes. Everyone knows that Peter does abortions. He is *the* abortionist, believe me."

"But J. D. never knew Karen had been aborted."

"That's correct."

"What's the connection between Mrs. Randall and Art Lee?"

"You are very acute today," Fritz said.

I waited for an answer. Fritz puffed twice on his cigar, producing a dramatic cloud around his face, and looked away from me.

"Oh," I said. "When?"

"Last year. Around Christmas, if I recall."

"J. D. never knew?"

"If you will remember," Fritz said, "J. D. spent the months of November and December in India last year working for the State Department. Some kind of goodwill tour, or public health thing."

"Then who was the father?"

"Well, there is some speculation about that. But nobody knows for sure —perhaps not even Mrs. Randall."

Once again, I had the feeling that he was lying.

"Come on, Fritz. Are you going to help me or not?"

"Dear boy, you are immensely clever." He stood, walked to the mirror, and straightened his jacket. He ran his hands over his shirt. It was something you always noticed about Fritz: he was continually touching his body, as if to assure himself that he had not disappeared.

"I have often thought," Fritz said, "that the present Mrs. Randall might as well have been Karen's mother, since they are both such bitches in heat."

I lit a cigarette. "Why did J. D. marry her?"

Fritz gave a helpless shrug and fluffed a handkerchief in his pocket. He tugged his shirt cuffs down his jacket sleeves. "God only knows. There was great talk at the time. She comes from a good family, you know—a Rhode Island family—but they sent her to a Swiss school. Those Swiss schools will destroy a girl. In any event, she was a poor choice for a man in his sixties, and a busy surgeon. She grew rapidly bored sitting

round her cavernous home. The Swiss schools teach you to be bored in
ny case."

He buttoned his jacket and turned away from the mirror, with a final
lance over his shoulder at himself. "So," he said, "she amused herself."

"How long has this been going on?"

"More than a year."

"Did she arrange Karen's abortion?"

"I doubt it. One can't be sure, but I doubt it. More likely it would be
igne."

"Signe?"

"Yes. J. D.'s mistress."

I took a deep breath and wondered if Fritz was kidding me. I decided
e wasn't.

"J. D. had a mistress?"

"Oh, yes. A Finnish girl. She worked in the cardiology lab of the
Mem. Quite a stunner, I'm told."

"You never met her?"

"Alas."

"Then how do you know?"

He smiled enigmatically.

"Karen liked this Signe?"

"Yes. They were good friends. Rather close in ages, actually."

I ignored the implications in that.

"You see," Fritz continued, "Karen was very close to her mother, the
irst Mrs. Randall. She died two years ago of cancer—rectum, I think—
nd it was a great blow for Karen. She never liked her father much, but
ad always confided in her mother. The loss of a confidante at the age of
ixteen was a great blow to her. Much of her subsequent . . . activity
an be attributed to bad advice."

"From Signe?"

"No. Signe was quite a proper girl, from what I'm told."

"I don't get it."

"One of the reasons Karen disliked her father was that she knew about
is propensities. You see, he has always had women friends. Young ones.
The first was Mrs. Jewett, and then there was——"

"Never mind," I said. I had already gotten the picture. "He cheated
n his first wife, too?"

"Wandered," Fritz said. "Let us say wandered."

"And Karen knew?"

"She was quite a perceptive child."

"There's one thing I don't understand," I said. "If Randall likes variety why did he remarry?"

"Oh, that's quite clear. One look at the present Mrs. Randall and you'd know. She is a fixture in his life, a decoration, an ornament to his existence. Rather like an exotic potted plant—which is not far from the truth, considering how much she drinks."

"It doesn't make sense," I said.

He gave me an amused, askance look. "What about that nurse you have lunch with twice a week?"

"Sandra is a friend. She's a nice girl." As I said it, it occurred to me that he was astonishingly well informed.

"Nothing further?"

"Of course not," I said, a little stiffly.

"You just happen to run into her at the cafeteria on Thursdays and Fridays?"

"Yes. Our schedules——"

"What do you think this girl feels about you?"

"She's just a girl. She's ten years younger than I am."

"Aren't you flattered?"

"What do you mean?" I said, knowing exactly what he meant.

"Don't you derive satisfaction from talking with her?"

Sandra was a nurse on the eighth-floor medical service. She was very pretty, with very large eyes and a very small waist, and a way of walking. . . .

"Nothing has happened," I said.

"And nothing will. Yet you meet her twice a week."

"She happens to be a welcome change from my work," I said. "Twice a week. A rendezvous in the intimate, sexually charged atmosphere of the Lincoln Hospital cafeteria."

"There's no need to raise your voice."

"I'm not raising my voice," I said, lowering it.

"You see," Fritz said, "men handle things differently. You feel no compulsion to do more than talk to this girl. It is enough that she be there, hanging on your every word, mildly in love with you—"

"Fritz—"

"Look," Fritz said. "Let's take a case from my experience. I had a patient who felt a desire to kill people. It was a very strong desire, difficult to control. It bothered the patient; he was in constant fear of actually killing someone. But this man finally got a job in the Midwest, working as an executioner. He electrocuted people as his livelihood. And he did it very well; he was the best electrocutioner in the history of the state. He holds several patents, little techniques he has developed to do the job faster, more painlessly. He is a student of death. He likes his work. He is dedicated. He sees his methods and his advances much as a doctor does: a relief of suffering, an improvement, a bettering."

"So?"

"So I am saying that normal desires can take many forms, some legitimate, some not. Everyone must find a way to deal with them."

"We're a long way from Karen," I said.

"Not really. Have you ever wondered why she was so close to her mother and so estranged from her father? Have you ever wondered why, when her mother died, she chose the particular mode of behavior she did? Sex, drugs, self-humiliation? Even to the point of befriending her father's mistress?"

I sat back. Fritz was being rhetorical again.

"The girl," he said, "had certain stresses and strains. She had certain reactions, some defensive, some offensive, to what she knew was going on with her parents. She reacted to what she knew. She had to. In a sense, she stabilized her world."

"Some stability."

"True," Fritz said. "Unpleasant, nasty, perverse. But perhaps it was all she could manage."

I said, "I'd like to talk with this Signe."

"Impossible. Signe returned to Helsinki six months ago."

"And Karen?"

"Karen," Fritz said, "became a lost soul. She had no one to turn to, no friends, no aid. Or so she felt."

"What about Bubbles and Angela Harding?"

Fritz looked at me steadily. "What about them?"

"They could have helped her."

"Can the drowning save the drowning?"

We walked downstairs.

SIX

CRUSHER THOMPSON used to be a wrestler in the fifties. He was distinguished by a flat, spatulalike head, which he used to press down on his opponent's chest once the man was down, and thus crush him. For a few years, it was good for some laughs—and enough money to buy a bar which had become a hangout for young professional men. It was a well-run bar; Thompson, despite the shape of his head, was no fool. He had some corny touches—you wiped your feet on a wrestling mat as you entered— and the inevitable pictures of himself on the walls, but the overall effect was pleasing.

There was only one person in the bar when I arrived, a heavyset, well-dressed Negro sitting at the far end, hunched over a martini. I sat down and ordered a Scotch. Thompson himself was bartending, his sleeves rolled up to expose massive, hairy forearms.

I said, "You know a fellow named George Wilson?"

"Sure," Thompson said, with a crooked grin.

"Tell me when he comes in, will you?"

Thompson nodded to the man at the far end of the bar. "That's him, right there."

The Negro looked up and smiled at me. It was a half-amused, half-embarrassed look. I went over and shook his hand.

"Sorry," I said. "I'm John Berry."

"It's all right," he said, "this is new for me, too."

He was young, in his late twenties. There was a pale scar running down his neck from his right ear, disappearing below his shirt collar. But his eyes were steady and calm as he tugged at his red striped tie and said, "Shall we go to a booth?"

"All right."

As we walked to a booth, Wilson turned over his shoulder and said, "Two more of the same, Crusher."

The man behind the bar winked.

I said, "You're with Bradford's firm, is that it?"

"Yes. I was hired a little over a year ago."

I nodded.

"It was the usual thing," Wilson said. "They gave me a good office with a view out to the reception desk, so that people coming in and out could see me. That kind of thing."

I knew what he was saying, but I still felt a twist of irritation. I had several friends who were young lawyers, and none of them had gotten an office of any kind for several years after joining a firm. By any objective standard, this young man was lucky, but it was no good telling him that, because we both knew why he was lucky—he was a kind of freak, a product which society had suddenly deemed valuable, an educated Negro. His horizons were now open and his future was good. But he was still a freak.

"What kind of work have you been doing?"

"Tax, mostly. A few estates. One or two civil proceedings. The firm doesn't have many criminal cases, as you might expect. But when I joined them, I expressed an interest in trial work. I never expected they'd drop this one on me."

"I see."

"I just want you to understand."

"I think I do. They've stuck you with a dead horse, is that it?"

"Maybe." He smiled. "At least, that's what they think."

"And what do you think?"

"I think," he said, "that a case is decided in the courtroom, not before."

"You have an approach?"

"I'm working on one," Wilson said. "It's going to take a lot of work, because it will have to be good. Because that jury's going to see an uppity Negro defending a Chinese abortionist, and they won't like it."

I sipped my drink. The second round was brought and set at one side of the table.

"On the other hand," Wilson said, "this is a big break for me."

"If you win."

"That," he said evenly, "is my intention."

I suddenly thought that Bradford, whatever his reasons for giving Wilson the case, had made a very wise decision. Because this kid was going to want to win. Badly.

"Have you talked with Art?"

"This morning."

"What was your impression?"

"Innocent. I'm sure of it."

"Why?"

"I understand him," Wilson said.

OVER THE SECOND DRINK, I outlined what I had done for the last few days. Wilson listened in silence, not interrupting me, though he occasionally made notes. When I was through, he said, "You've saved me a lot of work."

"In what way?"

"From what you've already told me, we can close the case. We can get Dr. Lee off easily."

"You mean because the girl wasn't pregnant?"

He shook his head. "In several cases, among them *Commonwealth versus Taylor*, it was concluded that pregnancy is not an essential element. Nor does it matter if the fetus was already dead prior to the abortion."

"In other words, it makes no difference that Karen Randall wasn't pregnant?"

"None."

"But isn't it evidence that the job was done by an amateur, a person who did not first run a pregnancy test? Art would never perform an abortion without checking first."

"Is that going to be your case? That Dr. Lee is too skilled an abortionist to make so simple a mistake?"

I was chagrined. "No, I guess not."

"Look," Wilson said, "you can't conduct a defense based on the character of the accused. It won't work, no matter how you try it." He flipped through his notebook. "Let me give you a rundown on the legal situation. In 1845, a Massachusetts General Law stated that it was an offense to procure an abortion, by any means. If the patient did not die, the sentence was not more than seven years; if the patient did die, it was five to twenty. Since then the law has been enlarged upon. Some years later, it was decided that an abortion, if necessary to save the life of the mother, was not an unlawful abortion. That doesn't apply in this case."

"No."

"Later revisions include *Commonwealth versus Viera,* which decided that use of an instrument with intent constituted a crime, even without proof that miscarriage or death resulted. This might be very important. If the prosecution attempts, as I am sure they will, to show that Dr. Lee is an abortionist of many years' standing, they will then imply that an absence of direct evidence is not sufficient to get Lee off the hook."

"Can they do that?"

"No. But they can try, and it would be immensely damaging to our case."

"Go on."

"There are two other rulings that are important, because they show how the laws are slanted against the abortionist, with no interest in the woman involved. *Commonwealth versus Wood* ruled that the consent of the patient was immaterial and did not constitute a justification of abortion. The same court also concluded that the ensuing death of a woman is only an aggravation of the offense. In effect, this means that your investigation of Karen Randall is, from a legal standpoint, a waste of time."

"But I thought—"

"Yes," he said, "I said that the case is closed. And it is."

"How?"

"There are two alternatives. The first is to present the Randall family with the material at hand, before the trial. Point out the fact that Peter Randall, the deceased's personal physician, is an abortionist. The fact that he aborted her previously. The fact that Mrs. Randall, the wife, had had an abortion from Dr. Lee, and hence might be bearing a grudge against him, causing her to lie about what Karen had said. The fact that Karen was an unstable and unsavory young lady, whose dying words in any case were open to question. We could present all this to the family, in the hope of persuading them to drop charges before the trial."

I took a deep breath. This kid played rough. "And the second alternative?"

"The second is an extension, within the courtroom. Clearly, the crucial questions concern the relationships of Karen, Mrs. Randall, and Dr. Lee. The prosecution's case now stands on Mrs. Randall's testimony. We must discredit it, and her. We must destroy her until no juror dares believe a word she says. Then we must examine Karen's personality and behavior. We must demonstrate that she was an habitual drug-user, a promiscuous person, and a pathological liar. We must convince the jury that anything Karen said, whether to her stepmother or anyone else, is of doubtful veracity. We can also demonstrate that she was twice aborted by Peter Randall and that in all likelihood he performed the third abortion."

"I'm certain Peter Randall didn't do it," I said.

"That may be," Wilson said, "but it is immaterial."

"Why?"

"Because Peter Randall is not on trial. Dr. Lee is, and we must use anything we can to free him."

I looked at him. "I'd hate to meet you in a dark alley."

"You don't like my methods?" He smiled slightly.

"No, frankly."

"Neither do I," Wilson said. "But we are forced into this by the nature of the laws. In many instances, laws are slanted against a doctor in the doctor-patient relationship. We had a case only last year of an intern at the Gorly Clinic who performed a pelvic and rectal exam on a woman. At least, that was what he said. The woman claimed he raped her. There was no nurse present at the examination; no witnesses. The woman had been treated three times in mental institutions for paranoia and schizophrenia. But she won the case, and the intern was out of luck—and out of a profession."

"I still don't like it."

"View it rationally," Wilson said. "The law is clear. Right or wrong, it

is clear. It offers both the prosecution and the defense certain pattern
certain approaches, certain tactics in regard to the present statutes. Ur
fortunately, for both prosecution and defense, these approaches will com
down to character assassinations. The prosecution will attempt to di
credit Dr. Lee as thoroughly as they know how. We, the defense, wi
attempt to discredit the deceased, Mrs. Randall, and Peter Randall. Th
prosecution will have, as an advantage, the innate hostility of a Bosto
jury to anyone accused of abortion. We will have as an advantage th
desire of any random jury from Boston to witness the defilement of a:
old family."

"Dirty."

He nodded. "Very dirty."

"Isn't there another way to handle it?"

"Yes," he said. "Of course. Find the real abortionist."

"When will the trial be?"

"A preliminary hearing next week."

"And the trial itself?"

"Perhaps two weeks later. It's gotten some kind of priority. I don'
know how, but I can guess."

"Randall pushing his weight around."

Wilson nodded.

"And if an abortionist isn't found by the trial?" I asked.

Wilson smiled sadly. "My father," he said, "was a preacher. In Raleigh
North Carolina. He was the only educated man in the community. H
liked to read. I remember once asking him if all the people he read
like Keats and Shelley, were white. He said yes. I asked him if there wer
any coloreds that he read. He said no." Wilson scratched his forehead
hiding his eyes with his hands. "But anyway, he was a preacher, and h
was a Baptist, and he was strict. He believed in a wrathful god. He be
lieved in thunderbolts from heaven striking a sinner to the ground. H
believed in hellfire and damnation for eternity. He believed in righ
and wrong."

"Do you?"

"I believe," Wilson said, "in fighting fire with fire."

"Is the fire always right?"

"No," he said. "But it is always hot and compelling."

"And you believe in winning."

He touched the scar along his neck. "Yes."

"Even without honor?"

"The honor," he said, "is in winning."

"Is it?"

He stared at me for a moment. "Why are you so eager to protect the Randalls?"

"I'm not."

"You sound like you are."

"I'm doing what Art would want."

"Art," Wilson said, "wants to get out of jail. I'm telling you I can get him out. Nobody else in Boston will touch him; he's a hot potato. And I'm telling you I can get him out."

"It's dirty."

"Yes, Christ, it's dirty. What did you expect—a croquet game?" He finished his drink and said, "Look, Berry. If you were me, what would you do?"

"Wait," I said.

"For what?"

"The real abortionist."

"And if he doesn't turn up?"

I shook my head. "I don't know," I said.

"Then think about it," he said and left the bar.

SEVEN

WILSON HAD IRRITATED ME, but he had also left me with plenty to think about. I drove home, poured myself a vodka on the rocks, and sat down to put it together. I thought about everyone I had talked to, and I realized that there were significant questions I had never asked. There were gaps, big gaps. Like what Karen had done Saturday night, when she went out in Peter's car. What she had said to Mrs. Randall the next day. Whether she had returned Peter's car—it was now stolen; when had Peter gotten it back?

I drank the vodka and felt a calm settle over me. I had been too hasty; I had lost my temper too often; I had reacted more to people than to information, more to personalities than to facts.

I would be more careful in the future.

The telephone rang. It was Judith. She was over at the Lees.

"What's going on?"

In a very steady voice, she said, "You'd better come over here. There's some kind of demonstration outside."

"Oh?"

"There's a mob," Judith said, "on the lawn."

"I'll be right over," I said and hung up. I grabbed my coat and started for the car, then stopped.

It was time to be more careful.

I went back and quickly dialed the city desk of the *Globe*. I reported a demonstration at the Lees' address. I made it a breathless and melodramatic call; I was sure they'd act on it.

Then I got in my car and drove over.

When I got to the Lees', the wooden cross was still smoldering on the front lawn. A police car was there and a large crowd had gathered, mostly neighborhood kids and their stunned parents. It was still early evening; the sky was deepening blue and the smoke from the cross curled straight upward.

I pushed through the crowd toward the house. Every window that I could see had been smashed. Someone was crying inside. A cop stopped me at the door.

"Who're you?"

"Dr. Berry. My wife and children are inside."

He stepped aside and I went in.

They were all in the living room. Betty Lee was crying; Judith was taking care of the children. There was broken glass all around. Two of the children had been cut deeply but not seriously. A policeman was questioning Mrs. Lee. He wasn't getting anywhere. All she said was, "We asked for protection. We asked for it. We pleaded with you, but you never came. . . ."

"Jesus, lady," said the cop.

"We asked. Don't we have any rights?"

"Jesus, lady," he said again.

I helped Judith bandage the kids.

"What happened?"

Suddenly the cop turned on me. "Who're you?"

"I'm a doctor."

"Yeah, well, high time," he said and turned back to Mrs. Lee.

Judith was subdued and pale. "It started twenty minutes ago," she said. "We've been getting threats all day, and letters. Then it finally happened: four cars pulled up and a bunch of kids got out. They set up the cross and poured gasoline over it and lighted it. There must have been about twenty of them. They all stood there and sang 'Onward Christian Soldiers.' Then they started to throw rocks when they saw us looking at them through the window. It was like a nightmare."

"What did the kids look like? Were they well-dressed? What were the cars like?"

She shook her head. "That was the worst part. They were young, nice-looking kids. If they had been old bigots, I could understand, but they were just teen-agers. You should have seen their faces."

We finished bandaging the children and got them out of the room.

"I'd like to see the letters you've received," I said.

Just then the Lees' year-old baby crawled into the living room. He was smiling and making little gurgling, drooling noises. The glinting glass on the carpet obviously intrigued him.

"Hey!" I said to the cop at the door. "Get him!"

The cop looked down. He had been watching the baby all along.

Now he bent over and stopped the baby by holding onto his pudgy ankle.

"Pick him up," I said to the cop. "He can't hurt you."

Reluctantly, the cop picked him up. He handled the baby as if he might be diseased. You could see the distaste on his face: abortionist's baby.

Judith walked over, her shoes crunching on the glass. She took the baby from the cop. The baby didn't know how the cop felt. He had been happily playing with the cop's shiny buttons and drooling on his blue uniform. He didn't like it when Judith took him away from those buttons.

I heard the other cop say to Mrs. Lee, "Well, look, we get threats all the time. We can't respond to them all."

"But we called when they burned that . . . that *thing* on the lawn."

"That's a cross."

"I know what it is," she said. She was no longer crying. She was mad.

"We came as fast as we could," the cop said. "That's the truth, lady. As fast as we could."

Judith said to me, "It took them fifteen minutes. By that time, all the windows were broken and the teen-agers were gone."

I went over to the table and looked at the letters. They had been carefully opened and stacked in a neat pile. Most were handscrawled; a few were typewritten. They were all short, some just a sentence, and they all had the breathless hiss of a curse.

Dirty comminist Jewlover Nigger lover killer. You and youre kind will get what you deserve, baby killers. You are the scum of the Earth. You may think you are in Germany but you are not.
Unsigned.

Our Lord and Saviour spake this 'Suffer the little children to come to me.'
You have sinned against the Lord Jesus Our God and you will suffer
the retrobution at his Almighty Hands. Praise God in his infinite wisdom
and mercy.
　　Unsigned.

The decent Godfearing people of the Commonwealth will not sit idly
by. We shall fight you wherever the fight is to be. We shall drive you
from your homes, we shall drive you from this country. We shall drive
all of you out, until out Commonwealth is a decent place for all to
live.
　　Unsigned.

We caught you. We'll catch all your friends. Doctors think they can do
anything. a) Driving those big Cadillacs. b) charging high costs. c) mak-
ing patients wait that's why they call them patients because they wait
patiently. d) But you are all evil. You will be stopped.
　　Unsigned.

You like to kill kids? See how it feels to have yours killed.
　　Unsigned.

Abortion is a crime against God and man and society and the newborn
yet to be. You will pay on this earth. But the Lord in his infinite way
will burn you in hell forever.
　　Unsigned.

Abortion is worse than murder. What did they ever do to you? Answer
that and you will see I am right. May you rot in jail and your family die.
　　Unsigned.

There was a final letter, written in a neat feminine hand.

I am sorry to hear of your misfortune. I know this must be a trying
time for all of you. I only wanted to say that I am very grateful for
what you did for me last year, and that I believe in you and what you
are doing. You are the most wonderful doctor I have ever known, and the
most honest. You have made my life much better than it would be other-
wise, and my husband and I are eternally grateful. I shall pray for you
every night.
　　Mrs. Allison Banks

I slipped it into my pocket. It wouldn't do to have that one lying
around.

I heard voices behind me.

"Well, well, well. Fancy that."

I turned. It was Peterson.

"My wife called me."

"Fancy that." He looked around the room. With all the broken windows, it was getting chilly as night fell. "Quite a mess, isn't it?"

"You might say so."

"Yes, indeed." He walked around the room. "Quite a mess."

Watching him, I had a sudden horrifying vision of a uniformed man in heavy boots strutting among ruins. It was a generalized vision, nonspecific, attached to no particular time or place or era.

Another man pushed into the room. He wore a raincoat and had a pad in his hand.

"Who're you?" Peterson said.

"Curtis. From the *Globe,* sir."

"Now who called you, fella?"

Peterson looked around the room. His eyes rested on me.

"Not nice," Peterson said. "Not nice at all."

"It's a reputable newspaper. This boy will report the facts accurately. You surely can't object to that."

"Listen," Peterson said. "This is a city of two and a half million and the police department is understaffed. We can't investigate every crackpot complaint and lunatic threat that comes along. We can't do that if we want to do the regular things, like direct traffic."

"Family of an accused," I said. I was aware that the reporter was watching me closely. "Family of an accused receives threats by telephone and letter. Wife and young family. She's afraid. You ignore her."

"That's not fair and you know it."

"Then something big happens. They start to burn a cross and tear the place apart. The wife calls for help. It takes your boys fifteen minutes to get here. How far away is the nearest station?"

"That's not the point."

The reporter was writing.

"You'll look bad," I said. "Lots of citizens in this town are opposed to abortion, but still more are against the wanton, lawless destruction of private property by a band of young hoodlums—"

"They weren't hoodlums."

I turned to the reporter. "Captain Peterson expresses the opinion that the kids who burned the cross and broke every window in the house were not young hoodlums."

"That's not what I meant," Peterson said quickly.

"It's what he said," I told the reporter. "Furthermore, you may be interested to know that two children were seriously lacerated by flying glass. Children ages three and five, seriously lacerated."

"That's not what I was told," Peterson said. "The cuts were only——"

"I believe," I said, "that I am the only doctor present at this time. Or did the police bring a doctor when they finally answered the call for help?"

He was silent.

"Did the police bring a doctor?" the reporter asked.

"No."

"Did they summon a doctor?"

"No."

The reporter wrote swiftly.

"I'll get you, Berry," Peterson said. "I'll get you for this."

"Careful. You're in front of a reporter."

His eyes shot daggers. He turned on his heel.

"By the way," I said, "what steps will the police now take to prevent a recurrence?"

He stopped. "That hasn't been decided yet."

"Be sure," I said, "to explain to this reporter how unfortunate it all is and how you'll post a twenty-four-hour guard. Be sure to make that clear."

He curled his lip, but I knew he would do it. That's all I wanted—protection for Betty, and a little pressure on the police.

EIGHT

JUDITH TOOK THE KIDS HOME; I stayed with Betty and helped her board up the windows. It took nearly an hour, and with each one I did, I got angrier.

Betty's kids were subdued, but would not go to sleep. They kept coming downstairs to complain that their cuts hurt or that they wanted a glass of water. Young Henry in particular complained about his foot, so I removed the bandage to be certain I had not missed any glass. I found a small sliver still lodged in the wound.

Sitting there, with his small foot in my hand, and Betty telling him not to cry as I cleaned the wound again, I suddenly felt tired. The house smelled of burning wood, from the cross. It was chilly and drafty from the broken windows. Everything was a shambles; it would take days to clean it up.

All so unnecessary.

When I finished with Henry's foot, I went back to the letters Betty had received. Reading them made me feel more tired. I kept wondering how people could do it, what they must have been thinking. The obvious answer was that they were thinking nothing. They were simply reacting, as I had been reacting, as everyone had been reacting.

I suddenly wanted it finished. I wanted the letters to stop, the windows to be fixed, the wounds to heal, and life to return to normal. I wanted it very badly.

So I called George Wilson.

"I thought you might call," Wilson said.

"How'd you like to take a trip?"

"Where?"

"J. D. Randall's."

"Why?"

"To call off the dogs," I said.

"Meet me in twenty minutes," he said and hung up.

As we drove toward the South Shore and the Randall house, Wilson said, "What made you change your mind?"

"A lot of things."

"The kids?"

"A lot of things," I repeated.

We drove for a while in silence, then he said, "You know what this means, don't you? It means we put the squeeze on Mrs. Randall and on Peter."

"That's all right," I said.

"I thought he was your buddy."

"I'm tired."

"I thought doctors never got tired."

"Lay off, will you?"

It was late, approaching nine. The sky was black.

"When we get to the house," Wilson said, "I'll do the talking, right?"

"O.K.," I said.

"It's no good if we both talk. It has to be just one."

"You can have your moment," I said.

He smiled. "You don't like me much, do you?"

"No. Not much."

"But you need me."

"That's right," I said.

"Just so we understand each other," he said.

"Just so you do the job," I said.

I did not remember exactly where the house was, so I slowed the car as I approached. Finally I found it and was about to turn into the drive when I stopped. Up ahead, in the gravel turnabout in front of the house, were two cars. One was J. D. Randall's silver Porsche. The other was a gray Mercedes sedan.

"What's the matter?"

I doused my lights and backed away.

"What's going on?" Wilson said.

"I'm not sure," I said.

"Well, are we going in, or not?"

"No," I said. I backed across the road and parked on the opposite side, near the shrubs. I had a good view up the drive to the house and could see both cars clearly.

"Why not?"

"Because," I said, "there's a Mercedes parked there."

"So?"

"Peter Randall owns a Mercedes."

"All the better," Wilson said. "We can confront them together."

"No," I said. "Because Peter Randall told me his car was stolen."

"Oh?"

"That's what he said."

"When?"

"Yesterday."

I thought back. Something was beginning to bother me, to pick at my mind. Then I remembered: the car I had seen in the Randall garage when I had visited Mrs. Randall.

I opened my door. "Come on."

"Where are we going?"

"I want to see that car," I said.

We stepped out into the night, which was damp and unpleasant. Walking up the drive, I reached into my pocket and felt my little penlight. I always carried it; a throwback to my days as an intern. I was glad to have it now.

"You realize," Wilson whispered, "that we're trespassing on private property."

"I realize."

We moved from the crunching gravel to the soft grass and climbed the hill toward the house. There were lights burning on the ground floor, but the shades were drawn, and we could not see inside.

We came to the cars and stepped onto the gravel again. The sounds of our footsteps seemed loud. I reached the Mercedes and flicked on my penlight. The car was empty; there was nothing in the back seat.

I stopped.

The driver's seat was soaked in blood.

"Well, well," Wilson said.

I was about to speak when we heard voices and a door opening. We hurried back to the grass and slipped behind a bush near the drive.

J. D. Randall came out of the house. Peter was with him. They were arguing about something in low voices; I heard Peter say, "All ridiculous," and J. D. said, "Too careful"; but otherwise their voices were inaudible. They came down the steps to the cars. Peter got into the Mercedes and started the engine. J. D. said, "Follow me," and Peter nodded. Then J. D. got into the silver Porsche and started down the drive.

At the road, they turned right, heading south.

"Come on," I said.

We sprinted down the drive to my car, parked on the opposite side of the road. The other two cars were already far away; we could barely hear their engines, but we could see their lights moving down the coast. I started the car and followed them.

Wilson had reached into his pocket and was fiddling with something. "What have you got there?"

He held it over so I could see. A small, silver tube.

"Minox."

"You always carry a camera?"

"Always," he said.

I stayed back a good distance, so the other cars would not suspect. Peter was following J. D. closely.

After a five-minute drive, the two cars entered the ramp for the southeast expressway. I came on a moment later.

"I don't get it," Wilson said. "One minute you're defending the guy, and the next minute you're tracking him like a bloodhound."

"I want to know," I said. "That's all. I just want to know."

I followed them for half an hour. The road narrowed at Marshfield, becoming two lanes instead of three. Traffic was light; I dropped even farther back.

"This could be completely innocent," Wilson said. "The whole thing could be a——"

"No," I said. I had been putting things together in my own mind. "Peter loaned his car to Karen for the weekend. The son, William, told me that. Karen used that car. There was blood on it. Then the car was garaged in the Randall house, and Peter reported it as stolen. Now . . ."

"Now they're getting rid of it," Wilson said.

"Apparently."

"Hot damn," he said. "This one's in the bag."

The cars continued south, past Plymouth, down toward the Cape. The air here was chilly and tangy with salt. There was almost no traffic.

"Doing fine," Wilson said, looking at the taillights ahead. "Give them plenty of room."

As the road became more deserted, the two cars gained speed. They were going very fast now, near eighty. We passed Plymouth, then Hyannis, and out toward Provincetown. Suddenly, I saw their brake lights go on, and they turned off the road to the right, toward the coast.

We followed, on a dirt road. Around us were scrubby pine trees. I doused my lights. The wind was gusty and cold off the ocean.

"Deserted around here," Wilson said.

I nodded.

Soon I could hear the roar of the breakers. I pulled off the road and parked. We walked on foot toward the ocean and saw the two cars parked, side by side.

I recognized the place. It was the east side of the Cape, where there was a long, one-hundred-foot sandy drop to the sea. The two cars were at the ledge, overlooking the water. Randall had gotten out of his Porsche and was talking with Peter. They argued for a moment, and then Peter got back in the car and drove it until the front wheels were inches from the edge. Then he got out and walked back.

J. D. had meanwhile opened the trunk to the Porsche and taken out a portable can of gasoline. Together the two men emptied the can of gasoline inside Peter's car.

I heard a click near me. Wilson, with the little camera pressed to his eyes, was taking pictures.

"You don't have enough light."

"Tri-X," he said, still taking pictures. "You can force it to 2400, if you have the right lab. And I have the right lab."

I looked back at the cars. J. D. was returning the tank to his trunk. Then he started the Porsche engine and backed the car around, so it was facing the road, away from the ocean.

"Ready for the getaway," Wilson said. "Beautiful."

J. D. called to Peter and got out of the car. He stood by Peter, then

I saw the brief flare of a match. Suddenly the interior of the Mercedes burst into flames.

The two men immediately ran to the rear of the car and leaned their weight against the car. It moved slowly, then faster, and finally began the slide down the sandy slope. They stepped back and watched its descent. At the bottom, it apparently exploded, because there was a loud sound and a bright red flash of light.

They sprinted for the car, got in, and drove past us.

"Come on," Wilson said. He ran forward to the edge with his camera. Down below, at the edge of the water, was the burning, smashed hulk of the Mercedes.

Wilson took several pictures, then put his camera away and looked at me.

He was grinning broadly. "Baby," he said, "have we got a case."

NINE

ON THE WAY BACK, I turned off the expressway at the Cohasset exit.

"Hey," Wilson said, "what're you doing?"

"Going to see Randall."

"*Now?*"

"Yes."

"Are you crazy? After what we saw?"

I said, "I came out tonight to get Art Lee off the hook. I still intend to do it."

"Uh-uh," Wilson said. "Not now. Not after what we saw." He patted the little camera in his hand. "Now we can go to court."

"I told you before," I said, "we've got to keep this out of court."

"But there's no need. We have an iron case. Unbeatable. Unshakable."

I shook my head.

"Listen," Wilson said, "you can rattle a witness. You can discredit him, make him look like a fool. But you can't discredit a picture. You can't beat a photograph. We have them by the balls."

"No," I said.

He sighed. "Before, it was going to be a bluff. I was going to walk in there and bullshit my way through it. I was going to scare them, to frighten them, to make them think we had evidence when we didn't. But now, it's all different. We have the evidence. We have everything we need."

"If you don't want to talk to them, I will."

"Berry," Wilson said, "if you talk to them, you'll blow our whole case."

"I'll make them quit."

"Berry, you'll blow it. Because they've just done something very incriminating. They'll know it. They'll be taking a hard line."

"Then we'll tell them what we know."

"And if it comes to trial? What then? We'll have blown our cool."

"I'm not worried about that. It won't come to trial."

Wilson scratched his scar again, running his finger down his neck. "Listen," he said, "don't you want to win?"

"Yes," I said, "but without a fight."

"There's going to be a fight. Any way you cut it, there'll be a fight. I'm telling you."

I pulled up in front of the Randall house and drove up the drive. "Don't tell me," I said. "Tell them."

"You're making a mistake," he said.

"Maybe," I said, "but I doubt it."

We climbed the steps and rang the doorbell.

RELUCTANTLY, the butler led us into the living room. It was no larger than the average-size basketball court, an immense room with a huge fireplace. Seated around the roaring fire were Mrs. Randall, in lounging pajamas, and Peter and J. D., both with large snifters of brandy in their hands.

The butler stood erectly by the door and said, "Dr. Berry and Mr. Wilson, sir. They said they were expected."

J. D. frowned when he saw us. Peter sat back and allowed a small smile to cross his face. Mrs. Randall seemed genuinely amused.

J. D. said, "What do you want?"

I let Wilson do the talking. He gave a slight bow and said, "I believe you know Dr. Berry, Dr. Randall. I am George Wilson. I am Dr. Lee's defense attorney."

"That's lovely," J. D. said. He glanced at his watch. "But it's nearly midnight, and I am relaxing with my family. I have nothing to say to either of you until we meet in court. So if you will——"

"If you will pardon me, sir," Wilson said, "we have come a long way to see you. All the way from the Cape, in fact."

J. D. blinked once and set his face rigidly. Peter coughed back a laugh. Mrs. Randall said, "What were you doing on the Cape?"

"Watching a bonfire," Wilson said.

"A bonfire?"

"Yes," Wilson said. He turned to J. D. "We'd like some brandies, please, and then a little chat."

Peter could not suppress a laugh this time. J. D. looked at him sternly, then rang for the butler. He ordered two more brandies, and as the butler was leaving, he said, "Small ones, Herbert. They won't be staying long."

Then he turned to his wife. "If you will, my dear."

She nodded and left the room.

"Sit down, gentlemen."

"We prefer to stand," Wilson said. The butler brought two small crystal snifters. Wilson raised his glass. "Your health, gentlemen."

"Thank you," J. D. said. His voice was cold. "Now what's on your minds?"

"A small legal matter," Wilson said. "We believe that you may wish to reconsider charges against Dr. Lee."

"Reconsider?"

"Yes. That was the word I used."

"There is nothing to reconsider," J. D. said.

Wilson sipped the brandy. "Oh?"

"That's right," J. D. said.

"We believe," Wilson said, "that your wife may have been mistaken in hearing that Dr. Lee aborted Karen Randall. Just as we believe that Peter Randall was mistaken when he reported his automobile stolen to the police. Or hasn't he reported it yet?"

"Neither my wife, nor my brother, were mistaken," J. D. said.

Peter coughed again and lit a cigar.

"Something wrong, Peter?" J. D. asked.

"No, nothing."

He puffed the cigar and sipped his brandy.

"Gentlemen," J. D. said, turning to us. "You are wasting your time. There has been no mistake, and there is nothing to reconsider."

Wilson said softly, "In that case, it must go to court."

"Indeed it must," Randall said, nodding.

"And you will be called to account for your actions tonight," Wilson said.

"Indeed we may. But we will have Mrs. Randall's firm testimony that we spent the evening playing chess." He pointed to a chessboard in the corner.

"Who won?" Wilson asked, with a faint smile.

"I did, by God," Peter said, speaking for the first time. And he chuckled.

"How did you do it?" Wilson said.

"Bishop to knight's twelve," Peter said and chuckled again. "He is a terrible chess player. If I've told him once, I've told him a thousand times."

"Peter, this is no laughing matter."

"You're a sore loser," Peter said.

"Shut up, Peter."

Quite abruptly, Peter stopped laughing. He folded his arms across his massive belly and said nothing more.

J. D. Randall savored a moment of silence, then said, "Was there anything else, gentlemen?"

"YOU SON OF A BITCH," I said to Wilson. "You blew it."

"I did my best."

"You got him angry. You were forcing him into court."

"I did my best."

"That was the lousiest, rottenest——"

"Easy," Wilson said, rubbing his scar.

"You could have scared him. You could have told them how it would go—the way you explained it to me in the bar. You could have told them about the pictures. . . ."

"It wouldn't have done any good," Wilson said.

"It might."

"No. They are determined to take the case to court. They——"

"Yes," I said, "thanks to you. Strutting around like a self-satisfied bastard. Making cheap threats like a penny tough. Demanding a brandy—that was beautiful, that was."

"I attempted to persuade them," Wilson said.

"Crap."

He shrugged.

"I'll tell you what you did, Wilson. You pushed them into a trial, because you want one. You want an arena, a chance to show your stuff, a chance to make a name for yourself, to prove that you're a ruthless hotshot. You know, and I know, that if the case ever comes to trial, Art Lee —no matter what the outcome—will lose. He'll lose his prestige, his patients, maybe even his license. And if it comes to trial, the Randalls will also lose. They'll be smeared, shot through with half-truths and implications, destroyed. Only one person will come out on top."

"Yes?"

"You, Wilson. Only you can win in a trial."

ONE

I AWOKE FEELING MEAN. Like a caged animal, trapped, enclosed. I didn't like what was happening and didn't see any way to stop it. Worst of all, I didn't see any way to beat Wilson. It was hard enough to prove Art Lee was innocent; to prove Peter Randall was innocent as well was impossible.

Judith took one look at me and said, "Grumpy."

I snorted and showered.

She said, "Find out anything?"

"Yeah. Wilson wants to pin it on Peter Randall."

She laughed. "Jolly old Peter?"

"Jolly old Peter," I said.

"Has he got a case?"

"Yes."

"That's good," she said.

"No," I said, "it's not."

I turned off the shower and stepped out, reaching for a towel. "I can't believe Peter would do it," I said.

"Charitable of you."

I shook my head. "No," I said, "it's just that getting another innocent man for it solves nothing."

"It serves them right," Judith said.

"Who?"

"The Randalls."

"It isn't just," I said.

"That's fine for you to say. You can immerse yourself in the technicalities. I've been with Betty Lee for three days."

"I know it's been hard—"

"I'm not talking about me," she said. "I'm talking about her. Or have you forgotten last night?"

"No," I said, thinking to myself that last night had started it all, the whole mess. My decision to call in Wilson.

"Betty has been through hell," Judith said. "There's no excuse for it, and the Randalls are to blame. So let them boil in their own oil for a while. Let them see how it feels."

"But Judith, if Peter is innocent—"

"Peter is very amusing," she said. "That doesn't make him innocent."

"It doesn't make him guilty."

"I don't care who's guilty anymore. I just wanted it finished and Art set free."

"Yes," I said. "I know how you feel."

While I shaved, I stared at my face. A rather ordinary face, too heavy in the jowls, eyes too small, hair thinning. But all in all, nothing unusual about me. It gave me a strange feeling to know that I had been at the center of things, at the center of a crisis affecting a half-dozen people, for three days. I wasn't the sort of person for that.

As I dressed and wondered what I would do that morning. I also wondered if I had ever been at the center of things. It was an odd thought. Suppose I had been circling at the periphery, digging up unimportant facts? Suppose the real heart of the matter was still unexplored?

Trying to save Peter again.

Well, why not? He was as much worth saving as anyone else.

It occurred to me then that Peter Randall was as much worth saving as Art. They were both men, both doctors, both established, both interesting, both a little nonconformist. When you came down to it, there was nothing really to choose between them. Peter was humorous, Art was sarcastic. Peter was fat and Art was thin.

But essentially the same.

I pulled on my jacket and tried to forget the whole thing. I wasn't the judge; thank God for that. It wouldn't be my job to unsnarl things at the trial.

The telephone rang. I didn't answer it. A moment later, Judith called, "It's for you."

I picked up the receiver.

"Hello?"

A familiar, booming voice said, "John, this is Peter. I'd like you to come by for lunch."

"Why?" I said.

"I want you to meet the alibi I haven't got," he said.

"What does that mean?"

"Twelve-thirty?" he asked.

"See you then," I said.

TWO

PETER RANDALL LIVED WEST OF NEWTON, in a modern house. It was small but beautifully furnished: Breuer chairs, a Jacobsen couch, a Rachmann coffee table. The style was sleekly modern. He met me at the door with a drink in his hand.

"John. Come in." He led the way into the living room. "What will you drink?"

"Nothing, thanks."

"I think you'd better," he said. "Scotch?"

"On the rocks."

"Have a seat," he said. He went into the kitchen; I heard ice cubes in a glass. "What did you do this morning?"

"Nothing," I said. "I sat around and thought."

"About what?"

"Everything."

"You don't have to tell me, if you don't want to," he said, coming back with a glass of Scotch.

"Did you know Wilson took pictures?"

"I had a suspicion. That boy is ambitious."

"Yes," I said.

"And I'm in hot water?"

"It looks that way," I said.

He stared at me for a moment, then said, "What do you think?"

"I don't know what to think anymore."

"Do you know, for example, that I do abortions?"

"Yes," I said.

"And Karen?"

"Twice," I said.

He sat back in a Breuer chair, his rounded bulk contrasting with the sharp, linear angles of the chair. "Three times," he said, "to be precise."

"Then you—"

"No, no," he said. "The last was in June."

"And the first?"

"When she was fifteen." He sighed. "You see, I've made some mistakes. One of them was trying to look after Karen. Her father was ignoring her, and I was . . . fond of her. She was a sweet girl. Lost and confused, but sweet. So I did her first abortion, as I have done abortions for other patients from time to time. Does that shock you?"

"No."

"Good. But the trouble was that Karen kept getting pregnant. Three times in three years; for a girl of that age, it wasn't wise. It was pathological. So I finally decided that she ought to bear the fourth child."

"Why?"

"Because she obviously wanted to be pregnant. She kept doing it. She obviously needed the shame and trouble of an illegitimate child. So I refused the fourth time."

"Are you sure she was pregnant?"

"No," he said. "And you know why I had my doubts. That vision business. One wonders about primary pituitary dysfunction. I wanted to do tests, but Karen refused. She was only interested in an abortion, and when I wouldn't give it to her, she became angry."

"So you sent her to Dr. Lee."

"Yes," he said.

"And he did it?"

Peter shook his head. "Art is far too clever for that. He would have insisted on tests. Besides, she was four months' pregnant, or so she claimed. So he wouldn't have done it."

"And you didn't, either," I said.

"No. Do you believe that?"

"I'd like to."

"But you aren't fully convinced?"

I shrugged. "You burned your car. It had blood in it."

"Yes," he said. "Karen's blood."

"How did it happen?"

"I lent Karen my car for the weekend. I did not know at the time that she planned an abortion."

"You mean she drove your car to the abortion, had it, and drove it back to her home, bleeding? Then she switched to the yellow Porsche?"

"Not exactly," Peter said. "But you can get a better explanation from someone else." He called, "Darling. Come on out."

He smiled at me. "Meet my alibi."

Mrs. Randall came into the room, looking taut and hard and sexy. She sat in a chair next to Peter.

"You see," Peter said, "what a bind I am in."

I said, "Sunday night?"

"I am afraid so."

"That's embarrassing," I said, "but also convenient."

"In a sense," Randall said. He patted her hand and lifted himself heavily out of the chair. "I don't call it either embarrassing or convenient."

"You were with her all night Sunday?"

He poured himself another Scotch. "Yes."

"Doing what?"

"Doing," Peter said, "what I would rather not explain under oath."

"With your brother's wife?" I said.

He winked at Mrs. Randall. "Are you my brother's wife?"

"I've heard a rumor," she said, "but I don't believe it."

"You see, I am letting you into some quite private family affairs," Peter said.

"They are family affairs, if nothing else."

"You're indignant?"

"No," I said. "Fascinated."

"Joshua," Peter said, "is a fool. You know that, of course. So does Wilson. That is why he could be so confident. But unfortunately, Joshua married Evelyn."

"Unfortunately," Evelyn said.

"Now we are in a bind," Peter said. "She cannot divorce my brother to marry me. That would be impossible. So we are resigned to our life as it is."

"Difficult, I imagine."

"Not really," Peter said, sitting down again with a fresh drink. "Joshua is very dedicated. He often works long into the night. And Evelyn has many clubs and civic functions to attend."

"He'll find out sooner or later."

"He already knows," Peter said.

I must have reacted, because he said quickly, "Not consciously, of course. J. D. knows nothing consciously. But in the back of his mind, he realizes that he has a young wife whom he neglects and who is finding . . . satisfaction elsewhere."

I turned to Mrs. Randall, "Would you swear Peter was with you Sunday night?"

"If I had to," she said.

"Wilson will make you. He wants a trial."

"I know," she said.

"Why did you accuse Art Lee?"

She turned away from me and glanced at Peter.

Peter said, "She was trying to protect me."

"Art was the only other abortionist she knew?"

"Yes," Evelyn said.

"He aborted you?"

"Yes. Last December."

"Was it a good abortion?"

She shifted in the chair. "It worked, if that's what you mean."

"That's what I mean," I said. "Do you know Art wouldn't implicate you?"

She hesitated, then said, "I was confused. I was frightened. I didn't know what I was doing."

"You were screwing Art."

"Yes," she said, "that was how it turned out."

"Well," I said, "you can clear him now."

"How?"

"Drop the charges."

Peter said, "It's not that easy."

"Why not?"

"You saw for yourself last night. J. D. is fixed on the battle, once the lines are drawn. He has a surgeon's view of right and wrong. He sees only black and white, day and night. No gray. No twilight."

"No cuckolds."

Peter laughed. "He may be a lot like you."

Evelyn got up and said, "Lunch will be ready in five minutes. Will you have another drink?"

"Yes," I said, looking at Peter, "I'd better."

When Evelyn had gone, Peter said, "You see me as a cruel and heartless beast. Actually I'm not. There has been a long chain of errors here, a long list of mistakes. I would like to see it cleaned up—"

"With no harm done."

"More or less. Unfortunately my brother is no help. Once his wife accused Dr. Lee, he took it as gospel truth. He pounced upon it as truth the way a man grasps a life preserver. He will never relent."

"Go on," I said.

"But the central fact remains. I insist—and you can believe it or not—that I did not do the abortion. You are equally certain that Dr. Lee did not do it. Who is left?"

"I don't know," I said.

"Can you find out?"

"You're asking me to help you?"

"Yes," he said.

OVER LUNCH, I said to Evelyn, "What did Karen really say to you in the car?"

"She said, 'That bastard.' Over and over again. Nothing else."

"She never explained?"

"No."

"Did you have any idea who she meant?"

"No," Evelyn said, "I didn't."

"Did she say anything else?"

"Yes," she said. "She talked about the needle. Something about how she didn't want the needle, didn't want it in her, didn't want it around her. The needle."

"Was it a drug?"

"I couldn't tell," Evelyn said.

"What did you think at the time?"

"I didn't think anything," Evelyn said. "I was driving her to the hospital and she was dying right before my eyes. I was worried that Peter might have done it, even though I didn't think he had. I was worried that Joshua would find out. I was worried about a lot of things."

"But not her?"

"Yes," she said, "her, too."

THREE

THE MEAL WAS GOOD. Toward the end, staring at the two of them, I found myself wishing I had not come and did not know about them. I didn't want to know, didn't want to think about it.

Afterward, I had coffee with Peter. From the kitchen I heard the sounds of Evelyn washing dishes. It was hard to imagine her washing dishes, but she acted differently around Peter; it was almost possible to like her.

"I suppose," Peter said, "that it was unfair to ask you here today."

"It was," I said.

He sighed and straightened his tie down his massive belly. "I've never been in this kind of situation before."

"How's that?"

"Caught," he said.

I thought to myself that he had done it to himself, going in with both eyes wide open. I tried to resent him for that but could not quite manage it.

"The terrible thing," he said, "is to think back and wonder what you'd do differently. I keep doing that. And I never find the point I'm looking for, that one crucial point in time where I made the wrong turn in the maze. Getting involved with Ev, I suppose. But I'd do that again. Getting involved with Karen. But I'd do that again, too. Each individual thing was all right. It was the combination. . . ."

I said, "Get J. D. to drop the charges."

He shook his head. "My brother and I," he said, "have never gotten along. For as long as I can remember. We are different in every way, even physically. We think differently, we act differently. When I was young I used to resent the fact that he was my brother, and I secretly suspected that he was not, that he had been adopted or something. I suppose he thought the same thing."

He finished his coffee and rested his chin on his chest. "Ev has tried to convince J. D. to drop charges," he said. "But he's firm, and she can't really——"

"Think of an excuse?"

"Yes."

"It's too bad she ever named Lee in the first place."

"Yes," he said. "But what's done is done."

He walked with me to the door. I stepped outside into a gray, pale sunlight. As I went down to my car, he said, "If you don't want to get involved, I'll understand."

I looked back at him. "You knew damned well I'd have no choice."

"I didn't," he said. "But I was hoping."

WHEN I GOT INTO MY CAR, I wondered what I would do next. I had no idea, no leads, nothing. Perhaps I could call Zenner again and see if he could remember more of his conversation. Perhaps I could visit Ginnie at Smith, or Angela and Bubbles, and see if they remembered more. But I doubted they would.

I reached into my pocket for the keys and felt something. I brought it out: a picture of a Negro in a shiny suit. Roman Jones.

I had forgotten all about Roman. Somewhere along the line he had disappeared in the rush, the stream of faces. I stared at the picture for a long time, trying to read the features, to measure the man. It was impossible; the pose was standard, the cocky look of a silver-suited stud, swaggering, half grinning, half leering. It was a pose for the crowds, and it told me nothing at all.

I am not good with words, and it has always been surprising to me that my son, Johnny, is. When he is alone, he plays with his toys and makes up word games; he rhymes or tells himself stories. He has very sharp ears and always comes to me for explanations. Once he asked me what an ecdysiast was, pronouncing the word perfectly but carefully, as if it were fragile.

So I was not really surprised when, as I was minding my own business, he came up and said, "Daddy, what's an abortionist mean?"

"Why?"

"One of the policemen said Uncle Art was an abortionist. Is that bad?"

"Sometimes," I said.

He leaned against my knee, propping his chin on it. He has large brown eyes; Judith's eyes.

"But what's it mean, Daddy?"

"It's complicated," I said, stalling for time.

"Does it mean a kind of doctor? Like neurologist?"

"Yes," I said. "But an abortionist does other things." I hoisted him up on my knee, feeling the weight of his body. He was getting heavy, growing up. Judith was saying it was time for another.

"It has to do with babies," I said.

"Like obsetrician?"

"Obstetrician," I said. "Yes."

"He takes the baby out of the mommy?"

"Yes," I said, "but it is different. Sometimes the baby isn't normal. Sometimes it is born so it can't talk—"

"Babies can't talk," he said, "until later."

"Yes," I said. "But sometimes it is born without arms or legs. Sometimes it is deformed. So a doctor stops the baby and takes it away early."

"Before it's grown up?"

"Yes, before it's grown up."

"Was I taken away early?"

"No," I said and hugged him.

"Why do some babies have no arms or legs?"

"It's an accident," I said. "A mistake."

He stretched out his hand and looked at it, flexing the fingers.

"Arms are nice," he said.

"Yes."

"But everybody has arms."

"Not everybody."

"Everybody *I* know."

"Yes," I said, "but sometimes people are born without them."

"How do they play catch without arms?"

"They can't."

"I don't like that," he said. He looked at his hand again, closing his fingers, watching them.

"Why do you have arms?" he asked.

"Because." It was too big a question for me.

"Because what?"

"Because inside your body there is a code."

"What's a code?"

"It's instructions. It tells the body how it is going to grow."

"A code?"

"It's like a set of instructions. A plan."

"Oh."

He thought about this.

"It's like your erector set. You look at the pictures and you make what you see. That's a plan."

"Oh."

I couldn't tell if he understood or not. He considered what I had said, then looked at me. "If you take the baby out of the mommy, what happens to it?"

"It goes away."

"Where?"

"Away," I said, not wanting to explain further.

"Oh," he said. He climbed down off my knee. "Is Uncle Art really an abortionist?"

"No," I said. I knew I had to tell him that, otherwise I would get a call from his kindergarten teacher about his uncle the abortionist. But I felt badly, all the same.

"Good," he said. "I'm glad."

And he walked off.

JUDITH SAID, "YOU'RE NOT EATING."

I pushed my food away. "I'm not very hungry."

Judith turned to Johnny and said, "Clean your plate, Johnny."

He held the fork in a small, tight fist. "I'm not hungry," he said and glanced at me.

"Sure you are," I said.

"No," he said, "I'm not."

Debby, who was barely big enough to see over the table, threw her knife and fork down. "I'm not hungry either," she said. "The food tastes icky."

"I think it tastes very good," I said and dutifully ate a mouthful. The kids looked at me suspiciously. Especially Debby: at three, she was a very level-headed little girl.

"You just want us to eat, Daddy."

"I like it," I said, eating more.

"You're pretending."

"No, I'm not."

"Then why aren't you smiling?" Debby said.

Fortunately, Johnny decided at that moment to eat more. He rubbed his stomach. "It's good," he said.

"It is?" Debby said.

"Yes," Johnny said, "very good."

Debby nibbled. She was very tentative. She took another forkful, and as she moved it to her mouth, she spilled it on her dress. Then, like a normal woman, she got mad at everyone around her. She announced that it was terrible and she didn't like it; she wouldn't eat any more. Judith began to call her "Young lady," a sure sign that Judith was getting mad. Debby backed off while Johnny continued to eat until he held up his plate and showed it to us proudly: clean.

It was another half-hour before the kids were in bed. I stayed in the kitchen; Judith came back and said, "Coffee?"

"Yes. I'd better."

"Sorry about the kids," she said. "They've had a wearying few days."

"We all have."

She poured the coffee and sat down across the table from me.

"I keep thinking," she said, "about the letters. The ones Betty got."

"What about them?"

"Just what they mean. There are thousands of people out there, all around you, waiting for their chance. Stupid, bigoted, small-minded—"

"This is a democracy," I said. "Those people run the country."

"Now you're making fun of me."

"No," I said. "I know what you mean."

"Well, it frightens me," Judith said. She pushed the sugar bowl across the table to me and said, "I think I want to leave Boston. And never come back."

"It's the same everywhere," I said. "You might as well get used to it."

I KILLED TWO HOURS IN MY STUDY, looking over old texts and journal articles. I also did a lot of thinking. I tried to put it together, to match up Karen Randall, and Superhead, and Alan Zenner, and Bubbles and Angela. I tried to make sense of Weston, but in the end nothing made sense.

Judith came in and said, "It's nine."

I got up and put on my suit jacket.

"Are you going out?"

"Yes."

"Where?"

I grinned at her. "To a bar," I said. "Downtown."

"Whatever for?"

"Damned if I know."

The Electric Grape was located just off Washington Street. From the outside it was unimpressive, an old brick building with large windows. The windows were covered with paper, making it impossible to see inside. On the paper was written: "The Zephyrs Nightly. Go-Go Girls." I could hear jarring rock-'n'-roll sounds as I approached.

It was ten P.M. Thursday night, a slow night. Very few sailors, a couple of hookers down the block, standing with their weight on one hip, their pelvises thrust outward. One cruised by in a little sports car and batted her mascara at me. I entered the building.

It was hot, damp, smelly, animal heat, and the sound was deafening: vibrating the walls, filling the air, making it thick and liquid. My ears began to ring. I paused to allow my eyes to adjust to the darkness of the room. There were cheap wooden tables in the center booths along one wall, and a bar along another. A tiny dance floor near the bandstand; two sailors were dancing with two fat, dirty-looking girls. Otherwise the place was empty.

On stage, the Zephyrs were beating it out. Five of them—three steel guitars, a drummer, and a singer who caressed the microphone and wrapped his legs around it. They were making a lot of noise, but their faces were oddly bland, as if they were waiting for something, killing time by playing.

Two discothèque girls were stationed on either side of the band. They wore brief costumes, bikinis with fringes. One was chubby and one had a beautiful face on a graceless body. Their skins were chalky-white under the lights.

I stepped to the bar and ordered straight Scotch on the rocks. That way, I'd get Scotch and water, which was what I wanted.

I paid for my drink and turned to watch the group. Roman was one of the guitarists, a wiry muscular man in his late twenties, with a thick head of curly black hair. The grease shone in the pink stage lights. He stared down at his fingers as he played.

"They're pretty good," I said to the bartender.

He shrugged. "You like this kinda music?"

"Sure. Don't you?"

"Crap," the bartender said. "All crap."

"What kind of music do you like?"

"Opera," he said and moved down to another customer. I couldn't tell if he was kidding me or not.

I stood there with my drink. The Zephyrs finished their piece, and the sailors on the dance floor clapped. Nobody else did. The lead singer, still swaying from the song, leaned into the microphone and said, "Thank you, thank you," in a breathless voice, as if thousands were wildly applauding.

Then he said, "For our next song, we want to do an old Chuck Berry piece."

It turned out to be "Long Tall Sally." Really old. Old enough for me to know it was a Little Richard song, not Chuck Berry. Old enough for me to remember from the days before my marriage, when I took girls to places like this for a wild evening, from the days when Negroes were sort of amusing, not people at all, just a musical sideshow. The days when white boys could go to the Apollo in Harlem.

The old days.

They played the song well, loud and fast. Judith loathes rock 'n' roll, which is sad; I've always kept a taste for it. But it wasn't fashionable when our generation was growing up. It was crude and lower class. The deb set was still fixed on Lester Lanin and Eddie Davis, and Leonard Bernstein hadn't learned the twist yet.

Times change.

Finally the Zephyrs finished. They hooked a record player to their amplifiers and started the records going. Then they climbed down off the stage and headed for the bar. As Roman walked toward me, I came up to him and touched his arm.

"Buy you a drink?"

He gave me a surprised look. "Why?"

"I'm a fan of Little Richard."

His eyes swept up and down me. "Get off it," he said.

"No, seriously."

"Vodka," he said, sitting down next to me.

I ordered a vodka. It came, and he gulped it down quickly.

"We'll just have another," he said, "and then we can go talk about Little Richard, right?"

"O.K.," I said.

He got another vodka and carried it to a table across the room. I followed him. His silver suit shimmered in the near darkness. We sat down, and he looked at the drink and said, "Let's see the silver plate."

"What?"

He gave me a pained look. "The badge, baby. The little pin. I don't do nothing unless you got the badge."

I must have looked puzzled.

"Christ," he said, "when they gonna get some bright fuzz?"

"I'm not fuzz," I said.

"Sure." He took his drink and stood up.

"Wait a minute," I said. "Let me show you something."

I took out my wallet and flipped to my M.D. card. It was dark; he bent down to look at it.

"No kidding," he said, his voice sarcastic. But he sat down again.

"It's the truth. I'm a doctor."

"O.K.," he said. "You're a doctor. You smell like a cop to me, but you're a doctor. So let's have the rules: you see those four guys over there?" He nodded toward his group. "If anything happens, they all testify you showed me a doctor's card and no badge. That's entrapment, baby. Don't hold in court. Clear?"

"I just want to talk."

"No kidding," he said and sipped the drink. He smiled slightly. "Word sure does get around."

"Does it?"

"Yeah," he said. He glanced at me. "Who told you about it?"

"I have ways."

"What ways?"

I shrugged. "Just . . . ways."

"Who wants it?"

"I do."

He laughed. "You? Get serious, man. You don't want nothing."

"All right," I said. I stood up and started to go. "Maybe I got the wrong man."

"Just a minute, baby."

I stopped. He was sitting at the table, looking at the drink, twisting the glass in his hands. "Sit down."

I sat down again. He continued to stare at the glass. "This is good stuff," he said. "We don't cut it with nothing. It's the finest quality and the price is high, see?"

"O.K.," I said.

He scratched his arms and his hands in a quick, nervous way. "How many bags?"

"Ten. Fifteen. Whatever you have."

"I got as much as you want."

"Then fifteen," I said. "But I want to see it first."

"Yeah, yeah, right. You can see it first. It's good."

He continued to scratch his arms through the silver material, then smiled. "But one thing first."

"What's that?"

"Who told you?"

I hesitated. "Angela Harding," I said.

He seemed puzzled by this. I could not decide whether I had said something wrong. He shifted in his chair, as if making up his mind, then said, "She a friend of yours?"

"Sort of."

"When did you see her last?"

"Yesterday," I said.

He nodded slowly. "The door," he said, "is over there. I'll give you thirty seconds to get out of here before I tear you to pieces. You hear me, cop? Thirty seconds."

I said, "All right, it wasn't Angela. It was a friend of hers."

"Who's that?"

"Karen Randall."

"Never heard of her."

"I understand you knew her quite well."

He shook his head: "Nope."

"That's what I was told."

"You was told wrong, baby. Dead wrong."

I reached into my pocket and brought out his picture. "This was in her room at college."

Before I knew what was happening, he had snatched the picture from my hand and torn it up.

"What picture?" he said evenly. "I don't know no picture. I never even seen the girl."

I sat back.

He regarded me with angry eyes. "Beat it," he said.

"I came here to buy something," I said. "I'll leave when I have it."

"You'll leave now, if you know what's good for you."

He was scratching his arms again. I looked at him and realized that I would learn nothing more. He wasn't going to talk, and I had no way to make him.

"All right," I said. I got up, leaving my glasses on the table. "By the way, do you know where I can get some thiopental?"

For a moment, his eyes widened. Then he said, "Some what?"

"Thiopental."

"Never heard of it. Now beat it," he said, "before one of those nice fellas at the bar picks a fight with you and beats your head in."

I walked out. It was cold; a light rain had started again. I looked toward Washington Street and the bright lights of the other rock-'n'-roll joints, strip joints, clip joints: I waited thirty seconds, then went back.

My glasses were still on the table. I picked them up and turned to leave, my eyes sweeping the room.

Roman was in the corner, talking on a pay phone.

That was all I wanted to know.

FOUR

AROUND THE CORNER at the end of the block was a stand-up, self-service greasy spoon. Hamburgers twenty cents. It had a large glass window in front. Inside I saw a few teen-age girls giggling as they ate, and one or two morose derelicts in tattered overcoats that reached almost to their shoes. At one side, three sailors were laughing and slapping each other on the back, reliving some conquest or planning the next. A telephone was in the back.

I called the Mem and asked for Dr. Hammond. I was told he was on the EW that night; the desk put the call through.

"Norton, this is John Berry."

"What's up?"

"I need more information," I said, "from the record room."

"You're lucky," he said. "It seems to be a slow night here. One or two lacerations and a couple of drunken fights. Nothing else. What do you need?"

"Take this down," I said. "Roman Jones, Negro, about twenty-four or -five. I want to know whether he's ever been admitted to the hospital and whether he's been followed in any of the clinics. And I want the dates."

"Right," Hammond said. "Roman Jones. Admissions and clinic visits. I'll check it out right away."

"Thanks," I said.

"You going to call back?"

"No. I'll drop by the EW later."

That, as it turned out, was the understatement of the year.

WHEN I FINISHED THE CALL I was feeling hungry, so I got a hot dog and coffee. Never a hamburger in a place like this. For one thing, they often use horsemeat or rabbit or entrails or anything else they can grind up. For another, there's usually enough pathogens to infect an army. Take trichinosis—Boston has six times the national rate of infection from that. You can't be too careful.

I have a friend who's a bacteriologist. He spends his whole time running a hospital lab where they culture out organisms that have infected the patients. By now this guy is so worked up that he practically never goes to the dinner, even to Joseph's or Locke-Ober. Never eats a steak unless it's well done. He really worries. I've been to dinner with him, and it's terrible—he sweats all through the main course. You can see him imagining a blood agar petri dish, with those little colonies streaked out. Every bite he takes, he sees those colonies. Staph. Strep. Gram negative bacilli. His life is ruined.

Anyway, hot dogs are safer—not much, but some—so I had one and took it over to the stand-up counter with my coffee. I ate looking out the window at the crowd passing by.

Roman came to mind. I didn't like what he'd told me. Clearly, he was selling stuff, probably strong stuff. Marijuana was too easy to get. LSD was no longer being made by Sandoz, but lysergic acid, the precursor, is produced by the ton in Italy, and any college kid can convert it if he steals a few reagents and flasks from his chem lab. Psilocybin and DMT are even easier to make.

Probably Roman was dealing in opiates, morphine or heroin. That complicated matters a great deal—particularly in view of his reaction to mention of Angela Harding and Karen Randall. I wasn't sure what the connection was but I felt, somehow, that I'd find out very soon.

I finished the hot dog and drank my coffee. As I looked out the win-

(Ed. note: the three-step synthesis of lysergic acid diethylamine (LSD) from common precursors has been omitted from this manuscript.)

dow, I saw Roman hurry by. He did not see me. He was looking forward, his face intent and worried.

I gulped the rest of my coffee and followed him.

FIVE

I LET HIM GET HALF A BLOCK AHEAD OF ME. He was hurrying through the crowds, pushing and shoving. I kept him in sight as he walked toward Stuart Street. There he turned left and headed for the expressway. I followed him. This end of Stuart was deserted; I dropped back and lit a cigarette. I pulled my raincoat tighter and wished I had a hat. If he looked back over his shoulder, he would certainly recognize me.

Roman walked one block, then turned left again. He was doubling back. I didn't understand, but I played it more cautiously. He was walking in a quick, jerky way, the movements of a frightened man.

We were on Harvey Street now. There were a couple of Chinese restaurants here. I paused to look at the menu in one window. Roman was not looking back. He went another block, then turned right.

I followed.

South of the Boston Commons, the character of the town changes abruptly. Along the Commons, on Tremont Street, there are elegant shops and high-class theaters. Washington Street is one block over, and it's a little sleazier: there are bars and tarts and nude movie houses. A block over from that, things get even tougher. Then there's a block of Chinese restaurants, and that's it. From then on, you're in the wholesale district. Clothes mostly.

That's where we were now.

The stores were dark. Bolts of cloth stood upright in the windows. There were large corrugated doors where the trucks pulled up to load and unload. Several little dry-goods stores. A theatrical supply shop, with costumes in the window—chorus girl stockings, an old military uniform, several wigs. A basement pool hall, from which came the soft clicking of balls.

The streets were wet and dark. We were quite alone. Roman walked quickly for another block, then he stopped.

I pulled into a doorway and waited. He looked back for a moment and kept going. I was right after him.

Several times, he doubled back on his own path, and he frequently stopped to check behind him. Once a car drove by, tires hissing on the wet pavement. Roman jumped into a shadow, then stepped out when the car had gone.

He was nervous, all right.

I followed him for perhaps fifteen minutes. I couldn't decide whether he was being cautious or just killing time. He stopped several times to look at something he held in his hand—perhaps a watch, perhaps something else. I couldn't be sure.

Eventually he headed north, skirting along side streets, working his way around the Commons and the State House. It took me a while to realize that he was heading for Beacon Hill.

Another ten minutes passed, and I must have gotten careless, because I lost him. He darted around a corner, and when I turned it moments later, he was gone: the street was deserted. I stopped to listen for footsteps, but heard nothing. I began to worry and hurried forward.

Then it happened.

Something heavy and damp and cold struck my head, and I felt a cool, sharp pain over my forehead, and then a strong punch to my stomach. I fell to the pavement and the world began to spin sickeningly. I heard a shout, and footsteps, and then nothing.

SIX

IT WAS ONE OF THOSE PECULIAR VIEWS YOU HAVE, like a dream where everything is distorted. The buildings were black and very high, towering above me, threatening to collapse. They seemed to rise forever. I felt cold and soaked through, and rain spattered my face. I lifted my head up from the pavement and saw that it was all red.

I pulled up on one elbow. Blood dripped down onto my raincoat. I looked stupidly down at the red pavement. Hell of a lot of blood. Mine?

My stomach churned and I vomited on the sidewalk. I was dizzy and the world turned green for a while.

Finally, I forced myself to get to my knees.

In the distance, I heard sirens. Far off but getting closer. I stood shakily and leaned on an automobile parked by the curb. I didn't know where I was; the street was dark and silent. I looked at the bloody sidewalk and wondered what to do.

The sirens were coming closer.

Stumbling, I ran around the corner, then stopped to catch my breath. The sirens were very close now; a blue light flashed on the street I had just left.

I ran again. I don't know how far I went. I don't know where I was. I just kept running until I saw a taxi. It was parked at a stand, the motor idling.

I said, "Take me to the nearest hospital."

He looked at my face.

"Not a chance," he said.

I started to get in.

"Forget it, buddy." He pulled the door shut and drove away, leaving me standing there.

In the distance, I heard the sirens again.

A wave of dizziness swept over me. I squatted and waited for it to pass. I was sick again. Blood was still dripping from somewhere on my face. Little red drops spattered into the vomit.

The rain continued. I was shivering cold, but it helped me to stay conscious. I got up and tried to get my bearings; I was somewhere south of Washington Street; the nearest signpost said Curley Place. It didn't mean anything to me. I started walking, unsteady, pausing frequently.

I hoped I was going in the right direction. I knew I was losing blood, but I didn't know how much. Every few steps, I had to stop to lean on a car and catch my breath.

The dizziness was getting worse.

I stumbled and fell. My knees cracked into the pavement and pain shot through me. For an instant, it cleared my head, and I was able to get back to my feet. The shoes, soaked through, squeaked. My clothes were damp with sweat and rain.

I concentrated on the sound of my shoes and forced myself to walk. One step at a time. Three blocks ahead, I saw lights. I knew I could make it.

One step at a time.

I leaned against a blue car for a moment, just a moment, to catch my breath.

"THAT'S IT. That's the boy." Somebody was lifting me up. I was in a car, being lifted out. My arm was thrown over a shoulder, and I was walking. Bright lights ahead. A sign: "Emergency Ward." Blue-lighted sign. Nurse at the door.

"Just go slow, boy. Just take it easy."

My head was loose on my neck. I tried to speak but my mouth was too dry. I was terribly thirsty and cold. I looked at the man helping me, an old man with a grizzled beard and a bald head. I tried to stand better so he wouldn't have to support me, but my knees were rubber, and I was shivering badly.

"Doing fine, boy. No problem at all."

His voice was gruffly encouraging. The nurse came forward, floating in the pool of light near the EW door, saw me, and ran back inside. Two interns came out and each took an arm. They were strong; I felt myself lifted up until my toes were scraping through the puddles. I felt rain on the back of my neck as my head drooped forward. The bald man was running ahead to open the door.

They helped me inside where it was warm. They put me on a padded table and started pulling off my clothes, but the clothes were wet and blood-soaked; they clung to my body, and finally they had to cut them off with scissors. It was all very difficult and it took hours. I kept my eyes closed because the lights overhead were painfully bright.

"Get a crit and cross-match him," said one of the interns. "And set up a four kit with sutures in room two."

People were fussing with my head; I vaguely felt hands and gauze pads being pressed against my skin. My forehead was numb and cold. By now they had me completely undressed. They dried me with a hard towel and wrapped me in a blanket, then transferred me to another padded table. It started to roll down the hall. I opened my eyes and saw the bald man looking down at me solicitously.

"Where'd you find him?" one of the interns asked.

"On a car. He was lying on a car. I saw him and thought he was a drunk passed out. He was half in the street, you know, so I figured he could get run over and stopped to move him. Then I saw he was nicely dressed and all bloody. I didn't know what happened, but he looked bad, so I brought him here."

"You have any idea what happened?" the intern asked.

"Looks beat up, if you ask me," the man said.

"He didn't have a wallet," the intern said. "He owe you money for the fare?"

"That's all right," the bald man said.

"I'm sure he'll want to pay you."

"That's all right," the cabby said. "I'll just go now."

"Better leave your name at the desk," the intern said.

But the man was already gone.

They wheeled me into a room tiled in blue. The surgical light over my head switched on. Faces peered down at me. Rubber gloves pulled on, gauze masks in place.

"We'll stop the bleeding," the intern said. "Then get some X rays." He looked at me. "You awake, sir?"

I nodded and tried to speak.

"Don't talk. Your jaw may be broken. I'm just going to close this wound on your forehead, and then we'll see."

The nurse bathed my face, first with warm soap. The sponges came away bloody.

"Alcohol now," she said. "It may sting a little."

The interns were talking to each other, looking at the wound. "Better mark that as a six-centimeter superficial on the right temple."

I barely felt the alcohol. It felt cool and tingled slightly, nothing more.

The intern held the curved suture needle in a needle holder. The nurse stepped back and he moved over my head. I expected pain, but it was nothing more than a slight pricking on my forehead. The intern who was sewing said, "Damned sharp incision here. Looks almost surgical."

"Knife?"

"Maybe, but I doubt it."

The nurse put a tourniquet on my arm and drew blood. "Better give him tetanus toxoid as well," the intern said, still sewing. "And a shot of penicillin." He said to me, "Blink your eyes once for yes, twice for no. Are you allergic to penicillin?"

I blinked twice.

"Are you sure?"

I blinked once.

"O.K.," said the intern. He returned to his sewing. The nurse gave me two injections. The other intern was examining my body, saying nothing.

I must have passed out again. When I opened my eyes, I saw a huge X-ray machine poised by my head. Someone was saying, "Gently, gently," in an irritated voice.

I passed out again.

I awoke in another room. This was painted light green. The interns were holding the dripping-wet X rays up to the light, talking about them. Then one left and the other came over to me.

"You seem all right," he said. "You may have a few loose teeth, but no fractures anywhere that we can see."

My head was clearing; I was awake enough to ask, "Has the radiologist looked at those films?"

That stopped them cold. They froze, thinking what I was thinking, that skull films were hard to interpret and required a trained eye. They also didn't understand how I knew to ask such a question.

"No, the radiologist is not here right now."

"Well, where is he?"

"He just stepped out for coffee."

"Get him back," I said. My mouth was dry and stiff; my jaw hurt. I touched my cheek and felt a large swelling, very painful. No wonder they had been worried about a fracture.

"What's my crit?" I said.

"Pardon, sir?"

It was hard for them to hear me, my tongue was thick and my speech unclear.

"I said, what's my hematocrit?"

They glanced at each other, then one said, "Forty, sir."

"Get me some water."

One of them went off to get water. The other looked at me oddly, as if he had just discovered I was a human being. "Are you a doctor, sir?"

"No," I said, "I'm a well-informed Pygmy."

He was confused. He took out his notebook and said, "Have you ever been admitted to this hospital before, sir?"

"No," I said. "And I'm not being admitted now."

"Sir, you came in with a laceration——"

"Screw the laceration. Get me a mirror."

"A mirror?"

I sighed. "I want to see how good your sewing is," I said.

"Sir, if you're a doctor——"

"Get the mirror."

With remarkable speed, a mirror and a glass of water were produced. I drank the water first, quickly; it tasted marvelous.

"Better go easy on that, sir."

"A crit of forty isn't bad," I said. "And you know it." I held up the mirror and examined the cut on my forehead. I was angry with the interns, and it helped me forget the pain and soreness in my body. I looked at the cut, which was clean and curved, sloping down from above one eyebrow toward my ear.

They had put about twenty stitches in.

"How long since I came in?" I said.

"An hour, sir."

"Stop calling me sir," I said, "and do another hematocrit. I want to know if I'm bleeding internally."

"Your pulse is only seventy-five, sir, and your skin color——"

"Do it," I said.

They took another sample. The intern drew five cc's into a syringe. "Jesus," I said, "it's only a hematocrit."

He gave me a funny apologetic look and quickly left. Guys on the EW get sloppy. They need only a fraction of a cc to do a crit; they could get it from a drop of blood on a finger.

I said to the other intern, "My name is John Berry. I am a pathologist at the Lincoln."

"Yes, sir."

"Stop writing it down."

"Yes, sir." He put his notebook aside.

"This isn't an admission and it isn't going to be officially recorded."

"Sir, if you were attacked and robbed——"

"I wasn't," I said. "I stumbled and fell. Nothing else. It was just a stupid mistake."

"Sir, the pattern of contusions on your body would indicate——"

"I don't care if I'm not a textbook case. I'm telling you what happened and that's it."

"Sir——"

"No," I said. "No arguments."

I looked at him. He was dressed in whites and he had some spatterings of blood on him; I guessed it was my blood.

"You're not wearing your nametag," I said.

"No."

"Well, wear it. We patients like to know who we're talking to."

He took a deep breath, then said, "Sir, I'm a fourth-year student."

"Jesus Christ."

"Sir——"

"Look, son. You'd better get some things straight." I was grateful for the anger, the fury, which gave me energy. "This may be a kick for you to spend one month of your rotation in the EW, but it's no kicks at all for me. Call Dr. Hammond."

"Who, sir?"

"Dr. Hammond. The resident in charge."

"Yes, sir."

He started to go, and I decided I had been too hard on him. He was, after all, just a student, and he seemed a nice enough kid.

"By the way," I said, "did you do the suturing?"

There was a long, guilty pause. "Yes, I did."

"You did a good job," I said.

He grinned. "Thanks, sir."

"Stop calling me sir. Did you examine the incision before you sutured it up?"

"Yes, s—. Yes."

"What was your impression?"

"It was a remarkably clean incision. It looked like a razor cut to me." I smiled. "Or a scalpel?"

"I don't understand."

"I think you're in for an interesting night," I said. "Call Hammond."

ALONE, I had nothing to think about but the pain. My stomach was the worst; it ached as if I had swallowed a bowling ball. I rolled over onto my side, and it was better. After a while, Hammond showed up, with the fourth-year student trailing along behind.

Hammond said, "Hi, John."

"Hello, Norton. How's business?"

"I didn't see you come in," Norton said, "otherwise—"

"Doesn't matter. Your boys did a good job."

"What happened to you?"

"I had an accident."

"You were lucky," Norton said, bending over the wound and looking at it. "Cut your superficial temporal. You were spurting like hell. But your crit doesn't show it."

"I have a big spleen," I said.

"Maybe so. How do you feel?"

"Like a piece of shit."

"Headache?"

"A little. Getting better."

"Feel sleepy? Nauseated?"

"Come on, Norton—"

"Just lie there," Hammond said. He took out his penlight and checked my pupils, then looked into the fundi with an ophthalmoscope. Then he checked my reflexes, arms and legs, both sides.

"You see?" I said. "Nothing."

"You still might have a hematoma."

"Nope."

"We want you to stay under observation for twenty-four hours," Hammond said.

"Not a chance." I sat up in bed, wincing. My stomach was sore. "Help me get up."

"I'm afraid your clothes——"

"Have been cut to shreds. I know. Get me some whites, will you?"

"Whites? Why?"

"I want to be around when they bring the others in," I said.

"What others?"

"Wait and see," I said.

The fourth-year student asked me what size whites I wore, and I told him. He started to get them when Hammond caught his arm.

"Just a minute." He turned to me. "You can have them on one condition."

"Norton, for Christ's sake, I don't have a hematoma. If it's subdural, it may not show up for weeks or months anyway. You know that."

"It might be epidural," he said.

"No fractures on the skull films," I said. An epidural hematoma was a collection of blood inside the skull from a torn artery, secondary to skull fracture. The blood collected in the skull and could kill you from the compression of the brain.

"You said yourself, they haven't been read by a radiologist yet."

"Norton, for Christ's sake. You're not talking to an eighty-year-old lady. I——"

"You can have the whites," he said calmly, "if you agree to stay here overnight."

"I won't be admitted."

"O.K. Just so you stay here in the EW."

I frowned. "All right," I said finally, "I'll stay."

The fourth-year student left to get me the clothes. Hammond stood there and shook his head at me.

"Who beat you up?"

"Wait and see."

"You scared hell out of the intern and that student."

"I didn't mean to. But they were being kind of casual about things."

"The radiologist for the night is Harrison. He's a fuck-off."

"You think that matters to me?"

"You know how it is," he said.

"Yes," I said, "I do."

The whites came, and I climbed into them. It was an odd feeling; I hadn't worn whites for years. I'd been proud of it then. Now the fabric seemed stiff and uncomfortable.

They found my shoes, wet and bloody; I wiped them off and put them on. I felt weak and tired, but I had to keep going. It was all going to be finished tonight. I was certain of it.

I got some coffee and a sandwich. I couldn't taste it, it was like eating newspaper, but I thought the food was necessary. Hammond stayed with me.

"By the way," he said, "I checked on Roman Jones for you."

"And?"

"He was only seen once. In the GU[1] clinic. Came in with what sounded like renal colic, so they did a urinalysis."

"Yes?"

"He had hematuria, all right. Nucleated red cells."

"I see."

It was a classic story. Patients often showed up in clinic complaining of severe pain in the lower abdomen and decreased urine output. The most likely diagnosis was a kidney stone, one of the five most painful conditions there are; morphine is given almost immediately when the diagnosis is made. But in order to prove it, one asks for a urine sample and examines it for slight blood. Kidney stones are usually irritating and cause a little bleeding in the urinary tract.

Morphine addicts, knowing the relative ease of getting morphine for kidney stones, often try to mimic renal colic. Some of them are very good at it; they know the symptoms and can reproduce them exactly. Then when they're asked for a urine sample, they go into the bathroom, collect the sample, prick their fingers, and allow a small drop of blood to fall in.

But some of them are squeamish. Instead of using their own blood, they use the blood of an animal, like a chicken. The only trouble is that chicken red cells have nuclei, while those of humans do not. So nucleated red cells in a patient with renal colic almost always meant someone faking the symptoms, and that usually meant an addict.

"Was he examined for needle marks?"

"No. When the doctor confronted him, he left the clinic. He's never been seen again."

"Interesting. Then he probably is an addict."

"Yes. Probably."

After the food, I felt better. I got to my feet, feeling the exhaustion and the pain. I called Judith and told her I was at the Mem OPD and that I was fine, not to worry. I didn't mention the beating or the cut. I knew she would have a fit when I got home, but I wasn't going to excite her now.

I walked down the corridor with Hammond, trying not to wince from the pain. He kept asking me how I felt, and I kept telling him I felt fine. In fact, I didn't. The food was beginning to make me nauseated, and

[1] Genito-urinary.

my headache was worse standing up. But the worst thing was the fatigue. I was terribly, terribly tired.

We went to the emergency entrance of the EW. It was a kind of stall, an open-ended garage where the ambulances backed up and unloaded their cargoes. Swinging, automatic doors, operated by foot-pressure pads, led into the hospital. We walked out and breathed the cool night air. It was a rainy, misty night, but the cool air felt good to me.

Hammond said, "You're pale."

"I'm O.K."

"We haven't even begun to evaluate you for internal hemorrhage."

"I'm O.K.," I said.

"Tell me if you're not," Hammond said. "Don't be a hero."

"I'm not a hero," I said.

We waited there. An occasional automobile drove past us, tires hissing on the wet streets; otherwise it was silent.

"What's going to happen?" Hammond said.

"I'm not sure. But I think they're going to bring in a Negro and a girl."

"Roman Jones? Is he involved in all this?"

"I think so."

In fact, I was almost certain that it had been Roman Jones who had beaten me up. I didn't remember exactly any more; the events right before the accident were hazy. I might have expected that. I didn't have true retrograde amnesia, which is common with concussions and extends back for fifteen minutes before the accident. But I was a little confused.

It must have been Roman, I thought. He was the only logical one. Roman had been heading for Beacon Hill. And there was only one logical reason for that, too.

We would have to wait.

"How do you feel?"

"You keep asking," I said. "And I keep telling you I'm fine."

"You look tired."

"I am tired. I've been tired all week."

"No. I mean you look drowsy."

"Don't jump the gun," I said. I glanced at my watch. Nearly two hours had passed since I had been beaten up. That was plenty of time. More than enough time.

I began to wonder if something had gone wrong.

At that moment, a police car came around the corner, tires squealing, siren going, blue light flashing. Immediately afterward an ambulance pulled up, followed by a third car. As the ambulance backed in, two men in business suits jumped out of the third car: reporters. You could tell by their eager little faces. One had a camera.

"No pictures," I said.

The ambulance doors were opened and a body on a stretcher was brought out. The first thing I saw was the clothes—slashed and ripped across the trunk and upper limbs, as if the body had been caught in some kind of monstrous machine. Then, in the cold fluorescent light of the EW entrance, I saw the face: Roman Jones. His skull was caved in on the right side like a deflated football, and his lips were purple-black.

The flashbulbs popped.

Right there in the alley-way, Hammond went to work. He was quick: in a single movement, he picked up the wrist with his left hand, put his ear over the chest, and felt the carotids in the neck with his right hand. Then he straightened and without a word began to pound the chest. He did it with one hand flat and the heel of the other thumping against the flat hand in sharp, hard, rhythmic beats.

"Call anesthesia," he said, "and get the surgical resident. Get an arrest cart here. I want aramine, one-in-a-thousand solution. Oxygen by mask. Positive pressure. Let's go."

We moved him inside the EW and down to one of the little treatment rooms. Hammond continued the cardiac massage all the time, not breaking his rhythm. When we got to the room the surgical resident was there.

"Arrested?"

"Yes," Hammond said. "Apneic, no pulses anywhere."

The surgeon picked up a paper packet of size-eight gloves. He didn't wait for the nurse to open them for him; he took them out of the paper himself and yanked them over his fingers. He never took his eyes off the motionless figure of Roman Jones.

"We'll open him up," the surgeon said, flexing his fingers in the gloves.

Hammond nodded, continuing his pounding of the chest. It didn't seem to be doing much good: Roman's lips and tongue were blacker. His skin, especially in the face and ears, were blotchy and dark.

An oxygen mask was slapped on.

"How much, sir?" said the nurse.

"Seven liters," said the surgeon. He was given a scalpel. Roman's already shredded clothes were torn away from his chest; nobody bothered to strip him down completely. The surgeon stepped forward, his face blank, the scalpel held tightly in his right hand with his index finger over the blade.

"All right," he said and made the incision, sloping across the ribs on the left side. It was a deep incision and there was bleeding, which he ignored. He exposed the whitish glistening ribs, cut between them, and then applied retractors. The retractors were pulled wide and there was a crunching snapping sound as the ribs snapped. Through the gaping incision, we could see Roman's lungs, collapsed and wrinkled-looking, and his heart, large, bluish, not beating, but wriggling like a bag of worms.

The surgeon reached into the chest and began to massage. He did it smoothly, contracting his little finger first, then all the others in his hand up to the index finger, expelling blood from the heart. He squeezed very hard and grunted rhythmically.

Someone had slapped on a blood-pressure cuff and Hammond pumped it up to take a reading. He watched the needle for a moment, then said, "Nothing."

"He's fibrillating," the resident said, holding the heart. "No epinephrine. Let's wait."

The massage continued for one minute, then two. Roman's color turned darker still.

"Getting weaker. Give me five cc's in one to a thousand."

A syringe was prepared. The surgeon injected it directly into the heart, then continued squeezing.

Several more minutes passed. I watched the squeezing heart, and the rhythmic inflation of the lungs from the respirator. But the patient was declining. Finally, they stopped.

"That's it," the surgeon said. He removed his hand from the chest, looked at Roman Jones, and stripped off his glove. He examined the lacerations across the chest and arms and the dent in the skull.

"Probably primary respiratory arrest," he said. "He was hit pretty hard over the head." To Hammond: "You going to do the death certificate?"

"Yeah," Hammond said, "I'll do it."

At that moment, a nurse burst into the room. "Dr. Hammond," she said, "Dr. Jorgensen needs you. They've got a girl in hemorrhagic shock."

OUT IN THE HALL, the first one I saw was Peterson. He was standing there in a suit, looking both confused and annoyed. When he saw me he did a double take and plucked at my sleeve.

"Say, Berry——"

"Later," I said.

I was following Hammond and the nurse down to another treatment room. A girl was there, lying flat, very pale. Her wrists were bandaged. She was conscious, but just barely—her head rolled back and forth, and she made moaning sounds.

Jorgensen, the intern, was bent over her.

"Got a suicide here," he said to Hammond. "Slashed wrists. We've stopped the bleeding and we're getting whole blood in."

He was finding a vein for the IV feeder. Working on the leg.

"She's cross-matched," he said, slipping the needle in. "We're getting more blood from the bank. She'll take at least two units. Hematocrit's O.K., but that doesn't mean anything."

"Why the legs?" Hammond said, nodding to the IV.

"Had to bandage her wrists. Don't want to fool with upper extremities."

I stepped forward. The girl was Angela Harding. She did not look so pretty now; her face was the color of chalk, with a grayish tinge around the mouth.

"What do you think?" Hammond said to Jorgensen.

"We'll keep her," he said. "Unless something goes wrong."

Hammond examined the wrists, which were bandaged.

"Is this the lesion?"

"Yes. Both sides. We've sutured it."

He looked at the hands. The fingers were stained dark brown. He looked at me. "Is this the girl you were talking about?"

"Yes," I said, "Angela Harding."

"Heavy smoker," Hammond said.

"Try again."

Hammond picked up one hand and smelled the stained fingers.

"These aren't tobacco," he said.

"That's right."

"Then . . ."

I nodded. "That's right."

". . . she's a nurse."

"Yes."

The stains were from tincture of iodine, used as a disinfectant. It was a brownish-yellow liquid, and it stained tissues it came in contact with. It was employed for scrubbing a surgical incision before cutting, and for such other practices as introduction of an IV feeder.

"I don't get it," Hammond said.

I held up her hands. The balls of the thumb and the backs of the hands were covered with minute slashes which were not deep enough to draw blood.

"What do you make of this?"

"Testing." A classic finding in suicides by wrist-slashing is one or more preliminary cuts on the hand as if the suicide victim wishes to test the sharpness of the blade or the intensity of the pain that would result.

"No," I said.

"Then what?"

"Ever seen a fellow who's been in a knife fight?"

Hammond shook his head. Undoubtedly, he never had. It was the kind of experience one had only as a pathologist: small cuts on the hands were the hallmark of a knife fight. The victim held up his hands to ward off the knife; he ended up with small cuts.

"Is this the pattern?"

"Yes."

"You mean she was in a knife fight?"

"Yes."

"But why?"

"Tell you later," I said.

I went back to Roman Jones. He was still in the same room, along with Peterson and another man in a suit, examining the eyes of the body.

"Berry," Peterson said, "you show up at the damnedest times."

"So do you."

"Yeah," Peterson said, "but it's my job."

He nodded toward the other man in the room.

"Since you were so worried the last time, I brought a doctor along. A police doctor. This is a coroner's case now, you know."

"I know."

"Fellow by the name of Roman Jones. We got that from the wallet."

"Where'd you find him?"

"Lying on the street. A nice quiet street in Beacon Hill. With his skull bashed in. Must have fallen on his head. There was a broken window two floors up, in an apartment owned by a girl named Angela Harding. She's here, too."

"I know."

"You know a lot tonight, don't you?"

I ignored him. My headache was worse; it was throbbing badly, and I felt terribly tired. I was ready to lie down and go to sleep for a long, long time. But I wasn't relaxed; my stomach was churning.

I bent over the body of Roman Jones. Someone had stripped off the clothing to expose multiple, deep lacerations of the trunk and upper arms. The legs were untouched. That, I thought, was characteristic.

The doctor straightened and looked at Peterson. "Hard to tell now what the cause of death was," he said. He nodded to the gaping chest wound. "They've messed it up pretty bad. But I'd say crush injury to the cranium. You said he fell from a window?"

"That's the way we figure it," Peterson said, glancing at me.

"I'll handle the forms," the doctor said. "Give me the wallet."

Peterson gave him Roman Jones' wallet. The doctor began to write on a clipboard at one side of the room. I continued to look at the body. I was particularly interested in the skull. I touched the indentation, and Peterson said, "What're you doing?"

"Examining the body."

"On whose authority?"

I sighed. "Whose authority do I need?"

He looked confused then.

I said, "I'd like your permission to conduct a superficial examination of the body."

As I said it, I glanced over at the doctor. He was making notes from the wallet, but I was sure he was listening.

"There'll be an autopsy," Peterson said.

"I'd like your permission," I said.

"You can't have it."

At that point, the doctor said, "Oh, for shit's sake, Jack."

Peterson looked from the police doctor, to me, and back again. Finally he said, "Okay, Berry. Examine. But don't disturb anything."

I looked at the skull lesion. It was a cup-shaped indentation roughly the size of a man's fist, but it hadn't been made by any fist. It had been made by the end of a stick, or a pipe, swung with considerable force. I looked more closely and saw small brown slivers of wood sticking to the bloody scalp. I didn't touch them.

"You say this skull fracture was caused by a fall?"

"Yes," Peterson said. "Why?"

"Just asking."

"Why?"

"What about the lacerations of the body?" I said.

"We figure he got those in the apartment. Apparently he had a fight with this girl, Angela Harding. There was a bloody kitchen knife in the apartment. She must have gone after him. Anyway, he fell out of the window or was pushed out. And he got this fracture, which killed him."

He paused and looked at me.

"Go on," I said.

"That's all there is to tell," he said.

I nodded, left the room, and returned with a needle and syringe. I bent over the body and jabbed the needle into the neck, hoping for the jugular vein. There was no point in fooling with arm veins, not now.

"What're you doing?"

"Drawing blood," I said, pulling back the syringe and drawing out several milliliters of bluish blood.

"What for?"

"I want to know whether he was poisoned," I said. It was the first thought, the first answer, that came into my head.

"Poisoned?"

"Yes."

"Why do you think he was poisoned?"

"Just a hunch," I said.

I dropped the syringe into my pocket and started to leave. Peterson watched me, then said, "Just wait a minute."

I paused.

"I have one or two questions for you."

"Oh?"

"The way we figure it," Peterson said, "this fellow and Angela Harding had a fight. Then Jones fell, and the girl attempted suicide."

"You already told me that."

"There's only one problem," Peterson said. "Jones is a big fellow. He must have gone one-ninety, two hundred. You think a little girl like Angela Harding could have shoved him out?"

"Maybe he fell."

"Maybe she had help."

"Maybe she did."

He looked at my face, at the bandage covering my cut. "Have some trouble tonight?"

"Yes."

"What happened?"

"I fell on the wet streets."

"Then you have an abrasion?"

"No. I fell against one of the city's excellent parking meters. I have a laceration."

"A jagged laceration."

"No, quite fine."

"Like Roman Jones'?"

"I don't know."

"Ever met Jones before?"

"Yes."

"Oh? When?"

"Tonight. About three hours ago."

"That's interesting," Peterson said.

"Do your best with it," I said. "I wish you luck."

"I could take you in for questioning."

"Sure you could," I said. "But on what charge?"

He shrugged. "Accessory. Anything."

"And I'd have a lawsuit on you so fast your head would swim. I'd have two million dollars out of your hide before you knew what hit you."

"Just for questioning?"

"That's right," I said. "Compromising a doctor's reputation. A doctor's reputation is his life, you know. Anything, even the slightest shadow of suspicion, is potentially damaging—financially damaging. I could very easily prove damages in court."

"Art Lee doesn't take that attitude."

I smiled. "Want to bet?"

I continued on. Peterson said, "How much do you weigh, Doctor?"

"One hundred and eighty-five pounds," I said. "The same as I weighed eight years ago."

"Eight years ago?"

"Yes," I said, "when I was a cop."

MY HEAD FELT AS IF IT WERE IN A VISE. The pain was throbbing, aching, agonizing. On my way down the corridor, I felt sudden and severe nausea. I stopped in the men's room and vomited up the sandwich and coffee I had eaten. I felt weak, with cold sweat afterward, but that passed and I was better. I went back and returned to Hammond.

"How do you feel?"

"You're getting monotonous," I said.

"You look like hell," he said. "Like you're about to be sick."

"I'm not," I said.

I took the syringe with Jones' blood from my pocket and set it on the bedside table. I picked up a fresh syringe and went.

"Can you find me a mouse?" I said.

"A mouse?"

"Yes."

He frowned. "There are some rats in Cochran's lab; it may be open now."

"I need mice."

"I can try," he said.

We headed for the basement. One the way, a nurse stopped Hammond to say that Angela Harding's parents had been called. Hammond said to let him know when they arrived or when the girl recovered consciousness.

We went down to the basement and moved through a maze of corridors, crouching beneath pipes. Eventually we came to the animal-storage area. Like most large hospitals connected with a university, the Mem had a research wing, and many animals were used in experiments. We heard barking dogs and the soft flutter of birds' wings as we passed room after room. Finally we came to one which said MINOR SUBJECTS. Hammond pushed it open.

It was lined, floor to ceiling, with row after row of rats and mice. The smell was strong and distinctive. Every young doctor knew that smell, and it was just as well, because it had clinical significance. The breath of patients in hepatic failure from liver disease had a peculiar odor known as *fetor hepaticus*; it was very similar to the smell of a room full of mice.

We found one mouse and Hammond plucked it from the cage in the accepted manner, by the tail. The mouse squirmed and tried to bite Hammond's hand, but had no success. Hammond set it down on the table and held the animal by a fold of loose flesh just behind the head.

"Now what?"

I picked up the syringe and injected some of the blood from Roman Jones' body. Then Hammond dropped the mouse in a glass jar.

For a long time, the mouse did nothing but run around the jar in circles.

"Well?" Hammond said.

"It's your failing," I said. "You aren't a pathologist. Have you ever heard of the mouse test?"

"No."

"It's an old test. It used to be the only bioassay available."

"Bioassay? For what?"

"Morphine," I said.

The mouse continued to run in circles. Then it seemed to slow, its muscles becoming tense, and the tail stuck straight up in the air.

"Positive," I said.

"For morphine?"

"Right."

There were better tests now, such as nalorphine, but for a dead person, the mouse test remained as good as any.

"He's an addict?" Hammond said.

"Yes."

"And the girl?"

"We're about to find out," I said.

She was conscious when we returned, tired and sad-eyed after taking three units[2] of blood. But she was no more tired than I was. I felt a deep, overpowering fatigue, a kind of general weakness, a great desire to sleep.

There was a nurse in the room who said, "Her pressure's up to one hundred over sixty-five."

"Good," I said. I fought back the fatigue and went up to her, patted her hand. "How are you feeling, Angela?"

Her voice was flat. "Like hell."

"You're going to be all right."

"I failed," she said in a dull monotone.

"How do you mean?"

A tear ran down her cheek. "I failed, that's all. I tried it and I failed."

"You're all right now."

"Yes," she said. "I failed."

"We'd like to talk to you," I said.

She turned her head away. "Leave me alone."

"Angela, this is very important."

"Damn all doctors," she said. "Why couldn't you leave me alone? I wanted to be left alone. That's why I did it, to be left alone."

"The police found you."

She gave a choking laugh. "Doctors and cops."

"Angela, we need your help."

"No." She raised her bandaged wrists and looked at them. "No. Never."

"I'm sorry, then." I turned to Hammond and said, "Get me some nalorphine."

I was certain the girl had heard me, but she did not react.

"How much?"

"Ten milligrams," I said. "A good dose."

Angela gave a slight shiver, but said nothing.

"Is that all right with you, Angela?"

She looked up at me and her eyes were filled with anger and something else, almost hope. She knew what it meant, all right.

"What did you say?" she asked.

"I said, is it all right if we give you ten milligrams of nalorphine."

"Sure," she said. "Anything. I don't care."

Nalorphine was an antagonist of morphine.[3] If this girl was an addict, it would bring her down with brutal swiftness—possibly fatal swiftness, if we used enough.

[2] A liter and a half.
[3] Actually a partial agonist, meaning that in low doses it has a morphinelike effect, but in high doses in an addict, it induces withdrawal symptoms.

A nurse came in. She blinked when she did not recognize me, but recovered quickly. "Doctor, Mrs. Harding is here. The police called her."

"All right. I'll see her."

I went out into the corridor. A woman and man were standing there nervously. The man was tall, wearing clothes he had obviously put on hurriedly—his socks didn't match. The woman was handsome and concerned. Looking at her face, I had the strange feeling I had met her before, though I was certain I had not. There was something very, almost hauntingly, familiar about her features.

"I'm Dr. Berry."

"Tom Harding." The man held out his hand and shook mine quickly, as if he were wringing it. "And Mrs. Harding."

"How do you do."

I looked at them both. They seemed like nice fifty-year-old people, very surprised to find themselves in a hospital EW at four in the morning with a daughter who'd just slashed her wrists.

Mr. Harding cleared his throat and said, "The, uh, nurse told us what happened. To Angela."

"She's going to be all right," I said.

"Can we see her?" Mrs. Harding said.

"Not right now. We're still conducting some tests."

"Then it isn't——"

"No," I said, "these are routine tests."

Tom Harding nodded. "I told my wife it'd be all right. Angela's a nurse in this hospital, and I told her they'd take good care of her."

"Yes," I said. "We're doing our best."

"Is she really all right?" Mrs. Harding said.

"Yes, she's going to be fine."

Mrs. Harding said to Tom, "Better call Leland and tell him he doesn't have to come over."

"He's probably already on his way."

"Well, try," Mrs. Harding said.

"There's a phone at the admitting desk," I said.

Tom Harding left to call. I said to Mrs. Harding, "Are you calling your family doctor?"

"No," she said, "my brother. He's a doctor, and he was always very fond of Angela, ever since she was a little girl. He——"

"Leland Weston," I said, recognizing her face.

"Yes," she said. "Do you know him?"

"He's an old friend."

Before she could answer, Hammond returned with the nalorphine and syringe. He said, "Do you really think we should——"

"Dr. Hammond, this is Mrs. Harding," I said quickly. "This is Dr. Hammond, the chief medical resident."

"Doctor." Mrs. Harding nodded slightly, but her eyes were suddenly watchful.

"Your daughter's going to be fine," Hammond said.

"I'm glad to hear that," she said. But her tone was cool.

We excused ourselves and went back to Angela.

"I HOPE TO HELL you know what you're doing," Hammond said as we walked down the hall.

"I do." I paused at a water fountain and filled a cup with water. I drank it down, then filled it again. My headache was now very bad, and my sleepiness was terrible. I wanted to lie down, to forget everything, to sleep. . . .

But I didn't say anything. I knew what Hammond would do if he found out.

"I know what I'm doing," I said.

"I hope so," he said, "because if anything goes wrong, I'm responsible. I'm the resident in charge."

"I know. Don't worry."

"Worry, hell. Ten milligrams of this stuff will shove her into cold turkey so fast—"

"Don't worry."

"It could kill her. We ought to be doing graded doses. Start with two, and if there's no effect in twenty minutes, go to five, and so on."

"Yes," I said. "But graded doses won't kill her."

Hammond looked at me and said, "John, are you out of your mind?"

"No," I said.

We entered Angela's room. She was turned away from us, rolled over on her side. I took the ampoule of nalorphine from Hammond and set it with the syringe on the table just alongside her bed; I wanted to be sure she read the label.

Then I walked around to the other side of the bed, so her back was to me.

I reached across her and picked up the ampoule and syringe. Then I quickly filled the syringe with water from the cup.

"Would you turn around, Angela, please?"

She rolled onto her back and held out her arm. Hammond was too astonished to move; I put the tourniquet on her arm and rubbed the veins in the crook of her elbow until they stood out. Then I slipped the needle in and squeezed out the contents. She watched me in silence.

When it was done, I stood back and said. "There now."

She looked at me, then at Hammond, then back to me.

"It won't be long," I said.

"How much did you give me?"

"Enough."

"Was it ten? Did you give me ten?"

She was becoming agitated. I patted her arm reassuringly. "There's nothing to worry about."

"Was it twenty?"

"Well, no," I said. "It was only two. Two milligrams."

"Two!"

"It won't kill you," I said mildly.

She groaned and rolled away from us.

"Disappointed?" I said.

"What are you trying to prove?" she said.

"You know the answer to that, Angela."

"But two milligrams. That's——"

"Just enough to give you symptoms. Just the cold sweats and the cramps and the pain. Just the beginnings of withdrawal."

"Jesus."

"It won't kill you," I said again. "And you know it."

"You bastards. I didn't ask to come here, I didn't ask to be——"

"But you are here, Angela. And you have nalorphine in your veins. Not much, but enough."

She began to break out into a sweat. "Stop it," she said.

"We can use morphine."

"Stop it. Please. I don't want it."

"Tell us," I said. "About Karen."

"First stop it."

"No."

Hammond was bothered by all this. He started forward toward the bed. I pushed him back.

"Tell us, Angela."

"I don't know anything."

"Then we'll wait until the symptoms start. And you'll have to tell us while you scream from the pain."

Her pillow was soaked with sweat. "I don't know, I don't know."

"Tell us."

"I don't know anything."

She began to shiver, slightly at first, and then more uncontrollably, until her whole body shook.

"It's starting, Angela."

She gritted her teeth. "I don't care."

"It will get worse, Angela."

"No . . . no . . . no. . . ."

I produced an ampoule of morphine and set it on the table in front of her.

"Tell us."

Her shivering got worse, until her whole body was wracked with spasms. The bed shook violently. I would have felt pity if I had not known that she was causing the reaction herself, that I had not injected any nalorphine at all.

"Angela."

"All right," she said, gasping. "I did it. I had to."

"Why?"

"Because of the heat. The heat. The clinic and the heat."

"You'd been stealing from the surgery?"

"Yes . . . not much, just a little . . . but enough . . ."

"How long?"

"Three years . . . maybe four . . ."

"And what happened?"

"Roman robbed the clinic . . . Roman Jones."

"When?"

"Last week."

"And?"

"The heat was on. They were checking everybody . . ."

"So you had to stop stealing?"

"Yes . . ."

"What did you do?"

"I tried to buy from Roman."

"And?"

"He wanted money. A lot."

"Who suggested the abortion?"

"Roman."

"To get money?"

"Yes."

"How much did he want?"

I already knew the answer. She said, "Three hundred dollars."

"So you did the abortion?"

"Yes . . . yes . . . yes. . . ."

"And who acted as anesthetist?"

"Roman. It was easy. Thiopental."

"And Karen died?"

"She was all right when she left. . . . We did it on my bed . . . the whole thing. . . . It was all right, everything . . . on my bed. . . ."

"But later she died."

"Yes. . . . Oh God, give me some stuff. . . ."

"We will," I said.

I filled a syringe with more water, squeezed out the air until a fine stream shot into the air, and injected it intravenously. Immediately she calmed. Her breathing became slower, more relaxed.

"Angela," I said, "did you perform the abortion?"

"Yes."

"And it resulted in Karen's death?"

A dull voice. "Yes."

"All right." I patted her arm. "Just relax now."

WE WALKED DOWN THE CORRIDOR. Tom Harding was waiting there with his wife, smoking a cigarette and pacing up and down.

"Is she all right, Doctor? Did the tests——"

"Fine," I said. "She'll recover beautifully."

"That's a relief," he said, his shoulders sagging.

"Yes," I said.

Norton Hammond gave me a quick glance, and I avoided his eyes. I felt like hell; my headache was much worse and I was beginning to have moments when my vision blurred. It seemed much worse in my right eye than my left.

But someone had to tell them. I said, "Mr. Harding, I am afraid your daughter has been implicated in business that involves the police."

He looked at me, stunned, disbelieving. Then I saw his face melt into a peculiar acceptance. Almost as if he had known it all along. "Drugs," he said, in a low voice.

"Yes," I said and felt worse than ever.

"We didn't know," he said quickly. "I mean, if we had . . ."

"But we suspected," Mrs. Harding said. "We never could control Angela. She was a headstrong girl, very independent. Very self-reliant and sure of herself. Even as a child, she was sure of herself."

HAMMOND wiped the sweat from his face with his sleeve. "Well," he said, "that's that."

"Yes."

Even though he was close to me, he seemed far away. His voice was suddenly faint and insignificant. Everything around me was insignificant. The people seemed small and faded. My headache now came in bursts of severe pain. Once, I had to stop for a moment and rest.

"What's the matter?"

"Nothing. Just tired."

He nodded. "Well," he said, "it's all over. You should be pleased."

"Are you?"

We went into the doctors' conference room, a small cubbyhole with two chairs and a table. There were charts on the walls, detailing procedure for acute emergencies: hemorrhagic shock, pulmonary edema, MI, burns, crush injuries. We sat down and I lit a cigarette. My left hand felt weak as I flicked the lighter.

Hammond stared at the charts for a while; neither of us said anything. Finally, Hammond said, "Want a drink?"

"Yes," I said. I was feeling sick to my stomach, disgusted, and annoyed. A drink would do me good, snap me out of it. Or else it would make me sicker.

He opened a locker and reached into the back, producing a flask. "Vodka," he said. "No smell. For acute medical emergencies." He opened it and took a swallow, then passed it to me.

As I drank, he said, "Jesus. Tune in, turn on, drop dead. Jesus."

"Something like that."

I gave the flask back to him.

"She was a nice girl, too."

"Yes."

"And that placebo effect. You got her into withdrawal on water, and you snapped her out of it with water."

"You know why," I said.

"Yeah," he said, "she believed you."

"That's right," I said. "She believed me."

I looked up at a chart illustrating the pathological lesion and emergency steps for diagnosis and treatment of ectopic pregnancy. I got down to the place where they talked about menstrual irregularity and cramping right-lower-quadrant pain when the words began to blur.

"John?"

It took me a long time to answer. It seemed as if it took me a long time to hear the words. I was sleepy, slow-thinking, slow-acting.

"John?"

"Yes," I said. My voice was hollow, a voice in a tomb. It echoed.

"You O.K.?"

"Yes, fine."

I kept hearing the words repeated in a kind of dream: fine, fine, fine. . . .

"You look terrible."

"I'm fine. . . ." Fine, fine, fine . . .

"John, don't get mad—"

"I'm not mad," I said and shut my eyes. The lids were hard to keep open. They stuck down, were heavy, sticking to the lower lids. "I'm happy."

"Happy?"

"What?"

"Are you happy?"

"No," I said. He was talking nonsense. It meant nothing. His voice was squeaky and high like a baby, a chattering childish voice. "No," I said, "I'm not mad at all."

"John—"

"Stop calling me John."

"That's your name," Norton said. He stood up, slowly, moving in dreamy slowness, and I felt very tired as I watched him move. He reached into his pocket and produced his light and shined it into my face. I looked away; the light was bright and hurt my eyes. Especially my right eye.

"Look at me."

The voice was loud and commanding. Drill sergeant's voice. Snappish and irritable.

"Fuck off," I said.

Strong fingers on my head, holding me, and the light shining into my eyes.

"Cut it out, Norton."

"John, hold still."

"Cut it out." I closed my eyes. I was tired. Very tired. I wanted to sleep for a million years. Sleep was beautiful, like the ocean washing the sand, lapping up with a slow, beautiful, hissing sound, cleaning everything.

"I'm O.K., Norton. I'm just mad."

"John, hold still."

John, hold still.

John, hold still.

John, hold still.

"Norton, for Christ's sake—"

"Shut up," he said.

Shut up, shut up.

He had his little rubber hammer out. He was tapping my legs. Making my legs bounce up and down. It tingled and irritated me. I wanted to sleep. I wanted to go fast, fast asleep.

"Norton, you son of a bitch."

"Shut up. You're as bad as any of them."

As any of them, as any of them. The words echoed in my head. As any of what? I wondered. Then the sleep, creeping up on me, fingers stretching out, plastic, rubbery fingers, closing over my eyes, holding them shut. . . .

"I'm tired."

"I know you are. I can see."

"I can't. I can't see anything."

Anything.

Can't see.

I tried to open my eyes. "Coffee. Need coffee."

"No," he said.

"Give me a fetus," I said and wondered why I said it. It made no sense. Did it? Didn't it? So confusing. Everything was confused. My right eye hurt. The headache was right behind my right eye. Like a little man with a hammer, pounding the back of my eyeball.

"A little man," I said.

"What?"

"A little man," I explained. It was obvious. He was stupid not to understand. It was perfectly obvious, a reasonable statement from a reasonable man. Norton was just playing games, pretending he didn't understand.

"John," he said, "I want you to count backward from one hundred. Subtract seven from one hundred. Can you do that?"

I paused. It wasn't easy. In my mind, I saw a piece of paper, a shining white piece of paper, with pencil on it. One hundred minus seven. And a line, for the subtraction.

"Ninety-three."

"Good. Continue."

That was harder. It needed a new piece of paper. I had to tear the old one off the pad before I could begin with a new piece. And when I had torn the old one off, I had forgotten what was on it. Complicated. Confusing.

"Go on, John. Ninety-three."

"Ninety-three minus seven." I paused. "Eighty-five. No. Eighty-six."

"Go on."

"Seventy-nine."

"Yes."

"Seventy-three. No. Seventy-four. No, no. Wait a minute."

I was tearing off pieces of paper, but slowly now. It was so much work to tear off pieces of paper. So hard. And so very confusing. It was so much *work* to concentrate.

"Eighty-seven."

"No."

"Eighty-five."

"John, what day is this?"

"Day?"

What a silly question. Norton was full of silly questions today. What day is this?

"Today," I said.

"What is the date?"

"The date?"

"Yes, the date."

"May," I said. It was the date of May.

"John, where are you?"

"I am in the hospital," I said, looking down at my whites. I opened my eyes a fraction, because they were heavy and I was groggy and the light hurt my eyes. I wished he would be quiet and let me sleep. I wanted to sleep. I needed the sleep. I was very, very tired.

"What hospital?"

"The hospital."

"What hospital?"

"The—" I started to say something, but couldn't remember what I intended to say. My headache was fierce now, pounding on the right eye, on the front of my head on the right side, a terrible pounding headache.

"Raise your left hand, John."

"What?"

"Raise your left hand, John."

I heard him, heard the words, but they were foolish. No one would pay attention to those words. No one would bother.

"What?"

The next thing I felt was a vibration, on the right side of my head. A funny rumbling vibration. I opened my eyes and saw a girl. She was pretty, but she was doing strange things to me. Brown fluffy things were falling off my head. Drifting down. Norton was watching and calling for something, but I did not understand the words. I was nearly asleep, it was all very strange. After the fluff came a lather.

And the razor. I looked at it, and the lather, and I was suddenly sick, no warning, no nothing, but vomit all over and Norton was saying, "Hurry it up, let's go."

And then they brought in the drill. I could barely see it, my eyes kept closing, and I was sick again.

The last thing I said was "No holes in my head."

I said it very clearly and slowly and distinctly.

I think.

FRIDAY, SATURDAY & SUNDAY

October
14, 15, & 16

ONE

IT FELT LIKE SOMEBODY had tried to cut off my head and hadn't done a very good job. When I woke up I buzzed for the nurse and demanded more morphine. She said I couldn't have it in a smiling, difficult-patient way and I suggested she go to hell. She didn't much like that but I didn't much like her. I reached up and felt the bandages on the side of my skull and made a few comments. She didn't like those any better so she left. Pretty soon Norton Hammond came in.

"You're a hell of a barber," I said, touching my head.

"I thought we did pretty well."

"How many holes?"

"Three. Right parietal. We took out quite a bit of blood. You remember any of that?"

"No," I said.

"You were sleepy, vomiting, and one pupil was dilated. We didn't wait for the X rays; we put the burr holes right in."

"Oh," I said. "When do I get out of here?"

"Three or four days, at most."

"Are you kidding? Three or four days?"

"An epidural," he said, "is a rugged thing. We want to be sure you rest."

"Do I have any choice?"

"They always say," he said, "that doctors make the worst patients."

"More morphine," I said.

"No," he said.

"Darvon."

"No."

"Aspirin?"

"All right," he said. "You can have some aspirin."

"Real aspirin? Not sugar pills?"

"Watch it," he said, "or we'll call a psychiatric consult."

"You wouldn't dare."

He just laughed and left the room.

I slept for a while, and then Judith came in to see me. She acted annoyed with me for a while, but not too long. I explained to her that it wasn't my fault and she said I was a damned fool and kissed me.

Then the police came, and I pretended to be asleep until they left.

In the evening, the nurse got me some newspapers and I searched for news about Art. There wasn't any. Some lurid stories about Angela Harding and Roman Jones, but nothing else. Judith came again during evening visiting hours and told me that Betty and the kids were fine and that Art would be released the next day.

I said that was great news and she just smiled.

THERE IS NO SENSE OF TIME IN A HOSPITAL. One day blends into the next; the routine—temperatures, meals, doctors' rounds, more temperatures, more meals—was everything. Sanderson came to see me, and Fritz, and some other people. And the police, only this time I couldn't fake sleep. I told them everything I knew and they listened and made notes. Toward the end of the second day I felt better. I was stronger, my head was clearer, and I was sleeping less.

I told Hammond and he just grunted and said to wait another day.

Art Lee came to see me in the afternoon. He had the old, wry grin on his face but he looked tired. And older.

"Hi," I said. "How's it feel to be out?"

"Good," he said.

He looked at me from the foot of the bed and shook his head. "Hurt much?"

"Not any more."

"Sorry it happened," he said.

"It's all right. It was interesting, in a way. My first epidural hematoma."

I paused. There was a question I wanted to ask him. I had been thinking about a lot of things and kicking myself for my foolish mistakes. The worst had been calling that reporter into the Lees' house that night. That had been very bad. But there were other bad things. So I wanted to ask him.

Instead, I said, "The police have things wrapped up now, I imagine."

He nodded. "Roman Jones was supplying Angela. He made her do the abortion. When it failed—and you got curious—he went over to Angela's house, probably to kill her. He decided he was being followed and caught you. Then he went to her place and went after her with a razor. That was what happened to your forehead."

"Nice."

"Angela fought him with a kitchen knife. Slashed him up a little. It must have been a pleasant scene, him with the razor and her with the knife. Finally she managed to hit him with a chair and knock him out the window."

"She said that?"

"Yes, apparently."

I nodded.

We looked at each other for a while.

"I appreciate your help," he said, "in all this."

"Any time. You sure it was help?"

He smiled. "I'm a free man."

"That's not what I mean," I said.

He shrugged and sat down on the edge of the bed. "The publicity wasn't your fault," he said. "Besides, I was getting tired of this town. Ready for a change."

"Where will you go?"

"Back to California, I guess. I'd like to live in Los Angeles. Maybe I'll deliver babies for movie stars."

"Movie stars don't have babies. They have agents."

He laughed. For a moment, it was the old laugh, the momentary self-pleasure that came when he had just heard something that amused him and had hit upon an amusing response. He was about to speak, then closed his mouth and stared at the floor. He stopped laughing.

I said, "Have you been back to the office?"

"Just to close it up. I'm making arrangements for the movers."

"When will you go?"

"Next week."

"So soon?"

He shrugged. "I'm not eager to stay."

"No," I said, "I imagine you're not."

I SUPPOSE EVERYTHING THAT HAPPENED afterward was the result of my anger. It was already a rotten business, stinking rotten, and I should have left it alone. There was no need to continue anything. I could let it go and forget about it. Judith wanted to have a farewell party for Art; I told her no, that he wouldn't like it, not really.

That made me angry, too.

On the third hospital day I bitched to Hammond until he finally agreed to discharge me. I guess the nurses had been complaining to him as well. So they let me go at 3:10 in the afternoon, and Judith brought me clothes and drove me home. On the way, I said, "Turn right at the next corner."

"Why?"

"I have to make a stop."

"John—"

"Come on, Judith. A quick stop."

She frowned, but turned right at the corner. I directed her across Beacon Hill, to Angela Harding's street. A police car was parked in front of her apartment. I got out and went up to the second floor. A cop stood outside the door.

"Dr. Berry, Mallory Lab," I said in an official tone. "Have the blood samples been taken yet?"

The cop looked confused. "Blood samples?"

"Yes. The scrapings from the room. Dried samples. For twenty-six factor determinations. You know."

He shook his head. He didn't know.

"Dr. Lazare is worried about them," I said. "Wanted me to check."

"I don't know anything about it," the cop said. "There were some medical guys here yesterday. Those the ones?"

"No," I said, "they were the dermatology people."

"Uh. Oh. Well, you better check for yourself." He opened the door for me. "Just don't touch anything. They're dusting."

I entered the apartment. It was a shambles, furniture overturned, blood spattered on couches and tables. Three men were working on a glass, dusting powder onto it and blowing it off, then photographing the fingerprints. One looked up, "Help you?"

"Yes," I said. "The chair—"

"Over there," he said, jerking his thumb toward a chair in the corner. "But don't touch it."

I went over and stared at the chair. It was not very heavy, a cheap wood kitchen chair, rather nondescript. But it was sturdily made. There was some blood on one leg.

I looked back at the three men. "You dusted this one yet?"

"Yeah. Funny thing. There's hundreds of prints in this room. Dozens of people. It's going to take us years to unravel it all. But there were two things we couldn't get prints from. That chair and the doorknob to the outside door."

"How's that?"

The man shrugged. "Been wiped."

"Wiped?"

"Yeah. Somebody cleaned up the chair and the doorknob. Anyhow, that's the way it looks. Damned funny. Nothing else was wiped, not even the knife she used on her wrists."

I nodded. "The blood boys been here yet?"

"Yeah. Came and went."

"O.K.," I said. "Can I make a call? I want to check back with the lab."

He shrugged. "Sure."

I went to the phone, picked it up, and dialed the weather bureau. When the voice came on, I said, "Give me Dr. Lazare."

"—sunny and cool, with a high in the mid-fifties. Partly cloudy in late afternoon—"

"Fred? John Berry. I'm over at the room now."

"—with fifty-percent chance of showers—"

"Yeah, they say the samples were taken. You sure you haven't gotten them yet?"

"—tomorrow, fair and colder with a high in the forties—"

"Oh. I see. O.K. Good. Right. See you."

—"wind from the east at fifteen miles per hour—"

I hung up and turned to the three men. "Thanks," I said.

"Sure."

Nobody paid any attention to me as I left. Nobody really cared. The men who were there were doing routine duty. They'd done things like this before, dozens of times. It was just routine.

October
17

I WAS IN A BAD MOOD MONDAY. I sat around for most of the morning drinking coffee and smoking cigarettes and tasting a lousy sour taste in my mouth. I kept telling myself that I could drop it and nobody would care. It was over. I couldn't help Art and I couldn't undo anything. I could only make things worse.

Besides, none of this was Weston's fault, not really. Even though I wanted to blame somebody, I couldn't blame him. And he was an old man.

It was a waste of time. I drank coffee and told myself that, over and over. A waste of time.

I did it anyway.

Shortly before noon I drove over to the Mallory and walked into Weston's office. He was going over some microscopic slides and dictating his findings into a small desk recorder. He stopped when I came in.

"Hello, John. What brings you over here?"

I said, "How do you feel?"

"Me?" He laughed. "I feel fine. How do you feel?" He nodded to the bandages on my head. "I heard what happened."

"I'm okay," I said.

I looked at his hands. They were under the table, in his lap. He had dropped them down as soon as I had come into the room.

I said, "Hurt much?"

"What?"

"Your hands."

He gave me a puzzled look or tried to. It didn't work. I nodded to his hands and he brought them out. Two fingers of his left hand were bandaged.

"Accident?"

"Yes. Clumsy of me. I was chopping an onion at home—helping out in the kitchen—and I cut myself. Just a superficial wound, but embarrassing. You'd think after all these years I'd know how to handle a knife."

"You bandaged it yourself?"

"Yes. It was just a small cut."

I sat down in the chair opposite his desk and lit a cigarette, aware that he was watching me carefully. I blew a stream of smoke out, toward the ceiling. He kept his face calm and blank; he was making it hard for me. But that was his right, I guess. I'd probably do the same.

"Was there something you wanted to see me about?" he asked.

"Yes," I said.

We stared at each other for a moment, and then Weston pushed his microscope to one side and turned off the recorder.

"Was it about the path diagnosis on Karen Randall? I'd heard you were concerned."

"I was," I said.

"Would you feel better if someone else looked them over? Sanderson?"

"Not now," I said. "It doesn't really matter now. Not legally, anyway."

"I suppose you're right," he said.

We stared at each other again, a long silence falling. I didn't know how to bring it up, but the silence was killing me.

"The chair," I said, "was wiped. Did you know that?"

For a moment, he frowned, and I thought he was going to play dumb. But he didn't; instead, he nodded.

"Yes," he said. "She told me she'd wipe it."

"And the doorknob."

"Yes. And the doorknob."

"When did you show up?"

He sighed. "It was late," he said. "I had worked late at the labs and was on my way home. I stopped by Angela's apartment to see how she was. I often did. Just stopped in. Looked in on her."

"Were you treating her addiction?"

"You mean, was I supplying her?"

"I mean, were you treating her?"

"No," he said. "I knew it was beyond me. I considered it, of course, but I knew that I couldn't handle it, and I might make things worse. I urged her to go for treatment, but . . ."

He shrugged.

"So instead, you visited her frequently."

"Just to try and help her over the rough times. It was the least I could do."

"And Thursday night?"

"He was already there when I arrived. I heard scuffling and shouts, so I opened the door, and I found him chasing her with a razor. She had a kitchen knife—a long one, the kind you use for bread—and she was fighting back. He was trying to kill her because she was a witness. He said that, over and over. 'You're a witness, baby,' in a low voice. I don't remember exactly what happened next. I had always been fond of Angela. He said something to me, some words, and started at me with the razor. He looked terrible; Angela had already cut him with the knife, or at least, his clothes . . ."

"So you picked up the chair."

"No. I backed off. He went after Angela. He was facing her, away from me. That was when . . . I picked up the chair."

I pointed to his fingers. "And your cuts?"

"I don't remember. I guess he did it. There was a little slash on the sleeve of my coat, too, when I got home. But I don't remember."

"After the chair—"

"He fell down. Unconscious. Just fell."

"What did you do then?"

"Angela was afraid for me. She told me to leave immediately, that she could take care of everything. She was terrified that I would be involved. And I . . ."

"You left," I said.

He looked at his hands. "Yes."

"Was Roman dead when you left?"

"I don't really know. He had fallen near the window. I guess she just pushed him out and then wiped up. But I don't know for sure. I don't know for sure."

I looked at his face, at the lines in the skin and the white of the hair, and remembered how he had been as a teacher, how he had prodded and pushed and cajoled, how I had respected him, how he had taken the residents every Thursday afternoon to a nearby bar for drinks and talk, how he used to bring a big birthday cake in every year on his birthday and share it with everyone on the floor. It all came back, the jokes, the good times, the bad times, the questions and explanations, the long hours in the dissecting room, the points of fact and the matters of uncertainty.

"Well," he said with a sad smile, "there it is."

I lit another cigarette, cupping my hands around it and ducking my head, though there was no breeze in the room. It was stifling and hot and airless, like a greenhouse for delicate plants.

Weston didn't ask the question. He didn't have to.

"You might get off," I said, "with self-defense."

"Yes," he said, very slowly. "I might."

OUTSIDE, cold autumnal sun splashed over the bare branches of the skeletal trees along Massachusetts Avenue. As I came down the steps of Mallory, an ambulance drove past me toward the Boston City EW. As it passed I glimpsed a face propped up on a bed in the back, with an oxygen mask being held in place by an attendant. I could see no features to the face; I could not even tell if it was a man or a woman.

Several other people on the street had paused to watch the ambulance go by. Their expressions were fixed into attitudes of concern, or curiosity, or pity. But they all stopped for a moment, to look, and to think their private thoughts.

You could tell they were wondering who the person was, and what the disease was, and whether the person would ever leave the hospital again. They had no way of knowing the answers to those questions, but I did.

This particular ambulance had its lights flashing, but the siren was off, and it moved with almost casual slowness. That meant the passenger was not very sick.

Or else he was already dead. It was impossible to tell which.

For a moment, I felt a strange, compelling curiosity, almost an obligation, to go to the EW and find out who the patient was and what the prognosis was.

But I didn't. Instead I walked down the street, got into my car, and drove home. I tried to forget about the ambulance, because there were millions of ambulances, and millions of people, every day, at every hospital. Eventually, I did forget. Then I was all right.

APPENDIX I:

Delicatessen Pathologists

PART OF ANY PATHOLOGIST'S JOB is to describe what he sees quickly and precisely; a good path report will allow the reader to see in his mind exactly what the pathologist saw. In order to do this, many pathologists have taken to describing diseased organs as if they were food, earning themselves the name, delicatessen pathologists.

Other pathologists are revolted by the practice; they deplore path reports that read like restaurant menus. But the device is so convenient and useful that nearly all pathologists use it, at one time or another.

Thus there are currant jelly clots and postmortem chicken-fat clots. There is ripe raspberry mucosa or strawberry gallbladder mucosa, which indicates the presence of cholesterol. There are nutmeg livers of congestive heart failure and Swiss-cheese endometria of hyperplasia. Even something as unpleasant as cancer may be described as food, as in the case of oat-cell carcinoma of the lung.

APPENDIX II:

Cops and Doctors

DOCTORS ARE GENERALLY MISTRUSTFUL of the police and try to avoid police business. One reason:

A brilliant resident at the General was called out of bed one night to examine a drunk brought in by the police. The police know that certain medical disorders—such as diabetic coma—may closely imitate inebriation, even including an "alcoholic" breath. So this was routine. The man was examined, pronounced medically sound, and carted off to jail.

He died during the night. At autopsy, he was found to have a ruptured spleen. The family sued the resident for negligence, and the police were extraordinarily helpful to the family in attempting to put the blame on the doctor. At the trial, it was decided that the doctor had indeed been negligent, but no damages were awarded.

This doctor later tried to obtain certification from the Virginia State Board to practice in that state, and succeeded only with the greatest difficulty. This incident will follow him for the rest of his life.

While it is possible that he missed the enlarged or ruptured spleen in his examination, it is highly unlikely considering the nature of the injury and extremely high caliber of the doctor. The conclusion of the hospital staff was that probably the man had received a good kick in the stomach by the police, after he had been examined.

There is, of course, no proof either way. But enough incidents such as this have occurred that doctors mistrust police almost as a matter of general policy.

APPENDIX III:
Battlefields and Barberpoles

THROUGHOUT HISTORY, surgery and war have been intimately related. Even today, of all doctors, young surgeons are the ones who least object to being sent to the battlefield. For it is there that surgeons and surgery have traditionally developed, innovated, and matured.

The earliest surgeons were not doctors at all; they were barbers. Their surgery was primitive, consisting largely of amputations, blood-letting, and wound-dressing. Barbers accompanied the troops during major campaigns and gradually came to learn more of their restorative art. They were hampered, however, by a lack of anesthesia; until 1890, the only anesthetics available were a bullet clenched between the victim's teeth and a shot of whiskey in his stomach. The surgeons were always looked down on by the medical doctors, men who did not deign to treat patients with their hands, but took a more lofty and intellectual approach. This attitude, to some extent, persists to the present day.

Now, of course, surgeons are not barbers, or vice versa. But the barbers retain the symbol of their old trade—the red-and-white-striped pole which represents the bloody white dressings of the battlefield.

But if surgeons no longer give haircuts, they still accompany armies. War gives them vast experience in treating trauma, wounds, crush injuries, and burns. War also allows innovation; most of the techniques now common to plastic or reconstructive surgery were developed during World War II.

All this does not necessarily make surgeons either prowar or antipeace. But the historical background of their craft does give them a somewhat different outlook from other doctors.

APPENDIX IV:
Abbreviations

DOCTORS LOVE ABBREVIATIONS, and probably no other major profession has so many. Abbreviations serve an important timesaving function, but there seems to be an additional purpose. Abbreviations are a code, a secret and impenetrable language, the cabalistic symbols of medical society.

For instance: "The PMI, corresponding to the LBCD, was located in the 5th ICS two centimeters lateral to the MCL." Nothing could be more mysterious to an outsider than that sentence.

X is the most important letter of the alphabet in medicine, because of its common use in abbreviations. Use ranges from the straightforward "Polio x3" for three polio vaccinations, to "Discharged to Ward X," a common euphemism for the morgue. But there are many others: dx is diagnosis; px, prognosis; Rx, therapy; sx, symptoms; hx, history; mx, metastases; fx, fractures.

Letter abbreviations are particularly favored in cardiology, with its endless usage of LVH, RVF, AS, MR to describe heart conditions, but other specialties have their own.

On occasion, abbreviations are used to make comments which one would not want to write out in full. This is because any patient's hospital record is a legal document which may be called into court; doctors must therefore be careful what they say, and a whole vocabulary and series of abbreviations have sprung up. For instance, a patient is not demented, but "disoriented" or "severely confused"; a patient does not lie, but "confabulates"; a patient is not stupid, but "obtunded." Among surgeons, a favorite expression to discharge a patient who is malingering is SHA, meaning "Ship his ass out of here." And in pediatrics is perhaps the most unusual abbreviation of all, FLK, which means "Funny looking kid."

APPENDIX V:
Whites

EVERYBODY KNOWS DOCTORS WEAR WHITE UNIFORMS, and nobody, not even the doctors, knows why. Certainly the "whites," as they are called, are distinctive, but they serve no real purpose. They are not even traditional.

In the court of Louis XIV, for example, all physicians wore black: long, black, imposing robes which were as striking and awe-inspiring in their day as shining whites are now.

Modern arguments for whites usually invoke sterility and cleanliness. Doctors wear white because it is a "clean" color. Hospitals are painted white for the same reason. This sounds quite reasonable until one sees a grubby intern who has been on duty for thirty-six consecutive hours, has slept twice in his clothes, and has ministered to dozens of patients. His whites are creased, wrinkled, dirty, and no doubt covered with bacteria.

Surgeons give it all away. The epitome of aseptic conditions, of germ-free living, is found in the operating room. Yet few OR's are white, and the surgeons themselves do not wear white clothing. They wear green, or blue, or sometimes gray.

So one must consider the medical "whites" as a uniform, with no more logic to the color than the designation of blue for a navy uniform or green for an army uniform. The analogy is closer than the casual observer might expect, for the medical uniform designates rank as well as service. A doctor can walk into a ward and can tell you the rank of everyone on the ward team. He can tell you who is the resident, who the intern, who the medical student, who the male orderly. He does this by reading small cues, just as a military man reads stripes and shoulder insignias. It comes down to questions like: is the man carrying a stethoscope? Does he have one notebook in his pocket or two? Filecards held by a metal clip? Is he carrying a black bag?

The process may even be extended to indicate the specialty of a doctor. Neurologists, for example, are readily identified by the three or four straight pins stuck through their left jacket lapels.

APPENDIX VI:

Arguments on Abortion

THERE ARE GENERALLY CONSIDERED to be six arguments for abortion, and six counterarguments.

The first argument considers the law and anthropology. It can be shown that many societies routinely practice abortion and infanticide without parental guilt or destruction of the moral fiber of the society. Usually examples are drawn from marginal societies, living in a harsh environment, such as the African Pygmies or Bushmen of the Kalahari. Or from societies which place a great premium on sons and kill off excess female infants. But the same argument has used the example of Japan, now the sixth-largest nation in the world and one of the most highly industrialized.

The reverse argument states that Western society has little in common with either Pygmies or the Japanese, and that what is right and acceptable for them is not necessarily so for us.

Legal arguments are related to this. It can be shown that modern abortion laws did not always exist; they evolved over many centuries, in response to a variety of factors. Proponents of abortion claim that modern laws are arbitrary, foolish, and irrelevant. They argue for a legal system which accurately reflects the mores and the technology of the present, not of the past.

The reverse argument points out that old laws are not necessarily bad laws and that to change them thoughtlessly invites uncertainty and flux in an already uncertain world. A less sophisticated form of the argument opposes abortion simply because it is illegal. Until recently, many otherwise thoughtful doctors felt comfortable taking this position. Now, however, abortion is being debated in many circles, and such a simplistic view is untenable.

The second argument concerns abortion as a form of birth control. Proponents regard abortion on demand as a highly effective form of birth control and point to its success in Japan, Hungary, Czechoslovakia, and elsewhere. Proponents see no essential difference between preventing a conception and halting a process which has not yet resulted in a fully-viable infant. (These same people see no difference between the rhythm method and the pill, since the intention of both practices is identical.) In essence, the argument claims that "it's the thought that counts."

Those who disagree draw a line between prevention and correction. They believe that once conception has occurred, the fetus has rights and cannot be killed. This viewpoint is held by many who favor conventional birth-control measures, and for these people, the problem of what to do if birth control fails—as it does in a certain percentage of cases—is troublesome.

The third argument considers social and psychiatric factors. It has variants.

The first states that the physical and mental health of the mother always takes precedence over that of the unborn child. The mother, and her already-existing family, may suffer emotionally and financially by the birth of another infant, and therefore, in such cases the birth should be prevented.

The second states that it is immoral and criminal to bring into the world an unwanted child. It states that, in our increasingly complex society, the proper rearing of a child is a time-consuming and expensive process demanding maternal attention and paternal financial support for education. If a family cannot provide this, they do a grave disservice to the child. The obvious extreme case is that of the unwed mother, who is frequently unprepared to rear an infant, either emotionally or financially.

The counterargument is vague here. There is talk of mothers who unconsciously wish to conceive; talk of the maternal urge to procreate; flat statements that "there never was a child born who wasn't wanted." Or an ex-post-facto approach: once the child is born, the family will adjust and love him.

The fourth argument states that a woman should never, under any circumstances, be required to bear a child if she does not wish to do so. Abortion on demand should be a right of every woman, like the right to vote. This is an interesting argument, but its usefulness has been diluted by many of its proponents, who often express a rather paranoid feeling that the world is dominated by men who cannot be expected to show any sympathy for the opposite sex.

Those who disagree with this argument usually point out that a modern, emancipated woman need not become pregnant if she does not wish it. A wide variety of birth-control methods and devices is available to her, and they believe that abortion is not a substitute for birth control. The case of

birth-control failure and inadvertent pregnancy—such as rape—are difficult to handle within this framework, however.

The fifth argument states that abortion is safe, easy, simple, and cheap;
thus there can be no practical objection to legalizing termination of pregnancy.

The counterargument states that abortion carries a finite risk or mortality, which, though small, nonetheless exists. Unfortunately for this
viewpoint, it is now perfectly clear that a hospital abortion is one-sixth
to one-tenth as dangerous as a hospital delivery. This means it is safer to
abort a child than to carry it to term.

The sixth argument is the newest and the most ingenious. It was first
proposed by Garrett Hardin, and it attacks the problem at a crucial
question: is abortion murder? Hardin says no. He argues that the embryo
does not become human until after birth and a long period of training.
He states that the embryo is nothing but a template, ultimately derived
from DNA, the information-carrying genetic substance. Information in
itself, he says, is of no value. It is like a blueprint. The blueprint of a
building, he says, is worthless; only the building has value and significance. The blueprint may be destroyed with impunity, for another can
easily be made, but a building cannot be destroyed without careful
deliberation.

This is a swift and oversimplified summary of his argument. Hardin
was trained both as an anthropologist and as a biologist, and his viewpoint is unique. It is interesting because it considers the question of *when*
is a person human in terms of *what* is a human being? Returning to the
analogy of blueprint and building, the blueprint specifies size, shape, and
general structure, but it does not state whether the building will be erected
in New York or Tokyo, whether in a slum or an affluent area, whether
it will be used effectively or fall into disrepair. By implication, Hardin
is defining a human being not only as an animal that walks on its hind
legs, has a large brain, and an opposable thumb; he includes in the definition enough maternal care and education to make the person a well-
adjusted and functioning unit of a social grouping.

The counterargument says that Hardin assumes DNA is a "non-unique"
copy of information, when in fact it is quite unique. All children of a
given mother and father are not identical; therefore the DNA cannot be
"non-unique."

To this Hardin replies that we already, quite by chance, select only
some of the potential DNA combinations of sperm and egg and allow

these to reach maturation. He notes that an average woman has 30,000 eggs in her ovaries, yet will bring only a few to term. The others are destroyed just as surely as if they had been aborted. And, as he says, one of them might have been "a super Beethoven."

Hardin's argument is still new and strikes many as abstruse. But undoubtedly his is just the first of many new arguments, for and against abortion, which will be proposed on an increasingly subtle scientific basis. It is a commentary on modern man that he must justify his morality on the basis of the molecular mechanisms at work within a single cell of his body.

There are other arguments, but they are mostly evasive and petty. There are economic arguments concerning the cost of turning hospitals into abortion mills; there are vague and wild-eyed arguments of unleashed libertinism, similar to the arguments heard before the introduction of birth-control pills. There are also reflex liberal arguments that anything freer is by definition good and meritocratic arguments that the outpouring of children from the lower classes should be stemmed. There is no point in considering these viewpoints. They are advanced for the most part, by thoughtless and irritable little men.

APPENDIX VII:
Medical Morals

IN MEDICINE TODAY, there are four great moral questions involving the conduct of medical practice. One is abortion. Another is euthanasia, the killing of a patient with a terminal and incurable illness. A third concerns the social responsibility of the doctor to administer care to as many people as possible. A fourth concerns the definition of death.

The interesting thing is that all these problems are new. They are products of our technology, moral and legal problems which have sprung up within the last decade or so.

Hospital abortion, for example, must now be regarded as a relatively inexpensive and safe procedure, carrying a mortality rate roughly similar to a tooth extraction. This was not always true, but in the modern context it is, and we must therefore deal with it.

Euthanasia was once much less serious a problem. When doctors had fewer "supportive" aids, artificial respirators, and knowledge of electrolyte balances, patients with terminal illnesses tended to die quickly. Now, medicine faces the fact that a person can be kept technically alive for an indefinite period, though he can never be cured. Thus the doctor must decide whether supportive therapy should be instituted and for how long. This is a problem because doctors have traditionally felt that they should keep their patients alive as long as possible, using every available technique. Now, the morality—and even the humanity—of such an approach must be questioned.

There is a corollary: whether the patient facing an incurable disease has the right to refuse supportive therapy; whether a patient facing weeks or months of terminal pain has a right to demand an easy and painless death; whether a patient who has put himself in a doctor's hands still retains ultimate life-and-death control over his own existence.

Social responsibility in its modern terms—responsibility to a community, not an individual—is something rather new to medicine. Formerly patients who were indigent were treated by kind doctors, or not at all; now, there is a growing feeling that medical care is a right, not a privilege. There is also a growing number of patients who were once charity cases but are now covered by health insurance or Medicare. The physician is today being forced to reconsider his role, not in terms of those patients who can afford to seek his help, but in terms of all the people in the community. Related to this is the increased medical emphasis on preventive care.

The definition of death is a problem with a single cause: organ transplants. As surgeons become more skilled in transplanting parts from the dead to the living, the question of when a man is dead becomes crucial, because transplantable organs should be removed as rapidly as possible from a dead man. The old, crude indicators—no pulse, no breathing—have been replaced by no EKG activity, or a flat EEG, but the question is still unresolved, and may be for many years to come.

There is another problem involving medical ethics, and that concerns the doctor and the drug companies. This is currently being fought over in a four-way tug-of-war involving patient, doctor, government, and drug manufacturer. The issues, and the eventual outcome, are still unclear.

ABOUT THE AUTHOR

Jeffery Hudson is the pseudonym of an American scientist who was educated in Boston and currently lives in London. A Case of Need is his first novel.